THE

POEMS OF VIRGIL

TRANSLATED INTO ENGLISH PROSE

BY

JOHN CONINGTON, M.A.

LATE CORPUS PROFESSOR OF LATIN IN THE UNIVERSITY OF OXFORD

British Library Cataloguing-in-Publication Data
A catalogue record for this book is available from
the British Library

PROFESSOR CONINGTON'S prose translation of Virgil has not been published hitherto in a separate form, and is now reprinted *verbatim* from his Miscellaneous Writings. It should be added that the translation had been finished some time before his death, but had not been revised for publication.

CONTENTS.

————0————

THE BUCOLICS.

ECLOGUE I.

TITYRUS.

M. You, Tityrus, as you lie under the covert of the spreading beech, are studying the woodland Muse on your slender reed, while we are leaving our country's borders and the fields of our love—we are exiles from our country, while you, Tityrus, at ease in the shade, are teaching the woods to resound the charms of Amaryllis.

T. O Melibœus, it is a god who has given us the peace you see—for a god he shall ever be to me; his altar shall often be wet with the blood of a tender lamb from our folds. He it is that has made my oxen free to wander at large, and myself to play at my pleasure on my rural pipe.

M. I do not grudge you, I. It is rather that I wonder, so great is the unsettledness in the whole country round. Look at me here! I am driving my goats feebly on before me; and here is one, Tityrus, which I can but just drag along. Why, it was here among these thick hazels only just now that she dropped twins, after hard labour—the last hope of my flock— alas! on the bare flint. Ah! often and often, I mind, this mischief was foretold me, had I but had sense, by the lightning

A

striking the oak. However, do kindly tell me, Tityrus, who this god of yours is.

T. That city which they call Rome I thought, Melibœus, was like this of ours, where we shepherds are in the habit of weaning and driving our young lambs. It was so that I had observed puppies to be like dogs, and kids like their dams ; so, in short, that I used to compare big things to little. But I found her carrying her head as high among all other cities as cypresses do among your bending hedgerow trees.

M. And what was the mighty reason of your visiting Rome ?

T. Freedom, which cast an eye on me in my laziness, late as it was, after my beard was beginning to look grey as it fell under the barber's shears. However, it did cast an eye on me, and came, though it was long first, after Amaryllis got the hold she has of me, and Galatea took leave of me. For, to tell the truth, while I was under Galatea I never looked forward to freedom nor attended to my pelf; though I had many a sheep for sacrifice going out of my folds, and many a rich cream-cheese made for the thankless town, yet my hand used never to come home with a load of money in it.

M. Aye, Amaryllis, I used to wonder why you were calling on the gods so piteously—for whom it was that you were letting the apples hang on their trees. It was Tityrus that was away. Why, Tityrus, the pines, and the springs, and the vineyards here, used all to call for you as loudly as she did.

T. How could I help it ? I had no other way of quitting slavery, and no other place where I could find gods so ready to help me. Here it was, Melibœus, that I saw that youth for whom I make my altars smoke twelve days a year. Here it was that I got from him my first gracious answer to my suit, ' Go on, swains, feeding your oxen as before, and breeding your bulls.'

M. Happy old man! so your land will remain your own, and enough, too, for your wants, though there may be bare flints all over it, and the marsh covering the pastures with slime and reeds. Still, no strange fodder will trouble your breeding ewes—no baleful contagion from a neighbour's flock will harm them. Happy old man! here you will lie among the streams you know so well, and the sacred springs, courting the coolness of the shade—from here, on the border of your neighbour's land, that hedge, whose willow-blossoms are browsed by Hybla's bees, shall often tempt you to sleep, as it has ever done, with its light whispering—from here, under the high rock's shelter, the dresser shall sing out into the air— while the hoarse wood-pigeons, those favourites of yours, and the turtle will still go on complaining from the skiey elm-top.

T. Yes; sooner shall the stags become buoyant and pasture in the sky, and the seas leave their fish bare on the shore— sooner shall the Parthian and German wander over each other's frontiers, one to drink the Arar in his exile, the other the Tigris —than that gracious look of his shall fade from my mind.

M. Meanwhile we are leaving our home; some going among the thirsty Africans, while others will reach Scythia, and Crete's swift Oaxes, and Britain, cut off utterly from the whole world. Tell me, will there ever be a day when I shall gaze wonderingly, after long years, on my native fields, and the turfheaped roof of my homely cottage, surveying my old domains, then, perhaps, a few ears of corn? Is a lawless soldier to be master of lands that I have broken up and tilled so well—a barbarian, of such crops as these? See to what a point civil discord has brought a wretched country! See for whom it is that we have sown our fields! Aye, Meliboeus, go on grafting your pears and setting your vines in rows! Away, my goats, away—you that were once so happy! No more shall I see you, as I lie in some green cavern, in the distance hanging from a briery crag—no more verses for me to sing—no more flowering lucerne and bitter willow leaves for you to crop, my goats, with me to tend you !

T. This night, at all events, you might rest here with me on a couch of green leaves. We have ripe apples, mealy chestnuts, and milk-cheeses in good store; and now the farm-house tops are smoking in the distance, and the shadows are falling larger from the mountain heights.

ECLOGUE II.

ALEXIS.

Corydon, the shepherd, was burning for the lovely Alexis, his master's darling, with no prospect for his hope. All he could do was to come daily among the thick beeches, with their shady summits, and there all alone to pour out wildly to the mountains and woods such unstudied strains as these in unavailing passion :

'Cruel Alexis! have you no care for my songs? no pity for me? You will drive me to death at last. It is the hour when even cattle are seeking the shade and its coolness—the hour when even green lizards are sheltering themselves in the brakes, and Thestylis is making for the reapers, as they come back spent with the vehement heat, her savoury mess of bruised garlic and wild thyme; but I, as I am scanning the prints of your feet, am left with a choir of hoarse cicalas that make the plantations ring again under the blazing sun. Was there not satisfaction in bearing Amaryllis's storms of passion and her scornful humours? or Menalcas, again—dark as he was —fair as are you? Do not, loveliest boy, do not presume too much on that bright bloom—white privet is left to fall, dark hyacinths are gathered for posies.

'You think scorn of me, Alexis, without even asking what
I am—how rich I am in cattle, how overflowing in milk
white as snow. Why, I have a thousand ewe lambs straying
at large over the mountains of Sicily—new milk never fails
me either summer or winter. I can sing as Amphion of Dirce
sang when calling the flocks home on the Attic Aracynthus.
I am not so unsightly either—the other day on the seashore I
looked at myself, as the sea was standing all glassy in a calm.
I should not fear competing with Daphnis in your judgment,
if the reflection never plays false.

'O if you would but take a fancy to live with me a homely
country life in a humble cottage, shooting the deer, and driving the herds of kids a-field to the green mallows! Living
with me, you shall soon rival Pan in singing in the woodland. Pan it was that first taught the fashion of fastening
several reeds together with wax. Pan it is that cares for
sheep and shepherds. Do not think you would be sorry to
chafe your lip with a reed—to learn this same lesson, what
used not Amyntas to go through? I have a pipe made out of
seven uneven hemlock stalks, which Damœtas once gave me
as a present—his dying words were, "It is yours now, as my
next heir." So said Damœtas. Amyntas, in his folly, felt
jealous. Besides, I have two young roes, which I found in
a dangerous valley, their skins still sprinkled with white,
sucking the same ewe twice a day. I am keeping them for
you. Thestylis, to be sure, has been long begging to get them
away from me—and so she shall, as you think my presents so
mean. Come to me, loveliest boy—see, the nymphs are
bringing basketsful of lilies, all for you—for you, the fair
naiad plucks yellow violets and poppy heads, and puts them
with the narcissus and the fragrant fennel flower, twines
them with casia and other pleasant plants, and picks out the
delicate hyacinth with the yellow marigold! I will gather

you myself quinces with their soft white down, and chestnuts, which my Amaryllis used to love so, and put in waxen plums —this fruit, too, shall come in for honour. You, too, I will pluck, ye bays, and you, myrtle, that always go with them— so placed you make a union of sweet smells.

'Corydon, you are nothing but a clown. Alexis cares nothing for such presents; nay, if presents are to be your weapons, Iollas will not yield the day to you. Alas, alas! what wretched wish have I been forming? I have been madman enough to let the south wind into my flower-beds, and the boars into my clear springs. Do you know whom you are flying from, infatuate as you are? Why, even the gods have lived in the country, aye, and Dardan Paris. Leave Pallas to live by herself in the great city towns she has built; let us love the country beyond any other place. The grim lioness goes after the wolf, the wolf, for his part, after the goat, the playful goat after the flowering lucerne, Corydon after you, Alexis—each is drawn by his peculiar pleasure. Look, the bullocks are drawing home the plough, with its share slung up, and the sun, as he withdraws, is doubling the lengthening shadows—yet still love is burning me up—for how should there be any stint for love? Ah, Corydon, Corydon! what madness has possessed you? Here are your vines half-pruned, and the elms they hang on overgrown with leaves. Come, you had better set about plaiting out some work for needful occasions with twigs or pliant rushes. You will find another Alexis, though the present one may scorn you.'

ECLOGUE III.

PALÆMON.

M. Tell me, Damœtas, whose cattle ? Melibœus's ?

D. No ; but Ægon's. They were just now handed over to me by Ægon.

M. Poor creatures, always unlucky ! He is courting Neæra, all afraid that she will be preferring me to him, while his hireling performs a shepherd's duty by milking the sheep twice an hour, and so the cattle are robbed of their life juice, and the lambs of their milk.

     *   *   *   *

M. Aye, of course, when they saw me with my felon-knife notching Micon's plantations of young vines.

D. Or rather, we will say, by the old beeches here, when you broke Daphnis's bow and arrows, which you were vexed about at the time—you, with your crooked ways—when you saw the boy get his present, and afterwards, if you had not found some way of spiting him, you would have died.

M. What are masters likely to do, if knaves venture so far ? Did not I see you, you scoundrel, snapping up stealthily Damon's goat, while his mongrel was barking furiously ? And then, when I was calling out, 'Where's he off to now ? Tityrus, muster your flock !' you skulked behind the sedge.

D. Why, after a fair beating in singing, was he not to pay me the goat which my pipe had earned for me by its songs ? If you must know, that goat was mine, and Damon owned it to me himself, but said he would not pay.

M. You beat him in singing ! Why, had you ever a pipe jointed with wax ? Used you not to perform at the crossings, executing vile, miserable songs, like an uneducated dolt, as you are, on a screaking straw ?

D. Well, what do you say to our trying together what each is made of, turn and turn about? This heifer—don't back out of it—she comes twice a day to the milk-pail and suckles a couple of calves—shall be my stake. Do you name what wager you will go in upon.

M. Why, out of my flock I dare not stake anything with you. The fact is, I have a father at home, aye, and I have a harsh step-mother; both count the flock twice a day, and one of them the kids too. But I will make what you will yourself own to be a greater venture, as you are minded to play so mad a game. I will stake a pair of cups of beechwood, the embossed work of the divine Alcimedon; the plastic graving-tool has wreathed them round with a limber vine, entwined with spreading clusters of pale-yellow ivy. In the field there are two figures, Conon and—who was the other, who marked out with his rod the whole heavens for mankind, that they might know the seasons which the reaper and the stooping ploughman were to have for their own? I have not yet put my lips to them either, but keep them in store.

D. Yes. I have two cups, too, made for me by the same Alcimedon, who has clasped their handles with pliant acanthus, and drawn Orpheus on the field and the woods going after him. I have not yet put my·lips to them either, but keep them in store. However, if you once look to the heifer, you will have nothing to say for the cups.

M. You are not going to run away this time. I will meet you wherever you appoint—only let there be some one to hear us. Palæmon—don't you see him coming up?—will do. I will take care that you challenge nobody to sing for the future.

D. Nay, come on, if you can; there will be no·hinderance on.my side. I don't run away from anybody—only, neighbour Palæmon, give your best attention to this: it is no trifling matter.

P. Sing, then, now that we are seated on the soft grass. It is the time when every field and every tree is yielding its fruit; the time when the woods are in leaf, and the year is at its loveliest. Begin, Damœtas; you follow him, Menalcas. You shall sing by turns; singing by turns is what the Muses love.

D. Jove shall be our first word, Muses. Jove is the filler of all things; he makes the earth fruitful, and he has a thought for verses like mine.

M. I am Phœbus's favourite. Phœbus always finds with me his own peculiar presents, the bay and the sweet ruddy hyacinth.

D. Galatea flings an apple at me, like a saucy girl, as she is, and then runs off to the willows, and would like to be seen first.

M. But I have my darling Amyntas, putting himself in my way unasked, so that my dogs have got to know him now as well as Delia.

D. I have got a present ready for my goddess. I have marked the spot with my own eyes where the wood-pigeons have been building up in the sky.

M. I have done my best for to-day; ten golden apples, picked from a tree in the orchard, I have sent my boy; tomorrow I will send as many more.

D. O the times Galatea has talked to me and the things she has said! Carry some of them, ye winds, to the ears of the gods!

M. What good is it that at heart you do not scorn me, Amyntas, if while you are following the boars, I am always watching the nets?

D. Send me Phyllis: it is my birthday, Iollas. When I sacrifice a heifer for the harvest, come yourself.

M. Phyllis is my own dearest love. Why, she wept on

parting from me, and dwelt long on the words, 'Farewell, farewell, my lovely Iollas!'

D. The bane of the folds is the wolf, of the ripe crops the rain, of the trees the sirocco—mine is Amaryllis's storms of passion.

M. The joy of the young corn is moisture, of weaned kids the arbute, of breeding cattle the limber willow—mine is none but Amyntas.

D. Pollio loves my muse—country-bred though she be. Pierian goddesses, breed a heifer for your gentle reader.

M. Pollio writes fresh verses himself. Breed a bull old enough to butt with the horn and spurn the sand with the hoof.

D. The man that loves you, Pollio, let him arrive where he is glad to see you; for him let honey distil, and let the prickly thorn-bush bear spices.

M. The man that hates not Bavius, let him love your verses, Mævius; let him, moreover, plough with a team of foxes, and milk he-goats.

D. You who gather flowers and strawberries that grow on the ground, there is a cold snake—off with you, my boys!—lurking in this grass.

M. Don't go on venturing too far, my sheep; the bank is not to be trusted. Why, the ram himself is just now drying his coat.

D. Tityrus, sling away those goats that are grazing there from the river. I'll wash them all myself in due time at the spring.

M. Get your sheep into the shade, my boys; if the heat steal a march on the milk, as it did the other day, it will be in vain that we shall tug at the udders.

D. Dear, dear, how lean my bull is among those fattening tares! it is the same love that wastes the cattle and the cattle's master.

M. These of mine certainly have not less the matter with them either—the flesh scarcely covers the bones; it must be some one's evil eye that bewitches such young lambs as mine are.

D. Tell me in what country—and you shall be my grand Apollo—the horizon is no broader than three ells across.

M. Tell me in what country flowers grow with the names of kings written on them, and have Phyllis all to yourself.

P. I am not the man to settle a difference like this between you. You deserve the heifer, and so does he; and every one who shall either mistrust love's sweets or taste its bitters as you have done. Shut off the water now, my boys; the meadows have had enough to drink.

ECLOGUE IV.

POLLIO.

Muses of Sicily, let us strike a somewhat louder chord. It is not for all that plantations have charms, or groundling tamarisks. If we are to sing of the woodland, let the woodland rise to a consul's dignity.

The last era of the song of Cuma has come at length; the grand file of the ages is being born anew; at length the virgin is returning, returning too the reign of Saturn; at length a new generation is descending from heaven on high. Do but thou smile thy pure smile on the birth of the boy who shall at last bring the race of iron to an end, and bid the golden race spring up all the world over—thou, Lucina—thine own Apollo is at length on his throne. In thy consulship it is—in thine, Pollio—that this glorious time shall come on, and the mighty months begin their march. Under thy conduct, any remaining trace of our national guilt shall become void, and release the world from the thraldom of perpetual fear. He shall have the life of the gods conferred on him, and shall see gods and heroes mixing together, and shall himself be seen of them, and with his father's virtues shall govern a world at peace.

For thee, sweet boy, the earth of her own unforced will shall pour forth a child's first presents—gadding ivy and fox-glove everywhere, and Egyptian bean blending with the bright smiling acanthus. Of themselves, the goats shall carry home udders distended with milk; nor shall the herds fear huge lions in the way. Of itself, thy grassy cradle shall pour out flowers to caress thee. Death to the serpent, and to the treacherous plant of poisoned juice. Assyrian spices shall spring up by the wayside.

But soon as thou shalt be of an age to read at length of the glories of heroes and thy father's deeds, and to acquaint thyself with the nature of manly work, the yellow of the waving corn shall steal gradually over the plain, and from briers, that know nought of culture, grapes shall hang in purple clusters, and the stubborn heart of oak shall exude dews of honey. Still, under all this show, some few traces shall remain of the sin and guile of old—such as may prompt men to defy the ocean goddess with their ships, to build towns with walls round them, to cleave furrows in the soil of earth. A second Tiphys shall there be in those days—a second Argo to convey the flower of chivalry; a second war of heroes, too, shall there be, and a second time shall Achilles be sent in his greatness to Troy.

Afterwards, when ripe years have at length made thee man, even the peaceful sailor shall leave the sea, nor shall the good ship of pine exchange merchandise—all lands shall produce all things; the ground shall not feel the harrow, nor the vine-yard the pruning-hook; the sturdy ploughman, too, shall at length set his bullocks free from the yoke ; nor shall wool be taught to counterfeit varied hues, but of himself, as he feeds in the meadows, the ram shall transform his fleece, now into a lovely purple dye, now into saffron-yellow—of its own will, scarlet shall clothe the lambs as they graze. Ages like these, flow on !—so cried to their spindles the Fates, uttering in concert the fixed will of destiny.

Assume thine august dignities—the time is at length at hand—thou best-loved offspring of the gods, august scion of Jove ! Look upon the world as it totters beneath the mass of its overhanging dome—earth and the expanse of sea and the deep of heaven—look how all are rejoicing in the age that is to be ! O may my life's last days last long enough and breath be granted me enough to tell of thy deeds ! I will be o'ermatched in song by none—not by Orpheus of Thrace, nor by Linus, though that were backed by his mother, and this by his father—Orpheus by Calliope, Linus by Apollo in his beauty. Were Pan himself, with Arcady looking on, to enter the lists with me, Pan himself, with Arcady looking on, should own himself vanquished.

Begin, sweet child, with a smile, to take notice of thy mother—that mother has had ten months of tedious sickness and loathing. Begin, sweet child—the babe on whom never parent smiled, never grew to deserve the table of a god or the bed of a goddess !

ECLOGUE V.

DAPHNIS.

Me. Why not sit down together, Mopsus, as we happen to have met, both good in our way—you at filling slender reeds with your breath, I at singing songs—here among this clump of elms and hazels ?

Mo. You are my elder; you have a right to give me the word, Menalcas, whether we should retire under those flickering shades which the zephyrs keep agitating, or rather into the cave. See how the cave is covered by the wild vine's straggling tendrils.

Me. In these hills of ours you have no rival but Amyntas.

Mo. What if he were to rival Phœbus, too, for the prize of singing?

Me. You go on first, Mopsus. If you happen to have any song about Phyllis's flame, or Alcon's glories, or Codrus's quarrels, go on. Tityrus will look after the kids while grazing.

Mo. I would rather try my hand at some verses which I wrote out the other day on the green beechen bark, and set them to music, with marks for the flute and voice. When I have done, put on my rival, Amyntas.

Me. As far as the limber willow is below the yellow-green olive, or the groundling Celtic nard below the bright red rosebeds, so far in my judgment does Amyntas rank lower than you.

Mo. Well, my boy, say no more; we are getting into the cave.

Over Daphnis, cut off by so cruel a fate, the nymphs were weeping; hazels and rivers, you heard the nymphs, when his mother, clasping her son's piteous corpse, is crying out on the cruelty of the gods and the stars, as only a mother can. None were there in those dreary days, Daphnis, to feed the oxen, and drive them down to the cool streams; no beast was there that tasted the river, or touched the blades of grass. Daphnis, thy death drew groans even from the lions of Carthage, so say the echoes of those wild mountains and forests. Daphnis, too, it was that set the fashion of harnessing the tigers of Armenia to the car. Daphnis, that showed how to bring on companies of Bacchanals, and twine quivering spear-shafts with soft foliage. As the vine is the glory of the trees it clasps, as the grapes of the vine, as the bull of the herd, as the standing corn of the fruitful field, thou and thou alone art the glory of those who love thee. Since the Fates have swept her off, Pales has taken *her* leave of the country, aye, and Apollo *his.* Often now-a-days, in the very furrows to whose care we give our largest barley grains, we see growing ungenerous darnel and unfruitful oats. In place of the delicate violet and the dazzling bright narcissus springs up the thistle, and the thorn with its sharp spikes. Sow the turf with flowers, embower the springs in shade, ye shepherds! It is Daphnis' charge that this should be done for him; and raise a tomb, and to the tomb append a verse, 'Here lie I, Daphnis, the woodlander, whose name is known from here to the stars; a lovely flock I had to keep, but I was more lovely than they.'

Me. Sweet is your strain to my ears, heavenly poet, as is sleep to tired limbs on the grass, as is the quenching of thirst in mid-day heat in the stream where sweet waters play. It is not only in piping, but in singing that you match your teacher. Happy shepherd boy! now you will be his fitting successor. Still, however, I will sing you in turn, as I best may, a strain here of my own, and will exalt your Daphnis to heaven. Yes, Daphnis I will carry up to heaven. I, too, was beloved by Daphnis.

Mo. As if there were anything I should value more than a boon like this. That glorious boy was a theme worthy of any one's song, and Stimicon ere now has dwelt to me with rapture on those strains of yours.

Me. Dazzling in beauty himself, Daphnis is now marvelling at the strange splendour of heaven's threshold as he crosses it, and looking down on the clouds and stars under his feet, whereat a wild and eager rapture is taking hold of the woods and the rest of rustic life, seizing on Pan and the

shepherds, and the Dryad maids. No more does the wolf
plan surprises for the cattle or the snares for the deer, for
they know that the gracious Daphnis loves all to be at
peace. The very mountains in their unshorn strength are
flinging the sound exultingly to the sky. The very rocks,
the plantations, too, are already taking up the song, 'We
have a new god, a new god, Menalcas!' Be gracious and
propitious to thy worshippers! See, here are four altars—
two, see, for thee, Daphnis; two of a larger build for
Phœbus; two cups, with new milk, foaming over the brim
each year, and two bowls will I set up for thee of rich olive
oil; and, above all, cheering the feast with abundance of the
wine-god's juice before the fire, if it be winter; if harvest-
time, in the shade, I will pour out into goblets the fresh
nectar of Ariusian wine. I will have songs sung by Damœtas
and Ægon of Lycta; the dances of the Satyrs shall be imita-
ted by Alphesibœus. Such honours shall be thine for ever,
both when we pay our yearly vows to the nymphs, and when
we have our lustral survey of the country. So long as the
wild boar shall love the mountain ridges, and the fish the
running stream; so long as thyme shall be the food of the bee,
and dew of the grasshopper, so long shall thy honour, and
thy name, and thy glory for ever remain. Like Bacchus and
Ceres, thou shalt have vows paid thee yearly by the countrymen. Thou, like them, shalt make thy worshippers thy
debtors.

Mo. What present, what shall I give you for a song like
this? Why, the whisper of the rising south is not so charming
to my ear, nor the beating of the waves on the shore, nor the
streams that run down among the rocky glens.

Me. Here is my present to you first—this frail reed; it was
this from which I learnt 'Corydon was burning for the lovely
Alexis,' and that other lesson, 'Whose cattle, Melibœus?'

Mo. But you must accept this sheep-hook, which, in spite of his frequent begging, Antigenes never got from me—and there was much to love in him, too, in those days—a handsome one, with regular knots and brass about it, Menalcas.

ECLOGUE VI.

VARUS.

First of all, my muse deigned to disport herself in the strains of pastoral Syracuse, and disdained not to make her home in the woods, goddess as she was. When I was venturing to sing of kings and battles, the Cynthian god touched my ear, and appealed to my memory. 'It is a shepherd's part, Tityrus, that the sheep that he feeds should be fat, and the songs that he sings thin.' So now I—for there will be enough and to spare, whose desire it will be to sing thy praises, Varus, and make battles their tragic theme—will choose the woodland muse for my study, and the slender reed for my instrument. It is not for me to sing strains unbidden. Still, if there *should* be any, any to read even a lowly lay like this with fond regard, thou, Varus, shouldst be the song of these tamarisks of mine— the song of the whole forestry—for Phœbus knows no more welcome page than that which bears on its front the name of Varus.

Proceed, Pierian maids. Young Chromis and Mnasylos saw old Silenus lying asleep in a cave, his veins swollen, as is his constant wont, by the wine-god, his friend of yesterday. There were the garlands a short way off, lying just as they dropped from his head, and his heavy jug was hanging by its battered handle. They commence the attack (for the old god had often balked both of a promised song), and put him in fetters made out of his own garlands. A companion comes up

B

to reassure their faltering, Ægle, Ægle, fairest of the Naiads, and as he begins to open his eyes, paints his forehead and his temples blood-red with mulberry juice. He, with a laugh at the stratagem, exclaims, 'What do you want with binding me? Untie me, boys; be content with the credit of having me in your power. The song you want is at your service.' With that he begins. This was the signal for fauns and wild beasts —you might see them—frolicking in measured dance, and stately unbending oaks nodding their tops to and fro; and as for the mountains, the rock of Parnassus is never so enraptured with Phœbus, nor are Rhodope and Ismarus so entranced by Orpheus.

For he began to sing how through the mighty void had been brought together the elements of earth and air and sea and streaming fire all at once; how from them as their origin all things had a beginning, and the new-born orb of the universe grew into shape. Next, the soil began to harden, and leave Nereus to be shut up in the sea, and by degrees to assume the forms of things, so that at length the earth is surprised to see a new sun break into light above it, and the rain has a longer fall as the clouds are drawn up higher, just as the woods first begin to rise from the ground, and living things wander thinly over mountains that never saw them before.

From this he comes to tell of the stones that Pyrrha threw behind her, the golden reign of Saturn, and the birds of Caucasus, and the theft of Prometheus. With this he couples the tale, how Hylas was left behind at the spring, and his shipmates called for him till the shore rang with Hylas! Hylas! from end to end. Turning next to her who would have been happy indeed had cattle never been created, Pasiphae, he soothes her with her passion for the snow-white bull. Unhappy girl! how came such frenzy to take hold of thee? Prœtus' daughters once filled the pastures with their counterfeited low-

ings, yet none of them ever fell to such disgrace, often as she
shrank from the thought of the yoke on her neck, and felt for
horns on her smooth woman's brow. Unhappy girl ! yes, thou
art wandering over the hills, while he, with that snowy side
pillowed on soft hyacinths, is chewing the yellow green grass
under the dark holm oak, or going after some heifer in the
populous herd. Close, ye nymphs, ye nymphs of Dicte, haste
and close the glades of the forest, if by any chance my eyes
may fall on the bull's truant footsteps ; perhaps he may have
been attracted by a patch of green herbage, or may have gone
after the herd, and some of the cows may bring him home to
the stalls of Gortyna.

Then he sings of the maiden who stopped to admire the
apples of the Hesperides ; next he clothes the sisters of Phaethon with a mossy bark of bitter taste, and bids them rise
from the ground as tall alders. Next he sings how, as Gallus
was wandering by the waters of Permessus, one of the sisters
took him up to the Aonian hills, and how the whole choir of
Phœbus stood up to receive their noble visitant ; how Linus,
shepherd and heavenly poet in one, his locks wreathed with
flowers and bitter parsley leaves, bespoke him thus :—'These
reeds the Muses present to thee, here they are. The same
which they gave the old bard of Ascra before thee. The same
with which he, as he sang to them, used to bring stately unbending ashes down from the mountain-side. With these do
thou tell the story of the planting of the Grynean forest, and
tell it so that there may be no grove on which Apollo prides
himself more.'

What need to repeat how he told of Scylla, Nisus' daughter,
her to whom the story clings, that, 'with a girdle of howling
monsters round her beauteous form, she made havoc of the
Dulichian vessels, and in the depths of the eddying waters
gave the poor trembling sailors to be torn limb from limb by

the dogs of the sea; or how he told of Tereus' transformed shape, of the food and the present which Philomela got ready for him, of the strange speed with which she made for the desert, and of the wings on which the unhappy queen hovered over the palace once her own?

All the themes, in short, to which, as once sung by Phœbus, Eurotas listened in ecstasy, and bade his bays get them by heart, Silenus sings: the valleys feel the shock of song and pass it on to the stars, till Vesper gave the word to fold the flocks and report the number, and began his unwelcome march over Olympus.

ECLOGUE VII.

MELIBŒUS.

Daphnis happened just to have seated himself under a holm oak that gave tongue to the wind, and Corydon and Thyrsis had driven their flocks to the same spot—Thyrsis' sheep, Corydon's goats swelling with milk—both in the bloom of life, Arcadians both, ready to sing first or second in a match. Just then, as I was busy sheltering some myrtles from the cold, my he-goat, the lord and master of the herd, had strayed to where they were, and I catch sight of Daphnis. As soon as he meets my eye—' Quick,' he says, ' come here, Melibœus, your goat and kids are all safe, and if you can afford to be idle a little, rest under the shade. Whére we are, your bullocks will come over the meadows of themselves to drink; here is Mincius fringing his green banks with a border of soft waving reeds, and there is a swarm humming from Jupiter's favourite oak.' What was I to do? On the one hand I had no Alcippe or Phyllis, to shut up my new-weaned lambs at home, and the match coming off, Corydon against Thyrsis, was sure to be great. However, I let their play take precedence of my work.

So in alternate songs they began to compete. Alternate songs were what the Muses within them chose to recall. These were repeated by Corydon, those by Thyrsis in regular order.

C. Nymphs of Libethra, my heart's delight, either vouchsafe me a strain such as you gave my Codrus—the songs *he* makes come next to Phœbus' own—or, if such power is not for all of us, see, my tuneful pipe shall be hung up here on your consecrated pine.

T. Shepherds, deck your rising poet with a crown of ivy; ye of Arcadia, that Codrus' sides may burst with envy; or should he try the power of extravagant praise, bind foxglove on my brows, that the ill tongue may do no harm to the bard that is to be.

C. This for thee, Delia, the head of a bristly boar, from young Micon, and the branchy horns of a long-lived stag. Should such luck be secured to him by right, thou shalt be set up full length in polished marble, with purple buskins tied round thy legs.

T. A bowl of milk and these cakes, Priapus, are enough for thee to look for year by year; the orchard thou guardest is but a poor one, so we have had to make thee marble with our present means; but if this year's births fill up our herds, then be of gold.

C. Galatea, child of Nereus, sweeter to me than Hybla's thyme, whiter than the swan, more delicate than the palest ivy, soon as the bullocks return home from pasture to their stalls, if thou hast any regard for thy Corydon, come, O come!

T. Nay, rather think me bitterer than Sardinian herbage, rougher than gorse, more worthless than the weed that rots on the shore, if I do not find this day longer already than a whole year. Home with you from your pasture; for shame, home with you, lazy bullocks!

C. Mossy springs, and grass more downy-soft than sleep,

and the arbute that embowers you greenly with its straggling shade, keep the solstice heat from my flock; already summer is coming on in its fierceness, already buds are swelling on the vine's luxuriant tendrils.

T. Here we have a good hearth, and pinewood with plenty of pitch, and a large fire always blazing, and the posts of our door black with continual soot; here as we sit we care for north winds and cold weather about as much as the wolf for the size of the flock, or torrents for their banks.

C. Here stand junipers and prickly chestnuts—there lie the fruits of summer scattered each under its parent tree— just now all nature is smiling; but if our lovely Alexis were to go away from these hills of ours, you would see even the rivers dried up.

T. The country is parched up; the grass is dying for thirst from the sickly air; the wine-god grudges the hills the shade of the vine they love; but when my own Phyllis arrives, all the woodland shall be green again, and Jupiter shall come down plenteously in fertilising showers.

C. The poplar is the favourite of Alcides, the vine of Bacchus, the myrtle of Venus, beauty's queen, the bay of Phœbus: Phyllis' passion is for the hazel—while Phyllis' passion lasts, the myrtle shall not take rank above the hazel, nor yet the bay of Phœbus.

T. The ash is the fairest in the woods, the pine in the gardens, the poplar on the river banks, the fir on the mountain heights; but if thou, Lycidas, beauty's king, shouldst visit me often and often, the ash would soon bow to thee in the woods, the pine in the gardens.

M. So much I remember, and how Thyrsis failed in the match. From that day forward it is all Corydon, Corydon with us.

ECLOGUE VIII.

PHARMACEUTRIA.

The pastoral muse that inspired Damon and Alphesibœus, at whose contention the heifer stood wondering and forgot to graze, whose strains held lynxes spell-bound, and made rivers suffer change, and arrest their flow—the Muse that inspired Damon and Alphesibœus shall be our song.

But thou, whether my heart is with thee as thou art surmounting the rocks of mighty Timavus or coasting the shore of the Illyrian sea, will that day ever come that will find me free to tell of thy deeds? Shall I ever be free to publish the whole world through those strains of thine, alone worthy of Sophocles' tragic march? From thee is my beginning, for thee shall be the end. Accept these strains commenced at thy bidding, and suffer this ivy to wind itself round thy brows among thy triumphal bays.

Scarce had night's cold shade parted from the sky, just at the time that the dew on the tender grass is sweetest to the cattle, when leaning on his smooth olive wand Damon thus began :—

Rise, Lucifer, and usher in the day, the genial day, while I, deluded by a bridegroom's unworthy passion for my Nisa, make my complaint, and turning myself to the gods, little as their witness has stood me in stead, address them nevertheless, a dying man, at this very last hour. Take up with me, my pipe, the song of Mænalus.

Mænalus it is whose forests are ever tuneful, and his pines ever vocal ; he is ever listening to the loves of shepherds, and to Pan, the first who would not have the reeds left unemployed. Take up with me, my pipe, the song of Mænalus.

Mopsus has Nisa given him : what may not we lovers

expect to see ? Matches will be made by this between griffins and horses, and in the age to come hounds will accompany timid does to their draught. Mopsus, cut fresh brands for to-night; it is to you they are bringing home a wife. Fling about nuts as a bridegroom should; it is for you that Hesperus is leaving his rest on Œta. Take up with me, my pipe, the song of Mænalus.

O worthy mate of a worthy lord! There as you look down on all the world, and are disgusted at my pipe and my goats, and my shaggy brow, and this beard that I let grow, and do not believe that any god cares aught for the things of men. Take up with me, my pipe, the song of Mænalus.

It was in our enclosure I saw you gathering apples with the dew on them. I myself showed you the way, in company with my mother—my twelfth year had just bidden me enter on it. I could just reach from the ground to the boughs that snapped so easily. What a sight! what ruin to me! what a fatal frenzy swept me away! Take up with me, my pipe, the song of Mænalus.

Now know I what love is; it is among savage rocks that he is produced by Tmarus, or Rhodope, or the Garamantes at earth's end; no child of lineage or blood like ours. Take up with me, my pipe, the song of Mænalus.

Love, the cruel one, taught the mother to embrue her hands in her children's blood; hard too was thy heart, mother. Was the mother's heart harder, or the boy god's malice more wanton? Wanton was the boy god's malice; hard too thy heart, mother. Take up with me, my pipe, the song of Mænalus.

Aye, now let the wolf even run away from the sheep; let golden apples grow out of the tough heart of oak; let narcissus blossom on the alder; let the tamarisk's bark sweat rich drops of amber; rivalry let there be between swans and screech-owls;

let Tityrus become Orpheus—Orpheus in the woodland, Arion among the dolphins. Take up with me, my pipe, the song of Mænalus.

Nay, let all be changed to the deep sea. Farewell, ye woods! Headlong from the airy mountain's watchtower I will plunge into the waves; let this come to her as the· last gift of the dying. Cease, my pipe, cease at length the song of Mænalus.

Thus far Damon; for the reply of Alphesibœus, do ye recite it, Pierian maids; it is not for all of us to have command of all.

Bring out water and bind the altars here with a soft woollen fillet, and burn twigs full of sap and male frankincense, that I may try the effect of magic rites in turning my husband's mind from its soberness; there is nothing but charms wanting here. Bring me home from the town, my charms, bring me my Daphnis.

Charms have power even to draw the moon down from heaven; by charms Circe transformed the companions of Ulysses; the cold snake as he lies in the fields is burst asunder by chanting charms. Bring me home from the town, my charms, bring me my Daphnis.

These three threads distinct with three colours I wind round thee first, and thrice draw the image round the altar thus; heaven delights in an uneven number. Twine in three knots, Amaryllis, the three colours; twine them, Amaryllis, do,· and say, 'I am twining the bonds of Love.' Bring me home from the town, my charms, bring me my Daphnis.

Just as this clay is hardened, and this wax melted, by one and the same fire, so may my love act doubly on Daphnis. Crumble the salt cake, and kindle the crackling bay leaves with bitumen. Daphnis, the wretch, is setting me on fire; I am setting this bay on fire about Daphnis. Bring me home from the town, my charms, bring me my Daphnis.

May such be Daphnis' passion, like a heifer's, when, weary of looking for her mate through groves and tall forests, she throws herself down by a stream of water on the green sedge, all undone, and forgets to rise and make way for the fargone night—may such be his enthralling passion, nor let me have a mind to relieve it. Bring me home from the town, my charms, bring me my Daphnis.

These cast-off relics that faithless one left me days ago, precious pledges for himself, them I now entrust to thee, Earth, burying them even on the threshold; they are bound as pledges to give me back Daphnis. Bring me home from the town, my charms, bring me my Daphnis.

These plants and these poisons culled from Pontus I had from Mæris' own hand. They grow in plenty at Pontus. By the strength of these often I have seen Mæris turn to a wolf and plunge into the forest, often call up spirits from the bottom of the tomb, and remove standing crops from one field to another. Bring me home from the town, my charms, bring me my Daphnis.

Carry the embers out of doors, Amaryllis, and fling them into the running stream over your head; and do not look behind you. This shall be my device against Daphnis. As for gods or charms, he cares for none of them. Bring me home from the town, my charms, bring me my Daphnis.

Look, look! the flickering flame has caught the altar of its own accord, shot up from the embers, before I have had time to take them up, all of themselves. Good luck, I trust! . . . Yes, there is something, I am sure . . . and Hylax is barking at the gate. Can I trust myself? or is it that lovers make their own dreams? Stop, he is coming from town; stop now, charms, my Daphnis!

ECLOGUE IX.

MÆRIS.

L. Whither away on foot, Mæris; following the road to the town?

M. O Lycidas! we have been kept on alive, to hear a stranger . . . what our fears never looked for . . . now, owner of our little farm, say to us, 'I am master here; you old tenants, take yourselves away;' and so now, beaten and cowed, since Fortune's wheel is on the roll everywhere, we are carrying him these kids, with a mischief to him.

L. Why, surely I had heard that all the land from where the hills begin to draw themselves up from the plain, and then let down the ridge with a gentle slope, on to the water, and those old beeches with their battered tops, your Menalcas had succeeded in saving by his songs.

M. Aye, so you had, and so the story went; but our songs, I can tell you, Lycidas, have as much power in the clatter of weapons of war as the doves of Chaonia, they say, have when the eagle is coming. So if I had not been warned before hand anyhow to cut this new quarrel short by the raven on the left from the hollow holm-oak, you would not have seen your servant Mæris here, nor Menalcas himself alive.

L. Alas! could any one be guilty of such a crime? alas! were we so nearly losing all the comfort you give us, along with yourself, Menalcas? Who would there be to sing of the nymphs? Who to sow the turf with flowers and herbage, and embower the springs in green shade? Or who would give us songs like that I caught slily from you the other day when you were making your way to that darling Amaryllis of ours?—'Tityrus, whilst I come back—it will not be long—feed my goats for me; and when fed drive them to water,

Tityrus, and in driving them don't come across the he-goat—
he has a trick of butting, beware.'

M. Or this, you might have said, the song he was making
for Varus and had not finished :—'Varus, thy name—only
let Mantua be spared us ; Mantua, too near a neighbour, alas !
to ill-starred Cremona—our swans in their songs shall carry
aloft to the stars.'

L. If you would have your swarms fail to light on the
yews of Corsica, and your heifers swell their udders with milk
from browsing on lucerne, begin with anything you have in
your mind. I, too, have been made a poet by the Muses, and
have verses, too, of my own. I am called a bard myself by
the shepherds, but I have no mind to trust them ; for as yet
I cannot think my singing worthy of Varius or of Cinna ; no,
it is the mere cackling of a goose among the melody of swans.

M. That is what I am trying to do, turning over in my
mind, Lycidas, while you have been speaking, in the hope of
being able to recollect ; for it is no vulgar song. 'Hither to
me, Galatea ! why, what sport can there be in the water ? Here
are the glorious hues of spring, here is the ground pouring
forth flowers of all dyes on the river-bank, here is the fair
white poplar stooping over the cave, and the limber vines
weaving a bower of shelter. Hither to me, and let the mad
waves beat the shore as they please.'

L. What of the song I heard you singing that clear night
all alone ? I remember the tune if I could but get the words.

M. 'Daphnis, why that upturned look at the old constellations rising ? See, the star of Cæsar, Dione's darling, has
begun its march—a star to make the corn-fields glad with produce, and the colour deepen on the grape in the sunny hills.
Graft your pears, Daphnis, and spare not ; the fruit you grow
will be gathered by the next generation.' Everything goes
with time, the brain among the rest. Many were the long

summer days, I remember, I used to send to their grave with singing as a boy, and now all my store of songs is forgotten. Nay, Mæris' voice is taking leave of him too; wolves have set eyes on Mæris first. But what you want you can hear repeated often enough by Menalcas.

L. All your put-offs only make my longing greater. Besides, just now the sea is all laid and hushed to hear you, and every breath of murmuring wind, as you may see, has fallen dead. Here we are just half-way, for the tomb of Bianor is becoming visible; here, where the husbandmen are lopping those thick leaves; here, Mæris, let us stop and sing; here put your kids down; we shall get to the town for all that; or, if we are afraid that night will get up a shower first, there is nothing to hinder our singing—it makes the journey hurt less—as we go right on. So now, that we may sing as we go, I will relieve you of this load of yours.

M. Press me no more, my boy; let us think only of what is before us; the songs we shall have a better voice for when we see *him* with us again.

ECLOGUE X.

GALLUS.

This my last effort, Arethusa, do thou vouchsafe me. A song for my Gallus, brief, yet such as may win even Lycoris' ear, I have to sing—who would refuse a song to Gallus? If, as thou glidest under the Sicilian billows, thou wouldest not have the salt goddess of Ocean mingle her waters with thine, begin the lay; let its theme be Gallus' vexing passion, while the silly flat-nosed goats are browsing on the growing brakes. Our songs are not to deaf ears: every note is echoed by the woods.

What forests, what lawns were your abode, virgin nymphs of the fountains, when Gallus was wasting under an unworthy passion? What indeed? for it was not any spot in the ridges of Parnassus or of Pindus that kept you there; no, nor Aonian Aganippe. Yet over him even the bays, even the tamarisks shed their tears; over him as he lay under the lonely rock even the pine-crowned head of Mænalus shed a tear, and the dull stones of cold Lycæus. There, too, standing about him are his sheep; they are not ashamed of humanity, nor do thou be ashamed of thy flock, heavenly poet as thou art; even Adonis in his beauty once fed sheep by the water. Up came the shepherd too: slowly up came the swineherds; dripping from the winter's mast up came Menalcas. Every mouth cries, Whence this passion of thine? Up came Apollo—Gallus, says he, why be a madman? thy heart's queen, Lycoris, has braved the snow and the savage life of camps to follow another. Up, too, came Silvanus with his woodland honours green on his brow, nodding his fennels in bloom and his giant lilies. Pan came, Arcadia's own god; him we saw with our own eyes, crimsoned all over with blood-red elderberries and vermilion. Is there ever to be an end of this? he cries. As for Love, such things move him not. Tears will no more sate Love's cruelty than sluices will your grass, or lucerne your bees, or fodder your goats. His answer came with a sigh— You will sing of me though, Arcadians, when I am gone, in the ears of your mountains; none know how to sing but Arcadians. O how soft a sleep would my bones enjoy, could I but feel that a pipe of yours one day would tell of my passion! Nay, indeed, would that I had been one of you myself—the shepherd of a flock of yours, or the dresser of those full ripe grapes! Then at least, whether it had been Phyllis, or Amyntas, or any other love; and what if Amyntas be brown? violets are dark too and so are hyacinths dark—I should have

had them ever by my side, among the willows, under the
limber vine; Phyllis plucking me flowers for a wreath,
Amyntas singing. See, here are cold springs and soft meadows,
Lycoris, and a forest of trees; here I could wear away with
thee by mere lapse of time. And now this mad passion for
the savage war-god is keeping me here in arms, with weapons
all about me and enemies drawn up before me, while thou,
far away from thy native land—would it were not mine to
believe the tale—art looking with those cruel, cruel eyes on
the Alpine snows and the frost-bound Rhine, alone without
me at thy side. Oh! may the frost forbear to harm thee!
may the sharp ice be kept from wounding thy tender feet! I
will be gone, and set the strains which I have framed in the
measure of Chalcis to the reed of the Sicilian shepherd. Sure
am I that it will be better to bear my fate in the woods, with
the dens of wild beasts round me, and engrave my love on the
young growing trees; they will shoot up, and my love will
shoot up with them. Meantime I will scour Mænalus along
with the nymphs, or have a hunt of fierce boars. No stress of
winter shall keep me from besetting with my hounds the
lawns of mount Parthenius. Yes, I can see myself already
on the move over rocks or amid the cry of the woods; I feel
the pleasure of winging shafts of Cydon from a bow of Parthia,
as though this were a medicine for madness like mine, or that
tyrant god would ever learn compassion for human suffering!
It is gone—wood nymphs have no charm for me now, nor
songs either. Woodlands, I must part from you, too, now.
He is a god whom no endurance of ours can change. No,
not if in midwinter we were to drink the waters of Hebrus, or
submit ourselves to the snows of Sithonia and its sleety cold.
All are conquered by Love; and let us, too, yield ourselves
Love's captives.

Let thus much suffice, Goddesses, for your poet's song,

sung as he sits and weaves a basket of slender willow. Goddesses of Pieria, you will enhance its worth to the highest in Gallus's eyes. Gallus, the love of whom grows on me hour by hour as fast as the green alder shoots up from the earth when the spring is new. Now let us rise; there is apt to be danger to singers in the shade; danger in the juniper's shade, and crops too suffer from shade. Home with you, such a meal as you have eaten. Hesper is coming, home with you, my goats.

THE GEORGICS.

BOOK I.

WHAT makes a corn-field smile; what star suits best for turning up the soil, and marrying the vine to the elm; what care oxen need; what is the method of breeding cattle; and what weight of men's experience preserves the frugal common-wealth of bees: such is the song I now essay. Brightest lights of the world, that guide the year's smooth course through heaven: father Liber and mother Ceres; if it was by your bounty that Earth changed the acorn of Chaonia for the plump well-favoured corn-ear, and found the grape where-with to temper her draught of Achelous: you too, Fauns, the countryman's propitious deities, trip hither in time, Fauns and Dryad maidens, I sing of your bounty too: and thou, for whom Earth first teemed forth the fiery horse under the stroke of thy mighty trident, Neptune; and thou, dresser of woods and groves, to pleasure whom Ceos' luxuriant brakes are browsed by three hundred snow-white bullocks; come thou, too, in thy power, from thy forest home and the Lycæan lawns, Pan, tender of sheep, by the love thou bearest thy Mænalus, O stand graciously at my side, god of Tegea; and thou, Minerva, who foundest the olive for man; and thou, blessed youth, who showedst him the crooked plough; and

Silvanus, carrying a young cypress, fresh torn up by its roots—gods and goddesses all, whose province is the guardianship of the country—both ye who foster the new-born produce that springs up unsown, and ye who send down on the sown crop plenteous rain from heaven. And thou, last not least, of whom we know not in what house of gods thou art in good time to sit—whether it be our Cæsar's pleasure to preside over cities and take charge of the earth, that so the vast world may welcome thee as the giver of its increase, and lord of its changeful seasons, crowning thy brows with thy mother's own myrtle; or whether thy coming shall be as the god of the unmeasured sea, the sole power to claim the seaman's homage, with furthest Thule for thy handmaid, and Tethys, buying thee for her daughter with the dower of all her waves; or whether thou art to give us a new star to quicken our lazy months, just where a space opens itself between Erigone and the Claws that come next in order:—see, there is the fiery Scorpion, already drawing in his arms for thee, and leaving thee more than thy fair share of the sky. Whatever thy future place—for let not Tartarus hope to have thee for its king, nor mayest thou ever feel so monstrous an ambition; though Greece see charms in her Elysian fields, and Proserpine, spite of her mother's journey, refuse to follow her back to earth—vouchsafe me a smooth course, and smile on my bold endeavours, and in pity, like mine, for the countryman as he wanders blind and unguided, assume the god, and attune thine ear betimes to the voice of prayer.

In the dawn of spring, when icy streams trickle melting from the hoar mountains, and the crumbling clod breaks its chain at the west wind's touch, even then I would fain see the plough driven deep till the bull groans again, and the share rubbed in the furrow till it shines. That is the cornfield to give an answer, full though late, to the grasping farmer's prayer, which has twice been laid bare to summer heat, and twice to winter cold—that is the corn-field to burst the barns with its unmeasured crop. Before, however, our share breaks the crust of an unknown soil, our care should be to understand the winds, and the divers humours of the sky, and the traditional culture and habitude of the land, what each clime produces and what each disowns. Here you see corn crops, there grapes have kindlier growth: other spots are green with the young of trees and grass that comes unbidden. Only see how it is Tmolus that sends us its saffron fragrance, India its ivory, the soft Arab his frankincense, the great naked Chalybs, again, his iron, Pontus its potent castor, Epirus the prizes of the mares of Elis! Such is the chain of law, such the eternal covenant with which Nature has bound certain climes, from the day when Deucalion first hurled his stones on the unpeopled earth—stones, whence sprang man's race, hard as they. Come, then, and let your rich soil, soon as ever the year begins, be turned up by the bullock's strength—let the clods be exposed for Summer to bake them to dust with its full mellow suns; but if the land be not fertile, be content to wait till Arcturus, and then just raise the surface with a shallow furrow—in the one case, that a luxuriant crop may not be choked with weeds; in the other, that the barren seed may not lose the little moisture it has.

Moreover, in alternate years, you will let your fields lie fallow after reaping, and suffer the scurf to harden on the inactive plain; or you will sow your golden spelt when another star arises; where you lately took off the rattling pods of a luxuriant bean crop, or the yield of the slender vetch and the bitter lupine's brittle stems and echoing jungle. For a plain is parched by a crop of flax; parched by the oat, parched by the poppy steeped in slumberous Lethe. Yet rotation will lighten the strain; only think of the dried-up soil, and be not afraid to give it its fill of rich manure—think of the exhausted field, and fling about the grimy ashes broadcast. Then, under the change of produce, the land gets equal rest, and you escape the thanklessness of an unploughed soil. Oft, too, has it been found of use to set a barren field on fire, and let the crackling flames burn up the light stubble. Whether it be that the land derives hidden strength and fattening nourishment from the process, or that the fire bakes out any distemper it may have, and sweats out its superfluous moisture, or that the heat opens fresh passages and secret apertures through which life-juice may come to the tender blades, or that it makes the land harder, and binds up its gaping pores, that so the subtle shower and the fierce sun's unusual tyranny, and the north wind's searching cold may have no power to parch it to the quick. Great, aye, great are his services to the land who breaks up its sluggish clods with the harrow, and drags over them his wicker hurdles : the golden corn-goddess eyes him from her Olympian height with no idle regard ; great, too, his, who having once broken through the land's crust, and made it lift its ridgy back, turns his plough, and drives through it a second time crosswise, and piles earth again and again, and bows her fields to his will.

A wet summer and a fine winter should be the farmer's prayer. From winter's dust comes great joy to the corn, joy to the land. No tillage gives Mysia such cause for boasting, or Gargarus for wondering at his own harvest. Why talk of the man who having cast his seed, follows up the blow with his rake, and levels the bare sandy ridges, and then when the corn is springing up, brings on it streaming waters,•that follow as he leads ; and when the scorched land is in a glow, and the corn blades dying—O joy ! from the brow of the channelled slope entices the floods? See ! down it tumbles, waking hoarse murmurs among the smooth stones, and allaying the sun-struck ground as it bubbles on. Why talk of him, who in his care lest the weight of the ear should overbear the stems, grazes down the luxuriance of the crop while yet in the blade, when the springing corn has just reached the furrow's top; or of him, who drains off the whole watery contents of a marsh by absorbent sand—especially where, in the treacherous seasons, a river overflows, and covers whole acres with a coat of mud, making the hollow furrows steam again with the reeking moisture?

Do not think either, after all that the labour of man and beast has gone through in turning the soil over and over, that no harm is to be feared from the tormenting goose, the crane from the Strymon, or the bitter fibres of chicory; no injury from excess of shade. No, the wise Father of all has willed that the farmer's path should be no easy one. He was the first to break up the land by human skill, using care to sharpen men's wits, nor letting the realm he had made his own grow dull under the weight of lethargy. Before Jove's time never husbandman subdued the country. Even to set a mark on the champaign or divide it with a boundary line was a thing unlawful. Men's gettings were for the common stock, and earth of her own free will produced everything, and that more freely than now, though none asked it of her. He it was that gave the black snake its baleful venom, and ordered the wolf to prowl and the sea to swell, stripped the leaves of their honey, and put the fire away, and stopped the wine that used to flow in common river-beds—that experience, through patient thought, might hammer out divers arts by slow degrees— might get at the corn blade by delving the furrow, and smite out from the heart of the flint the hidden fire. Then it was that the hollowed alder first touched the river—then the mariner numbered and named the stars—Pleïades, and Hyades, and Lycaon's glittering child, the Bear. Then men found how to capture game with the noose, to beguile them with lime, and how to let their hounds round the mighty lawns. And one man has learned already to flog a wide river with his casting net, making for the deep, while another is dragging his dripping meshes through the sea. Then came stubborn iron and the thin creaking saw—for the first men clove their wood with the wedge—then came the divers arts of life. So Toil conquered the world, relentless Toil, and Want that grinds in adversity.

Ceres was the first to teach men to break up the earth with iron, in days when the sacred forests had begun to fall short in acorns and arbutes, and Dodona to withhold her sustenance. Soon, however, the wheat had plagues of its own—the baleful mildew was bidden to eat the stems, and the lazy thistle to set up its spikes in the fields. The crops begin to die, and a prickly jungle steals into their place, burrs, caltrops and the like; and among the glistening corn towers like a king the unkindly darnel and the unfruitful oat. So, unless your rake is ever ready to exterminate weeds, your shout to scare away birds, your hook to restrain the shade which darkens the land, and your prayers to call down rain, poor man, you will gaze on your neighbour's big heap of grain, with unavailing envy. Betake yourself to the woods again, and shake the oak to allay your hunger.

I must tell you, too, what are the stout farmer's weapons of war, without whose aid none has ever sown or raised a crop. First the share, and the bent plough's heavy wood, and the slow lumbering wains of the mighty Mother of Eleusis, sledges and drags, and the rakes with their cruel weight, and the cheap wicker-work furniture of Celeus, bush-harrows of arbute twigs, and Iacchus' mystic fan—implements these which you will remember to store up long before the day of need, if you are destined to win and wear the full glories of the divine country.

From its youth up in the woods the elm is bent by main force and trained into a beam, taking the form of the crooked plough; to suit this a pole is shaped, stretching eight feet in length with two earth-boards, and a share-beam with its back on each side. So the light linden tree is cut down betimes for the yoke, and the tall beech which is to be the handle to guide the carriage from behind, and the wood is hung up over the hearth for the smoke to season it.

I could repeat to you many rules of old experience, but I see you start off and weary of listening to such petty cares. The threshing-floor in particular has to be smoothed with a heavy roller, kneaded with the hand, and made solid with astringent chalk, lest weeds should creep into it, or dust get into it and break it into holes, and then all manner of plagues make their game of it—the tiny mouse for example often sets up a home and builds a granary under ground, or the blind mole scrapes out a lurking place, or toads are found in the hollows, and all the other loathly creatures that the earth produces, and ravages are made in a huge heap of corn by the weevil, and the ant which ever fears for an old age of poverty.

Observe, too, when the walnut-tree in the plantation bursts into blossom all over and makes its fragrant boughs bend again, if the bulk of them turn to fruit, grain will follow in like proportion, and there will be a great day for the threshing and a great one for the heat; but if it is a luxuriance of leaves that makes the shade so abundant, the threshing-floor will be tasked in vain, bruising stems laden only with chaff.

As for pulse, I have known many men steep it ere they sowed it, drenching it first with nitre and black mother-of-oil, that the treacherous pods might yield a larger produce, and one that would boil readily over a small fire. Yet spite of all patience in choosing, spite of all pains in examining, I have seen the race die out, unless where men's power, year by year, picked out the largest one by one. So is it—all earthly things are doomed to fall away and slip back into chaos, like a boatman who just manages to make head against the stream, if the tension of his arms happens to relax, and the current whirls away the boat headlong down the river's bed.

Moreover it is as much our interest to watch Arcturus' sign, and the rising of the Kids, and the glittering Snake, as theirs who sailing homeward over the stormy water explore Pontus and the jaws of oyster-breeding Abydus. When the Balance has apportioned the hours equally between daytime and sleep, and is giving half the circle of the sky to light and half to shade; come, my brave men, task your oxen, sow barley broadcast over the field, till the very verge of the cold winter rains, when no hand can be put to work. Then, too, is the time to bury in the earth your future crop of flax, and the poppy that the corn-goddess loves, aye, and more than time to stoop vigorously over the plough, while the dry earth will let you, while the clouds hang unbroken. Spring is the sow-ing time for beans—then, too, the lucerne is welcomed by the fallow furrows, and millet claims its yearly care, when the snow-white Bull with his gilded horns throws open the year, and the Dog sets in retreat before the star's advancing front. But if it is for a harvest of wheat and hardy spelt that you would task the soil, pressing on with ardour which only corn can satisfy, first see Atlas' children take their morning departure, and the star of Gnossus, the blazing crown, recede from view, ere you charge the furrows with the seed they have begun to want, or force the care of a whole year's Hopes on a reluctant soil. Many have begun ere the setting of Maia; but they have found their expected crop mock them with a show of empty corn-ears. But if you are for sowing vetches and cheap kidney-beans, and do not think time ill-spent over the lentile of Pelusium, you cannot misread the prognostic given by Boötes at his setting—begin, and carry on your sowing into the heart of the frosty season.

It is to this end that the orbit of the golden sun, divided into fixed portions, is guided through the world's twelve signs. Five zones comprise the heaven; one of them, ever glowing under the sun's glance, ever scorched by his flame; on each side of which, right and left, two others stretch away into the far distance—frozen homes of dull green ice and black storms. Between these and the central zone yet other twain have been vouchsafed to over-toiled humanity by the clemency of Heaven, and betwixt them has been cut a path, along which the succession of the signs may turn obliquely. High as the globe rises towards Scythia and the pinnacles of Rhipæan hills, so deep is its downward slope to Libya and its southern clime. The one pole ever stands towering above our heads; the other is thrust down beneath the feet of murky Styx and her abysmal spectres. Here, with his monstrous spiral coils, shoots out the Snake, winding like a river around and between the two Bears—the Bears who ever shrink from the touch of ocean's waters. There, some say, all is wrapped in eternal night, with its silence that knows no seasons, and its thick pall deepening the gloom; or, as others think, Aurora visits them when she leaves us, and brings them back the day; and as we feel the first breath of her orient steeds panting up our sky, among them Vesper, all crimson, is lighting its evening torch. Hence it is that we can foretell the changes of the fitful heaven, the harvest-tide, and the time for sowing, and what season is best for breaking with our oars the sea's treacherous calm; what for rigging and launching a fleet, or laying low the pine among its forest brethren when its time is come. Aye, hence it is that we watch, not in vain, for the signs as they rise and set, and for the four Seasons whose diversity regulates the year.

Whenever a cold rainy day keeps the farmer a prisoner, it is but a boon, enabling him to get ready in time many things which he would have had to hurry through ere long in fine weather. See, the ploughman sits hammering out the fang of his ploughshare, which has been blunted, or hollowing a trough out of a tree, or he has set marks on his cattle, or numbers on his corn-sacks ; others are sharpening stakes and two-pronged forks, and making bands of Amerian willows for tying up the limber vine. Now is your time ; plait baskets of the pliant bramble-twig, parch your corn at the fire, or bruise it with the millstone. Why, even on holy-days, some work is permitted by the laws of heaven and earth. The strictest worshipper has never scrupled to let off a river, plant a hedge to protect his crop, set traps for birds, fire the brambles, or wash his bleating flock for health's sake in the stream. Often, too, has the slow ass his sides laden with oil or plenty of cheap apples by his driver, who comes back from town with a dented millstone, or a lump of black pitch for his trouble.

The moon herself has assigned her several days to man, as each in its several degree propitious to labour. Avoid the fifth ; then was born the ghastly God of Death and the Furies ; then it was that the Earth produced her monster brood—Cœus and Iapetus and fell Typhoeus, and the brethren who banded together to tear down heaven's gates. Thrice, indeed, did they essay to heap Ossa on Pelion, and upheave on to Ossa the forests of Olympus ; thrice the Father with his thunderbolt dashed their mountain pile to pieces. The seventeenth is lucky for planting out the vine, taking and breaking in young oxen, and adding the leashes to the warp. The ninth smiles on runaways, but frowns on thieving.

Nay, there are many cases where nature submits to man

more readily in chilly night, or when the sun is young, and the morning star sends dew on the earth. Night is the best for cutting the light stubble, night for the dry meadows; night has always good store of moisture to supple the grass. I know a man who will sit by the light of a winter fire the whole night through, with a sharp knife notching his brands, while his wife, solacing her tedious task with song, draws her shrill comb quickly over the warp, or with the fire-god's help boils down the sweet liquid must, and skims with a leaf the wave of the simmering caldron.

But the ruddy corn-goddess is reaped in midsummer heat, and in midsummer heat the parched ears are bruised on the threshing-floor. Strip to plough, strip to sow; winter is a lazy time for the farmer. In cold weather the husbandman thinks rather of enjoying what he has got, and making merry with his neighbours in friendly companies. Winter is the entertainer, calling out man's happier self, and unbinding his load of care, as it were the end of a long voyage, when the heavy-laden vessel has at length touched the harbour's bar, and the sailors in ecstasy are wreathing her stern with garlands. Then, however, is the time to strip acorns for fodder, and the berries of the bay, the olive, and the blood-red myrtle; the time to set springes for cranes and nets for deer, and chase the long-eared hare; the time to strike the doe with a vigorous sweep of the hempen lash of your Balearic sling, in the days when the snow lies in deep drifts, when the floods roll down their ice.

Why talk of the fitful changes of Autumn and its signs, and the dangers against which men must watch when the days begin to shorten, and the summer heat to soften! or when Spring pours down in showers, when the plain already bristles with waving ears, and the corn on its green stem is swelling with milky juice? Oft have I, when the farmer

was taking his reaper into the yellow field, and just beginning
to top the barley's frail stalk, seen all the armies of the winds
meet in the shock of battle, tearing up by the roots whole
acres of heavy corn, and whirling it on high, just as a common
hurricane would sweep down its dark current light straw and
flying stubble. Oft, too, comes rushing from the sky a vast
column of waters, the clouds mustering from the length and
breadth of heaven, and making their dark storms into one
great murky tempest; down crashes the whole dome of the
firmament, washing away before the mighty rain-deluge all
those smiling crops, all for which the ox toiled so hard. The
dykes are filled, the deep streams swell with a roar, and the
sea glows again through every panting inlet. The great
Father himself, intrenched in a night of storm-clouds, wields
the huge thunderbolt with flashing arm: at that shock the
giant earth trembles, the beasts have disappeared, and men's
hearts all the world over lie quailing low in terror; he with
his blazing javelin strikes Athos or Rhodope on the high
Ceraunian range: doubly loud howls the south wind, doubly
thick gathers the cloud of rain, and under the blast's mighty
stroke forest and shore by turns wail in agony.

With this terror before you, look watchfully to the heaven,
its seasons and its signs. Mark into what dreary regions
Saturn's cold star withdraws itself; what celestial orbit com-
prises the wanderings of the Cyllenian fire. First of all, worship the gods, and year by year pay great Ceres her recurring
honour, with a sacrifice on the luxuriant sward, when winter
has at last fallen, and spring begins to clear the sky. Those
are the days when lambs are fat, and wine at its mellowest,
when sleep is pleasant, and the trees on the mountains thick
of shade. Then summon all your rustic force to worship
Ceres; to pleasure her, mix the honeycomb with milk, and
the wine-god's mellow juice, and thrice let the auspicious

victim be led round the young corn, with the whole quire of your mates following it in triumph, and shouting invitations to Ceres to come and dwell with them ; nor let any put the sickle into the ripe corn, ere in Ceres' honour he wreath his brow with the oaken chaplet, join in the uncouth dance, and take part in the song !

Moreover, it is that these dangers may be known to us by infallible tokens—the heat, I mean, and the rain, and the wind that brings the cold—that the great Father himself has ordained what should be the lesson taught by each month's moon, what the signal for the south wind to fall asleep, what the symptom which, repeatedly observed, makes the husband-man keep his herds within sight of their stalls. From the first, when the wind is getting up, either the inlets of the sea begin to work and swell, and a dry crashing sound is heard shivering down the high mountains, or a confused roar echoes far along the beach, and the whispering of the forests comes fast and thick. By this time the wave can scarcely keep itself from falling on the vessel's keel, at the moment when the gulls fly swiftly home from over the sea, and their noise travels with them to the shore ; at the moment, when the cormorants, whose element is the water, are sporting on the land, and the heron forsakes its home in the marsh, and flies aloft above the clouds. Often, too, when wind is near, you will see stars shooting headlong from the sky, with long trails of flame behind them, glimmering white through the blackness of night ; often you will see light chaff and fallen leaves flying about, and films of gossamer in sportive conjunction floating on the water's brim. But when from the quarter of the savage North come lightnings, and thunder rolls through the halls of the East and the West, every field is flooded from the dyke's overflow, and every sailor afloat furls his dripping sails. Never man was surprised by rain at unawares. He might either have seen the crows dropping from the sky to the depths of the valley, to shelter themselves from it as it rises, or the heifer turning its face to heaven, and sniffing up the air with its broad nostrils, or the swallow flying twitteringly round and round the pool, and the frogs sitting in the slime, and singing their old complaining note. Often, too, the ant is seen carrying its eggs out of its secret cells along that narrow well-worn path, and the great rainbow drinking, and the army of rooks, as it draws off from its pasture in long column, crying and flapping its serried wings. Again, the tribes of sea-birds, and such as dig for treasure far and wide in the Asian meads among Cayster's sweet waters, may be observed in rivalry with each other, pouring showers of spray over their backs, now presenting their heads to the waves, now running into the sea, rejoicing, as it were, in the mere aimless delight of bathing. Then the raven, in her deep tones, like an ill spirit, calls down the rain, and stalks in stately solitude along the dry sea sand. Even at night, maidens at their tasks can still tell stormy weather, when in the blazing lamp they see the oil sputter, and fungus clots form round the wick.

Not less sure are the signs by which to foresee and learn a change from rain to sunshine and clear open sky. Then there is no bluntness about the edge of the stars, nor does the moon seem to rise in deep debt to her brother's light, nor are thin fleeces of wool seen to float over the sky. Nor do the Halcyons, whom the sea-goddess loves, stand on the shore, spreading their wings to the warm sun; nor does it occur to the uncleanly swine to toss in their snouts loosened wisps of hay. But the clouds fly lower and stretch themselves along the plain, and as she watches the sunset on her tower, the owl, all for nothing, keeps plying her weary task of song. Nisus is seen soaring in the clear sky, while Scylla suffers vengeance for the purple ringlet. Wherever her flying wings

cut through the thin ether, see there is Nisus, her savage foe,
with a mighty sound chasing her through the air. Where
Nisus flies up into the air there is she, with her flying wings
cutting scuddingly through the thin ether. Then the rooks,
narrowing their throats, utter a clear note, three or four times
over, and repeatedly in their nests on the tree top, moved by
some mysterious ecstasy beyond their wont, make a chatter
among the leaves for pleasure belike, when the rain is over,
at seeing their young and their own dear nests again. Not,
if I may judge, that Heaven has given them any spark of wit
like ours, or Fate any deeper insight into things, but that
when the weather and the fitful moisture of the sky has
changed its course, and the god of the air with his wet gales
from the south condenses particles, which ere-while were thin,
and releases what was dense, there is a change in the phases
of their life, and movements rise in their breasts, unlike those
they felt while the wind was gathering the clouds. There lies
the secret of the birds' rural chorus, and the ecstasy of the
cattle, and the rook's triumphant pæan.

But if you will watch the whirling sun and the array of the
moons, the morrow will never play you false, nor will you fall
into the snare set by a clear night. When the moon is first
mustering her rallied fires, if her horns are dull, with dark
atmosphere between, there will be a mighty storm brewing
for farming-men and sea. But if her face should be suffused
with a maiden blush, then there will be wind : the approach
of wind ever flushes the cheek of golden Phœbe. But if, on
her fourth rising, for that is your safest counsellor, she shall
sail through the sky clear, and with unblunted horn, then that
whole day, aye, and the days which shall be born from it to
the month's end, shall be untroubled by rain or wind, and seamen safely landed, shall pay their vows on the beach to Glaucus
and Panopea, and Ino's darling, Melicerta.

The sun, too, alike when rising and when going under the wave, will give you tokens : no train of tokens is surer than the sun's, those which attend his morning return, and those which recur with the rising stars. For him, when you find him flecking his infant dawn with spots, buried in a cloud, and shrinking from the middle of his disk, beware of showers : for there is looming overhead a south wind, foe to tree, and crop, and cattle. Again, when at daybreak his rays come shivered and scattered through a thick mass of cloud, or when Aurora rises pale from Tithonus' saffron bed, alas, the vine branch that day will be a poor shelter to your ripe grapes, so pelting are the spokes of hail that bound and crackle on your roof. This warning, too, it will serve you more to bear in mind when he has finished his course, and is quitting the sky, for then we often see various hues wandering over his countenance : the dusky portends rain, the fiery-red east winds ; but if dark spots and red fire begin to blend, then you will see the whole firmament in one fierce turmoil of wind and storm-cloud. Let no one advise me to take a journey on the sea that night, or pluck the cable from the shore. But if both when he restores the day, and when he hides away again the restored treasure, his disk is bright, your alarms of storm-clouds will be vain, and you will see the woods swaying to and fro in a clear north wind.

In short, the secrets which evening carries on his wing, the quarter whence a fair wind will blow to drive away the clouds, the hidden purposes of the rainy South, of all these the Sun will give you prognostics. The Sun—who will dare to call him untrue? Nay, he it is who often betrays the stealthy approach of battle alarms, the heavings of treason and concealed rebellion. Nay, he it was that had compassion for Rome at her Cæsar's death, when he veiled his shining head with a gloom of iron-grey, and a godless world was afraid of

everlasting night. Though that in truth was a crisis when
Earth and the expanse of Ocean, dogs of evil name and birds
of ill omen gave their prognostics too. How often have we
seen the fire-god's cells burst, and Ætna in a stream blazing
forth on the Cyclops' domain, with balls of flame and molten
stones sweeping along! The clashing of arms was heard by
Germany from sky to sky; strange convulsions sent a trembling through the Alps. There was a voice, too, heard by many
through the still temple-groves, deeper than human; and
spectres of unearthly pallor were seen at the dead of night,
and cattle—the tale is too dire to tell—spoke like men: see!
the rivers stay their courses, the earth yawns, the ivory in the
fanes sheds tears for sorrow, and the brass sweats. With the
sweep of its frenzied torrent it bears down whole forests, that
king of rivers, Eridanus, hurling before it far as the plain ex-
tends, stall and cattle alike. No respite was there in those
fearful days to the threatening filaments that overcast the
entrails with sadness, or to the blood that welled from springs
in the ground, or to the howling of wolves by night, echoing
through our steep-built towns. Never also fell there more
thunder-bolts from a clear sky; never blazed comets with fre-
quence so appalling. Hence it was that the spectacle of two
Roman hosts, armed alike, meeting in the shock of fight, was
seen once more by Philippi, nor did the Powers above think
it shame that our best blood should twice serve to fatten the
land of Emathia and Hæmus' broad plains. Yes, and the
time will come when in those borders the husbandman, as with
his crooked plough he upheaves the mass of earth, will find,
devoured by a scurf of rust, Roman javelins, or strike his heavy
rake on empty helms, and gaze astounded on the gigantic bones
that start from their broken sepulchres.

Gods of our fathers, native powers, and Romulus and Vesta,
our great mother, who preservest the Etruscan Tiber and

Rome's palaces, at least let this younger champion come to the aid of a world o'erthrown, with none to hinder him. To the full, long since, has our best blood atoned for the perjuries of Laomedon and his Troy. Long since, Cæsar, has heaven's kingly home been grudging thee to this our earth, complaining that thy thoughts are all for human triumphs—triumphs among a race where right and wrong are confounded, in a globe that teems with war and swarms with the myriad forms of crime; where the plough meets with nought of its due honour; where the tiller is swept off and the land left to weeds, and the hook has its curve straightened into the swordblade. In the East, Euphrates is stirring up war, in the West Germany; nay, close-neighbouring cities break their mutual league and draw the sword—and the war-god's unhallowed fury rages the whole earth through; even as when in the Circus the chariots burst from their floodgates, they dash into the course, and pulling desperately at the reins, the driver lets the horses drive him, and the car is deaf to the curb.

BOOK II.

THUS far of the tillage of the fields and of the stars of heaven. Now of thee, Bacchus, will I sing, and of the young forest trees as united with thee, and of the progeny of the slowly-growing olive. Come hither, father of the wine-press—everything here is filled with thy gifts—for thee the land looks gay, as it teems with the viny harvest, the vintage is foaming in the brimming vats. Come hither, father of the wine-press —strip off thy buskins, bare thy legs, and plunge them with me in the new must.

First, the law of the production of trees is various. For some, under no compulsion from men, grow up of themselves, of their own accord, and spread widely over the plains and the winding river banks, like the pliant osier and the limber broom, the poplar, and the willow groves that look so hoary with their grey leaves. Some again spring up from the dropping of seed, like the tall chestnuts, and the forest-monarch which puts forth its royal leaves for Jove, the æsculus, and the oaks, in Greece deemed oracular. With others a dense forest of suckers shoots up from their roots, as with cherry-trees and elms—nay, the bay of Parnassus rears its infant head under the mighty covert of its mother's shade. These are the modes which Nature first gave to men unasked—to these the whole race of forest-trees and shrubs and sacred groves owe their verdure.

Other modes there are which experience, working by

method, has found out for itself. One has thought of tearing
off suckers from their mother's tender frame, and planting
them in furrows; another has buried stocks in the ground,
truncheons cleft in four, and stakes sharpened to a point.
Some forest-trees yearn for the arch of the depressed layer,
and for slips which partake of their life and spring from their
soil. Others want nothing of the root; the gardener as he
prunes the tree confidently takes the topmost branch and
restores it as a trust to its native earth. Nay, the olive, when
cut down to a stump, marvellous to relate, strikes a root out
of the dry wood. Often, too, we see the branches of one tree
transformed to those of another by harmless magic—the pear-
tree is changed and bears a crop of engrafted apples—the
stony cornels look red on the plum-tree.

Come, then, husbandmen, and learn the culture proper to
each according to its kind, and so mellow your wild fruits by
cultivation, nor let the ground lie idle. What joy, to plant
Ismarus all over with the progeny of Bacchus, and clothe the
mighty sides of Taburnus with a garment of olives. Be thou,
too, at my side, and traverse with me the task that I have
essayed, thou who art my glory, to whom the largest share of
my fame of right belongs, and spread thy flying sails over this
broad ocean. Not that I aim at embracing all with my song.
I could not, had I a hundred tongues, a hundred mouths, a
voice of brass. Come with me and coast along the line of the
shore—the land is close at hand. I will not detain thee here
with mythic strains, or circuitous detail, or lengthy preambles.

The trees which of their own accord rear themselves up into
the realms of light grow up unfruitful, but luxuriant and vigorous—for there are latent forces of nature in the soil. Yet unfruitful as they are, if grafted with others or transplanted to pits
where the earth has been well worked, they will be found to have
put off their savage temper, and under constant cultivation to

learn readily whatever lessons you may choose to teach them.
So with the barren sucker that springs from the root, if it be
planted out with clear ground to expatiate in—as it now is,
the towering foliage and branches of its mother overshadow it,
and rob it of its fruit as it grows up, and wither up the pro-
ductive powers it exerts. Again, the tree which owes its
birth to chance-dropt seed comes up slowly, reserving its
shade for generations yet unborn—apples degenerate, having
lost the traditions of their ancient flavour, and the vine bears
ignoble clusters for birds to pillage. The fact is, all must
have labour spent on them—all must be drilled into trenches
and subdued with toil and pain. Olives, however, answer
best from truncheons, vines from layers, Paphian myrtles
from the solid wood. From suckers are raised the sturdy
hazels, and the huge ash, and the tree whose shade crowns
the brows of Hercules, and the acorns of our Chaonian father
—raised, too, is the lofty palm, and the fir which will one
day behold the disasters of the deep. But the prickly
arbutus is grafted with the fruit of the nut, and plane-trees,
though barren, have borne heavy apples in their day—the
chestnut's blossom has whitened the beech, the pear's the
mountain ash, and swine have crunched acorns that they
found under the elm. Nor is the method of grafting and of
inoculation one and the same. Where the buds sprout forth
from the middle of the bark and burst the thin coats, there
is a small orifice in the knot thus caused ; into it they intro-
duce a bud from a strange tree, and teach it to grow into the
bark that gives it the sap of life. Or again incision is made
in the stem where there are no knots, and a deep passage is
cloven by wedges into solid wood. Then shoots that will
bear are let in—a little while, and the tree has started up
towards the sky with a weight of teeming branches, marvelling at its strange foliage, and a fruitage not its own.

Further, there is not one kind only of stalwart elms, or of the willow and the lotus, or the cypresses of Ida, nor are fat olives all produced after one type—orchads and radii—and pausians with their bitter fruit; nor yet the apple-forests of Alcinous; nor is the scion the same which produces Syrian and Crustumian pears and big hand-fillers. The vintage that hangs from our trees is not the same which Lesbos gathers from the tendrils of Methymna. There are Thasian vines, there are Mareotids, which are white; these suited for rich soils, those for the lighter sort; and the Psithian, which does better for raisin-wine; and the Lageos, whose thin light juice will one day trouble the feet and tie up the tongue; and purples, and early-ripes—thou, too, grape of Rhætia, how shall I sing thy praises? Yet measure not thyself, therefore, against cellars of Falernum. Then there are the Aminæan vines—best of wines to keep—to which the Tmolian veils his crest, and the royal Phanæus himself, and the lesser Argitis, with which none will be found to vie, either for the streams of juice that it yields, or for the length of years that it lasts. Far be it from me to pass over thee, Rhodian—welcome to the gods and to the banquet's second course—or Bumastus, with thy big swelling clusters. But there is no number to tell how many kinds there are, or what their names; indeed, it skills not to measure them by number. The man who would have such knowledge would wish also to know how many sand-grains are lashed by the zephyr on the Libyan waste, or when the east wind falls with violence on the shipping, to tell how many waves the Ionian sea sends rolling to the shore.

Nor, indeed, is every soil able to produce everything. Willows grow by rivers, alders in rank boggy ground, barren ashes in a stony mountainous country. The most luxuriant myrtle groves are on the shore. Lastly, Bacchus is partial to

broad sunny hills, the yew-tree to north winds and cold.
Look also at the extremities of the earth as subdued by tillage, the Eastern homes of the Arabs and the tattooed Gelonians.
There you will find trees with their countries portioned out to
them. None but India produces black ebony; the spray of
frankincense belongs to none but the Sabæans. Why tell thee
of the balsams, the sweat of the fragrant wood, or of the berries
of the evergreen acanthus? Why speak of the woods of the
Ethiopians, with their hoary locks of soft wool, or how the
Seres comb silky fleeces from the lambs? Or the forests which
India bears, hard by the ocean, the utmost corner of the world
—forests where no shot of an arrow can reach the sky that
tops the trees; and the natives are not slow, either, when they
take up the quiver? Media produces the bitter juice and
lingering flavour of the benignant citron; no more present help
than that, if ever cruel stepdames have drugged the draught,
mingling herbs and charms not less baleful, to come and expel
the deadly poison from the frame. The tree itself is large,
and very like a bay to look at; nay, if the scent it flings
about were not different, a bay it had been. No wound can
make it shed its leaves, and the blossom, too, holds fast as few.
The Medes use it for purifying noisome breath, and relieving
the asthma of old age.

But neither Median forests, wealthiest of climes, nor lovely
Ganges, nor Hermus, whose mud is gold, may vie with the
glories of Italy. No, nor Bactria, nor Ind, nor Panchaïa, with
all the richness of its incense-bearing sands. Here is a land
where no bulls, breathing fire from their nostrils, have ploughed
the soil; where no enormous dragons' teeth were ever sown;
where no human harvest started up, bristling with helms and
crowded lances; but teeming corn and the vine-god's Massic
juice have made it their own; its tenants are olives and luxuriant herds of cattle. Hence comes the war-horse, that prances

proudly into the battle-field. Hence, Clitumnus, those white flocks, and the bull, that majestic victæ, which oft ere now, bathed in thy sacred flood, have ushered a Roman triumph to the temples of the gods. Here is ceaseless spring, and summer in months where summer is strange. Twice the cattle give increase, twice the tree yields its service of fruit. But far away are fierce tigers and the savage seed of lions; nor does aconite grow to beguile the wretched herb-gatherer; nor does the serpent roll his huge circles swiftly along the ground, or gather his scales into a coil with so vast a sweep. Think, too, of all those stately cities and trophies of human toil, all those towns piled by man's hand on beetling rocks, with rivers flowing beneath their time-honoured walls. Or shall I speak of the two seas that wash it above and below? or of those mighty lakes—of thee, Larius, the greatest, and thee, Benacus, heaving with the swell and the roar of ocean? or tell of the harbours and the barrier thrown across the Lucrine, and the rage and loud thunder of the baffled waters, where the sound of the sea. beaten back echoes far over the Julian wave, and the Tyrrhenian billows come foaming up into the creeks of Avernus? It is a land, too, which has disclosed currents of silver and of copper ore mantling in its veins, and has streamed profusely with gold—a land that has produced tribes of manly temper— the Marsian, the Sabine stock, the Ligurian, inured to hardship, and the Volscian spearmen; the families of the Decii and the great Camilli, the Scipios—those iron warriors—and thee, Cæsar, greatest of all, who now, crowned with conquest in Asia's utmost bounds, art driving back the unwarlike Indian from the towers of Rome. Hail to thee, land of Saturn, mighty mother of noble fruits and noble men! For thee I essay the theme of the glory and the skill of olden days. For thee I adventure to break the seal of those hallowed springs, and sing the song of Ascra through the towns of Rome.

Now for the tempers of fields—what are the powers of each, what the distinguishing colour, and what the natural aptitude for gendering things. First, then, those churlish soils and niggardly hills, where hungry marl and gravel form a bed for brambles, rejoice in the forest-growth of Minerva's long-lived olive. You may tell it by the many wild olives that spring up in the same line of country, and the ground strewn all over with their woodland berries. But a rich soil, which luxuriates in the moisture of fresh springs, a plain with abundant herbage and a teeming bosom, such as we often see at the bottom of a mountain hollow—for the streams pour down into it from the tops of the rocks, and carry with them fertilising slime ; a plain which rises to the south, and produces fern, that enemy of the crooked ploughshare ; such a soil will one day bear you good store of vines of excellent health, and yielding rivers of Bacchic juice : it will teem with grapes, and with liquor, such as we pour in libations from golden cups, when the plump Etruscan at the altar blows through the pipe, and we offer entrails smoking hot in chargers that bend under the weight. But if your care be rather to rear cattle, bullocks, lambs, or goats that kill young shoots, go to the distant lawns of luxuriant Tarentum, or plains such as that which poor Mantua lost, supporting silver swans with its weedy stream : there will be no lack of clear springs or grass for your cattle. Nay, all that your herds can devour on a summer's day, will be replaced by the cold fresh dew of one short night.

For corn, the best land in the main is that which is black, and shows itself rich when the ploughshare is driven into it, and whose soil is crumbling, that being what we seek to reproduce by ploughing ; there is no sort of ground from which you will see more wains dragged home by sturdy toiling bullocks ; or again, land from which timber has been carted away by the provoked husbandman, levelling wood

which has been doing no good these many years, and upset-
ting the leafy homes of the birds, roots and all—the tenants,
ejected from their nests, have gone up into the air, while the
rude field has been brightened up by dint of the ploughshare.
As for the hungry gravel of the hill country, it can barely
furnish shrubs like casia and rosemary for bees; and the
rugged tufa and the marl all eaten away by black snakes, tell
you plainly that no other ground is so good at supplying
serpents with food that they like, and holes where they may
wind and lurk.   But the land which exhales thin vapours
and light steam, which drinks in moisture, and gives it off
again at pleasure, which keeps itself constantly clothed with
the verdure of its own grass, and breeds no scurfy salt rust
to corrode the plough—here is a land which will yield you
luxuriant vines to twine round your elms—a land which produces olives abundantly—a land which the experience of
cultivation will show to be at once well natured for cattle and
submission to the crooked share.   Such is the land that is
fenced by wealthy Capua and the coast neighbouring the
Vesuvian ridge, and Clanius, the oppressor of desolate Acerræ.
   Now I will tell you how you may distinguish each.   If
you want to know whether a soil be loose or exceedingly stiff,
seeing that the one is partial to corn, the other to vines; the
stiffer to the corn-goddess, the loosest to the wine-god, fix on
a spot of ground, and cause a pit to be sunk in the solid earth,
then put all the mould back again, and stamp the surface
level.   If there is too little, the soil will be loose and more
suited for pasture and fruitful vines; but if it refuses to go
into its place, so that when the hole is full the earth still
dominates, the clay is thick—prepare yourself for resistance
in the clods and stiffness in the ridges, and let the oxen with
which you break up the ground be strong.
   As for a salt or bitter soil, as it is called, which is unkindly

to produce, never softening under ploughing—where the grape
is not true to its race, or the apple to its name, it will test
itself thus : pull down from your smoke-dried roof the thick
plaited baskets and wine-strainers, and into them stamp to the
full that malignant land, along with fresh water from the
spring—all the water, you will see, will force itself out, and
big drops will trickle through the plaits—the taste will tell
the tale plainly, warping the mouths of the triers into a frown
by the sense of bitterness.

Again, the fatness of a soil, to be brief, is ascertained in
this way : toss it about in the hand, it never crumbles, but
in the act of holding clings to the fingers like pitch. A moist
soil grows large weeds, and its powers of production are more
luxuriant than need be. Ah ! may I never be troubled by
its over-fertility, or the excess of strength that it puts forth
for a first crop ! As for heavy or light soils, their weight
betrays them without a word said. Your eye will tell you at
once which is black, and, in short, which is of what colour.
But the detection of that vile cold is difficult ; all that can be
said is, that pines, and noxious yews, and black ivy, occasion-
ally give signs of it.

All this duly observed, remember to get the ground well
baked, and the mountains ploughed up with trenches through
their length and breadth, and the clods all turned up and
exposed to the north winds, before you plant the scion of the
luxuriant vine. Fields where the soil is crumbling are the
best ; for that we must thank winds and sharp frosts, and the
main force of the spade labourer, disturbing and loosening the
ground. But men, whose watchfulness nothing escapes, look
out first for two similar soils, where the young shoots are to be
nursed for the trees, and where they are afterwards to be taken
and transplanted, that the sudden change may not make the
plants feel strangely to their mother. Nay, they mark the

quarter of the heavens on the bark, that they may be able to reproduce the way in which each used to stand, the part on which it bore the brunt of the southern heat, the side which it presented to the north pole. So powerful are habits formed in tender years.

Let your first question be, whether the vine would be better planted on a hill or on the plain. If you decide on laying out tracts of rich level ground, plant thick; thick setting will not dull the powers of the wine-god. But if you fix on land rising into hillocks and broad slopes, give free scope to your rows— all the same let the line of each avenue that you draw tally with the rest when the trees are planted—as you may often see when a legion has deployed at full length into cohorts for a great battle, and the column has taken its stand in the open plain, and the lines are drawn out and all the earth is gleaming like a sea with the wavy sheen of brass, while the grim melée of the fight has not yet begun, but the war-god hovers dubiously between the armies. Let all be laid out in regular symmetrical avenues, not only that the view may feed the idle fancy, but because there is no other way of getting the earth to give an equal share of support to all, or enabling the branches to spread freely into open air.

Perhaps too you may like to know about the depth of your pits. I would not mind trusting the vine to a shallow trench, but its supporter strikes down deeper into the heart of the earth, especially the æsculus, which does not push its head further towards the altitudes of heaven than it pushes its roots towards the dark world beneath. Hence it is that winter storm and blast and rain cannot tear it from its seat : it abides unmoved : many are the posterities, many the generations of men that it rolls along and lives down victoriously; while stretching out its sinewy branching arms on all sides, it supports with its central bulk the vast weight of their shade.

Do not let your vineyards slant towards the setting sun, nor plant a hazel among your vines, nor take the topmost spray of the vine, or pluck the suckers that are to support it from the top of the tree—the affection for the soil is so great —nor injure your buds by using blunt steel, nor plant truncheons of wild olive in your vineyard ; for careless husbandmen will often drop a spark, which after being first concealed and sheltered under the unctuous rind, catching the tree, mounts in a moment into the foliage, and sends a loud sound up into the air, then runs along and dominates victoriously among the branches and the summits that tower so high, and wraps the whole plantation in flame, and throws up black clouds of thick pitchy vapour to the sky, especially if a gale happens to come sweeping down over the woods and a driving wind gathers and spreads the blaze. In an event like this, the power of the root is gone ; they cannot be restored by amputation, or shoot up green as before from the depth of the soil : the wild olive with its bitter leaves is left master of the field.

Let no adviser have such credit for foresight as to persuade you to meddle with the earth while it is lying stiff under the breath of the northern blasts, for then winter seals up the ground with cold and does not suffer the plant when set to strike its frozen root into the soil. The best planting season for vines is the bloom of spring, at the return of that white bird, which the long vipers hate so, or in the first cold days of autumn, when the sun's fiery coursers have not yet reached winter, though summer is well over. Spring it is, spring that does good to woodland foliage and forestry ; in spring the soil swells and demands impregnation. It is then that Æther, the Almighty Father of Nature, penetrates the womb of earth with his fruitful showers and blending his mighty frame with hers gives life to all the embryos within. It is then that the pathless brakes are vocal with the songs of birds, and the cattle pair in their season. The parent soil brings forth, and the warm western breezes unseal the womb of the fields. A gentle moisture rises over all, and as the new suns dawn, the herbage ventures to encounter them with safety, and the young vine-branch has no fear that the south wind will get up or that the mighty north will shed a burst of rain from the sky, but puts out its buds and unfolds all its leaves. I do not believe that the days were brighter or their course more blissful when the young world first came into being : it was spring then—it was spring-tide that the great globe was keeping, and the east winds of winter were forbearing to blow, when the earliest cattle opened their eyes on the light, and an iron race of men rose from the hard soil of earth, and beasts were turned into the woods, and stars into the sky. Indeed things so delicate would not be able to endure such hardships, unless there were a great breathing time like this coming between cold and heat, and a clement sky ready to receive the earth.

For the rest, whatever cuttings you set in your land, be sure to sprinkle them with rich manure and cover them with plenty of earth ; or bury with them a porous stone or rough shells, for the water will penetrate between the crevices, and the searching breath of air will steal in, and the sets will pluck up heart. Men too have been known ere now to place a stone over them or a great heavy potsherd, as a protection against showers of rain, or when the sultry dog-star splits the thirsty jaws of the soil.

When your sets are planted, you have to loosen the ground repeatedly about the roots, and make play with your strong spades, or work the earth by dint of the ploughshare, and even turn your restiff team between the rows of your vine-yard ; further, you must get ready smooth canes and spearlike wands of peeled rods and stakes of the ash, and stout forks, by whose support the vines may be trained to climb and defy the winds, and run from story to story along the elm-tops.

In the time of their young growth and their first leaves you should spare their infancy, and even when the vine-branch is pushing its way exultingly into the sky, launched into the void in full career, the tree should not as yet be operated on by the pruning hook, but the leaves should be gathered by the fingers and picked off here and there. Then when they have shot up their stems strong and closely wound round the elms, is the time to lop the leaves and clip the branches; before that they shrink from the knife. Then is the time to set up a strong government and keep down the luxuriance of the boughs.

You must make close hedges too and keep out cattle of every sort, especially while the branches are young and un-accustomed to rough living. Besides the danger from cruel winters and oppressive suns, wild buffaloes and restless goats are constantly disporting themselves with it. Sheep and heifers feed on it greedily. Indeed no cold that hoarfrost ever congealed, no summer that ever smote heavily on the parching rocks has been so fatal to it as the flocks and the venom of their sharp tooth, and the wound impressed on the stem that they have gnawed to the quick. It is in fact for this crime that the goat appears at all altars as a victim to Bacchus, when the favourite old plays are brought on the stage. So the sons of Theseus set up prizes for wit in their village and cross-road gatherings, and in drunken jollity jumped over greased bags of goatskin in the velvet meads. The Ausonian rustics, too, who owe their descent to Troy, have their sport in artless verses and unbridled laughter, and put on frightful masks of hollowed bark and call on thee, Bacchus, in songs of joy, and in thy honour hang up images with pleasant faces to swing from the tall pine. This makes every vineyard luxuriate in plenteous increase. There is fulness in hollow valley and deep hill-gorge, and in every place to which the god has turned his comely head. Duly then will we husbandmen give Bacchus the celebration he claims in the songs our fathers sung, with offerings of loaded platters and steaming cakes; led by the horn the consecrated goat shall be set before the altar, and the dainty entrails shall be roasted on spits of hazel.

Again, too, there is that other heavy toil of dressing vines, a drain which is never satisfied; for the whole soil has to be broken up every year thrice and again, and the clods to be crushed incessantly with the hoe's back; the whole plantation has to be lightened of its foliage. Back upon the husbandman comes his labour in a round, as the year retraces its own footsteps and rolls round upon itself. And now already when the vineyard has shed its lingering leaves, and the cold north wind has stripped the woods of their beauty, even thus early a keen farmer stretches his forethought to meet the coming year, and with Saturn's hooked fang in hand pursues the forlorn vine, clipping it as it grows, and prunes it to the shape he will. Be the first to dig the ground, the first to cast away and burn the lopped boughs, the first to carry back the poles under cover, the last to put in the sickle. Twice a year the leaves encroach on the vines; twice a year the crop is overgrown with weeds and clustering briars; the one task is as hard as the other. Praise a large estate as you will, but farm a small one. Then, too, there are the rough twigs of butchers' broom to be cut up and down the woods, and the water-reed on the river-side, and the dressing of the untended willow to keep your hand at work. And now suppose that the vines are tied up, the plantations have done with the pruning hook, and the last dresser is singing the song of 'all rows finished,' still there is the earth to be disturbed and the dust raised, and the grape when fully ripe has to meet the terrors of Jupiter.

On the other hand olives need no dressing at all ; they claim nothing from curving hook or tearing rake, when once they have struck root into the soil and weathered the air. The earth itself, when the crooked fang unlocks it, gives the young plants moisture, and yields teeming produce by the plough-share's aid. Do this, and rear the olive to the fatness which makes it Peace's darling.

Apples again, so soon as they have felt their trunks firm under them and come into their strength, climb their way rapidly to the sky by their own power, and need no help from us.

Meanwhile the whole forest is teeming with young life no less, and the birds' wild haunts are .ablush with blood-red berries. The lucerne is eaten for fodder, the tall wood supplies pine torches, and night-fires are fed and give light to the house. And can men stand in doubt about planting and expending pains? Why go through the greater trees? take but willows and lowly brooms, even they afford leaves for cattle and shelter for shepherds, hedges for crops and food for honey. Ay, and what joy to gaze on Cytorus all waving with box, and those groves of Narycian pitch ! what joy to look on fields that owe no debt to the rake, none to aught of man's culture ! Nay, those barren forests on the top of Caucasus, which the gusty eastern blasts are for ever wasting and whirling, yield each tree a produce of its own, yield good timber for shipping in their pines, for houses in their cedars and cypresses. Hence the farmer turns spokes for wheels, drum-boards for waggons, and curved keels for vessels. Twigs are freely yielded by the willow, leaves by the elm, strong spear-shafts by the myrtle and the cornel, the warrior's friend ; yews are bent into Ituræan bows. Nor does the smooth linden or the lathe-polished box

E

refuse to take shape and be hollowed by the sharp steel. The
light alder, too, swims the torrent wave, sped down the
Po ; bees too hive their swarms in the hollow cork-bark and
the trough of the decaying ilex. What of equal account has
come from Bacchus' gifts to man ? Bacchus ! he has even
given occasion to crime ; it was he that tamed with the death-
stroke the Centaurs he had first maddened, their Rhoetus and
their Pholus, and their Hylaeus, menacing the Lapithæ with
his mighty bowl.

O happy, beyond human happiness, had they but a sense of
their blessings, the husbandmen, for whom of herself, far away
from the shock of arms, Earth, that gives all their due, pours
out from her soil plenteous sustenance. What if they have
not a lofty palace with proud gates disgorging from every room
a vast tide of morning visitors ; if they have not doors inlaid
with sumptuous tortoiseshell to gloat on, and tapestry with
fancy work of gold, and bronzes of Ephyra ; if their white
wool is not stained by Assyrian drugs, or their clear oil's
service spoiled by the bark of casia, still they have repose
without care and a life where fraud and pretence are unknown,
with stores of manifold wealth ; they have the liberty of broad
domains, grottos and natural lakes, cool Tempe-like valleys,
and the lowing of oxen, and luxurious slumbers in the shade
are there at their call. There are lawns and dens where wild
beasts hide, and a youth strong to labour and inured to scanty
fare. Here, too, is religion and reverend elders ; among them
it was that Justice left the last print of her feet as she with-
drew from earth.

As for me, first of all I would pray that the charming Muses,
whose minister I am, for the great love that has smitten me,
would receive me graciously, and teach me the courses of the
stars in heaven, the various eclipses of the sun and the agonies
of the moon, whence come quakings of the earth, what is the

force by which the deep seas swell to the bursting of their barriers and settle down again on themselves—why the winter suns make such haste to dip in ocean, or what is the retarding cause which makes the nights move slowly. But if I should be restrained from sounding these depths of nature by cold sluggish blood stagnating about my heart, then let me delight in the country and the streams that freshen the valleys—let me love river and woodland with an unambitious love. O for those plains—for Spercheius and Taygete, the revel-ground of Spartan maidens ! O for one to set me down in the cool glens of Hæmus, and shelter me beneath the giant shade of its boughs !

Happy the man who has gained a knowledge of the causes of things, and so trampled under foot all fears and fate's relentless decree, and the roar of insatiate Acheron. Yet not the less blest is he who has won the friendship of the rural gods, Pan, and old Silvanus, and the sisterhood of Nymphs. He is not moved by honours that the people confer, or the purple of empire, or civil feuds, that make brothers swerve from brothers' duty; or the Dacian coming down from the Hister, his sworn ally ; no, nor by the great Roman state and the death throes of subject kingdoms : he never felt the pang of pity for the poor, or of envy for the rich. The fruits which the arms of the trees present, which the country yields cheerfully of its own sweet will, these he gathers ; the iron rigour of law, the mad turmoil of the forum, the public archives, he has looked on none of them. Others are disturbing the darkness of the deep with their oars, rushing on the sword's point, winding their way into courts and kings' chambers. One is carrying havoc into a city and its wretched homes, all that he may have a gem to drink out of, and Tyrian purple to sleep on ; another is hoarding up wealth, and lying on the burying-place of his gold ; one is staring in rapt admiration at the Rostra; another, open-mouthed, is swept away by the plaudits of commons and senate as they roll, aye, again and again along the benches; men are bathed in their brothers' blood, and glory in it; they exchange the home and hearth-stone of their love for a life of exile, and seek out a country that lies under another sun. Meanwhile the husbandman has displaced the soil with his crooked plough-share—thence comes his year's employment—thence comes sustenance for his country and his own little homestead alike, and for his herds of oxen and the bullocks that have served him so well. The stream of plenty knows no pause; the year is always teeming either with apples or with animal produce, or the sheaf of Ceres' corn-ears, loading the furrows with increase, and bursting the barns. Winter is come : the berry of Sicyon is being bruised in the oil presses; see how fat the swine come off from their meal of acorns; there are arbutes in the woods for the picking, or for a change, autumn is dropping its various produce at his feet, and high up on the sunny rocks the vintage is being baked into ripeness. Then, too, there are his sweet children ever hanging on his lips— his virtuous household keeps the tradition of purity; the cows are letting down their milky udders, and fat kids in grass luxuriant as they, are engaging together horn against horn. He, the master, keeps holidays, and stretched at ease on the grass, with a turf-fire in the middle, and a merry company wreathing the bowl, calls on thee, god of the wine press, with a libation, and sets up on the elm a mark for spearing matches among the herdsmen, and they strip their bodies, hard as iron, for a country wrestle. Such were the arts of cultivation practised of old by the Sabines, and by Remus and his brother; such, in fact, the life in which Etruria grew to strength, and in which Rome has become the glory of the earth, embracing seven hills with the wall of a single city. Nay, in days before the rule of the Cretan king, before our race in its impiety began to regale itself on slaughtered bullocks—this was the life that was led on earth by Saturn, monarch of the golden age—days when the blast of the trumpet and the hammering of the sword on the stubborn anvil were sounds unknown.

But we have traversed a tract of boundless length and breadth, and it is high time to unyoke the steaming necks of our horses.

BOOK III.

Of thee, too, mighty Pales, shall be my song, and of thee, the poet's worthy theme, the swain from Amphrysus' bank—of you also, ye woods and streams of Lycæus. Other subjects, which once could have laid on the idle mind the spell of poesy, are all of them hackneyed now. Who knows not Eurystheus, hardest of masters, or the altars of Busiris, whom never tongue praised? Who has not told the tale of the lost boy Hylas, of Latona and her Delos, of Hippodamia and Pelops, hero of the ivory shoulder and keen charioteer? I must essay a course by which I too may rise from the ground, and ride in triumph over the heads of mankind. Yes, I will be the first, if but life hold out, to dislodge the Aonian muses from their mountain home, and carry them with me in my victorious progress into my native land. I will be the first to bring back to thee, my Mantua, the palms of Idumea, and on the broad green sward I will build a temple of marble by the water's side, where Mincius trails his great breadth along in lazy windings, and fringes his banks with soft rushes as he goes. In the shrine I will have Cæsar, the tutelar god of the temple. In his honour I, the hero of the day, in full pomp of Tyrian purple, will have driven by the river's bank a hundred four-horse cars. My fame shall draw all Greece away from Alpheus and the grove of Molorchus, to contend in the footrace and with the gloves of raw hide, while I with stripped olive leaves wreathed round my brow, will offer gifts at the altar. The time is come—what joy, to lead the stately procession to the temple, and see the bullocks slaughtered, or to mark on the stage how the fronts turn round and the scene withdraws, and how the embroidered Britons lift that grand purple curtain from the ground! On the temple doors I will have sculptured, all of gold and solid ivory, the battle of the Ganges, and the conquering arms of our own Quirinus; ay, and there, in full tide of war, swelling high, shall be seen the Nile, and columns built high with sailors' brass. I will throw in, too, Asia's vanquished cities, and Niphates with his shattered crest, and the Parthian, who stakes his all on flight and treacherous volleys from behind, and those two trophies torn from foes at the two ends of earth—those two nations led in triumph from the two coasts of ocean. I will set up, too, Parian marble in breathing statues, the lineage of Assaracus, and the great names of the house that comes down from Jove, old father Tros, and the builder of Troy, the Cynthian god—while Envy shall be seen, hiding her miserable head from the Furies and the gloomy flood of Cocytus, and the snakes that coil round Ixion, the enormous wheel, and the never baffled stone. Meanwhile, pursue we the Dryads' woods and glades, virgin as they, the hard task that you have laid on me, my Mæcenas. Uninspired by you, no lofty work can my mind essay. Come along—no loitering or delay—here is Cithæron calling us in full cry, and the hounds of Taygete, and Epidaurus with her well-trained horses—a cry rebounding in echoes from the applauding woods. But erelong I will gird myself to sing of those fiery fights of Cæsar, and waft his name in glory down a length of centuries, long as those which separate the cradle of Tithonus from Cæsar himself.

Whether a man in admiring ambition of the prize of the Olympic palm, breed horses, or breed bullocks, that shall be strong for ploughing, let his first care be to choose dams of the mould required. That cow is best shaped that is grim-looking, with an ugly head, an abundance of neck, and dewlaps hanging down from jaw to leg; with no end to length of her side, and everything large about her down to her foot, her horns curved inwards and her ears under them hairy. Nor should I dislike to see her dappled with spots of white or rebelling against the yoke, and sometimes savage with her horns, her countenance approaching a bull's, tall altogether, and, as she moves, sweeping her footsteps with the tip of her tail. The age for service to the child-birth goddess and the just claims of wedlock is over before ten years, as it begins after four; in the rest of life there is no aptness for breeding, no strength for the plough. Meantime, while the luxuriance of your cattle's youth is still unspent give your males liberty; be the first to send in your herds, and supply race after race by successive propagation. Poor mortals that we are, our brightest days of life are ever the first to fly; on creeps disease and the gloom of age, and suffering sweeps us off, and the ruthless cruelty of death. Constantly there will be those whose weakly mould you would gladly exchange; as constantly recruit your stock; and that you may not deplore losses when too late, prevent them, and every year pick for your herd a young supply.

Your breed of horses, too, must be chosen with no less care. Mark me, and let those whom you mean to rear as the propagators of their line have even from their first youth the advantage of your special pains. See, from the day of his birth, a colt of a noble family, how high he steps in the pasture, and with what spring he brings down his legs. Fearlessly he leads the way, is the first to brave the threatening flood and trust his weight on the untried bridge—no terror for him have idle alarms. Look at the height of his neck, the sharp cut of his head, the shortness of his belly, the plumpness

of his back, and the luxuriance of the firm flesh about that
chest which swells so with life. For colour, your best are
bay and blue-grey; the white and the dun are the worst.
Now, if he happens to hear the sound of arms in the distance,
no standing still for him; he pricks his ears, his whole body
quivers, he snorts, and works in his nostrils the gathered fire.
His mane is thick, and as he tosses it, rests on his right
shoulder. The spine which runs between his loins is hollow;
his hoof goes deep into the ground, and has the deep ring of
solid horn. Such was the steed that learnt to obey the rein
of Amyclæan Pollux, Cyllarus, and those of which Greek song
has preserved the memory, the horses of Mars, and the pair
of the mighty Achilles; ay, such was the great god, Saturn,
when quick as lightning he flung his mane over that horse's
neck of his as he heard his wife's step, and as he ran, thrilled
through the height and depth of Pelion with his clear sharp
neigh.

Yet even him too, when the burden of disease or the
increasing slowness of years makes him fail, you must shut
up at home, nor suffer his old age to be a disgrace; for an
old horse is a cold lover.[1]

*   *   *   *   *

Your first care then will be in each case to take note of
the horse's spirit, and of his age; passing thence to observe
the rest of his character, the breed of his sire and dam, and
how keen the pang of defeat or the thrill of victory. Who
has not watched the headlong speed of a racer, the chariots
swallowing the ground before them as they pour along in a
torrent from their floodgates, when the drivers' youthful hopes
are at their height, and the bounding heart is drained by each
eager pulsation? There are they, with their ever ready lash
circling in the air, bending forward to let the reins go; on flies

---

[1] The MS. is interrupted for three lines.—[ED.]

the wheel, swift and hot as fire; now they ride low, now they seem to tower aloft, shooting through the void air, and rising against the sky; no stint, no stay, while the yellow sand mounts up in a cloud, and each is sprinkled with the foam and breath of those behind him : that is what ambition can do, that is the measure of their zeal for success. Erichthonius was the first who rose to the feat of coupling a car and four horses together, standing erect above the wheels that swept him on in triumph. The bridle and the ring were a present from the Lapithæ of Mount Pelion, who mounted the steed's back, and taught the horseman, arms and all, to spurn the ground and complicate his haughty paces. Each task is arduous alike; for each the trainer looks out for a young one, with a high spirit and a fleet foot; though the veteran may have turned the foe to flight in many a battle, though his birthplace be Epirus or good Mycenæ itself, and the founder of his line no less than Neptune.

These points first noted, they are all zeal as the time draws near, and bestow their whole pains to swell out with firm fat the horse whom they have chosen as the leader of the herd and named as its lord. They cut for him flowering herbage and ply him with springs and with corn, lest he prove unequal to the task he loves, and the sire's insufficiency be reflected in a weak offspring. But the herd itself, of set purpose they bring down and make lean, and when the first promptings of love are felt, refuse them fodder and keep them off from running streams. Often too they shake them with galloping and tire them in the sun, when the threshing floor is groaning heavily with the pounding of the corn, and when the empty chaff is tossed to the rising western breeze.

Now the care of the sires begins to wane, and that of the dams to take its place. When the mares' time is out and they go about in foal, let no one suffer them to pull in harness to a heavy waggon, or clear the road with a high leap, scour the plain with the speed of fire, or breast a violent torrent. Wide lawns are the places for them to graze in, and the sides of brimming rivers, where they may have moss and a bank of the greenest grass, and the shelter of a cave, and the shadow of a rock flung full over the ground. About the groves of Silarus and the oaks that make Alburnum so green, swarms an insect whose Latin name is *asilus*, rendered in Greek by *œstrus*, a pest with a harsh loud hum, which scares the cattle and makes them fly right and left through the woodland, while the air is stunned and maddened with their bellowings, the air and the woodland and the banks of Tanager which runs dry in the sun. This was the monster of old with which Juno wreaked that fearful vengeance of hers, the scourge which she devised for the heifer of Inachus, and so you too—for mid-day heat makes its persecutions more savage—should shield your teeming herds from its sting, letting them graze only when the sun is just up or the stars are ushering in the night.

After delivery, the farmer's whole care is transferred to the calves. At once he brands them with tokens and names to mark the race, distinguishing those whom he chooses to rear for breeding, those whom he prefers to reserve for the altar's sacred uses, and those who are meant to break up the ground.[1] The rest of the cattle are grazing, as well they may, wherever the grass is green. Meantime do you take those whom you would train to the love and service of the land, school them while they are yet calves, and set out on the path of discipline while the youthful mind is docile and the time of life pliable. Let loose rings of slender osier be their first collars.

---

[1] This phrase stands in the M.S. for :—

Aut scindere terram,

Et campum horrentem fractis invertere glebis.—[ED.]

Then, when the freeborn neck has grown familiar with bondage, use these necklaces as the means of yoking them together in a well-matched pair, and make them step side by side. By this time too let them have an empty waggon often and often dragged at their heels, just printing the wheel-rut on the surface-dust. That done, you should next have the rattle of the beechen axle, as it pulls against a good stout weight, and a copper-plated pole to draw the wheels thereto attached. Meantime, ere their youth is broken in, you will not only give them grass or starveling willow leaves and marsh sedge, but standing corn plucked by the hand; and again, when your cows have just been bearing, do not, as our fathers did, force them to fill the snowy milk pail, but let them spend their udders entire on the offspring they love.

But if your bent is rather towards battle and fierce brigades, or to glide at Pisa by Alpheus' waters on wheels smooth as they, and in the grove of Jupiter drive the flying car, learn that a horse's first task is to bear the sight of martial fury and the harness of war, the sound of the clarion, the long-drawn rumbling of the wheel, and the jingle of the bridle as he stands in the stall; keener, too, and keener should grow his pleasure in his master's caressing voice, and more intense the luxury as he hears his neck patted. To this he should be inured from the moment of his weaning from his mother's milk; ever and anon too he should submit his head to bands of soft osier, ere his strength is set, or his nerves steady, or his hold on life firm. But when three summers are past and the fourth arrived, let him begin at once to scour the ring, his paces ringing a regular time, and his legs successively gathered into a curve, and let him show that he is working against his will; then, then let him challenge the winds to a race, flying along over the open spaces, as if he had no bridle in his mouth, and scarcely setting his footprint on the sand's surface—as when from polar climes the north wind stoops in full force, driving before him the storms of Scythia and the rainless clouds; the tall waving corn and the billowy plains are ruffled by the first light breeze, and a rustling is heard in the forest tops, and the long waves come pushing to the shore—on he flies, on wings that sweep land and sea alike. A horse like this will be seen all sweat at the goal of Elis and its mighty circles, spurting out flakes of bloody foam, or will draw the Belgian car with a grace, with that gentle neck of his. Then at last let their mighty bulk be distended at will with the fattening corn mess after the breaking-in is well over—for before, such food will raise their spirit too high, and make them refuse to bear the education of the pliant lash, or obey the sharp curb.

But there is nothing that tells more towards invigorating their strength, than to shield them with all your care from the stings of secret passion, whether your preference is for the service of oxen or of horses. To that end, the bull is sent into distant exile in solitary pastures, with a mountain before and a broad river between him and his home; or is shut in close confinement in his well-stored crib. For the female keeps insensibly preying on his strength, and consuming it by the very sight of her, and leaves him no thought for forest shelter or grassy food. Nay, those endearing charms of hers often drive her haughty lovers to use their horns for settling their rival claims. There she is grazing in Sila's mighty wood, the lovely heifer; they are in the thick of battle, dealing wounds with all their force, now one, now another; the black blood is bathing their frames, and pushing horn meets pushing horn with loud bellowing, that echoes through the woods and the length of the firmament. Nor, when all is over, are the combatants wont to stall together; the beaten champion retires to distant banishment in an unknown clime, with many a groan for his disgrace and the cruel wounds of his haughty conqueror, and many for his unredressed loss, the loss of his love—a wistful look at his stall, and the king has quitted his ancestral domain. So now all his care is to practise his powers — on the hard rocks the whole night long he makes his unpillowed bed—his food the bristly leaf and the pointed sedge; and he proves himself, and learns to throw his rage into his horns by butting at a tree's trunk, and assails the winds with his blows, and spurns the flying sand in prelude for the fray. Then, when his powers are mustered and his strength recruited, he raises the standard, and comes headlong down on his oblivious foe—like a billow that begins to whiten far away in the mid sea, and draws up from the main its bellying curve—like it, too, when rolling to the shore, it roars terrific among the rocks, and bursts in bulk as huge as their parent cliff—while the water below boils up in foaming eddies, and discharges from its depths the murky sand.

Nay, it is the wont of the whole race of men and beasts all the world through, the tribes of the waters, cattle, and gay-coloured birds, to rush headlong into this fiery madness; love fastens on all alike. At no other season has the lioness forgotten her cubs, and roamed the plains in fiercer mood; never has the monstrous bear spread death and havoc more widely through the forest; then is the wild boar savage, then the tigress at her worst. Ah! it is bad wandering then alone in the Libyan waste. Mark you not how horses thrill through their whole frame, if but a scent conveys to them the breath they know so well? No power to check them now has the rider's rein or the lash plied with fury, or rocks and beetling crags, or rivers crossing their path, tearing up mountains and hurling them down the tide. See! there is the great Sabine boar, rushing along and sharpening his tusks, pounding the

earth before him with his feet, rubbing his sides against the
tree, and in this way and that hardening his shoulders against
wounds. What of the youth, whose marrow the fierceness of
love has turned to flame ? The storm has broken loose, and
the night is dark, yet he swims the troubled sea ; over his
head thunders heaven's huge gate, and the waves that dash on
the rocks shout in his ears ; in vain ; nor can the tears of his
parents call him back, nor the maiden of his love, whose cruel
death must follow his. What of Bacchus' spotted lynxes, and
the fierce tribes of wolves and dogs ? What of the fight which
unwarlike stags are known to show ? Them I pass by ; for
indeed above all others conspicuous is the rage of the mares—
such was the boon with which Venus' grace endowed them,
what time Glaucus had his limbs devoured by his Potnian
chariot-steeds. On they are drawn by love, over Gargarus, over
the roar of Ascanius ; the mountain they scale, the river they
swim ; and soon as ever the spark touches their craving marrow,
in spring chiefly, for it is in spring that heat revisits their
frames, they stand all of them with their faces turned west-
ward on the cliff-top, and catch the light-floating breezes ; and
oft, without wedlock of any sort, impregnated by the wind,
over hill and rock and dipping vale, they fly here and there
—not towards thy birthplace, Eurus, or the Sun's, but to
north, or north-west, or where the south, blackest of winds,
is born, to sadden heaven's face with his rain and chill. Then
it is there trickles from them a thick fluid, which the shepherds rightly call horse-madness—horse-madness, which fell
step-dames have oft gathered up, to form a mess with herbs
and charms as baleful.

But time is flying, flying past recall, while we in fond
interest are making our circuit from point to point. Enough
of herds, another part of our charge is yet to do—the treat-
ment of woolly flocks and hairy goats. Here is a task indeed ;

here fix your hopes of renown, ye brave sons of the soil. For myself, I too am well assured how hard the struggle will be for language to plant her standard here, and invest a theme so slender with her own peculiar glory; but there is a rapturous charm that whirls me along over Parnassus' lonely steeps—a joy in surmounting heights where no former wheel has worn a way, no easy slope leads down to the Castalian spring.

Now, dread Pales, now for a louder and loftier strain. On my inauguration I proclaim that the sheep crop their grass in soft-laid sheds till summer, in due course, comes back with its leaves, and that plenty of straw and handfuls of fern be strewn on the hard ground under them, lest the chill of the ice harm your delicate cattle, and engender scab and, foot-rot, to your disgrace and disgust. Passing thence, I order that the goats have good store of arbute leaves and supplies of fresh running water, and that their sheds be placed away from the wind, full fronting the winter sun in his mid-day quarter, at the time when the cold bearer of the water urn is setting and sprinkling the skirts of the departing year. Yes, our goats should be shielded with care as serious as our sheep; nor will their service stand you in less stead, high as is the rate of exchange of Milesian wool engrained deep with Tyrian scarlet. From them comes a more swarming progeny, from them milk in plenteous abundance; the fuller the froth of your morning's pail from the dry-drained teat, the more luxuriant will flow the stream from the same udder when pressed at night. Nor is this all—the he-goat of Cinyps has his beard and hoary chin, aye, all his shaggy hair, clipped for the use of the camp, or to cover some poor shivering seaman. For their food, they graze among the forests and the summits of Lycæus, among stiff prickly bushes and brakes that cling to the heights, and of themselves, with never-failing memory, they come back home, showing their young the way, and just heave their full-charged udders over the threshold. Spend all your pains then in fencing them from ice and sleety blasts, considering how few their calls on the care of man; give them provender and twigs for food with luxuriant hand, and put no lock on your hayloft the whole winter through.

But when the zephyr's call is heard, and summer's genial smile sends both flocks alike into mountain lawn and mountain pasture, then let us be ready with the first dawn of the morning star to batten on the cool fresh fields while daybreak is young, while the grass is hoar, and the dew on the tender herbage is most grateful to cattle. Afterwards, when a sense of thirst crowds on the fourth hour of the day, and the cicalas split the woods with their plaintive note, bid your flocks stand at the well-side, or by the deep pool, to drink water running through oaken troughs; but in mid-day heat let them hunt out a shady vale, where, belike, Jove's mighty oak, strong in time-honoured power, spreads its enormous boughs; or where the grove, black with countless ilexes, reposes in hallowed shadow. Then once more give them the thin clear stream, once more feed them till set of sun, when the cool of eve allays the air, and the dews now falling from the moon revive the lawns, and the kingfisher sings along the shore, the goldfinch through the brake.

Why should my verse take you along with the shepherds of Libya, their pastures, and their camps, settlements of thin-spread huts? Often, day and night together, and a whole month in succession, their cattle graze, travelling on into a length of desert, without shelter of any sort, so vast is the extent of plain. The African herdsman carries with him all his goods—house, and hearth, and arms; his dog from Amyclæ, and his quiver from Crete—just as the keen Roman, when, armed and equipped in Roman fashion, he makes his march under his tyrannous load, and, ere he is looked for,

F

has his camp ready pitched, and is drawn up before his foe.
What a change to the tribes of Scythia and the water of
Mæotis—to the scene where Ister rolls turbidly his yellow
sands, and Rhodope stretches herself full under the pole, and
turns again ! There they keep their herds shut up in stalls—
never a blade of grass is seen on the plain, never a leaf on
the tree ; but the land lies a formless mass of snowy heaps
and deep ice, and rises seven ells high. Every day is winter,
every air the north wind's frosty breath.' Nay, the sun never
dispels the wan shades of night, not when he mounts his car
and scales the height of the sky, nor when he laves his headlong wheels in ocean's glowing flood. Sudden crusts form on
the running stream, and the water can now support on its
back the iron-bound wheel—the water that once welcomed
ships, and now welcomes the broad wain. Coppers are daily
split, and clothes congeal on the back, and clear-flowing wine
is chopped with hatchets ; whole pools are turned to solid
ice, and stiffening icicles harden on the untrimmed beard.
Meantime, as if there were no frost, snow is falling from all
the sky : the cattle perish—great hulks of oxen stand with
frost all about them—stags massed into a troop are numbed
by a weight not their own, and hardly lift the tips of their
horns above it. No need of letting in dogs on them, hunting them with nets, or scaring them with the terror of the
crimson feather ; as they are pushing in vain with their
chests at the mountain of snow, men kill them weapon in
hand, butcher them bellowing loud, and carry them off with
shouts of triumph. For the people, they keep careless holiday
in caves delved deep under the earth, with store of timber,
nay, whole elms pushed up to the hearth, and heaped on
the blaze—there they lengthen out the night in games, and
jovially imitate draughts of the vine with fermented grains
and acid service-juice. Such is the life of that ungoverned

race of men who dwell exposed to the seven Hyperborean stars, ever buffeted by the east winds of a Rhipæan sky, ever sheltering their frames, with the rough tawny coats of beasts.

If wool be your care, first remove the prickly jungle, burrs, caltrops, and the like; avoid luxuriant pastures, and at once choose flocks with white, soft fleeces. But the ram, however white himself, who has but a black tongue under his mouth's moist roof, set aside, lest he blur the fleece of the young lambs with dark spots, and look about the teeming plain till you find another. It was thus, with a present of wool, white as snow, if we may trust the tale, that Pan, Arcadia's patron, beguiled thee, bright'goddess of the Moon, calling thee under the tall forest trees; nor didst thou slight the call.

But if milk is the farmer's passion, let him with his own hand carry to the stalls lucerne and lotus in plenty, and salted herbage. Hence they love the water more, and have their udders more distended, and reproduce in their milk a hidden flavour of salt. Many separate the kid from its dam when fresh dropped, and at once front its mouth with an iron-pointed muzzle. The milk they have taken at dawn and in hours of daylight they churn at night; the milk taken at twilight and at sundown they carry away in baskets at day-break (it is a shepherd's visit to town), or sprinkle it spar-ingly with salt, and lay it by for winter.

Nor let your dogs be the last thing thought of; but bring up together swift Spartan hounds and a keen Molossian on fattening whey. Never, with them to guard you, need you quake for your stalls at a nightly robber or an invasion of wolves, or at Iberian outlaws in your rear. Often, too, you will chase the wild ass, so quickly scared, and hark your hounds on the hare, your hounds on the doe. Often you will rouse the wild boar, and dislodge him from his woody lair, baying and driving; and along the steep mountains, in full cry, force into your net an enormous stag.

Be taught also to burn fragrant cedar in your stalls, and with the steam of the Syrian gum chase away noisome serpents. Often under sheds long undisturbed you find that a viper, ill to handle, has been lurking, escaped in fear from the light of day; or a cobra, fond of haunting the shelter and the shade, and scattering its venom on the cattle—cruel scourge of oxen—has nestled in the ground. Quick, shepherds, quick, with your stones and staves—his terrors are rising, his throat swollen and hissing—smite him down. See! he is flying, his timid head already deep in the ground, while his writhing body and the waving line of his tail are untwisting themselves, and the final coil is dragging its slow spires along. Then, too, there is that deadly serpent in the gorges of Calabria, with breast erect and wreathed scaly back, flecked with great spots throughout his belly's length; who, while there are any rivers welling from their fountains, and while the earth is wet with the moist spring and the rainy south, haunts the still waters, and, dwelling on the banks there, with fish and clamorous frogs satiates the glutton craving of his black swollen maw.. Then, after the pool is burnt to the bottom, and the earth is gaping with heat, leaps to land, and, rolling eyes of fire, carries death into the fields, savage with thirst, and maddened by the sunstroke. May it never enter my mind to indulge the pleasure of open-air sleep, or to lie on the grass on the mountain's wood-grown ridge, at the moment when he, his skin shed, in new life and in the beauty of youth, leaving his young at home, hatched or in the shell, gathers himself up, towering to the sun, and flashes in his mouth his three-forked tongue.

About diseases, too, I will tell you, their causes and their symptoms. Sheep are tormented by a noisome scab, when

the cold rain and hoar-frost of cruel winter have sunk deep
into their flesh ; or when, after shearing, sweat unwashed has
clung to the skin, or rough brambles have wounded the body.
For fear of this, shepherds bathe the whole flock with fresh
streams, and the ram is plunged into the flood, his wool all
wet about him, and once launched, goes floating down the
river ; or they anoint the body after shearing with bitter
mother-of-oil, and mix scum of silver, and native sulphur,
and pitch from Ida, and wax softened by oil, and sea onions
and potent hellebore, and black bitumen. But never is the
fortune of the distemper so gracious as when a man has the
nerve to open the mouth of the sore with the knife : the
mischief keeps thriving, and lives upon concealment, while
the shepherd is refusing to apply a healing hand to the
wound, or sits praying the gods to send more favourable prognostics. Moreover, when the pain has pierced to the bleating
sufferer's bones, and is raging there, and a parching fever is
preying on its limbs, it has been found well to carry off the
fiery heat by opening a vein full throbbing with blood at the
bottom of the foot, as is the wont of the Bisaltæ and the keen
Gelonian, when he flies to Rhodope and to the steppes of the
Getæ, and drinks milk curdled with mare's blood. If you
observe a sheep often seeking refuge in the luxurious shade,
or indolently browsing the tops of the herbage, lagging after
you the last, or lying down in the middle of the field while
grazing, and at last retiring all alone before the late approach
of night, check the evil at once with the knife, ere the dire
contagion spread through the unwary multitude. Not so fast
sweeps a whirlwind over the sea, with a storm in its train, as
the thousand distempers that seize on cattle. It is not single
bodies here and there that the plague bears off, but the whole
of a summer's fold all in a moment—the flock of the future
with that which now is—an entire tribe, root and branch.

Let him become my witness who chances to see the skiey Alps, and the hillside forts of Noricum, and the fields of Iapydian Timavus, even as they now are, after time has done so much —the shepherds' domain unpeopled, and the lawns desolate through their length and breadth.

Here once, from a distemper of the sky, a season of piteous ruin set in, glowing with all the furnace-heat of autumn, and swept off to death the whole race of beasts, tame and wild; tainted the pools of water, and infected the herbage with venom. Nor was the path of death straight and without turning: but after fiery thirst, coursing through every vein, had drawn the poor limbs close together, there was a fresh overflow of fluid moistures, absorbing into itself piece by piece the whole bony frame, dissolved by pestilence. Often, in the middle of a sacrifice, as the victim was standing at the altar, and the snowy band of the woollen fillet was being placed round its brow, it fell dying between the attendants' faltering hands; or if the steel of the priest had given any an earlier death, that victim's entrails make no blaze on the altar they load, nor can the prophet learn from them responses to the votary's questions. A thrust from beneath scarcely stains the knives with blood, and the thin gore but just darkens the surface of the sand. Thus you might see calves dying everywhere among luxuriant herbage, or yielding the lives they love at the well-filled crib they cannot taste. Thus madness comes on the dog, man's playfellow, and a panting cough shakes the diseased swine, and stops the breath in their swollen throats. See! he droops, his occupation gone, his pasture neglected, the victorious steed; he recoils from running streams, and beats the ground rapidly with his hoof; his ears drop, a fitful sweat breaks out on them, striking cold as death draws on; the skin is dry, and when touched, meets the hand with hardness. Such are the signs that, go before death in the early days of the malady ; but when in its advance it begins to grow fierce, then at last the eyes are ablaze, the breath deep drawn, and sometimes groaningly heavy ; they distend their flanks to the bottom with a long-heaved sob, black blood trickles from their nostrils, and their obstructed jaws are closed on a roughened tongue. It was found well to drench them with the wine-god's streams, through a horn placed in the mouth; this seemed the one way of life to the dying; soon, that too was seen to lead to death : they were revived by madness into fever heat, and, even in the weakness of dissolution (grant, ye gods, better things to us your worshippers, and reserve this delusion for our foes), with their own bare teeth mangled their own rent flesh. Look there—the bull, smoking under the plough-share's stubborn weight, falls in a heap, disgorges from his mouth blood mingled with foam, and heaves a last sigh. The ploughman moves sadly away, unyokes the surviving bullock, itself mourning for its brother's fate, and leaves the work half done, and the plough still buried in the soil. The tall forest's shade, the soft meadow grass, cannot quicken that failing heart— no, nor the river that tumbles down the stones, purer than amber, and hurries to the plain : the flank is relaxed from end to end ; a stupor weighs the heavy eyelids down, and the weight of the neck bears it drooping to the earth. What profit has he of his labour and his good deeds to man ? what of all the heavy clods that he has upturned with the share ? Yet he and such as he have never known the poison of the wine-god's Massic gifts, nor of feast succeeding feast; they feed on leaves, on the diet of undressed herbage. Their cups are clear springs and rivers that freshen as they run ; and care never comes to break short their healthful slumbers. Then and then only in that country—*

* Here the MS. of this part of the translation ceases abruptly. I cannot find that the third Georgic was ever completed by Professor Conington.—[ED.]

BOOK IV.

I AM now in due order to tell of Heaven's gift, the honey of the sky. To this, as to the rest of my task, Mæcenas, vouchsafe your regard. A marvellous exhibition of things slight in themselves—high-souled leaders, and the life of a whole nation, its character, its genius, its races, its battles, shall all be successively unfolded to you. It is a small field for labour, but far from small is the glory to be reaped by one, if there be such, whose evil star leaves him free, and whose invoking voice is heard of Apollo.

First of all the bees must have a settlement and a station found them, in a spot to which the winds have no access— for the winds will not let them carry their food home—and where no sheep or wanton kids are likely to trample on the flowers, no wandering heifer to brush the dew from the meadow and beat down the rising herbage. Nor let the speckled lizard's scaly back be seen in their precious homesteads, nor the apiaster nor. other birds; no, nor Procne, with the marks of her bloody hands still on her breast—for they spread havoc through the domain far and wide, and catching its owners on the wing, carry them in their mouths to their ungentle nest- lings a delicate morsel. But let there be a clear spring close at hand, and a pool fringed with green moss, and a thread of water coursing through the grass, and let a palm-tree or a tall wild olive throw its shade over the vestibule, that, when the infant swarm marches out under their new kings in the spring

that they love, and the youth issuing from the comb disport
themselves at will, there may be a bank hard by, to tempt
them to retire from the heat, and a tree in the way to keep
them long under its leafy shelter. Into the middle of the
water, whether it be sluggish and standing, or fresh and running, throw willows crosswise and huge stones, that there
may be frequent bridges for them to settle on and spread
their wings to the summer sun, in case the east wind should
have sprinkled them while pausing in their flight, or sent
them headlong into Neptune's lap. All about let there be a
luxuriant growth of green casia, and wild thyme with its
spreading perfume, and abundance of strongly-scented savory,
and beds of violets to drink in the irrigation of the spring.
As for your hives, whether they be stitched, of hollow cork,
or woven, of pliant osier, let them have narrow entrances—
for in cold the wintry air congeals the honey, while heat
melts it and sets it free. Each is a tyrant that the bees have
alike to dread ; nor is it in vain that with emulous zeal they
smear the tiny crevices in their dwellings with wax, and fill
up the orifices with the pollen of flowers, and keep a store of
glue laid up for that very purpose, more tenacious than bird-
lime or than the pitch of Phrygian Ida. Often, too, in holes
underground, if fame speak truth, they have made them a
warm home, and have been found deep in the hollow of a
porous rock, and in the cavern of a decayed tree. Nevertheless do you give their crannied chambers the warmth of a
smooth mud-plaister, and strew them with a sprinkling of
leaves. Do not suffer a yew tree near their dwelling, nor
roast scarlet crabs at the fire, nor put any faith in a deep
swampy place, or where the mire smells strong, or where the
hollow rock rings with the impact of sound, and the reflection of the voice strikes it and rebounds again.

For the rest, when the golden sun has driven winter to hide

his vanquished head under the earth, and thrown open the gates of heaven by the force of summer's rays, immediately they are ranging lawn and woodland through, cropping the bright-hued flowers, and sipping the streamlet's brim with their tiny mouths. Hence it is that with a delicious sense of unknown sweetness they cherish their nestling young; hence it is that with workman's skill they forge fresh wax and mould the clammy honey. So then when looking up you see the body of bees issuing at last from their prison towards the sky and all afloat in the clear summer-tide, and wonder at the murky cloud which the wind is swaying to and fro, mark them well; they always make for fresh water and sheltering foliage. There then sprinkle the odours I prescribe, bruised balm, and the wax-flower, mean weed though it be, and raise a tinkling noise, and beat the cymbals of the mighty mother all around: unbidden they will settle on the medicated spot, unbidden they will nestle, as is their wont, in the furthest corners of their new cradle.

But if it is for battle that they have left the hive—for oft when there are two kings strife visits them with her dire convulsions, and at once you may learn even from a distance the temper of the masses, and hear their very hearts beating for war, for there is that hoarse brazen music that the war-god loves stirring up the loiterers, and a note is heard imitating the trumpet's short broken blasts; then in eager alarm they flock together, and flash their wings, and sharpen their beaks, and string their arms, and throng and swarm round their king and about the very door of the royal tent, and with loud cries bid the foe come on. So when then they have got a clear spring day, and the field is open before them, forth they rush for the gates; the battle joins high in air; the din mounts up; they are mingled and massed into a mighty ball, and come tumbling down. Never hail fell thicker through the

air, never did shaken oak rain such a shower of acorns. The
monarchs themselves move through the ranks, distinguished
by their wings, their giant souls ranging through their pigmy
bosoms, firm-set never to give way till the conqueror's heavy
hand has forced one or other of the hosts to turn its back in
flight. These storms of passion, this conflict of giants, the
sprinkling of a little dust controls and lays to rest.

But when you have succeeded in recalling the two generals
from the field, take him who looks the worse, and save the
hive from the harmful excess by doing him to death; let the
better reign in solitary state. One you will find emblazed
with stiffening drops of gold—for there are two royal races,
the better of distinguished mien, brilliant with red flashing
scales; the other sunk in squalor and inaction, and dragging
with him the ignoble weight of a huge belly. As the royal
features are of two kinds, so are the bodies of the common-
alty; for one sort are loathly and squalid, like the traveller
when he emerges from his bath of dust, and spits the clay
from his dry throat, parched and thirsty; the others shine out
and flash resplendently, blazing in gold, and with regular spots
flecking their bodies. This is the worthier progeny; this, in
the sky's due season, will give you sweet honey to strain, and
not only sweet, but clear, and of power to subdue the wine-
god's harsher flavour.

But when the swarms fly aimlessly about and disport them
in the sky, scorning their cells, and leaving their homes to
chill, you must restrain their fickle spirits from such empty
trifling. Nor is restraint a hard task—do you deprive the
monarchs of their wings: when they hang back, no subject
will venture to encounter the upward journey, or pluck up the
standard from the encampment. Let there be a garden to
tempt them with the fragrance of its saffron flowers, and the
guardianship of Priapus, god of the Hellespont, standing

sentinel against thieves and birds with scythe of willow, to keep them safe. Let him, and none other, carry thyme and pine-trees down from the mountain-tops, and set them all about the hive, whose charge such things are; let him, and none other, make the hand sore with hard toil; let him, and none other, put into the ground plants that will bear, and sprinkle the friendly shower.

Aye, and for myself—were I not now at the very end of my enterprise, furling my sails, and hastening to bring my prow to land, it may be that I should extend my song to the luxuriant garden. What care of husbandry decks it with flowers, and the rosaries of twice-bearing Pæstum; and what is the joy that the endive feels in the stream which it drinks, and the green banks in the parsley that fringes them, and how the cucumber winds along the grass and swells into a belly; nor had I passed in silence the late-flowering narcissus, or the acanthus' bending stem, or the pale yellow ivy, or the myrtle that loves the coast. For I remember how once, under the shadow of Œbalia's lofty towers, where dark Galæsus bathes the yellow fields, I saw an old man of Corycus, who had a few acres of unappropriated land, soil with no productiveness for bullocks, no fitness for cattle, no friendliness for the wine-god. Yet he, while planting pot-herbs thinly among the boskage, and round them white lilies, and vervain, and scant poppies, had a heart that matched the wealth of kings; and often as he came home at night, he would pile his table high with unbought viands. None so early as he to pluck the rose in spring, the apple in autumn; and when winter in its bitterest mood was still splitting the very rocks with the frost, and bridling with ice the rush of the water, there was he, already gathering the hyacinth's delicate flower, with many a gibe at that late summer and those loitering zephyrs. Thus he was the first to swarm with mother-bees and their plenteous young, and to collect the honey as it frothed out from the squeezed comb; for he had limes and pines in luxuriant plenty; and all the fruit with which each prolific tree had clad itself in its early bloom, it retained undiminished in the ripeness of autumn. He, too, had been known to plant out in rows elms, well on in life, and pears grown hard as iron, and thorns which had begun to bear plums, and plane-trees, already tendering to drinkers the service of their shade. All this, however, I must pass by for myself, precluded as I am by my ungracious limits, and leave to others to record when my work is over.

Now listen, and I will tell of the nature which almighty Jove of his own act conferred on the bees, the wages for which they went after the musical sounds of the Curetes and the tinkling of the brass, and fed the king of Heaven under the cave of Dicte. They alone have their children in common, their dwellings associated into a city; they alone lead a life of submission to the majesty of law; they alone know the claims of country and the permanence of home, think of winter before it comes, try in summer what toil can do, and lay up in store what each has earned for the public. For some with sleepless care watch over the general sustenance, and go out by a set rule to labour abroad; some within the walls of their homes lay down the narcissus' tear and the clammy gum from the bark of trees as the first foundation of the comb, and then hang in air the roof of clinging wax; others lead out the nation's hope, the young now grown; others again mass together honey of the purest water, and strain the cells to bursting with its clear nectarous sweets; some there are on whom the sentry's work of the gates devolves by lot, and who take their turn in looking out for showers and gathering clouds, or relieve those who are coming in of their burdens, or collect a troop and expel from their stall the drones—that lazy, thriftless herd. The work is all fire, and a scent of thyme breathes from the fragrant honey. Even as when the Cyclopes to meet a sudden call are forging thunderbolts from the reluctant ore—some with their leathern bellows are taking in and giving out the wind, others are dipping the hissing copper in the lake, while Ætna groans under the anvil's weight; they, one with another, with all a giant's strength, are lifting their arms in measured cadence, and turning with their griping tongs the iron here and there—so, if it be right to compare small things with great, the bees of Cecrops' clime are stimulated to labour by an inborn love of acquiring, each in his own function. The old have charge of the town, of rearing walls of comb, and building dwellings of cunning frame; the younger sort drag themselves home late at night, tired, with their thighs laden with thyme; they feed dispersedly on arbutes and gray willow leaves, and casia and crocus glowing red, and luxuriant limes, and purple hyacinths. All have one time for rest from their work, all have one time for labour: at daybreak they pour from the gates—no delaying; again, when the star of eve has warned them to quit their pasture at last, and withdraw from the plains, at once they seek their homes, at once they bethink them of refreshment; a noise is heard—they hum about the entrance, and on the threshold. Afterwards, when they have settled into their beds, there is silence for the night, and their weary limbs are lapped in the sleep that they love. Again, they do not go far away from their stalls when there is rain overhead, or put faith in the sky while east winds are on the wing, but about the hive, under the shelter of the city's wall, they fetch in water, and try short excursions, and often take up pebbles, as the tossing wave makes unsteady boats take up ballast, and with these balance themselves as they move through the unsubstantial clouds. There is another custom which you will wonder should have found favour with the bees, that they do not give way to sexual intercourse, but unaided pick up their young in their mouths from leaves and grateful herbage; unaided they supply their Rome with a new monarch and tiny citizens, and so remodel the palace and the whole waxen realm. Often, too, while straying among rugged rocks they have been known to crush their wings and yield their patriot lives under their load—so intense is their love of flowers, so paramount the pride of gendering honey. Hence it is, that though each single bee is born to a narrow span of life—for their summers never stretch beyond the seventh—the family abides undying, and for many, many years, the star of the house delays to go down, and fathers' fathers of fathers' fathers are counted on the roll.

Moreover, royalty never receives such homage from Egypt, or from mighty Lydia, from the nations of Parthia, or from Median Hydaspes. While the king is safe, all are of one mind; when he perishes, the bond is broken; they themselves plunder the honey that they stored with such skill, and tear in pieces the comb's cunning wicker-work. He is the master of the works; to him they look up; the whole nation surrounds him, thronging and humming, and swarms as a guard about his person; and often they lift him on their shoulders, and shield him with their bodies from the shock of battle, and in the shower of wounds seek a glorious death.

From these tokens, and with these instances to guide them, some have said that bees have received a share of the divine intelligence, a draught of the pure ethereal stream; the Deity, they tell us, pervades all, earth and the expanse of sea, and the deep vault of heaven; from Him flocks, herds, men, wild beasts of every sort, each creature at its birth draws the bright thread of life; further, to Him all things return, are restored and reduced—death has no place among them; but they fly

up alive into the ranks of the stars, and take their seats aloft
in the sky.

If ever you would break the seal of their narrow dwelling,
and of the treasury where their honey is stored, first cleanse
your mouth with a sprinkling draught of water, and arm your
hand with the searching power of smoke. Twice they gather
in their teeming produce, twice a year comes their harvest—
once when Taygete, the Pleiad, displays to the earth her
graceful head, and spurns the ocean stream with her scornful
foot; and again when, flying from the sign of the watery
Fish, she makes her sad descent from heaven into the wintry
wave. Their fury, too, is all in excess; hurt them, and they
shoot poison into the bite they give, fasten on a vein, and
leave in it their unseen stings, and thus bury their own lives
in the wound.

But if you fear for them the tyranny of winter, and so
would deal gently with their future, pitying the thought of
a nation's spirit crushed and a common weal ruined, yet to
fumigate the hive with thyme, and to cut away the empty
cells of wax, who would shrink from that? for often has the
comb been gnawed away unknown by the eft and by the
cradled young of the light-hating beetle; and the drone, who
sits down, an unworking citizen, to another's food; or the
fierce hornet has dashed among their unequal forces; or moths,
a terrible race; or Minerva's foe, the spider, has hung her
loose-threaded nets across their doorway. The greater the
drain on them has been, the greater the zeal with which all
will exert themselves to repair the wreck of the fallen house,
filling up the rows of their cells, and planking their granaries
with the spoils of the flowers.

But if, seeing that bees, like men, must meet the chances
of life, their frames should be unstrung by grievous sickness
—a thing which you will be able to tell at once by signs of

no doubtful meaning—as they sicken their colour at once
changes, a squalid leanness disfigures their features ; soon
they carry out from their homes the corpses of those who
have lost life's light, and lead the melancholy procession to
the grave ; either they hang about the door with their feet
linked together, or keep lingering within in their closed
dwelling, one and all languid with hunger and torpid with
pinching cold. Then a hoarse noise strikes the ear, and they
hum droningly and long, like the sigh of the bleak south
through the forest, like the crash of the troubled sea as its
waves retire from the beach, like the roar of the surging
blaze in the closed furnace. Now, aye and before now, I
would counsel you to burn the scent of galbanum, and to
convey honey through pipes of reed, anticipating them with
your encouragement, and inviting the poor tired creatures to
the food they know and love. It will be well too to mix
with the honey the flavour of pounded galls, and dried rose
leaves, or wine thickened to syrup over a hot fire, or the
juice of the raisin-cluster from the Psithian vine, and the
thyme of Cecrops' land, and the pungent-smelling centaury.
A flower, too, there grows in the meadows, to which the
countrymen have attached the name of *amellus*, a plant which
gives little trouble to those who seek it, for it shoots up a
great vegetation from the one spot of turf where it springs :
itself of golden hue, but in the leaves which cluster round
that golden centre there are gleams of purple under a dark
violet tint : many a time have the altars of the gods been
decked with its twined festoons ; it leaves a bitter taste in
the mouth: among the nibbled herbage of the valley, the
shepherds gather it, near the winding stream of Mella. Take
it and boil its roots in the wine-god's generous perfume, and
place it for their food in the doorway in piled baskets.

But should there be any whose whole stock has failed him

G

suddenly, and left no means of calling back the line to life
in a new race, it is time that I should also disclose the
memorable discovery of the great Arcadian keeper, and the
way in which, oft ere now, from the slaughter of bullocks,
tainted gore has generated bees. I will expound the whole
legend, mounting up to the source, and tracing it thence.
For where the favoured race of Macedon's Canopus dwell by
the stagnant Nile and its overflowing waters, and travel in
painted boats about the lands they till, where quivered
Persia's contiguity presses hard on the frontier, and the rapid
river parts into seven separate mouths, and with its black
slime fertilises the green land of Egypt—the river that has
come down all the way from among the sun-baked Indians—
that entire clime rests the weal of its hives with confidence
on this device.

In the first place, a spot small and confined for the very
purpose is chosen out ; this they close in with narrow roof-
tiling, and straitened walls, and insert four windows, with
slanting light from the four quarters of heaven. . Next they
look out for a bull-calf, whose horns have begun to arch
over a brow that has seen two summers; they take him
and seal up his two nostrils and his mouth's breath, spite
of furious struggles ; and after he has been slain by their
blows, his flesh through his unbroken hide is beaten to a jelly.
As he lies, they leave him in his barred prison, placing under
his ribs broken bits of bough, and thyme, and fresh-plucked
casia. This goes on when the west winds first play upon the
waters, ere the meadows are empurpled with fresh spring-tide
hues, ere the chattering swallow hangs her nest from the
rafters. Meanwhile, in his softened bones the sap has been
heated and begins to ferment, and living things of strange
manner to look upon, at first with no feet to crawl on, but
soon even with wings to buzz and fly with, swarm confusedly,

and skim the empty air more and more, till, like a burst of
rain from a summer cloud, out they break, or like arrows
from the rebounding cord, whenever the light-armed Parthian
strikes up the prelude of the battle.

Who of the gods, ye muses, who, beat out for us men this
skilled device? Whence did this fresh growth of men's
experience take its rise?

It was the shepherd, Aristæus, turning his back on Tempe
and her Peneus, when his bees were all dead—so runs the
tale—of disease and famine, that stood in sorrow at the sacred
head where the river rises, with many a plaint, and in words
like these bespoke her that bore him: 'Mother Cyrene,
mother, whose dwelling is at the bottom of this gulf, why
didst thou bear me, a son of an illustrious line of gods—if at
least he of whom thou tellest me is my father, Thymbra's
Apollo—to a life under an evil star? Whither has thy love
for me and mine been banished? Wherefore didst thou bid
me look forward to the sky? See now, even this very crown
of my poor mortality, which a life of skilful watching over
corn and cattle had barely won for me, every effort tried, I
must resign—and thou art my mother still! Why then, come
on—put thine own hand to the work, uproot my fruitful
forests, bring into my stalls the fire they hate, kill my crops,
burn my young plants, and wield against my vines the heaviest
axe thou canst find, if the access of thy disgust at hearing me
praised be indeed so strong.'

But his mother caught the sound as she sat in the bed-
chamber of the deep stream. Around her the nymphs were
spinning wool of Miletus, ingrained with hyaline's saturating
dye, Drymo, and Xantho, and Ligeia, and Phyllodoce, their
bright locks floating over their snowy necks, and Cydippe,
and yellow-haired Lycorias—a maiden one, the other having
just proved the first pangs of the goddess of travail—and Clio,

and Beroe, her sister, children of Ocean both, both girt with
gold, both with dresses of dappled hide, and Ephyre, and
Opis, and Asian Deiopeia, and Arethusa fleet of foot, her
huntress' shafts at last laid by ; among them Clymene was
telling the tale of Vulcan's vain jealousy, of Mars' stratagem
and the joy he stole, and from chaos downwards was counting
the crowded muster-roll of the loves of the gods.   As they sit
entranced by the song, and the spindle carries down their fleecy
tasks, yet again there smote on the mother's ear the wail of
Aristæus, and all were confounded on their crystal seats ; but
Arethusa, anticipating the rest of the sisterhood, looked forth,
and raised her yellow head from the water's surface, and cried
from the distance—'O thou whom a groan so loud has not
scared for nought, sister Cyrene, it is himself, thy chiefest
care, Aristæus, that stands at the wave of our father Peneus
weeping to thee, and calling on thy cruel name.'   Struck to
the soul with a strange terror, 'Go, bring him, bring him
to us; he may touch the floor that gods tread,' cries the
mother.   With that she bids the deep stream retire far and wide,
making a path on which the youth might walk.   Round him
closed the wave arched into mountain form, took him into its
giant bosom, and sped him down under the river.   And now
he is on his way marvelling at his mother's palace and the
whole watery realm, pools locked by caves and forests echoing
wide, and, all confounded by the mighty rush of the waters,
is gazing on all the rivers of earth as they flow under its vast
surface each in its several bed—Phasis, and Lycus, and the
source whence first breaks forth the deep Enipeus, whence
Tiber, the Roman's father, and whence the streams of Anio,
and rocky roaring Hypanis, and Mysian Caicus, and he that
bears two gilded horns on his bull's brow, Eridanus, than
whom no river pours himself more forcefully through his rich
cultured plains into the blue flushing deep.   After he had

come under the chamber's stone-hung roof, and Cyrene had
taken knowledge of her son's bootless weeping, the sisterhood,
each in her course, offer him clear spring water for his hands,
and present towels with the nap duly shorn, while others load
the table with viands, and set on cups brimming again and
again : the altars mount up with Panchaian fires ; and 'Take,'
says the mother, ' the bowl of Mæonia's wine-god ; make we
libation to Ocean.' So speaking, she offers herself a prayer to
Ocean, father of creation, and the sisterhood of nymphs, the
hundred guardians of the woods, the hundred of the rivers.
Thrice with the clear nectar she sprinkled the blazing fire-
queen ; thrice the flame shot up to the roof-top and shone
again. Cheering his heart with the omen, she thus begins
her speech :—

' In the sea-god's Carpathian gulf there lives a seer, Proteus,
of the sea's own hue, who takes the measure of the mighty
deep with his fishes, even with his harnessed car of two-legged
steeds. He is at this moment visiting again the havens of
Emathia and Pallene, the country of his birth. To him we
nymphs all do reverence, aye, and Nereus too, the old and
grey ; for all things are known to the seer, those which are,
those which have been, those which drag their length through
the advancing future. So it seemed good to Neptune, whose
monstrous herds of loathly sea-calves he pastures under the
deep. Him, my son, you must first make prisoner and bind,
that he may unfold all the history of the disease and prosper
the issue. For without force he will give no counsel, nor will
your praying bend him ; force, stern force, and fetters must be
put upon the captive ; against them his baffled wiles will at
last be broken. I myself, when the sun has kindled his
mid-day furnace, when the herbage is athirst, and cattle
begin to feel the joy of the shade, will lead you into the old
one's privacy, the place where he retires from his labours in

the water, that you may easily fall on him as he lies asleep. But when you have caught him in the grasp of hand and fetter, then the divers forms and features of wild beasts will be put on to mock you. He will change suddenly to a bristly boar, and a grim black tiger, a scaly dragon, and a lioness with tawny mane ; or he will send forth the sharp crackling of flame, and thus slip out of your bonds, or will trickle away into unsubstantial water and be gone. But the more you find him turn himself into shape after shape, the tighter, my son, strain the gripe of your bonds, till, his last change over, he appear in the form in which you saw him when sleep had set in and his eyes were curtained.'

So saying, she bids ambrosia send forth its liquid perfume, which she spreads over her son's whole frame ; at once he felt his new-trimmed locks exhale a breath of fragrance, and a supple vigour pass into his limbs. There is a vast cave eaten out in a mountain's side, whereinto wave upon wave is driven by the wind, and breaks in the retreating inlet—to the mariner, when the storm is upon him, at times a roadstead of safest shelter. There, far within, Proteus screens himself with the barrier of an enormous rock. Here the nymph places the youth in hiding, away from the light; she herself stands off in the dusk of a mist she raises. Already Sirius was all ablaze in the sky, with that fierce glow that scorches the Indians with thirst, and the sun's fiery car had exhausted the half of its circuit; the herbage was parching, and the hollow rivers, their dry jaws agape, were being baked by the sunbeams into a heated mass of mud, when Proteus was on his way from the surge, making for the accustomed cave ; around him the moist generation of the broad sea, leaping gamesomely, flung about the salt spray. They lay themselves to sleep, the sea-calves, here and there along the beach ; he, like the warder of a fold one day among the hills, when the star of eve brings the calves home from pasture, and the sound of the lamb's bleating whets the wolf's maw, sits down in the middle of the rock and tells over their tale. Soon as Aris- tæus saw the facility within his grasp, scarcely giving the old one time to settle his tired limbs, he bursts on him with a tremendous cry, and invades him with manacles there as he lies. The god on his part, his craft then, as ever, in his mind, transforms himself into all that is monstrous in nature—the fire, the hideous beast, the flowing stream. But when no stratagem finds him escape, vanquished, he becomes himself again, and at last from human lips speaks thus :—' Why, who has bid thee, most assured of all youths that are, to visit us in our home ? or what wouldst thou have hence ?' But he, ' Thou knowest, Proteus, thou knowest of thyself—nought can cheat thee ; but do thou leave off the will to cheat. Following the instructions of gods I am come, to ask an oracle for my o'erlaboured fortunes.' So far he spoke. At this the seer at length, with mighty force, darted on him the glass- green glare of his fiery eyes, and heavily gnashing his teeth, thus broke the seal of his lips with the voice of destiny :—

' No—think not it is no angry god that has laid his hand on thee—thy suffering is for a great crime : this thy punish- ment Orpheus, a wretched man by no fault of his own, should fate not interpose, is still stinging into life, still raging implac- ably for his ravished bride. She, in her headlong flight from thee, along the river meadow, saw not, the young doomed one that she was, in the deep grass an enormous water-serpent right before her feet, keeping ward over the river-bank. But the choir of her peers, the Dryads, filled the very mountain- peaks with their crying : her dirge was sung by the steeps of Rhodope, and high Pangæa and Rhesus' land, the land of the war-god, by the Getæ, by Hebrus, and Orithyia, Acte's child ; while he, solacing with the hollow shell his distempered love, made thee, darling wife, thee, all to himself on the lonely shore, thee at dawn of day, thee at set of sun, his unending song. Aye, and he entered the jaws of Tænarus, the abysmal gates of Pluto's court, and the grove that darkles with a horror of blackness; he went to the shades, and their terrible king, and knocked at the heart which never learnt to soften at human prayer. Startled by the song, came trooping from Erebus' deepest prison thin spectres and phantoms of those who lie in darkness, many as the myriads of birds that hide them in the leaves, when eve or winter's rain chases them from the hills—matrons, and husbands, and frames of high-souled heroes discharged of life, boys and unwedded girls, and youths that had been carried to death in their parents' sight, round whom the blackening ooze and the loathly reeds of Cocytus, and the sluggish waters of that unlovely swamp throw their chains, and Styx, wound nine times about them, holds them in durance. Nay, a charm fell on the very house of death, on the abyss of Tartarus itself, and the Furies, with livid snakes wreathing in their hair, and Cerberus riveted his three mouths attentive and agape, and Ixion's circling wheel stood fixed in wind-bound slumber. And now he was returning home, and every chance was just escaped, and Eurydice, surrendered to his prayer, was passing into the air of heaven, following behind—for such the condition that Proserpine had imposed—when a sudden frenzy took hold of the unthinking lover—a sin that might plead for pardon, were pardon an art known to the shades—he stopped. Eurydice was now his own, treading on the very threshold of daylight —his memory fled, alas! his soul was `mastered—he looked back on her. That instant all his pains were spilt like so much water, the covenant of the ruthless monarch was broken, and a thunder peal was heard thrice through Avernus' sluggish depths. She cried—"Oh! what madness, what monstrous

madness has undone me, poor me, and thee too, my Orpheus?
Look! again that cruel destiny is calling me back, and sleep
is burying my swimming eyes. And now farewell. I am
borne away, swathed in night's vast pall, and stretching
towards thee powerless hands—thine own, alas! no longer."
She said, and suddenly from his sight, like smoke that mingles
with thin air, she fled by another way, and though he caught
in vain at the shadows, and essayed to say a thousand things,
never saw him more: nor did the ferryman of Orcus suffer
him any further to pass the barrier of marsh-water. What
was he to do? whither was he to turn him, thus widowed
a second time? where was there a new wail to touch the
shades, new accents to melt the gods below? And she—
she was floating off in the boat of Styx, death-chilled
already. Seven whole months, one with another, they
say, under a skiey rock, by the waters of lonely Strymon,
he made his moan, and unfolded this his tale beneath the
wintry caverns, in strains that softened the tiger and drew the
oak to follow him—as the nightingale wailing in the poplar
shade plains for her lost young, that the rustic churl, with his
prying eye, has taken unfledged from the nest: while she
weeps the night through, and sitting on a bough, reproduces
her piteous melody, and fills the country round with the
plaints of her sorrow. No queen of love, no bridal rites had
power over his soul. Alone, over Hyperborean ice, and Tanais
the snowy, and fields whose marriage-bond with Rhipæan
frost is never severed, he would ramble, sorrowing for his lost
Eurydice and Pluto's cancelled boon—a service resented as
scorn by the Cicon dames, who, on a night of sacrifice to
heaven and orgies to Bacchus, tore the youth in pieces, and
scattered him broadcast over the plain. Even then, while the
head, rent from that pale marble neck, was swept floating
down the midst of Œagrian Hebrus' flood, *Eurydice*, the bare

voice of the cold tongue—*Ah ! my poor Eurydice*—kept calling as life parted. *Eurydice*, the banks returned all down
the stream.'

So far Proteus, and flounced into the deep sea, and when
he plunged wreathed the water in foam under the circling
eddy.

Not so Cyrene—at once she turned to the trembling
listener :—' My son, you are free to unburden your mind of
its grievous care. This is the whole secret of the plague : for
this the nymphs, with whom she wont to dance in the tall
green wood, have sent among your bees such piteous havoc.
Be it yours to tender a suppliant's offerings, praying to be
reconciled, and pay homage to the gracious sisters of the groves:
for they will grant forgiveness at your prayer, and abate their
wrath. But the method of supplication shall first be explained
in due course. Pick out four choice bulls of goodly frame, now
grazing among thy herds on the top of green Lycæus, and
as many heifers whose neck never yoke has touched. For
these set up four altars by the gods' lofty fanes, and let from
their throats the stream of sacred blood, and leave the bodies
of the kine to themselves in the leafy grove. After, when the
ninth morn-goddess shall have displayed the dawn, to Orpheus
you will send a funeral sacrifice of Lethe's poppies, and slay
a black sheep, and visit the grove again : then, when you find
Eurydice appeased, you will pay her the thank-offering of a
slaughtered calf.'

Not an hour's delay : at once he does his mother's bidding :
to the fane he comes : he uprears the prescribed altars, four
choice bulls of goodly frame he leads thither, and as many
heifers whose neck never yoke has touched. After, when the
ninth morn-goddess had ushered in the dawn, he sends to
Orpheus a funeral sacrifice, and visits the grove again. And
now a portent, sudden and marvellous to tell, meets their

view : through the whole length of the kine's dissolving flesh bees are seen, buzzing in the belly and boiling out through the bursten ribs, and huge clouds lengthen and sway, till at last they pour altogether to the tree's top, and let down a cluster from the bending boughs.

Such was the song I was making; a song of the husbandry of fields and cattle, and of trees ; while Cæsar, the great, is flashing war's thunderbolt over the depths of Euphrates, and dispensing among willing nations a conqueror's law, and setting his foot on the road to the sky. In those days I was being nursed in Parthenope's delicious lap, embowered in the pursuits of inglorious peace—I, Virgil, who once dallied with the shepherd's muse, and with a young man's boldness, sang of thee, Tityrus, under the spreading beechen shade.

THE ÆNEID.

—o—

BOOK I.

ARMS and the man I sing, who at the first from Troy's shores the exile of destiny, won his way to Italy and her Latian coast—a man much buffeted on land and on the deep by violence from above, to sate the unforgetting wrath of Juno the cruel—much scourged too in war, as he struggled to build him a city, and find his gods a home in Latium—himself the father of the Latian people, and the chiefs of Alba's houses, and the walls of high towering Rome.

Bring to my mind, O Muse, the causes—for what treason against her godhead, or what pain received, the queen of heaven drove a man of piety so signal to turn the wheel of so many calamities, to bear the brunt of so many hardships! Can heavenly natures hate so fiercely and so long?

Of old there was a city, its people emigrants from Tyre, Carthage, over against Italy and Tiber's mouths, yet far removed—rich and mighty, and formed to all roughness by war's iron trade—a spot where Juno, it was said, loved to dwell more than in all the world beside, Samos holding but the second place. Here was her armour, here her chariot —here to fix by her royal act the empire of the nations, could Fate be brought to assent, was even then her aim, her cherished scheme. But she had heard that the blood of Troy was sowing the seed of a race to overturn one day those Tyrian towers—from that seed a nation, monarch of broad realms and glorious in war, was to bring ruin on Libya—such the turning of Fate's wheel. With these fears Saturn's daughter, and with a lively memory of that old war which at first she had waged at Troy for her loved Argos' sake— nor indeed had the causes of that feud and the bitter pangs they roused yet vanished from her mind—no, stored up in her soul's depths remains the judgment of Paris, and the wrong done to her slighted beauty, and the race abhorred from the womb, and the state enjoyed by the ravished Ganymede. With this fuel added to the fire, the Trojans, poor remnants of Danaan havoc and Achilles' ruthless spear, she was tossing from sea to sea, and keeping far away from Latium ; and for many long years they were wandering, with destiny still driving them, the whole ocean round. So vast the effort it cost to build up the Roman nation !

Scarce out of sight of the land of Sicily were they spread- ing their sails merrily to the deep, and scattering with their brazen prows the briny spray, when Juno, the everlasting wound still rankling in her heart's core, thus communed with herself : 'And am I to give up what I have taken in hand, baffled, nor have power to prevent the king of the Teucrians from reaching Italy—because, forsooth, the Fates forbid me ? What ! was Pallas strong enough to burn up utterly the Grecian fleet, and whelm the crews in the sea, for the offence of a single man, the frenzy of Ajax, Oileus' son ? Aye, she with her own hand launched from the clouds Jove's winged fire, dashed the ships apart, and turned up the sea-floor with the wind—him, gasping out the flame which pierced his bosom, she caught in the blast, and impaled on a rock's point —while I, who walk the sky as its queen, Jove's sister and consort both, am battling with a single nation these many years. And are there any found to pray to Juno's deity after this, or lay on her altar a suppliant's gift ? '

With such thoughts sweeping through the solitude of her enkindled breast, the goddess comes to the storm-cloud's birthplace, the teeming womb of fierce southern blasts, Æolia. Here, in a vast cavern, King Æolus is bowing to his sway struggling winds and howling tempests, and bridling them with bond and prison. They, in their passion, are raving at the closed doors, while the huge rock roars responsive : Æolus is sitting aloft in his fortress, his sceptre in his hand, soothing their moods and allaying their rage ; were he to fail in this, why sea and land, and the deep of heaven, would all be forced along by their blast, and swept through the air. But the almighty sire has buried them in caverns dark and deep, with this fear before his eyes, and placed over them giant bulk and tall mountains, and given them a king who, by the terms of his compact, should know how to tighten or slacken the reins at his patron's will. To him it was that Juno then, in these words, made her humble request :—

'Æolus—for it is to thee that the sire of gods and king of men has given it with the winds now to calm, now to rouse the billows—there is a race which I love not now sailing the Tyrrhene sea, carrying Ilion into Italy and Ilion's vanquished gods ; do thou lash the winds to fury, sink and whelm their ships, or scatter them apart, and strew the ocean with their corpses. Twice seven nymphs are of my train, all of surpassing beauty ; of these her whose form is fairest, Deiopea, I will unite to thee in lasting wedlock, and consecrate her thy own, that all her days, for a service so great, she may pass with thee, and make thee father of a goodly progeny.'

Æolus returns : 'Thine, great Queen, is the task to search out on what thou mayest fix thy heart ; for me to do thy bidding is but right. Thou makest this poor realm mine, mine the sceptre and Jove's smile; thou givest me a couch at the banquets of the gods, and makest me lord of the storm-cloud and of the tempest.'

So soon as this was said, he turned his spear, and pushed the hollow mountain on its side; and the winds, as though in column formed, rush forth where they see an outlet, and sweep over the earth in hurricane. Heavily they fall on the sea, and from its very bottom crash down the whole expanse—one and all, east and south, and south-west, with his storms thronging at his back, and roll huge billows shoreward. Hark to the shrieks of the crew, and the creaking of the cables! In an instant the clouds snatch sky and daylight from the Teucrians' eyes—night lies on the deep, black and heavy—pole thunders to pole; heaven flashes thick with fires, and all nature brandishes instant death in the seaman's face. At once Æneas' limbs are unstrung and chilled—he groans aloud, and, stretching his clasped hands to the stars, fetches from his breast words like these:—'O happy, thrice and again, whose lot it was, in their fathers' sight, under Troy's high walls to meet death! O thou, the bravest of the Danaan race, Tydeus' son, why was it not mine to lay me low on Ilion's plains, and yield this fated life to thy right hand? Aye, there it is that Hector, stern as in life, lies stretched by the spear of Æacides—there lies Sarpedon's giant bulk—there it is that Simois seizes and sweeps down her channel those many shields and helms, and bodies of the brave!'

Such words as he flung wildly forth, a blast roaring from the north strikes his sail full in front and lifts the billows to the stars. Shattered are the oars; then the prow turns and presents the ship's side to the waves; down crashes in a heap a craggy mountain of water. Look! these are hanging on the surge's crest—to those the yawning deep is giving a glimpse of land down among the billows; surf and sand are raving together. Three ships the south catches, and flings upon hidden rocks—rocks which, as they stand with the waves all about them, the Italians call Altars, an enormous ridge rising above the sea. Three the east drives from the main on to shallows and Syrtes, a piteous sight, and dashes them on shoals, and embanks them in mounds of sand. One in which the Lycians were sailing, and true Orontes, a mighty sea strikes from high on the stem before Æneas' very eyes; down goes the helmsman, washed from his post, and topples on his head, while she is thrice whirled round by the billow in the spot where she lay, and swallowed at once by the greedy gulf. You might see them here and there swimming in that vast abyss—heroes', arms, and planks, and Troy's treasures glimmering through the water. Already Ilioneus' stout ship, already brave Achates', and that in which Abas sailed, and that which carried old Aletes, are worsted by the storm; their side-jointings loosened, one and all give entrance to the watery foe, and part failingly asunder.

Meantime the roaring riot of the ocean and the storm let loose reached the sense of Neptune, and the still waters disgorged from their deep beds, troubling him grievously; and casting a broad glance over the main he raised at once his tranquil brow from the water's surface. There he sees Æneas' fleet tossed hither and thither over the whole expanse—the Trojans whelmed under the billows, and the crashing ruin of the sky —nor failed the brother to read Juno's craft and hatred there. East and West he calls before him, and bespeaks them thus: —'Are ye then so wholly o'ermastered by the pride of your birth? Have ye come to this, ye Winds, that, without sanction from me, ye dare to confound sea and land, and upheave these mighty mountains? ye! whom I—— but it were best to calm the billows ye have troubled. Henceforth ye shall pay me for your crimes in far other coin. Make good speed with your flight, and give your king this message. Not to him did the lot assign the empire of the sea and the terrible trident, but to me. His sway is over those enormous rocks, where you, Eurus, dwell, and such as you; in that court let Æolus lord it, and rule in the prison-house of the winds when its doors are barred.'

He speaks, and ere his words are done soothes the swelling waters, and routs the mustered clouds, and brings back the sun in triumph. Cymothoe and Triton combine their efforts to push off the vessels from the sharp-pointed rock. The god himself upheaves them with his own trident, and levels the great quicksands, and allays the sea, and on chariot-wheels of lightest motion glides along the water's top. Even as when in a great crowd tumult is oft stirred up, and the base herd waxes wild and frantic, and brands and stones are flying already, rage suiting the weapon to the hand—at that moment, should their eyes fall on some man of weight, for duty done and public worth, tongues are hushed and ears fixed in attention, while his words sway the spirit and soothe the breast—so fell all the thunders of the ocean, so soon as the great father, with the waves before him in prospect, and the clear sky all about him, guides his steeds at will, and as he flies flings out the reins freely to his obedient car.

Spent with toil, the family of Æneas labour to gain the shore that may be nearest, and are carried to the coasts of Libya. There is a spot retiring deep into the land, where an island forms a haven by the barrier of its sides, which break every billow from the main and send it shattered into the deep indented hollows. On either side of the bay are huge rocks, and two great crags rising in menace to the sky; under their summits far and wide the water is hushed in shelter, while a theatric background of waving woods, a black forest of stiffening shade, overhangs it from the height. Under the brow that fronts the deep is a cave with pendent crags; within there are fresh springs and seats in the living rock—the home of the nymphs; no need of cable here to confine the weary bark or anchor's crooked fang to grapple her to the shore. Here with seven ships mustered from his whole fleet Æneas enters; and with intense yearning for dry land the Trojans disembark and take possession of the wished-for shore, and lay their brine-drenched limbs upon the beach. And first Achates from a flint struck out a spark, and received the fire as it dropped in a cradle of leaves, and placed dry food all about it, and spread the strong blaze among the tinder. Then their corn, soaked and spoiled as it was, and the corn-goddess' armoury they bring out, sick of fortune; and make ready to parch the rescued grain at the fire, and crush it with the millstone.

Æneas meanwhile clambers up a rock, and tries to get a full view far and wide over the sea, if haply he may see aught of Antheus, driven by the gale, and the Phrygian biremes, or Capys, or high on the stern the arms of Caicus. Sail there is none in sight; three stags he sees at distance straying on the shore; these the whole herd follows in the rear, and grazes along the hollows in long array. At once he took his stand, and caught up a bow and fleet arrows, which true Achates chanced to be carrying, and lays low first the leaders themselves, as they bear their heads aloft with tree-like antlers, then the meaner sort, and scatters with his pursuing shafts the whole rout among the leafy woods; nor stays his hand till he stretches on earth victoriously seven huge bodies, and makes the sum of them even with his ships. Then he returns to the haven and gives all his comrades their shares. The wine next, which that good Acestes had stowed in casks on the Trinacrian shore, and given them at parting

with his own princely hand, he portions out, and speaks
words of comfort to their sorrowing hearts :—

'Comrades! for comrades we are, no strangers to hardships
already; hearts that have felt deeper wounds! for these too
heaven will find a balm. Why, men, you have even looked
on Scylla in her madness, and heard those yells that thrill the
rocks; you have even made trial of the crags of the Cyclops.
Come, call your spirits back, and banish these doleful fears—
who knows but some day this too will be remembered with
pleasure? Through manifold chances, through these many
perils of fortune, we are making our way to Latium, where
the Fates hold out to us a quiet settlement; there Troy's empire has leave to rise again from its ashes. Bear up, and
reserve yourselves for brighter days.'

Such were the words his tongue uttered; heart-sick with
overwhelming care, he wears the semblance of hope in his face,
but has grief deep buried in his heart. They gird themselves
to deal with the game, their forthcoming meal; strip the hide
from the ribs, and lay bare the flesh—some cut it into pieces,
and impale it yet quivering on spits, others set up the caldrons
on the beach, and supply them with flame. Then with food
they recall their strength, and, stretched along the turf, feast
on old wine and fat venison to their hearts' content. Their
hunger sated by the meal, and the boards removed, they vent
in long talk their anxious yearning for their missing comrades
—balanced between hope and fear, whether to think of them
as alive, or as suffering the last change, and deaf already to the
voice that calls on them. But good Æneas' grief exceeds the
rest; one moment he groans for bold Orontes' fortune, another
for Amycus', and in the depth of his spirit laments for the cruel
fate of Lycus; for the gallant Gyas and the gallant Cloanthus.

And now at last their mourning had an end, when Jupiter
from the height of ether, looking down on the sea with its

fluttering sails, on the flat surface of earth, the shores, and the broad tribes of men, paused thus upon heaven's very summit, and fixed his downward gaze on Libya's realms. To him, revolving in his breast such thoughts as these, sad beyond her wont, with tears suffusing her starry eyes, speaks Venus: 'O thou, who by thy everlasting laws swayest the two common-wealths of men and gods, and awest them by thy lightning! What can my poor Æneas have done to merit thy wrath? What can the Trojans? yet they, after the many deaths they have suffered already, still find the whole world barred against them for Italy's sake. From them assuredly it was that the Romans, as years rolled on—from them were to spring those warrior chiefs, aye from Teucer's blood revived, who should rule sea and land with absolute sway—such was thy promise: how has thy purpose, O my father, wrought a change in thee? This, I know, was my constant solace when Troy's star set in grievous ruin, as I sat balancing destiny against destiny. And now here is the same Fortune, pursuing the brave men she has so oft discomfited already. Mighty king, what end of sufferings hast thou to give them? Antenor, indeed, found means to escape through the midst of the Achæans, to thread in safety the windings of the Illyrian coast, and the realms of the Liburnians, up at the gulf's head, and to pass the springs of Timavus, whence through nine months, 'mid the rocks' responsive roar, the sea comes bursting up, and deluges the fields with its thundering billows. Yet in that spot he built the city of Patavium for his Trojans to dwell in, and gave them a place and a name among the nations, and set up a rest for the arms of Troy: now he reposes, lapped in the calm of peace. Meantime we, of thine own blood, to whom thy nod secures the pinnacle of heaven, our ships, most mon-strous, lost, as thou seest, all to sate the malice of one cruel heart, are given up to ruin, and severed far from the Italian shores. Is this the reward of piety? Is this to restore a king to his throne?'

Smiling on her, the planter of gods and men, with that face which calms the fitful moods of the sky, touched with a kiss his daughter's lips, then addressed her thus: 'Give thy fears a respite, lady of Cythera: thy people's destiny abides still unchanged for thee; thine eyes shall see the city of thy heart, the promised walls of Lavinium; thine arms shall bear aloft to the stars of heaven thy hero Æneas; nor has my purpose wrought a change in me. Thy hero—for I will speak out, in pity for the care that rankles yet, and awaken the secrets of Fate's book from the distant pages where they slumber—thy hero shall wage a mighty war in Italy, crush its haughty tribes, and set up for his warriors a polity and a city, till the third summer shall have seen him king over Latium, and three winters in camp shall have passed over the Rutulians' defeat. But the boy Ascanius, who has now the new name of Iulus—Ilus he was, while the royalty of Ilion's state stood firm—shall let thirty of the sun's great courses fulfil their monthly rounds while he is sovereign, then transfer the empire from Lavinium's seat, and build Alba the Long, with power and might. Here for full three hundred years the crown shall be worn by Hector's line, till a royal priestess, teeming by the war-god, Ilia, shall be the mother of twin sons. Then shall there be one, proud to wear the tawny hide of the wolf that nursed him, Romulus, who will take up the sceptre, and build a new city, the city of Mars, and give the people his own name of Roman. To them I assign no limit, no date of empire: my grant to them is dominion without end. Nay, Juno, thy savage foe, who now, in her blind terror, lets neither sea, land, nor heaven rest, shall amend her counsels, and vie with me in watching over the Romans, lords of earth, the great nation of the gown. So it is willed. The time shall come, as Rome's years roll on, when the house of Assaracus shall bend to its yoke Phthia˙ and renowned Mycenæ, and queen it over vanquished Argos. Then shall be born the child of an illustrious line, one of thine own Trojans, Cæsar, born to extend his empire to the ocean, his glory to the stars,—Julius, in name as in blood the heir of great Iulus. Him thou shalt one day welcome in safety to the sky, a warrior laden with Eastern spoils; to him, as to Æneas, men shall pray and make their vows. In his days war shall cease, and savage times grow mild. Faith with her hoary head, and Vesta, Quirinus, and Remus his brother, shall give law to the world : grim, iron-bound, closely welded, the gates of war shall be closed; the fiend of Discord a prisoner within, seated on a pile of arms deadly as himself, his hands bound behind his back with a hundred brazen chains, shall roar ghastly from his throat of blood.'

So saying, he sends down from on high the son of Maia, that Carthage the new, her lands and her towers, may open themselves to welcome in the Teucrians, lest Dido, in her ignorance of Fate, should drive them from her borders. Down flies Mercury through the vast abyss of air, with his wings for oars, and has speedily alighted on the shore of Libya. See ! he is doing his bidding already : the Punic nation is resigning the fierceness of its nature at the god's pleasure ; above all the rest, the queen is admitting into her bosom thoughts of peace towards the Teucrians, and a heart of kindness.

But Æneas the good, revolving many things the whole night through, soon as the gracious dawn is vouchsafed, resolves to go out and explore this new region ; to inquire what shores be these on which the wind has driven him ; who their dwellers, for he sees it is a wilderness, men or beasts ; and bring his comrades back the news. His fleet he hides in the wooded cove under a hollow rock, with a wall of trees and stiffening shade on each side. He moves on with Achates, his single companion, wielding in his hands two spear shafts, with heads of broad iron. He had reached the middle of the wood, when his way was crossed by his mother, wearing a maiden's mien and dress, and a maiden's armour, Spartan, or even as Harpalyce of Thrace, tires steed after steed, and heads the swift waters of her own Hebrus as she flies along. For she had a shapely bow duly slung from her shoulders in true huntress fashion, and her hair streaming in the wind, her knee bare, and her flowing scarf gathered round her in a knot. Soon as she sees them, ' Ho! youths,' cries she, ' if you have chanced to see one of my sisters wandering in these parts, tell me where to find her—wandering with a quiver, and a spotted lynx hide fastened about her; or, it may be, pressing on the heels of the foaming boar with her hounds in full cry.'

Thus Venus spoke, and Venus' son replied :—' No sight or hearing have we had of any sister of thine, O thou—what name shall I give thee? maiden; for thy face is not of earth, nor the tone of thy voice human: some goddess surely thou art. Phœbus' sister belike, or one of the blood of the nymphs? be gracious, whoe'er thou art, and relieve our hardship, and tell us under what sky now, on what realms of earth we are thrown. Utter strangers to the men and the place, we are wandering, as thou seest, by the driving of the wind and of the mighty waters. Do this, and many a victim shall fall to thee at the altar by this hand of mine.'

Then Venus :—' Nay, I can lay claim to no such honours. Tyrian maidens, like me, are wont to carry the quiver, and tie the purple buskin high up the calf. This that you now see is the Punic realm, the nation Tyrian and the town Agenor's; but on the frontiers are the Libyans, a race ill to handle in war. The queen is Dido, who left her home in Tyre to escape from her brother. Lengthy is her tale

of wrong, lengthy the windings of its course; but I will pass
rapidly from point to point. Her husband was Sychæus,
wealthiest of Phœnician landowners, and loved by his poor
wife with fervid passion; on him her father had bestowed
her in her maiden bloom, linking them together by the
omens of a first bridal. But the crown of Tyre was on
the head of her brother, Pygmalion, in crime monstrous
beyond the rest of men. They were two, and fury came
between them. Impious that he was, at the very altar of
the palace, the love of gold blinding his eyes, he surprises
Sychæus with his stealthy steel, and lays him low, without
a thought for his sister's passion; he kept the deed long
concealed, and with many a base coinage sustained the
mockery of false hope in her pining love-lorn heart. But lo!
in her sleep there came to her no less than the semblance of
her unburied spouse, lifting up a face of strange unearthly
pallor; the ruthless altar and his breast gored with the steel,
he laid bare the one and the other, and unveiled from first to
last the dark domestic crime. Then he urges her to speed her
flight, and quit her home for ever, and in aid of her journey
unseals a hoard of treasure long hid in the earth, a mass of
silver and gold which none else knew. Dido's soul was stirred;
she began to make ready her flight, and friends to share it.
There they meet, all whose hate of the tyrant was fell or whose
fear was bitter; ships, that chanced to lie ready in the harbour,
they seize, and freight with gold. Away it floats over the
deep, the greedy Pygmalion's wealth; and who heads the
enterprise? a woman! So they came to the spot where you
now see yonder those lofty walls, and the rising citadel of
Carthage the new; there they bought ground, which got from
the transaction the name of Byrsa, as much as they could
compass round with a bull's hide. But who are you after all?
What coast are you come from, or whither are you holding on

your journey?' That question he answers thus, with a heavy sigh, and a voice fetched from the bottom of his heart :—

'Fair goddess! should I begin from the first and proceed in order, and hadst thou leisure to listen to the chronicle of our sufferings, eve would first close the Olympian gates and lay the day to sleep. For us, bound from ancient Troy, if the name of Troy has ever chanced to pass through a Tyrian ear, wanderers over divers seas already, we have been driven by a storm's wild will upon your Libyan coasts. I am Æneas, styled the good, who am bearing with me in my fleet the gods of Troy rescued from the foe ; a name blazed by rumour above the stars. I am in quest of Italy, looking there for an ancestral home, and a pedigree drawn from high Jove himself. With twice ten ships I climbed the Phrygian main, with a goddess mother guiding me on my way, and a chart of oracles to follow. Scarce seven remain to me now, shattered by wind and wave. Here am I, a stranger, nay, a beggar, wandering over your Libyan deserts, driven from Europe and Asia alike.' Venus could bear the complaint no longer, so she thus struck into the middle of his sorrows :—

'Whoever you are, it is not, I trow, under the frown of heavenly powers that you draw the breath of life, thus to have arrived at our Tyrian town. Only go on, and make your way straight hence to the queen's palace. For I give you news that your comrades are returned and your fleet brought back, wafted into shelter by shifting gales, unless my learning of augury was vain, and the parents who taught me cheats. Look at these twelve swans exultant in victorious column, which the bird of Jove, swooping from the height of ether, was just now driving in confusion over the wide unsheltered sky ; see now how their line stretches, some alighting on the ground, others just looking down on those alighted. As they, thus rallied, ply their whirring wings in sport, spreading their train round the sky, and uttering songs of triumph, even so your vessels and your gallant crews are either safe in the port, or entering the haven with sails full spread. Only go on, and where the way leads you direct your steps.'

She said, and as she turned away, flashed on their sight her neck's roseate hue; her ambrosial locks breathed from her head a heavenly fragrance; her robe streamed down to her very feet; and in her walk was revealed the true goddess. Soon as he knew his mother, he pursued her flying steps with words like these :—'Why wilt thou be cruel like the rest, mocking thy son these many times with feigned semblances? Why is it not mine to grasp thy hand in my hand, and hear and return the true language of the heart?' Such are his up-braidings, while he yet bends his way to the town. But Venus fenced them round with a dim cloud as they moved, and wrapped them as a goddess only can in a spreading mantle of mist, that none might be able to see them, none to touch them, or put hindrances in their path, or ask the reason of their coming. She takes her way aloft to Paphos, glad to revisit the abode she loves, where she has a temple and a hundred altars, smoking with Sabæan incense, and fragrant with garlands ever new.

They, meanwhile, have pushed on their way, where the path guides them, and already they are climbing the hill which hangs heavily over the city, and looks from above on the towers that rise to meet it. Æneas marvels at the mass of building, once a mere village of huts; marvels at the gates, and the civic din, and the paved ways. The Tyrians are alive and on fire—intent, some on carrying the walls aloft and up-heaving the citadel, and rolling stones from underneath by force of hand; some on making choice of a site for a dwelling, and enclosing it with a trench. They are ordaining the law and its guardians, and the senate's sacred majesty. Here are some digging out havens; there are others laying deep the foundations of a theatre, and hewing from the rocks enormous columns, the lofty ornaments of a stage that is to be. Such are the toils that keep the commonwealth of bees at work in the sun among the flowery meads when summer is new, what time they lead out the nation's hope, the young now grown, or mass together honey, clear and flowing, and strain the cells to bursting with its nectarous sweets, or relieve those who are coming in of their burdens, or collect a troop and expel from their stalls the drones, that lazy, thriftless herd. The work is all fire, and a scent of thyme breathes from the fragrant honey. ' O happy they, whose city is rising already !' cries Æneas, as he looks upward to roof and dome. In he goes, close fenced by his cloud, miraculous to tell, threads his way through the midst, and mingles with the citizens, unperceived of all.

A grove there was in the heart of the city, most plenteous of shade—the spot where first, fresh from the buffeting of wave and wind, the Punic race dug up the token which queenly Juno had bidden them expect, the head of a fiery steed—for even thus, said she, the nation should be renowned in war and rich in sustenance for a life of centuries. Here Dido, Sidon's daughter, was building a vast temple to Juno, rich in offerings and in the goddess's especial presence; of brass was the threshold with its rising steps, clamped with brass the door-posts, the hinge creaked on a door of brass. In this grove it was that first a new object appeared, as before, to soothe away fear: here it was that Æneas first dared to hope that all was safe, and to place a better trust in his shattered fortunes. For while his eye ranges over each part under the temple's massy roof, as he waits there for the queen—while he is marvelling at the city's prosperous star, the various artist-hands vying with each other, their tasks and the toil they cost, he beholds, scene after scene, the battles of

Ilion, and the war that Fame had already blazed the whole
world over—Atreus' sons, and Priam, and the enemy of
both, Achilles. He stopped short, and breaking into tears,
' What place is there left ?' he cries, ' Achates, what clime on
earth that is not full of our sad story? See there Priam.
Here, too, worth finds its due reward ; here, too, there are
tears for human fortune, and hearts that are touched by mortality. Be free from fear : this renown of ours will bring you
some measure of safety.' So speaking, he feeds his soul on the
empty portraiture, with many a sigh, and lets copious rivers
run down his cheeks. For he still saw how, as they battled
round Pergamus, here the Greeks were flying, the Trojan
youth in hot pursuit ; here the Phrygians, at their heels in his
car Achilles, with that dreadful crest. Not far from this he
recognises with tears the snowy canvas of Rhesus' tent, which,
all surprised in its first sleep, Tydeus' son was devastating
with wide carnage, himself bathed in blood—see ! he drives
off the fiery steeds to his own camp, ere they have had time
to taste the pastures of Troy or drink of Xanthus. There in
another part is Troilus in flight, his arms fallen from him—
unhappy boy, confronted with Achilles in unequal combat—
hurried away by his horses, and hanging half out of the
empty car, with his head thrown back, but the reins still in
his hand ; his neck and his hair are being trailed along the
ground, and his inverted spear is drawing lines in the dust.
Meanwhile to the temple of Pallas, not their friend, were
moving the Trojan dames with locks dishevelled, carrying the
sacred robe, in suppliant guise of mourning, their breasts
bruised with their hands—the goddess was keeping her eyes
riveted on the ground, with her face turned away. Thrice
had Achilles dragged Hector round the walls of Ilion, and was
now selling for gold his body, thus robbed of breath. Then,
indeed, heavy was the groan that he gave from the bottom

of his heart, when he saw the spoils, the car, the very body
of his friend, and Priam, stretching out those helpless hands.
Himself, too, he recognises in the forefront of the Achæan
ranks, and the squadrons of the East, and the arms of the
swarthy Memnon. There, leading the columns of her Amazons, with their moony shields, is Penthesilea in her martial
frenzy, blazing out, the centre of thousands, as she loops up her
protruded breast with a girdle of gold, the warrior queen, and
nerves herself to the shock of combat, a maiden against men.

While these things are meeting the wondering eyes of
Æneas the Dardan—while he is standing bewildered, and
continues riveted in one set gaze—the queen has moved
towards the temple, Dido, of loveliest presence, with a vast
train of youths thronging round her. Like as on Eurotas'
banks, or along the ridges of Cynthus, Diana is footing the
dance, while attending her, a thousand mountain nymphs
are massing themselves on either side; she, her quiver on
her shoulder, as she steps, towers over the whole goddess
sisterhood, while Latona's bosom thrills silently with delight;
such was Dido—such she bore herself triumphant through
the midst, to speed the work which had empire for its prospect. Then, at the doors of the goddess, under the midmost
vaulting of the temple, with a fence of arms round her, supported high on a throne, she took her seat. There she was
giving laws and judgments to her citizens, and equalising the
burden of their tasks by fair partition, or draughting it by lot,
when suddenly Æneas sees coming among the great crowd
Antheus and Sergestus, and brave Cloanthus, and other of
the Teucrians, whom the black storm had scattered over the
deep, and carried far away to other coasts. Astounded was
he, overwhelmed, too, was Achates, all for joy and fear:
eagerly were they burning to join hands with theirs, but the
unexplained mystery confounds their minds. They carry on

the concealment, and look out from the hollow cloud that wraps them, to learn what fortune their mates have had, on what shore they are leaving their fleet, what is their errand here—for they were on their way, a deputation from all the crews, suing for grace, and were making for the temple with loud cries.

After they had gained an entrance, and had obtained leave to speak in the presence, Ilioneus, the eldest, thus began, calm of soul :—

'Gracious queen, to whom Jupiter has given to found a new city, and to restrain by force of law the pride of savage nations, we, hapless Trojans, driven by the winds over every sea, make our prayer to you—keep off from our ships the horrors of fire, have pity on a pious race, and vouchsafe a nearer view to our affairs. We are not come to carry the havoc of the sword into the homes of Libya—to snatch booty and hurry it to the shore; such violence is not in our nature ; such insolence were not for the vanquished. There is a place —the Greeks call it Hesperia—a land old in story, strong in arms and in the fruitfulness of its soil; the Œnotrians were its settlers; now report says that later generations have called the nation Italian, from the name of their leader. Thither were we voyaging, when, rising with a sudden swell, Orion, lord of the storm, carried us into hidden shoals, and far away by the stress of reckless gales over the water, the surge mastering us, and over pathless rocks scattered us here and there : a small remnant, we drifted hither on to your shores. What race of men have we here ? What country is so barbarous as to sanction a native usage like this? Even the hospitality of the sand is forbidden us—they draw the sword, and will not let us set foot on the land's edge. If you defy the race of men, and the weapons that mortals wield, yet look to have to do with gods, who watch over the right and the wrong. Æneas was our king, than whom never man breathed more just, more eminent in piety, or in war and martial prowess. If the Fates are keeping our hero alive— if he is feeding on this upper air, and not yet lying down in death's cruel shade—all our fears are over, nor need you be sorry to have made the first advance in the contest of kindly courtesy. The realm of Sicily, too, has cities for us, and store of arms, and a hero-king of Trojan blood, Acestes. Give us leave but to lay up on shore our storm-beaten fleet, to fashion timber in your forests, and strip boughs for our oars, that, if we are allowed to sail for Italy, our comrades and king restored to us, we may make our joyful way to Italy and to Latium; or, if our safety is swallowed up, and thou, best father of the Teucrians, art the prey of the Libyan deep, and a nation's hope lives no longer in Iulus, then, at least, we may make for Sicania's straits, and the houses standing to welcome us, whence we came hither, and may find a king in Acestes.' Such was the speech of Ilioneus; an accordant clamour burst at once from all the sons of Dardanus.

Then briefly Dido, with downcast look, makes reply:— 'Teucrians! unburden your hearts of fear, lay your anxieties aside. It is the stress of danger and the infancy of my kingdom that make me put this policy in motion and protect my frontiers with a guard all about. The men of Æneas and the city of Troy—who can be ignorant of them?—the deeds and the doers, and all the blaze of that mighty war? Not so blunt are the wits we Punic folk carry with us, not so wholly does the sun turn his back on our Tyrian town when he harnesses his steeds. Whether you make your choice of Hesperia the great, and the old realm of Saturn, or of the borders of Eryx and their king Acestes, I will send you on your way with an escort to protect you, and will supply you with stores. Or would you like to

settle along with me in my kingdom here? Look at the city
I am building, it is yours, lay up your ships, Trojan and
Tyrian shall be dealt with by me without distinction. Would
to heaven your king were here too, driven by the gale that
drove you hither—Æneas himself! For myself, I will send
trusty messengers along the coast, with orders to traverse the
furthest parts of Libya, in case he should be shipwrecked and
wandering anywhere in forest or town.'

Excited by her words, brave Achates and father Æneas,
too, were burning long ere this to break out of their cloud.
Achates first accosts Æneas:—'Goddess-born, what purpose
now is foremost in your mind? All you see is safe, our fleet
and our mates are restored to us. One is missing, whom our
own eyes saw in the midst of the surge swallowed up, all the
rest is even as your mother told us.'

Scarce had he spoken when the cloud that enveloped them
suddenly parts asunder and clears into the open sky. Out
stood Æneas, and shone again in the bright sunshine, his face
and his bust the image of a god, for his great mother had shed
graceful tresses over her son's brow, and the glowing flush of
youth, and had breathed the breath of beauty and gladness
into his eyes, loveliness such as the artist's touch imparts to
ivory, or when silver or Parian marble is enchased with yellow
gold. Then he addresses the queen, and speaks suddenly to
the astonishment of all:—'Here am I whom you are seeking,
before you. Æneas, the Trojan, snatched from the jaws of the
Libyan wave. O heart that alone of all has found pity for
Troy's cruel agonies—that makes us, poor remnants of Danæan
fury, utterly spent by all the chances of land and sea, destitute
of all, partners of its city, of its very palace! To pay such a
debt of gratitude, Dido, is more than we can do—more than
can be done by all the survivors of the Dardan nation, now
scattered the wide world over. May the gods—if there are

powers that regard the pious, if justice and conscious rectitude count for aught anywhere on earth—may they give you the reward you merit! What age had the happiness to bring you forth? what godlike parents gave such nobleness to the world? While the rivers run into the sea, while the shadows sweep along the mountain-sides, while the stars draw life from the sky, your glory and your name and your praise shall still endure, whatever the land whose call I must obey.' So saying, he stretches out his right hand to his friend Ilioneus, his left to Serestus, and so on to others, gallant Gyas and gallant Cloanthus.

Astounded was Dido, Sidon's daughter, first at the hero's presence, then at his enormous sufferings, and she bespoke him thus :—' What chance is it, goddess-born, that is hunting you through such a wilderness of perils? what violence throws you on our savage coasts? Are you, indeed, the famed Æneas, whom to Anchises the Dardan, Venus, queen of light and love, bore by the stream of Simois? Aye, I remember Teucer coming to Sidon, driven from the borders of his fatherland, hoping to gain a new kingdom by the aid of Belus. Belus, my sire, was then laying waste the rich fields of Cyprus, and ruling the isle with a conqueror's sway. Ever since that time I knew the fate of the Trojan city, and your name, and the Pelasgian princes. Foe as he was, he would always extol the Teucrians with signal praise, and profess that he himself came of the ancient Teucrian stock. Come then, brave men, and make our dwellings your home. I, too, have had a fortune like yours, which, after the buffeting of countless sufferings, has been pleased that I should find rest in this land at last. Myself no stranger to sorrow, I am learning to succour the unhappy.' With these words, at the same moment she ushers Æneas into her queenly palace, and orders a solemn sacrifice at the temples of the gods. Meantime, as if this were nought,

I

she sends to his comrades at the shore twenty bulls, a hundred huge swine with backs all bristling, a hundred fat lambs with their mothers, and the wine-god's jovial bounty.

But the palace within is laid out with all the splendour of regal luxury, and in the centre of the mansion they are making ready for the banquet; the coverlets are embroidered, and of princely purple—on the tables is massy silver, and chased on gold the gallant exploits of Tyrian ancestors, a long, long chain of story, derived through hero after hero ever since the old nation was young.

Æneas, for his fatherly love would not leave his heart at rest, sends on Achates with speed to the ships to tell Ascanius the news and conduct him to the city. On Ascanius all a fond parent's anxieties are centred. Presents, moreover, rescued from the ruins of Ilion, he bids him bring—a pall stiff with figures of gold, and a veil with a border of yellow acanthus, adornments of Argive Helen, which she carried away from Mycenæ, when she went to Troy and to her unblessed bridal, her mother Leda's marvellous gift; the sceptre, too, which Ilione had once borne, the eldest of Priam's daughters, and the string of pearls for the neck, and the double coronal of jewels and gold. With this to despatch, Achates was bending his way to the ships.

But the lady of Cythera is casting new wiles, new devices in her breast, that Cupid, form and feature changed, may arrive in the room of the charmer Ascanius, and by the presents he brings influence the queen to madness, and turn the very marrow of her bones to fire. She fears the two-faced generation, the double-tongued sons of Tyre; Juno's hatred scorches her like a flame, and as night draws on the care comes back to her. So then with these words she addresses her winged Love :—' My son, who art alone my

strength and my mighty power, my son, who laughest to
scorn our great father's Typhœan thunderbolts, to thee I fly
for aid, and make suppliant prayer of thy majesty, How
thy brother Æneas is tossed on the ocean the whole world
over by Juno's implacable rancour I need not tell thee—nay,
thou hast often mingled thy grief with mine. He is now the
guest of Dido, the Phœnician woman, and the spell of a
courteous tongue is laid on him, and I fear what may be the
end of taking shelter under Juno's wing ; she will never be
idle at a time on which so much hangs. Thus then I am
planning to be first in the field, surprising the queen by
stratagem, and encompassing her with fire, that no power
may be able to work a change in her, but that a mighty
passion for Æneas may keep her mine. For the way in
which thou mayest bring this about, listen to what I have
been thinking. The young heir of royalty, at his loved
father's summons, is making ready to go to this Sidonian
city—my soul's darling that he is—the bearer of presents
that have survived the sea and the flames of Troy. Him I
will lull in deep sleep and hide him in my hallowed dwelling
high on Cythera or Idalia, that by no chance he may know
or mar our plot. Do thou then for a single night, no more,
artfully counterfeit his form, and put on the boy's usual look,
thyself a boy, that when Dido, at the height of her joy, shall
take thee into her lap while the princely board is laden and
the vine-god's liquor flowing, when she shall be caressing
thee and printing her fondest kisses on thy cheek, thou
mayest breathe concealed fire into her veins, and steal upon
her with poison.'

At once Love complies with his fond mother's words, puts
off his wings, and walks rejoicing in the gait of Iulus. As
for Ascanius, Venus sprinkles his form all over with the
dew of gentle slumber, and carries him, as a goddess may,

lapped in her bosom, into Idalia's lofty groves, where a soft couch of amaracus enfolds him with its flowers, and the fragrant breath of its sweet shade. Meanwhile Cupid was on his way, all obedience, bearing the royal presents to the Tyrians, and glad to follow Achates. When he arrives, he finds the queen already settled on the gorgeous tapestry of a golden couch, and occupying the central place. Already father Æneas, already the chivalry of Troy are flocking in, and stretching themselves here and there on coverlets of purple. There are servants offering them water for their hands, and deftly producing the bread from the baskets, and presenting towels with shorn nap. Within are fifty maidens, whose charge is in course to pile up provisions in lasting store, and light up with fire the gods of the hearth. A hundred others there are, and male attendants of equal number and equal age, to load the table with dishes, and set on the cups. The Tyrians, too, have assembled in crowds through the festive hall, and scatter themselves as invited over the embroidered couches. There is marvelling at Æneas' presents, marvelling at Iulus, at those glowing features, where the god shines through, and those words which he feigns so well, and at the robe and the veil with the yellow acanthus border. Chief of all, the unhappy victim of coming ruin cannot satisfy herself with gazing, and kindles as she looks, the Phœnician woman, charmed with the boy and the presents alike. He, after he has hung long in Æneas' arms and round his neck, gratifying the intense fondness of the sire he feigned to be his, finds his way to the queen. She is riveted by him—riveted, eye and heart, and ever and anon fondles him in her lap—poor Dido, unconscious how great a god is sitting heavy on that wretched bosom. But he, with his mind still bent on his Acidalian mother, is beginning to efface the name of Sychæus letter by letter, and endeavouring to surprise by a living passion affections long torpid, and a heart long unused to love.

When the banquet's first lull was come, and the board removed, then they set up the huge bowls and wreathe the wine. A din rings to the roof—the voice rolls through those spacious halls; lamps hang from the gilded ceiling, burning brightly, and flambeau-fires put out the night. Then the queen called for a cup, heavy with jewels and gold, and filled it with unmixed wine; the same which had been used by Belus, and every king from Belus downward. Then silence was commanded through the hall. 'Jupiter, for thou hast the name of lawgiver for guest and host, grant that this day may be auspicious alike for the Tyrians and the voyagers from Troy, and that its memory may long live among our posterity. Be with us, Bacchus, the giver of jollity, and Juno, the queen of our blessings; and you, the lords of Tyre, may your goodwill grace this meeting.' She said, and poured on the table an offering of the wine, and, the libation made, touched the cup first with her lips, then handed it to Bitias, rallying his slowness. Eagerly he quaffed the foaming goblet, and drenched himself deep with its brimming gold. Then came the other lords in order. Iopas, the long-haired bard, takes his gilded lyre, and fills the hall with music; he, whose teacher was the mighty Atlas. His song is of the wanderings of the moon and the agonies of the sun, whence sprung man's race and the cattle, whence rain-water and fire; of Arcturus and the showery Hyades, and the twin Bears; why the winter suns make such haste to dip in ocean, or what is the retarding cause that bids the nights move slowly. Plaudits redouble from the Tyrians, and the Trojans follow the lead. With varied talk, too, she kept lengthening out the night, unhappy Dido, drinking draughts of love long and deep, as she asked much about Priam, about Hector much; now what were the arms in which Aurora's son had come to battle; now what Diomede's steeds were like; now how great was Achilles. 'Or rather, gentle guest,' cries she, 'tell us the story from the very first—all about the stratagems of the Danaans, and the sad fate of your country, and your own wanderings—for this is now the seventh summer that is wafting you a wanderer still over every land and wave.'

BOOK II.

EVERY tongue was hushed, and every eye fixed intently, when, from his high couch, father Æneas began thus :—

'Too cruel to be told, great queen, is the sorrow you bid me revive—how the power of Troy and its empire met with piteous overthrow from the Danaans—the heartrending sights which my own eyes saw, and the scenes where I had a large part to play. Who, in such recital—be he of the Myrmidons or the Dolopes, or a soldier of ruthless Ulysses' band—would refrain from tears ? And now, too, night is rushing in dews down the steep of heaven, and the setting stars counsel repose. Still, if so great be your longing to acquaint yourself with our disasters, and hear the brief tale of Troy's last agony, though my mind shudders at the remembrance, and starts back in sudden anguish, I will essay the task.

' Broken by war and foiled by destiny, the chiefs of the Danaans, now that the flying years were numbering so many, build a horse of mountain size, by the inspiration of Pallas' skill, and interlace its ribs with planks of fir. A vow for their safe journey home is the pretext : such the fame that spreads. In this they secretly enclose chosen men of sinew, picked out by lot, in the depth of its sides, and fill every corner of those mighty caverns, the belly of the monster, with armed warriors.

' In sight of Troy lies Tenedos, an island of wide-spread renown, powerful and rich while Priam's empire yet was, now a mere bay, a treacherous roadstead for ships. Thus far they sail out, and hide themselves on the forsaken coast. We thought them gone off with a fair wind for Mycenæ. And so all Trojan land shakes off the agony of years. Open fly the gates; what pleasure to go and see the Dorian camp, and the places deserted, and the shore forsaken! Yes, here were the troops of the Dolopes; here the tent of that savage Achilles; here the ships were drawn up; here they used to set the battle in array. Some of us are standing agaze at the fatal offering to the virgin goddess, and wondering at the hugeness of the horse; and Thymætes takes the lead, urging to have it dragged within the walls, and lodged in the citadel, either with treasonable intent, or that the fate of Troy had begun to set that way. But Capys, and the men of saner judgment, bid us send this snare of the Danaans, this suspicious present, headlong into the sea, or light a fire under and burn it; or, if not that, to pierce and probe that hollow womb that might hide so much. The populace, unstable as ever, divides off into opposite factions.

'Throwing himself before all, with a great crowd at his back, Laocoon, all on fire, comes running down the steep of the citadel, crying in the distance, "What strange madness is this, my unhappy countrymen? Think you that the enemy has sailed off, or that a Danaan could ever make a present that had no treachery in it? Is this your knowledge of Ulysses? Either the Achæans are shut up and hiding in this piece of wood, or it is an engine framed against our walls, to command the houses and come down on the city from above, or there is some other secret trick. Men of Troy, put no faith in the horse. Whatever it be, I fear a Greek even with a gift in his hand." With these words he hurled a mighty spear with all his force against the beast's side, the jointed arch of its belly. It lodged, and stood quivering; the

womb shook again, and an echo and a groan rang hollow from
its caverns; and then, had but heaven's destiny and man's
judgment been unwarped, he had led us to carry sword and
havoc into the Argive lurking-place, and Troy would now be
standing, and thou, Priam's tall fortress, still in being.

'Meanwhile, see! some Dardan shepherds are dragging
with loud shouts before the king a young man with his hands
tied behind him, who had thrown himself, a stranger, across
their way, to compass this very thing, and thus let the Achæans
into Troy—bold of heart, and ready for either issue, either to
play off his stratagem, or to meet inevitable death. From all
sides, in eager curiosity, the Trojan youth come streaming
round, vying in their insults to the prisoner. Now then,
listen to the tale of Danaan fraud, and from one act of guilt
learn what the whole nation is. There as he stood, with all
eyes bent on him, bewildered, defenceless, and looked round
on the Phrygian bands, " Alas!" he cries, " where is there a
spot of earth or sea that will give me shelter now? or what
last resource is left for a wretch like me—one who has no
place among the Danaans to hide my head—while the children·
of Dardanus no less are in arms against me, crying for bloody
vengeance?" At that piteous cry our mood was changed, and
every outrage checked. We encourage him to speak—to tell
us what his parentage is; what his business; what he has to
rest on as a prisoner. " All, my lord, shall be avowed to you
truly, whatever be the issue. I will not deny that I am an
Argive by nation; this to begin with. Nor if Fortune has
made a miserable man out of Sinon, shall her base schooling
make him deceiver and liar as well. If haply in talk your
ears ever caught the name of Palamedes, of the house of Belus,
and his wide-spread renown—his, whom under false accusation, an innocent man, charged by the blackest calumny,
all because his voice was against the war, the Pelasgians

sent down to death, and now, when he is laid in darkness, lament him too late—know that it was as his comrade and near kinsman I was sent by a needy father to a soldier's life in earliest youth. While he stood with his royal state unimpaired, an honoured member of the kingly council, I, too, enjoyed my measure of name and dignity; but after the jealousy of false Ulysses—you know the tale—removed him from this upper clime—dashed from my height, I dragged on life in darkness and sorrow, and vented to my own heart my rage at the disaster of my innocent friend. Nor did I keep silence—madman that I was! No, if ever the chance were given me—if ever I came back with glory to my native Argos—I vowed myself his avenger, and my words stirred up bitter enmity. From that time my ruin began; from that time Ulysses was ever threatening me with some new charge, ever scattering abroad words of mystery, and looking for allies to plot with. Nor did he rest till by Calchas' agency—but why recall this unwelcome story with no end to gain? Why waste your time, if you hold all Achæans alike, and to hear *that* is to hear enough? Take the vengeance you should have taken long ago. It is just what would please the Ithacan, and earn a large reward from the sons of Atreus!"

'This makes us burn, indeed, to explore and inquire into the reason of his tale, not knowing that crime could be so monstrous, and Pelasgian art so cunning. He resumes, in faltering tones, spoken from his false heart:—

'"Often have the Danaans designed to turn their back on Troy and accomplish a retreat, and abandon the war that had wearied them so long; and would they had done it! As often has the fierce inclemency of the deep barred their purpose, and the south wind frightened them from sailing. Especially, when this horse was set up at last, a compacted mass of maple planks, the thunder of the storm-clouds was heard the whole firmament over. In our perplexity we send Eurypylus to inquire of Phœbus's oracle, and this is the gloomy message that he brings back from the shrine : ' With blood it was ye appeased the winds, even with a maiden's slaughter, when first ye came, Danaans, to the shore of Ilion. With blood it is ye must buy your return, and propitiate heaven by the life of an Argive ! ' Soon as the news reached the public ear, every mind was cowed, and a cold shudder thrilled the depths of every heart. For whom has Fate a summons ? Whom does Apollo demand as his prey ? And now the Ithacan, with boisterous vehemence, drags forward the prophet Calchas, insists on knowing what that announcement of heaven's will may mean ; and many even then were the prophetic mouths that warned me of the trickster's cruel villany, and many the eyes that silently foresaw the future. Ten days the seer holds his peace, and keeps his tent, refusing to utter a word that should disclose any name or sacrifice any life. At last, goaded by the Ithacan's vehement clamour, he breaks into a concerted utterance, and dooms me to the altar. All assented, well content that the danger which each feared for himself should be directed to the extinction of one poor wretch. And now the day of horror was come ; all was being ready for my sacrifice—the salt cakes for the fire, and the fillet to crown my brow—when I escaped, I own it, from death, and broke my bonds, and hid myself that night in a muddy marsh in the covert of the rushes, while they should be sailing, in the faint hope that they had sailed. My old country, I never expect to see it again, nor my darling children, and the father I have longed so for ! No ! they are likely to visit them with vengeance for my escape, and expiate this guilt of mine by taking their poor lives. O ! by the gods above, and the powers that know when truth is spoken, if there is yet abiding anywhere among men such a thing as unsullied faith, I conjure you, have pity on this weight of suffering, have pity on a soul that is unworthily borne down!"

'Such a tearful appeal gains him his life, and our compassion too. Priam himself is first to bid them relieve the man of his manacles and the chains that bound him, and addresses him in words of kindness, "Whoever you are, from this time forth have done with the Greeks, and forget them. I make you my man, and bid you answer truly the questions I shall put. What do they mean by setting up this huge mountain of a horse? Who was the prompter of it? What is their object? Some religious offering, or some engine of war?"

'Thus Priam: the prisoner, with all his Pelasgian craft and cunning about him, raised his unfettered hands to the stars:—

'"You, eternal fires, with your inviolable majesty, be my witnesses; you, altars and impious swords, from which I fled; and you, hallowed fillets, which I wore for the sacrifice! I am free to break all the sacred ties that bound me to the Greeks. I am free to treat them as my foes, and disclose all their secrets to the light of day, all the claims of the land of my birth notwithstanding. Only do thou abide by thy plighted word, and preserve faith with thy preserver, land of Troy, if he tells thee true, and makes thee large returns.

'"The strength of the Danaan hopes, and the soul of their confidence in the war they plunged into, has ever been the aid of Pallas. From the time when Tydeus' impious son and Ulysses, that coiner of villany, dared to drag away from her hallowed temple the fateful Palladium, slaughtering the guards who watched the citadel's height, thenceforth there was an ebb and a backsliding in the Danaan hopes, their forces shattered, the goddess estranged. Nor were the portents dubious that betokened Tritonia's change of mood. Scarce was the image lodged in the camp, when flashing fire glowed in her uplifted eyes, and salt sweat trickled over her frame, and thrice of herself she leaped from the ground, marvellous to relate, shield and quivering lance and all. Forthwith Calchas sounds the note for flight over the perilous deep, for that Pergamus can never be razed by Argive steel, unless they go to Argos for fresh omens, and bring back the divine aid which their crooked keels bore with them aforetime over the sea. And now this their voyage home to Mycenæ is to get new forces and gods to sail with them; they will recross the deep, and come upon you unforeseen. Such is Calchas' scanning of the omens. As for this image, he warned them *to* set it up in exchange for the Palladium, and, in expiation of injured deity, to atone for their fatal crime. Calchas, however, bade them raise it to the vast height you see, knitting plank to plank, till it was brought near to heaven, that it might not be admitted at the gates or dragged within the walls, and thus restore to the people the bulwark of their old worship. For if your hand should profane Minerva's offering, then (said he) a mighty destruction—may the gods turn the omen on his head ere it falls on yours!—would come on the empire of Priam and the Phrygian nation; but if these hands of yours should help it to scale your city's height, Asia would roll the mighty tide of invasion on the walls of Pelops, and our posterity would have to meet the fate he threatened."

'Such was the stratagem—the cursed art of perjured Sinon —that gained credence for the tale; and such the victory won over us by wiles and constrained tears—over us, whom not Tydeus' son, nor Achilles of Larissa, nor ten years of war subdued, nor a fleet of a thousand sail.

' And now another object, greater and far more terrible, is *forced on* my poor countrymen, to the confusion of their unprophetic souls. Laocoon, drawn by lot as Neptune's priest, was sacrificing a mighty bull at the wonted altar—when behold from Tenedos, over the still deep—I shudder as I recount the tale—two serpents coiled in vast circles are seen breasting the sea, and moving side by side towards the shore. Their breasts rise erect among the waves; their manes, of blood-red hue, tower over the water, the rest of them floats behind on the main, trailing a huge undulating length; the brine foams and dashes about them; they are already on shore, in the plain—with their glowing eyes bloodshot and fiery, and their forked tongues playing in their hissing mouths. We fly all ways in pale terror : they, in an unswerving column, make for Laocoon, and first each serpent folds round one of his two sons, clasping the youthful body, and greedily devouring the poor limbs. Afterwards, as the father comes to the rescue, weapon in hand, they fasten on him and lash their enormous spires tight round him—and now twice folded round his middle, twice embracing his neck with their scaly length, they tower over him with uplifted head and crest. He is straining with agonising clutch to pull the knots asunder, his priestly fillets all bedewed with gore and black poison, and raising all the while dreadful cries to heaven—like the bellowing, when a wounded bull darts away from the altar, dashing off from his neck the ill-aimed axe. But the two serpents escape glidingly to the temple top, making for the height where ruthless Tritonia is enthroned, and there shelter themselves under the goddess's feet and the round of her shield. Then, indeed, every breast is cowed and thrilled through by a new and strange terror—every voice cries that Laocoon has been duly punished for his crime, profaning the sacred wood with his weapon's point, and hurling his guilty lance against the back of the steed. Let the image be drawn to her temple, and let prayer be made to the goddess, is the general cry—we break through the walls and open the town within. All gird them to the work, putting wheels to run easily under its feet,

BOOK II. 143

and throwing lengths of hempen tie round its neck. It scales
the walls, that fateful engine, with its armed brood—boys and
unwedded girls, standing about it, chant sacred hymns,
delighted to touch the rope. In it moves, rolling with
threatening brow into the heart of the city. O my country!
O Ilion, home of the gods! O ye, Dardan towers, with your
martial fame! Yes—four times on the gateway's very threshold it stopped, four times the arms rattled in its womb. On,
however, we press, unheeding, in the blindness of our frenzy,
and lodge the ill-starred portent in our hallowed citadel. Even
then Cassandra unseals to speak of future fate those lips which
by the god's command no Trojan ever believed—while we, alas!
we, spend the day that was to be our last in crowning the
temples of the gods with festal boughs the whole city through.

'Meantime round rolls the sky, and on comes night from
the ocean, wrapping in its mighty shade earth and heaven and
Myrmidon wiles : through the city the Trojans are hushed in
careless repose, their tired limbs in the arms of sleep. Already
was the Argive host on its way from Tenedos, through the
friendly stillness of the quiet moon, making for the well-
known shore, when see! the royal ship mounts its fire signal,
and Sinon, sheltered by heaven's partial decree, stealthily sets
at large the Danaans, hid in that treacherous womb, and
opens the pine-wood door : they as the horse opens are restored
to upper air, and leap forth with joy from the hollow timber,
Thessander and Sthenelus leading the way, and the dreaded
Ulysses, gliding down the lowered rope, and Achamas and
Thoas, and Neoptolemus of Peleus' line, and first Machaon,
and Menelaus, and the framer of the cheat himself, Epeus.
They rush on the town as it lies drowned in sleep and revelry.
The watchers are put to the sword, the gates thrown open,
and all are welcoming their comrades, and uniting with the
conspiring bands.

'It was just the time when first slumber comes to heal
human suffering, stealing on men by heaven's blessing with
balmiest influence. Lo! as I slept, before my eyes Hector,
in deepest sorrow, seemed to be standing by me, shedding rivers of tears—mangled from dragging at the car,
as I remember him of old, and. black with gory dust,
and with his swollen feet bored by the thong. Ay me!
what a sight was there! what a change from that Hector of
ours, who comes back to us clad in the spoils of Achilles, or
from hurling Phrygian fire on Danaan vessels! with stiffened
beard and hair matted with blood, and those wounds fresh
about him, which fell on him so thickly round his country's
walls. Methought I addressed him first with tears like his
own, fetching from my breast the accents of sorrow—" O light
of Dardan land, surest hope that Trojans ever had! What
delay has kept you so long? From what clime is the Hector
of our longings returned to us at last? O the eyes with which,
after long months of death among your people, months of
manifold suffering to Troy and her sons, spent and weary, we
look upon you now! What unworthy cause has marred the
clear beauty of those features, or why do I behold these
wounds?" He answers nought, and gives no idle heed to my
vain inquiries, but with a deep sigh, heaved from the bottom
of his heart—"Ah! fly, goddess-born!" cries he, "and escape
from these flames—the walls are in the enemy's hand—Troy
is tumbling from its summit—the claims of country and king
are satisfied—if Pergamus could be defended by force of hand,
it would have been defended by mine, in my day. Your
country's worship and her gods are what she entrusts to you now
—take them to share your destiny—seek for them a mighty city,
which you shall one day build when you have wandered the
ocean over." With these words he brings out Queen Vesta with
her fillets and the ever-burning fire from the secret shrine.

'Meanwhile the city in its various quarters is being convulsed with agony—and ever more and more, though my father Anchises' palace was retired in the privacy of embosoming trees, the sounds deepen, and the alarm of battle swells. I start up from sleep, mount the sloping roof, and stand intently listening—even as when among standing corn a spark falls with a fierce south wind to fan it, or the impetuous stream of a mountain torrent sweeps the fields, sweeps the joyous crops and the bullocks' toil, and drives the woods headlong before it, in perplexed amazement a shepherd takes in the crash from a rock's tall summit. Then, indeed, all doubt was over, and the wiles of the Danaans stood confessed. Already Deiphobus' palace has fallen with a mighty overthrow before the mastering fire-god—already his neighbour Ucalegon is in flames—the expanse of the Sigean sea shines again with the blaze. Up rises at once the shouting of men and the braying of trumpets. To arms I rush in frenzy—not that good cause is shown for arms—but to muster a troop for fight, and run to the citadel with my comrades is my first burning impulse—madness and rage drive my mind headlong, and I think how glorious to die with arms in my hand.

'But see! Panthus, escaped from an Achæan volley, Panthus, Othrys' son, priest of Phœbus in the citadel, comes dragging along with his own hand the vanquished gods of his worship and his young grandchild, and making distractedly for my door. "How goes the day, Panthus? What hold have we of the citadel?" The words were scarcely uttered when with a groan he replies, "It is come, the last day, the inevitable hour—on Dardan land no more Trojans; no more of Ilion, and the great renown of the sons of Teucer; Jove, in his cruelty, has carried all over to Argos; the town is on fire, and the Danaans are its masters. There, planted high in the

K

heart of the city, the horse is pouring out armed men, and Sinon is flinging about fire in the insolence of conquest; some are crowding into the unfolded gates—thousands, many as ever came from huge Mycenæ; some are blocking up the narrow streets, with weapons pointed at all comers; the sharp steel with its gleaming blade stands drawn, ready for slaughter; hardly, even on the threshold, the sentinels of the gates are attempting resistance, in a struggle where the powers of war are blind."

'At these words of the son of Othrys, and heaven's will thus expressed, I plunge into the fire and the battle, following the war-fiend's yell, the din of strife, and the shout that rose to the sky. There join me Rhipeus and Epytus, bravest in fight, crossing my way in the moonlight, as also Hypanis and Dymas, and form at my side; young Coroebus, too, Mygdon's son; he happened to be just then come to Troy, with a frantic passion for Cassandra, and was bringing a son-in-law's aid to Priam and his Phrygians—poor boy! to have given no heed to the warnings of his heaven-struck bride! Seeing them gathered in a mass and nerved for battle, I begin thereon:—"Young hearts, full of unavailing valour, if your desire is set to follow a desperate man, you see what the plight of our affairs is—gone in a body from shrine and altar are the gods who upheld this our empire—the city you succour is a blazing ruin; choose we then death, and rush we into the thick of the fight. The one safety for vanquished men is to hope for none." These words stirred their young spirits to madness: then, like ravenous wolves in night's dark cloud, driven abroad by the blind rage of lawless hunger, with their cubs left at home waiting their return with parched jaws, among javelins, among foemen, on we go with no uncertain fate before us, keeping our way through the heart of the town, while night flaps over us its dark, overshadowing wings. Who could unfold in speech the carnage, the horrors of that night, or make his tears keep pace with our suffering? It is an ancient city, falling from the height where she queened it many a year; and heaps of unresisting bodies are lying confusedly in the streets, in the houses, on the hallowed steps of temples. Nor is it on Teucer's sons alone that bloody vengeance lights. There are times when even the vanquished feel courage rushing back to their hearts, and the conquering Danaans fall. Everywhere is relentless agony; everywhere terror, and the vision of death in many a manifestation.

'First of the Danaans, with a large band at his back, Androgeos crosses our way, taking us for a troop of his friends in his ignorance, and hails us at once in words of fellowship: "Come, my men, be quick. Why, what sloth is keeping you so late? Pergamus is on fire, and the rest of us are spoiling and sacking it, and here are you, but just disembarked from your tall ships." He said, and instantly, for no reply was forthcoming to reassure him, saw that he had fallen into the thick of the enemy. Struck with consternation, he drew back foot and tongue. Just as a man who at unawares has trodden on a snake among thorns and briers in his walk, and recoils at once in sudden alarm from the angry uplifted crest and the black swelling neck, so Androgeos, appalled at the sight, was retiring. But we rush on him, and close round, weapons in hand; and, in their ignorance of the ground, and the surprise of their terror, they fall before us everywhere. Fortune smiles on our first encounter. Hereon Coroebus, flushed with success and daring, "Come, my friends," he cries, "where Fortune at starting directs us to the path of safety, and reveals herself as our ally, be it ours to follow on. Let us change shields, and see if Danaan decorations will fit us. Trick or strength of hand, who, in dealing with an enemy, asks which? They shall arm us against themselves." So saying, he puts on Androgeos' crested helm, and his shield with its goodly device, and fastens to his side an Argive sword. So does Rhipeus, so Dymas too, and all our company, with youthful exultation, each arming himself.out of the new-won spoils. On we go, mixing with the Greeks, under auspices not our own, and many are the combats in which we engage in the blindness of night, many the Danaans whom we send down to the shades. They fly on all hands : some to the ships, making at full speed for safety on the shore; others, in the debasement of terror, climb once more the horse's huge sides, and hide themselves in the womb they knew so well.

'Alas! it is not for man to throw himself on the gods against their will !

'Lo ! there was a princess of Priam's house being dragged by her dishevelled hair from the temple, from the very shrine of Minerva, Cassandra, straining her flashing eyes to heaven in vain—her eyes—for those delicate hands were confined by manacles. The sight was too much for the infuriate mind of Coroebus : rushing to his doom, he flung himself into the middle of the hostile force. One and all, we follow, close our ranks, and fall on. And now, first from the temple's lofty top we are overwhelmed by a shower of our own countrymen's darts, and a most piteous carnage ensues, all along of the appearance of our arms and our mistaken Grecian crests. Then the Danaans, groaning and enraged at the rescue of the maiden, rally from all sides, and fall on us. Ajax, in all his fury, and the two sons of Atreus, and the whole array of the Dolopes—even as one day when the tempest is broken loose, and wind meets wind—west, and south, and east exulting in his orient steeds—there is crashing in the woods, and Nereus, in a cloud of foam, is plying his ruthless trident, and stirring up the sea from its very bottom. Such of the foe, moreover, as in the

darkness of night we had driven routed through the gloom—
thanks to our stratagem—and scattered the whole city over,
rally again : they are the first to recognise the imposture of
shield and weapon, and to mark the different sound of our
speech. All is over—we are overwhelmed by numbers : first
of all, Coroebus is stretched low ; his slayer Peneleos, his
place of death the altar of the Goddess of Arms ; slain, too,
is Rhipeus, the justest and most righteous man in Troy—
but heaven's will is not ours—down go Hypanis and Dymas
both, shot by their friends ; nor could all your acts of piety,
good Panthus, shield you in your fall ; no, nor the fillet of
Apollo on your brow. Ye ashes of Ilion, and thou, funeral
fire of those I loved, witness ye that in your day of doom I
shrank from no Danaan dart, no hand-to-hand encounter ;
nay, that had my fate been to fall, my hand had earned it
well. We are parted from the rest, Iphitus, Pelias, and I.
Iphitus, a man on whom years were already pressing ; Pelias,
crippled by a wound from Ulysses—all three summoned by
the shouting to Priam's palace.

'Here, indeed, the conflict was gigantic—just as if the rest
of the war were nowhere—as if none were dying in the whole
city beside : even such was the sight we saw—the war-god
raging untamed, the Danaans streaming up to the roof, the
door blockaded by a long penthouse of shields. The scaling
ladders are clasping the walls ; close to the very door men
are climbing, with their left hands presenting the buckler to
shelter them from darts, while with their right they are clasping the battlements. The Dardans, on their part, are tearing
up from the palace turret and roof—such the weapons with
which, in their dire extremity, in the last death-struggle, they
make ready for their defence—gilded rafters, the stately ornaments of elder days, they are hurling down ; while others,
their swords drawn, are stationed at the doors at the bottom,

and guarding them in close array. The fire revived within me, to bring succour to the royal roof, and relieve those brave men, and breathe new daring into the vanquished.

'A door there was, a hidden entrance, a thoroughfare through Priam's palace, a postern which you leave in the rear; by it the hapless Andromache, while yet the throne was standing, used often to repair unattended to her husband's parents, and pull the boy Astyanax into his grandsire's presence. Through it I make my way to the summit of the roof, whence the wretched Teucrians were hurling darts without avail. · There was a tower standing precipitous, its roof reared high to the stars, whence could be seen all Troy, and the Danaan fleet, and the Achæan camp; to this we applied our weapons, just where the lofty flooring made the joining insecure; we wrench it from its eminence, we have toppled it over—down it falls at once, a huge crashing ruin, and tumbles far and wide over the Danaan ranks. But others fill their place; while stones and every kind of missile keep raining unabated.

'There in the entry, at the very gate, is Pyrrhus in his glory, gleaming with spear and sword, and with all the brilliance of steel. Even as against the daylight a serpent gorged with baleful herbage, whom winter's cold of late was keeping swollen underground. Now, his skin shed, in new life and in the beauty of youth, rears his breast erect, and wreathes his shining scales, towering to the sun, and flashes in his mouth his three-forked tongue. With him gigantic Periphas and Automedon, his armour-bearer, once Achilles' charioteer, with him the whole chivalry of Scyros press to the walls, and hurl up fire to the roof. Himself among the foremost, a two-edged axe in hand, is bursting through the stubborn door and forcing from their hinges the valves coppersheathed; see! now he has cut out a plank and delved into that stout heart of oak, and made a wide gaping window in the middle. There is seen the house within, and the long vista of the hall; there is seen the august retirement of Priam, and the monarchs of past days, and armed warriors are disclosed standing in the entrance.

'But the palace within is a confused scene of shrieking and piteous disorder; the vaulted chambers wail from their hollow depths with female lamentation; the noise strikes the golden stars above. The terror-stricken matrons are running to and fro through the spacious courts, clinging claspingly to the gates and printing them with kisses. On presses Pyrrhus with all his father's might; neither barrier of oak nor yet living guard can resist him; the door gives way under the thick strokes of the battery, and the valves are torn from their hinges and brought down. Force finds its way; the Danaans burst a passage, rush in, and slaughter those they meet, and the whole wide space is flooded with soldiers. With far less fury, when the river, all foam, has broken the prison of its banks and streamed with triumphant tide over the barriers set to check it, down it comes tumbling along the corn-fields, and along the whole country sweeps away herd and stall. With my own eyes I saw Neoptolemus, mad with carnage, and the two Atridæ on the palace-floor. I saw Hecuba and her hundred daughters-in-law, and Priam at the altar, polluting with his blood the flames he had himself made holy. Those fifty marriage-chambers, the splendid promise of children's children, doors gorgeous with barbaric gold and plundered treasure, all sank in dust. Where the fire flags, the Danaans are masters.

'Perhaps, too, you may be curious to hear the fate of Priam. When he saw his city fallen and captured, the doors of his palace burst open, the foe in the heart of his home's sanctuary, poor old man! helplessly and hopelessly he puts about his shoulders, trembling with age, his armour, long disused, and girds on his unavailing sword, and is going to his doom among the thick of the foe. In the midst of the palace, under the naked height of the sky, stood a great altar, and by it a bay tree of age untold, leaning over the altar and enfolding the household gods in its shade. Here about the altar Hecuba and her daughters, all helpless, like doves driven headlong down by a murky tempest, huddled together and clinging to the statues of the gods, were sitting. But when she saw Priam —yes, Priam—wearing the arms of his youth—" What monstrous thought," cries she, " my most wretched spouse, has moved you to gird on these weapons? or to what are you hurrying? It is not help like this, not protections like those you wear, that the crisis needs. No, not even if my lost Hector were now at our side. Come, join us here at last; this altar shall be a defence for us all, or we will die together." With these words she took him to where she was, and lodged his aged frame in the hallowed resting-place.

' But, see! here is Polites, one of Priam's sons escaped from Pyrrhus' murderous hand, through showers of darts and masses of foemen, flying down the long corridors and traversing the empty courts, sore and wounded, while Pyrrhus, all on fire, is pursuing him with a deadly stroke, his hand all but grasping him, his spear close upon him. Just as at last he won his way into the view and presence of his parents, down he fell and poured out his life in a gush of blood. Hereon Priam, though hemmed in by death on all sides, could not restrain himself, or control voice and passion. " Aye," cries he, " for a crime, for an outrage like this, may the gods, if there is any sense of right in heaven to take cognizance of such deeds, give you the full thanks you merit, and pay you your due reward; you, who have made me look with my own eyes on my son's death, and stained a father's presence with the sight of blood. But he whom your lying tongue calls your sire,

Achilles, dealt not thus with Priam his foe—he had a cheek that could crimson at a suppliant's rights, a suppliant's honour. Hector's lifeless body he gave back to the tomb, and sent me home to my realms in peace." So said the poor old man, and hurled at him a dart unwarlike, unwounding, which the ringing brass at once shook off, and left hanging helplessly from the end of the shield's boss. Pyrrhus retorts : "You shall take your complaint, then, and carry your news to my father, Pelides. Tell him about my shocking deeds, about his degenerate Neoptolemus, and do not forget. Now die." With these words he dragged him to the very altar, palsied and sliding in a pool of his son's blood, wreathed his left hand in his hair, and with his right flashed forth and sheathed in his side the sword to the hilt. Such was the end of Priam's fortunes, such the fatal lot that fell upon him, with Troy blazing and Pergamus in ruins before his eyes— upon him, once the haughty ruler of those many nations and kingdoms, the sovereign lord of Asia ! There he lies on the shore, a gigantic trunk, a head severed from the shoulders, a body without a name.

'Now, for the first time grim horror prisoned me round— I was wildered—there rose up the image of my dear father, as I saw the king, his fellow in age, breathing out his life through that ghastly wound. There rose up Creusa unprotected, my house, now plundered, and the chance to which I had left my little Iulus. I cast my eyes back and look about to see what strength there is round me. All had forsaken me, too tired to stay; they had leapt to the ground, or dropped helplessly into the flames. And now I was there alone. When lodged in the temple of Vesta, and crouching mutely in its darkest recess, the daughter of Tyndareus meets my eye ; the brilliant blaze gives light to my wandering feet and ranging glance. Yes, she in her guilty fears, dreading at once the Teucrians whom the overthrow of Pergamus had made her foes, and the vengeance of the Danaans, and the wrath of the husband she abandoned—she, the common fiend of Troy ànd of her country, had hid herself away, and was sitting in hateful solitude at the altar. My spirit kindled into flame—a fury seized me to avenge my country in its fall, and to do justice on a wretch. " So she is to see Sparta and her native Mycenæ again in safety, and is to move as a queen in a triumph of her own ? She is to look upon her lord and her old home, her children and her parents, with a crowd of our Trojan ladies and Phrygian captives to wait on her ? Shall it be for this that Priam has died by the sword, that Troy has been burnt with fire, that the Dardan shore has gushed so oft with the sweat of blood ? No, never—for though there are no proud memories to be won by vengeance on a woman, no laurels to be reaped from a conquest like this, yet the extinction of so base a life and the exaction of vengeance so merited will count as a praise, and it will be a joy to have glutted my spirit with the flame of revenge and slaked the thirsty ashes of those I love." Such were the wild words I was uttering, such the impulse of my infuriate heart, when suddenly there appeared to me, brighter than I had ever seen her before, and shone forth in clear radiance through the night, my gracious mother, all her deity confessed, with the same mien and stature by which she is known to the dwellers in heaven. She seized me by the hand and stayed me, seconding her action with these words from her roseate lips : " My son, what mighty agony is it that stirs up this untamed passion ? What means your frenzy ? or whither has fled your care for me ? Will you not first see where you have left your father Anchises, spent with age as he is ? whether your wife, Creusa, be yet alive, and your child, Ascanius ? All about them the Grecian armies are ranging to

and fro, and were not my care exerted to rescue them, ere
this they had been snatched by the flame, devoured by the
foeman's sword. It is not the hated beauty of the daughter
of Tyndareus, the Spartan woman—not the reviled Paris.
No, it is heaven, unpitying heaven that is overturning this
great empire and levelling Troy from its summit. See here—
for I will take away wholly the cloud whose veil, cast over
your eyes, dulls your mortal vision and darkles round you damp
and thick—do you on your part shrink in naught from your
mother's commands, nor refuse to obey the instructions she
gives. Here, where you see huge masses rent asunder, and
stones wrenched from stones, and blended torrents of smoke and
dust, is Neptune with his mighty trident shaking the walls
and upheaving the very foundations ; here is Juno, cruellest of
foes, posted at the entry of the Scæan gate, and summoning in
tones of fury from the ships her confederate band, herself girt
with steel like them. Look behind you—there is Tritonian
Pallas, seated already on the summit of our towers, in the
lurid glare of her storm-cloud and grim Gorgon's head. The
great Father himself is nerving the Danaans with courage
and strength for victory—himself leading the gods against
our Dardan forces. Come, my son, catch at flight while you
may and bring the struggle to an end. I will not leave you,
till I have set you in safety at your father's door." She
had ceased, and veiled herself at once in night's thickest
shadows. I see a vision of awful shapes—mighty presences
of gods arrayed against Troy.

'Then, indeed, I beheld all Ilion sinking into flame, and
Neptune's city, Troy, overturned from its base. Even as
an ancient ash on the mountain-top, which woodmen have
hacked with steel and repeated hatchet strokes, and are trying
might and main to dislodge—it keeps nodding menacingly, its
leafy head palsied and shaken, till at last, gradually over-

borne by wound after wound, it has given its death-groan, and fallen uprooted in ruined length along the hill. I come down, and, following my heavenly guide, thread my way through flames and foemen, while weapons glance aside and flames retire.

'Now when at last I had reached the door of my father's house, that old house I knew so well, my sire, whom it was my first resolve to carry away high up the hills—who was the first object I sought—refuses to survive the razing of Troy and submit to banishment. "You, whose young blood is untainted, whose strength is firmly based and self-sustained, it is for you to think of flight. For me, had the dwellers in heaven willed me to prolong my life, they would have preserved for me my home. It is enough and more than enough to have witnessed one sack, to have once outlived the capture of my city. Here, O here as I lie, bid farewell to my corpse and begone. I will find me a warrior's death. The enemy will have mercy on me, and my spoils will tempt him. The loss of a tomb will fall on me lightly. Long, long have I been a clog on time, hated of heaven and useless to earth, from the day when the father of gods and sovereign of men blasted me with the wind of his lightning, and laid on me the finger of flame."

'Such the words he kept on repeating and continued unshaken, while we were shedding our hearts in tears—Creusa, my wife, and Ascanius and my whole house, imploring my father not to be bent on dragging all with him to ruin, and lending his weight to the avalanche of destiny. But he refuses, and will not be moved from his purpose or his home. Once more I am plunging into battle, and choosing death in the agony of my wretchedness—for what could wisdom or fortune do for me now? What, my father? that I could stir a step to escape, leaving you behind? was this your expectation? could aught so shocking fall from a parent's lips? No—if it is the will of heaven that naught of this mighty city should be spared—if your purpose is fixed, and you find pleasure in throwing yourself and yours on Troy's blazing pile, the door stands open for the death you crave. Pyrrhus will be here in a moment, fresh from bathing in Priam's blood—Pyrrhus, who butchers the son before the father's face, who butchers the father at the altar. Gracious mother! was it for this that thou rescuest me from fire and sword—all that I may see the foe in the heart of my home's sanctuary—may see my Ascanius, and my father, and my Creusa by them sacrificed in a pool of each other's blood? My arms, friends, bring me my arms! the call of the day of death rings in the ears of the conquered. Give me back to the Danaans, let me return and renew the combat. Never shall this day see us all slaughtered unresisting.

'Now I gird on my sword again, and was buckling and fitting my shield to my left arm, and making my way out of the house—when lo! my wife on the threshold, began to clasp and cling to my feet, holding out my little Iulus to his father. "If it is to death you are going, then carry us with you to death and all, but if experience gives you any hope in the arms you are resuming, let your first stand be made at your home. To whom, think you, are you leaving your little Iulus —your father, and me who was once styled your wife?"

'Thus she was crying, while her moaning filled the house, when a portent appears, sudden and marvellous to relate. Even while the hands and eyes of his grieving parents were upon him, lo, a flickering tongue of flame on the top of Iulus' head was seen to shoot out light, playing round his soft curly locks with innocuous contact and pasturing about his temples. We are all hurry and alarm, shaking out his blazing hair and quenching the sacred fire with water from the spring—but

Anchises my father raised his eyes in ecstasy to heaven, direct‑ing hand and voice to the stars : "Almighty Jove, if any prayer can bow thy will, look down on us—'tis all I crave— and if our piety have earned requital, grant us thy succour, father, and ratify the omen we now see." Scarce had the old man spoken, when there came a sudden peal of thunder on the left, and a star fell from heaven and swept through the gloom with a torchlike train and a blaze of light. Over the top of the house we see it pass, and mark its course along the sky till it buries itself lustrously in Ida's wood—then comes a long furrowed line of light, and a sulphurous smoke fills the space all about. Then at length overcome, my father raises himself towards the sky, addresses the gods, and does rever‑ence to the sacred meteor : "No more, no more delay from me. I follow your guidance, and am already in the way by which you would lead me. Gods of my country! preserve my house, preserve my grandchild. Yours is this augury— your shield is stretched over Troy. Yes, my son, I give way, and shrink not from accompanying your flight." He said— and by this the blaze is heard louder and louder through the streets, and the flames roll their hot volumes nearer. "Come then, dear father, take your seat on my back, my shoulders shall support you, nor shall I feel the task a burden. Fall things as they may, we twain will share the peril, share the deliverance. Let my little Iulus walk by my side, while my wife follows our steps at a distance. You, our servants, attend to what I now say. As you leave the city there is a mound, where stands an ancient temple of Ceres all alone, and by it an old cypress, observed these many years by the reverence of our sires. This shall be our point of meeting in one place from many quarters. You, my father, take in your hand these sacred things, our country's household gods. For me, just emerged from this mighty war, with the stains of carnage fresh upon me, it were sacrilege to touch them, till I have cleansed me in the running stream."

'So saying, I spread out my shoulders, bow my neck, cover them with a robe, a lion's tawny hide, and take up the precious burden. My little Iulus has fastened his hand in mine, and is following his father with ill-matched steps, my wife comes on behind. On we go, keeping in the shade—and I, who erewhile quailed not for a moment at the darts that rained upon me or at the masses of Greeks that barred my path, now am scared by every breath of air, startled by every sound, fluttered as I am, and fearing alike for him who holds my hand and him I carry. And now I was nearing the gates, and the whole journey seemed accomplished, when suddenly the noise of thick trampling feet came to my ear, and my father looks onward through the darkness. "Son, son," he cries, "fly : they are upon us. I distinguish the flashing of their shields and the gleam of their steel." In this alarm some unfriendly power perplexed and took away my judgment. For, while I was tracking places where no track was, and swerving from the wonted line of road, woe is me ! destiny tore from me my wife Creusa. Whether she stopped, or strayed from the road, or sat down fatigued, I never knew —nor was she ever restored to my eyes in life. Nay, I did not look back to discover my loss, or turn my thoughts that way till we had come to the mound and temple of ancient Ceres ; then at last, when all were mustered, she alone was missing, and failed those who should have travelled with her, her son and husband both. Whom of gods or men did my upbraiding voice spare ? what sight in all the ruin of the city made my heart bleed more ? Ascanius and Anchises my father and the Teucrian household gods I give to my comrades' care, and lodge them in the winding glade. I repair again to the city and don my shining armour. My mind is set to try every hazard again, and retrace my path through the whole of Troy, and expose my life to peril once more. First I repair again to the city walls, and the gate's dark entry by which I had passed out. I track and follow my footsteps back through the night, and traverse the ground with my eye. Everywhere my sense is scared by the horror, scared by the very stillness. Next I betake me home, in the hope, the faint hope that she may have turned her steps thither. The Danaans had broken in and were lodged in every chamber. All is over—the greedy flame is wafted by the wind to the roof, the fire towers triumphant—the glow streams madly heavenwards. I pass on, and look again at Priam's palace and the citadel. There already in the empty cloisters, yes, in Juno's sanctuary, chosen guards, Phœnix and Ulysses the terrible, were watching the spoil. Here are gathered the treasures of Troy torn from blazing shrines, tables of gods, bowls of solid gold and captive vestments in one great heap. Boys and mothers stand trembling all about in long array.

'Nay, I was emboldened even to fling random cries through the darkness. I filled the streets with shouts, and in my agony called again and again on my Creusa with unavailing iteration. As I was thus making my search and raving unceasingly the whole city through, the hapless shade, the spectre of my own Creusa appeared in my presence—a likeness larger than the life. I was aghast, my hair stood erect, my tongue clove to my mouth, while she began to address me thus, and relieve my trouble with words like these : "Whence this strange pleasure in indulging frantic grief, my darling husband ? It is not without Heaven's will that these things are happening ι that you should carry your Creusa with you on your journey is forbidden by fate, forbidden by the mighty ruler of heaven above. You have long years of exile, a vast expanse of ocean to traverse—and then you will arrive at the land of Hesperia, where Tiber, Lydia's river, rolls his gentle volumes through rich and cultured plains. There you have a smiling future, a kingdom and a royal bride waiting your coming. Dry your tears for Creusa, your heart's choice though she be. I am not to see the face of Myrmidons or Dolopes in their haughty homes, or to enter the service of some Grecian matron—I, a Dardan princess, daughter by marriage of Venus the immortal. No, I am kept in this country by heaven's mighty mother. And now farewell, and continue to love your son and mine." Thus having spoken, spite of my tears, spite of the thousand things I longed to say, she left me and vanished into unsubstantial air. Thrice, as I stood, I essayed to fling my arms round her neck—thrice the phantom escaped the hands that caught at it in vain—impalpable as the wind, fleeting as the wings of sleep.

'So passed my night, and such was my return to my comrades. Arrived there, I find with wonder their band swelled by a vast multitude of new companions, matrons and warriors both, an army mustered for exile, a crowd of the wretched. From every side they were met, prepared in heart as in fortune to follow me over the sea to any land where I might take them to settle. And now the morning star was rising over Ida's loftiest ridge with the day in its train—Danaan sentinels were blocking up the entry of the gates, and no hope of succour appeared. I retired at last, took up my father, and made for the mountains.

L

BOOK III.

'AFTER that it had seemed well to the powers above to over-throw Asia's fortunes and Priam's guiltless nation; after that Ilion fell headlong from its pride, and Troy, which Neptune reared, became one levelled smoking ruin, we are driven by auguries from heaven to look elsewhere for the exile's home in lands yet unpeopled. We build us a fleet under the shadow of Antandros, and the range of our own Phrygian Ida, all uncertain whither fate may carry us, where it may be our lot to settle, and muster men for sailing. Scarcely had summer set in, when my father, Anchises, was bidding us spread our sails to destiny. Then I give my last tearful look to my country's shores and her harbours, and those plains where Troy once stood but stands no longer. A banished man, I am wafted into the deep with my comrades and my son, my household gods and their mighty brethren.

'In the distance lies the land of the war-god, inhabited, in vast extent—the Thracians are its tillers—subject erewhile to Lycurgus' savage sway, bound by old hospitality to Troy, their household gods friends of ours, while our star yet shone. Hither I am wafted, and on the bending line of coast trace the outline of a city, a commencement made in an evil hour, and call the new nation Æneadæ, after my own name.

'I was sacrificing to my parent, Dione's daughter, and the rest of the gods, that they might bless the work I had begun, and was slaying to the heavenly monarch of the powers above a bull of shining whiteness on the shore. It happened that there was a mound near, on whose top were plants of cornel, and a myrtle bristling thick with spear-like wands. I drew near, and essayed to pull up from the ground the green forest growth, that I might have leafy boughs wherewith to shadow the altar, when I see a portent dreadful and marvellous to tell. For the first tree that I pull up from the soil, severing its roots, from that tree trickle drops of black blood, staining the earth with gore. For me, a freezing shudder palsies my frame, and my chilled blood curdles with affright. Again I go on to pluck the reluctant fibres of a second tree, and thus probe the hidden cause to the bottom; as surely from the bark of that second tree the black blood follows. Much musing in my mind, I began to call on the nymphs of the wood, and Gradivus, our father, patron of the land of Thrace, that they might duly turn the appearance to good, and make the heavy omen light. But when I come to tear up a third spear-shaft with a still greater effort, strain-ing with my knees against the sand which pressed on them— ought I to tell the tale or hold my peace?—a lamentable groan is heard from the bottom of the mound, and the utter-ance of a human voice reaches my ear : " Why, Æneas, mangle a wretch like me ? Spare me at length in my grave—spare those pious hands the stain of guilt. It was not an alien to you that Troy bore in bearing me—it is no alien's blood that is trickling from the stem. Ah ! fly from this land of cruelty, fly from this shore of greed, for I am Polydorus. Here I lie, pierced and buried by a growing crop of spears that has shot into sharp javelins."

'Then, indeed, terror, blank and irresolute, came over me— I was aghast—my hair stood erect, my tongue clove to my mouth. Yes, this Polydorus had long ago been sent secretly by Priam, unhappy then as ever, with a vast weight of gold, to be brought up by the king of Thrace, when he had already come to despair of the arms of Dardania, and saw the siege folding closer round his˙ city. When the power of the Thracians had been broken, and their star set, the Thracian followed Agamemnon's fortunes, and joined the standard of the conqueror—every tie of duty is snapped—he murders Polydorus, and by violence possesses himself of the gold. Cursed lust of gold, to what dost thou not force the heart of man? After the cold shuddering had ceased to tingle in my marrow, I lay this portent from heaven before the select senate of our nation, and my father as their chief, and ask them what they think. All are of the same mind, to depart from the land of crime, to leave the home of violated friendship, and indulge our fleet with the gales that wooed it. So we give Polydorus a solemn funeral : earth is heaped high upon his mound ; there stand the altars reared to his manes, in all the woe of dark fillets and sad-coloured cypress : and round them are daughters of Ilion, their hair unbound in mourner fashion : we offer bowls of new milk warm and frothing, and dishes of consecrated blood : so we lay the spirit to rest in its grave, and with a loud voice give the farewell call.

' Then, when the deep first looks friendly, and the winds offer a smooth sea, and the south's gentle whisper invites us to the main, our crews haul down their ships and crowd the shore. We sail out of the harbour, land and town leaving us fast. There is a sacred country with water all round it, chief favourite of the mother of the Nereids and the god of the Ægean. Once it drifted among the coasts and seaboards round about, till the heavenly archer in filial gratitude moored it to the rock of Myconos and to Gyaros, and gave it to be a fixed dwelling-place henceforth, and to laugh at the winds. Hither I sail : here it is that in a sheltered harbour our weary crews find gentlest welcome. We land, and worship the city of

Apollo. King Anius, king of men at once and priest of Phœbus, his temples wreathed with fillets and hallowed bay, comes running up ; in Anchises he owns an old friend, we knit hand to hand in hospitality and enter his roof.

'Behold me now worshipping the temple of the god, built of ancient stone. "Give us, god of Thymbra, a home that we can call our own : give us weary men a walled habitation, a posterity, a city that will last : keep from ruin Troy's second Pergamus, all that was left by the Danaans and their ruthless Achilles ! Who is our guide ? Whither wouldst thou have us go ? where set up our roof-tree ? Vouchsafe us a response, great father, and steal with power upon our souls ! "

'Scarce had I spoken, when methought suddenly came a trembling on the whole place, temple-gate and hallowed bay, a stir in the mountain from height to depth, a muttering from the tripod as the door of the shrine flew open. We fall low on earth, and a voice is wafted to our ears : "Sons of Dardanus, strong to endure, the land which first gave you birth from your ancestral tree, the same land shall welcome you back, restored to its fruitful bosom : seek for your old mother till you find her. There it is that the house of Æneas shall set up a throne over all nations, they, and their children's children, and those that shall yet come after." Thus Phœbus ; and a mighty burst succeeds of wild multitudinous joy, all asking as one man what that city is—whither is Phœbus calling the wanderers, and bidding them return. Then my father, revolving the traditions of men of old : "Listen," he cries, "lords of Troy, and learn where your hopes are. Crete lies in the midst of the deep, the island of mighty Jove. There is Mount Ida, and there the cradle of our race. It has a hundred peopled cities, a realm of richest plenty. Thence it was that our first father, Teucer, if I rightly recall what I have heard, came in the beginning to the Rhœtean coast, and fixed on the site of empire : Ilion and the towers of Pergamus had not yet been reared : the people dwelt low in the valley. Hence came our mighty mother, the dweller on Mount Cybele, and the symbols of the Corybants, and the forest of Ida : hence the inviolate mystery of her worship, and the lions harnessed to the car of their queen. Come, then, and let us follow where the ordinance of heaven points the way : let us propitiate the winds, and make for the realm of Gnossus—the voyage is no long one—let but Jupiter go with us, and the third day will land our fleet on the Cretan shore." He said, and offered on the altar the sacrifice that was meet—a bull to Neptune, a bull to thee, beauteous Apollo—a black lamb to the storm-wind, to the favouring Zephyrs a white one.

'Fame flies abroad that King Idomeneus has been driven to quit his paternal realm, that the shores of Crete are abandoned, houses cleared of the enemy, dwellings standing empty to receive us. So we leave Ortygia's harbour, and fly along the deep, past Naxos' bacchant mountains, and green Donysa, Olearos, and snowy Paros, and the Cyclades sprinkled over the waves, and seas thick sown with islands. Up rises the seaman's shout amid strain and struggle—each encourages his comrades, "For Crete and our forefathers, ho !" A wind gets up from the stern and escorts us on our way, and at length we are wafted to the Curetes' time-honoured shore.

'And now the site is chosen, and I am rearing a city's walls and calling it Pergamia : the new nation is proud to bear the name of the old : I bid them love hearth and home, and raise and roof the citadel. Already the ships had been hauled up high and dry on the shore, the crews were busied with marriage and tilling the new country, and I was appointing laws to live by, and houses to dwell in—when suddenly there came on the human frame a wasting sickness, shed from the whole tainted expanse of the sky, a piteous blight on trees and crops, a year charged with death. There were men leaving the lives they loved, or dragging with them the bodies that burdened them, while Sirius baked the fields into barrenness, the herbage was parching, the corn was sickening, and would not yield its food. Back again to Phœbus and his Ortygian oracle over the sea my father bids us go, and there sue for grace, asking the god to what haven he means to bring our overtoiled fortunes, whence he orders us to seek for help in our sufferings—whither to direct our course.

'It was night and all living things on earth were in the power of sleep, when methought the sacred images of the gods, the Phrygian household deities, whom I had borne away with me from Troy, even from the midst of the blazing town, stood before my eyes as I lay in slumber, clear in a flood of light, where the full moon was streaming through the windows of the house. Then they began to address me thus, and relieve my trouble with words like these: "The answer which Apollo has ready to give you when you reach Ortygia, he delivers here, sending us, see, of his own motion to your very door. We, the followers of you and your fortune since Dardanland sunk in flame—we, the comrades of the fleet which you have been guiding over the swollen main—we it is that will raise to the stars the posterity that shall come after you, and crown your city with imperial sway. Be it yours to build mighty walls for mighty dwellers, and not abandon the task of flight for its tedious length. Change your settlement: it is not this coast that the Delian god moved you to accept—not in Crete that Apollo bade you sit down. No, there is a place—the Greeks call it Hesperia —a land old in story, strong in arms and in the fruitfulness of its soil—the Œnotrians were its settlers. Now report says that later generations have called the nation Italian from the name of their leader. That is our true home : thence sprung Dardanus and father Iasius, the first founder of our line. Quick ! rise, and tell the glad tale, which brooks no question, to your aged sire : tell him that he is to look for Corythus and the county of Ausonia. Jupiter bars you from the fields of Dicte." Thus astonished by visions and voices of heaven —for sleep it was not : no—methought I saw them face to face, their wreathed locks and their features all in full view ; and a cold sweat, too, trickled down my whole frame. I leap from the bed, and direct upturned hand and voice to heaven, and pour on the hearth the undefiled libation. The sacrifice paid, with joy I inform Anchises, and expound the whole from first to last. He owns the double pedigree and the rival ancestors, and his own new mistake about the two old countries. Then he says : "My son, trained in the school of Troy's destiny, Cassandra's was the one voice which used to chant to me of this chance. Now I recollect, this was the fortune she presaged as appointed for our line, calling often for Hesperia, often for the land of Italy. But could any one think that Teucrians would ever reach the Hesperian shore ? Could Cassandra's prophesying in those days gain any one's credence ? Let us give way to Phœbus, and follow the better course enjoined." He said, and with one consent we gladly obey. So we quit this settlement as we quitted the last, and leaving a few behind, set sail, and make our hollow bark fly over the vast world of waters.

'Soon as the ships had gained the mid-sea, and land was no more to be seen, sky on every side, on every side ocean, then came a murky storm-cloud and stood over my head, charged with night and winter tempest, and darkness ruffled the billow's crest. At once the winds lay the sea in heaps, and the waters rise mountains high : a scattered fleet, we are tossed upon the vast abyss : clouds enshrouded the day, and dank night robbed us of the sky, while fire flashes momently from the bursting clouds. We are dashed out of our track, and wander blindly over the blind waters. Nay, even Palinurus owns he cannot tell day from night in a heaven like this, or recollect the footpath in the watery wilderness. Three dreary suns, blotted by blinding darkness, we wander on the deep : three nights with never a star. On the fourth day, at last, land was first seen to rise, and mountains with curling smoke wreaths to dawn in distant prospect. Down drop the sails : we rise on our oars : incessantly the crews, straining every nerve, toss the foam and sweep the blue.

'Escaped from the sea, I am first welcomed by the coast of the Strophades—the Strophades are known by the name Greece gave them, islands in the great Ionian, which fell Celæno and the rest of the Harpies have made their home, ever since Phineus' doors were closed against them, and fear drove them from the board which once fed them. A more baleful portent than this—a fiercer plague of heaven's vengeance never crawled out of the Stygian flood. Birds with maiden's faces, a foul discharge, crooked talons, and on their cheeks the pallor of eternal famine.

'On our arrival here, and entering the harbour, see ! we behold luxuriant herds of oxen grazing dispersedly in the fields, and goats all along the grass, with none to tend them. On we rush, sword in hand, inviting the gods and Jove himself to share the spoil with us : and then on the winding shore pile up couches for the banquet, and regale on the dainty fare. But on a sudden, with an appalling swoop from the hills, the Harpies are upon us, flapping their wings with a mighty noise—they tear the food in pieces, and spoil all with their filthy touch, while fearful screeches blend with foul smells.

Again, in a deep retreat under a hollow rock, with trees and crisp foliage all about us, we set out the board and put new fire on new altars. Again, from another quarter of the sky, out of their hidden lair, comes the troop, all rush and sound, flying about the prey with their hooked talons, tainting the food with their loathsome mouths. I give the word to my comrades to seize their arms and wage war with the fell tribe. As I ordered they do—they arrange their swords in hiding about the grass, and cover and conceal their shields. So soon as the noise of their swoop was heard along the winding shore, Misenus, from his lofty watch-tower, makes the hollow brass sound the alarm. On rush my comrades, and essay a combat of a new sort, to spoil with their swords the plumage of these foul sea-birds. But no violence will ruffle their feathers, no wounds pierce their skin : they are off in rapid flight high in the air, leaving their half-eaten prey and their filthy trail behind them. One of them, Celæno, perches on a rock of vast height—ill-boding prophetess—and gives vent to words like these : "What, is it war, for the oxen you have slain and the bullocks you have felled, true sons of Laomedon? is it war that *you* are going to make on *us*, to expel us, blameless Harpies, from our ancestral realm? Take then into your minds these my words, and print them there. The prophecy which the Almighty Sire imparted to Phœbus, Phœbus Apollo to me, I, the chief of the Furies, make known to you. For Italy, I know, you are crowding all sail : well, the winds shall be at your call as you go to Italy, and you shall be free to enter its harbours : but you shall not build walls round your fated city, before fell hunger and your murderous wrong against us drive you to gnaw and eat up your very tables." She said, and her wings carried her swiftly into the wood. But for my friends, a sudden terror curdled their blood, their hearts died within them ; no more arms—no, we must sue for grace, with vows and prayers, be the creatures goddesses or fell and loathsome birds. And my father Anchises, spreading his hands from the shore, invokes the mighty powers, and ordains meet sacrifice—" Great gods, forefend these menaces ! Great gods, avert a chance like this, and let your blessing shield your worshippers !" Then he bids us tear our moorings from the shore, and uncoil and stretch our ropes.

'The winds swell our sails, we scud over the foaming surge, where gale and pilot bid us go. Now rising from the wave are seen the woods of Zacynthos, and Dulichium, and Samos, and the tall cliffs of Neritos : we fly past the rocks of Ithaca, Laertes' realm, breathing a curse for the land that nursed the hard heart of Ulysses. Soon, too, the storm-capped peaks of Leucata dawn on the view, and their Apollo, the terror of sailors. In our weariness we make for him, and enter the little town : our anchors are thrown from the prow, our sterns ranged on the coast.

'So now, masters of the land beyond our hope, we perform lustrations to Jove, and set the altars ablaze with our vows, and solemnise the shores of Actium with the native games of Troy. My comrades strip, and practise the wrestle of the old country, all slippery with oil : what joy to have passed in safety by all those Argive cities, and held on our flight through the heart of the foe ! Meanwhile the sun rolls round the mighty year, and the north winds of icy winter roughen the sea. A shield of hollow brass, once borne by the great Abas, I fasten up full on the temple gate, and signalise the deed with a verse : " These arms are the offering of Æneas, won from his Danaan conquerors." Then I give the word to leave the haven and take seat on the benches. Each vying with each, the crews strike the water and sweep the marble surface. In due course we hide from view the airy summits of Phæacian land, coast the shore of Epirus,

enter the Chaonian haven, and approach Buthrotum's lofty
tower.

'Here a rumour of events past belief takes hold of our
ears—that Helenus, son of Príam, is reigning among Grecian
cities, lord of the wife and crown of Pyrrhus, Achilles' very
son, and that Andromache had again been given to a husband of her own nation. I was astounded: my heart
kindled with a strange longing to have speech of my old
friend, and learn all about this wondrous stroke of fortune.
So I advance into the country from the haven, leaving
fleet and coast behind, at the very time when Andromache, before the city, in a grove, by the wave of a mock
Simois, was celebrating a yearly banquet, the offering of
sorrow, to the dead, and invoking her Hector's shade at a
tomb called by his name, an empty mound of green turf
which she had consecrated to him with two altars, that she
might have the privilege of weeping. Soon as her wild eye
saw me coming with the arms of Troy all about me, scared
out of herself by the portentous sight, she stood chained to
earth while yet gazing—life's warmth left her frame—she
faints, and after long time scarce finds her speech :—" Is it a
real face that I see? are those real lips that bring me news?
Goddess-born, are you among the living? or, if the blessed
light has left you, where is my Hector?" She spoke—her
tears flowed freely, and the whole place was filled with her
shrieks. Few, and formed with labour, are the words I
address to her frenzied ear, broken and confused the accents
I utter :—" Aye, I live, sure enough, and through the worst
of fortunes am dragging on life still. Doubt it not, your eye
tells you true. Alas! on what chance have you alit, fallen
from the height where your first husband throned you? What
smile has Fortune bright enough to throw back on Hector's
Andromache? is it Pyrrhus' bed you are still tending?" She

dropped her eyes, and spoke with bated breath:—"O blest pre-eminently over all, Priam's virgin daughter, bidden to die at the grave of her foe, under Troy's lofty walls! she that had not to brook the chance of the lot, or a slave and a captive, to touch the bed of her lord and conqueror! While we, after the burning of our city, carried over this sea and that, have stooped to the scorn, the youthful insolence of Achilles' heir, the slave-mother of his child; he, after this, goes in quest of Leda's Hermione and her Spartan alliance, and gives me over to Helenus, the bondwoman to be the bondman's mate! Him, however, Orestes, fired by desperate passion for a ravished bride, and maddened by the frenzy-fiend of crime, surprises at unawares, and slays at his sire's own altar. At Neoptolemus' death a portion of this kingdom passed to Helenus, who called the fields Chaonian, and the land itself Chaonia, from Chaon, their Trojan namesake, and crowned, as you see, these heights with a new Pergamus, the citadel of Ilion. But you—what wind, what destiny has shaped your voyage? What god has driven you on a coast which you know not to be ours? What of the boy Ascanius? is he alive and breathing upper air? he, whom you on that night at Troy—say, can his boyish mind feel yet for the mother he has lost? Is he enkindled at all to the valour of old days, the prowess of a grown man, by a father like Æneas, an uncle like Hector?"

'Such were the sorrows she kept pouring 'out, weeping long and fruitlessly, when Priam's noble son, Helenus, presents himself from the city, with a train of followers, and knows his friends again, and joyfully leads them to his home, many a tear interrupting his utterance. As I go on, I recognise a miniature Troy, a Pergamus copied from the great one, a dry rivulet the namesake of Xanthus, and throw my arms round a Scæan gate. My Trojan comrades, too, are made free of the friendly town. The king made entertainment for them in spacious cloisters. There, in the midst of the hall, they were pouring libations from cups of wine, their meat served on gold, and goblets in their hands.

'And now suppose a day past, and yet another day : the breeze is inviting the sail, the swelling south inflating the canvas, when I accost the prophet with these words, and put to him the question I tell you :—" True Trojan born, heaven's interpreter,[1] whose senses inform you of the stars, and of the tongue of birds, and of the omens of the flying wing, tell me now—for revelation has spoken in auspicious words of the whole of my voyage, and all the gods have urged me with one voice of power to make for Italy, and explore that hidden clime. One alone, the Harpy Celæno, forebodes a strange portent, too horrible to tell, denouncing fierce vengeance and unnatural hunger. Tell me then, what perils do I shun first, or what must I observe to surmount the tremendous hardships before me ? " Then Helenus first implores the favour of Heaven by a solemn sacrifice of bullocks, and unbinds the fillet from his consecrated brow, and with his own hand leads me to thy temple, Phœbus, my mind lifted from its place by the effluence of divine power; which done, that priestly mouth chants these words from its prophetic lips :—

' " Goddess-born—for that presages of mighty blessing are attending you over the deep is clear beyond doubt—such is the casting of the lot of fate by heaven's king as he rolls event after event—such the ordained succession—a few things out of many, to make your voyage through strange waters safer, your settlement in Ausonia's haven more assured. My speech shall unfold to you but a few—for the rest the fatal sisters keep from Helenus' knowledge, and Saturnian Juno seals

---

[1] It will be observed that Mr. Conington has missed a line in his translation here.—[ED.]

his lips. First then for Italy, which you think close at hand, ready in your blindness to rush into the harbours that neighbour us, the length of a way where no way is, severs you from its length of territory. First must the oar be suppled in Trinacrian waters, and your ships must traverse the expanse of the Ausonian brine, and the spectral lake, and the isle of Ææan Circe, ere you can find a safe spot to build a peaceful city. I will tell you the tokens, be it yours to keep them lodged in your mind. When on an anxious day, by the side of a sequestered river, you shall find an enormous swine lying under the oaks on the bank with a litter of thirty head just born, white herself through all her lazy length, her children round her breasts as white as she—that shall be the site of your city—that your assured rest from toil and trouble. Nor need you shudder beforehand at the prospect of gnawing your tables—the fates will find you a path, and a prayer will bring you Apollo. But as for these lands, and this line of the Italian coast, which lies close at hand, and is washed by the spray of our waters, this you must fly : the cities, one and all, are peopled by enemies from Greece. Here the Narycian Locrians have built them cities, and the Sallentine fields have been occupied with an army by Lyctian Idomeneus : here is the Melibœan chief Philoctetes' tiny town Patelia, with a strong wall to prop it. Further, when your fleet stands moored on the other side the water, and you build altars and pay vows on the coast, shroud your head with the covering of a purple robe, lest, while the hallowed fires are blazing, and the worship of the gods yet unfinished, some enemy's eye should meet yours, and make the omens void. Be this ritual custom maintained by your comrades as by yourself : let the piety of generations to come abide in this observance. But when leaving Italy you are carried by the wind near the Sicilian coast, and Pelorus' narrow bars dimly open, make for the left

shore, for the left water, long as the circuit round may be; avoid
the right, its land and its seas. This whole region by the forceful throes of a mighty convulsion—such power of change is
there in long centuries of olden time—was rent in twain, so
runs the story, the two countries before having been one and
unbroken; at last the sea poured in violently between, and
with its waters cut off the Hesperian from the Sicilian side,
washing between fields and cities, their seaboards now parted,
with the waves of its narrow channel. There the right-hand
coast is held by Scylla, the left by Charybdis, ever hungering,
who, at the bottom of the whirling abyss, thrice a day draws
the huge waves down her precipitous throat, and in turn upheaves them to the sky, and lashes the stars with their spray.
But Scylla is confined in the deep recesses of a cave, whence
she thrusts out her mouths, and drags vessels on to her rocks.
At top, a human face, a maiden with beauteous bosom;
at bottom an enormous sea-monster—dolphins' ·tails attached
to a belly all of wolves' heads. Better far wearily to
round the goal of Trinacrian Pachynus and fetch about
a tedious compass, than once to have looked on the monster
Scylla in her enormous cave, and the rocks that echo
with her sea-coloured dogs. Moreover, if there be any foresight in Helenus, if you give any credence to his prophetic
tongue, if his mind be a fountain of Apollo's truth, one thing
there is, goddess-born, one thing outweighing all beside which
I will foreshow you, reiterating the warning again and again
—be Juno, great Juno, the first whose deity you worship—to
Juno chant your willing prayers: subdue that mighty
empress by suppliant offerings: thus at last victorious you
will leave Trinacria behind, and be sped to the borders
of Italy. When you are there at length, and have come
to the city of Cumæ, and the haunted lake, and the woods
that rustle over Avernus, you will have sight of the frenzied

prophetess, who, in the cavern under the rock, chants her fateful strain, and commits characters and words to the leaves of trees. All the strains that the maid has written on these leaves she arranges in order, shuts them up in her cave, and leaves them there. They remain as she has left them, their disposition unchanged. But, strange to say, when the hinge is turned, and a breath of air moves the leaves, and the opened door throws their light ranks into confusion, henceforth she never troubles herself for a moment to catch them as they fly about the cavern, to restore them to their places, or to fit each strain to each. The inquirers retire with their doubts unsolved, and a hatred of the sibyl's seat. Arrived here, let no cost of time or delay weigh with you so much—though your comrades should chide, and the voyage loudly call your sails to sea, and a sheet-full of fair wind be there at your choice—but that you visit the prophetess, and beg and pray her herself to chant the oracle, loosing speech and tongue with a ready will. She shall tell you of the nations of Italy, and the wars of the future, and the way to shun or stand the shock of every peril, and shall vouchsafe to your prayer the boon of a prosperous voyage. Such are the counsels which it is given you to receive from my lips. Go on your way, and by your own actions lift to heaven the greatness of Troy."

'Soon as the seer had thus uttered these words of kindness, he next orders massy gifts of gold and carved ivory to be carried on shipboard, and stores in the keels, a weight of silver and caldrons of Dodona, a cuirass of chain-mail, three-threaded in gold, and a splendid helmet with cone and flowing crest, the armour of Neoptolemus. My father, too, has presents of his own. Horses, too, he gives, and guides too ; makes up the complement of oars, and arms the crews. Meanwhile Anchises was giving the word to rig the fleet, not to wear out

M

the patience of a fair wind. Him the interpreter of Phœbus
addresses with much pomp of courtesy : " Anchises, graced with
the proud privilege of Venus's wedded love, the special care of
the gods, whom they twice interposed to save from the fall of
Pergamus, lo ! there lies Ausonia's land ; for this make all sail.
Yet what have I said ? This coast you must needs sail past ;
far away yonder lies that part of Ausonia which Apollo
reveals to you. Go on your way," cries he, "blessed in a
son so duteous ! Why proceed further, and make the rising
gales wait while I talk ?" As freely, too, Andromache, saddened with the grief of parting, presents Ascanius with robes
pictured with gold embroidery, and a Phrygian scarf. She
tires not in her bounty, but loads him with gifts of needlework, and bespeaks him thus : " Take, too, these, dear boy,
to be a memorial of what my hands can do—a token for
long years of the affection of Andromache, Hector's wife.
Yes, take the last presents your kin can bestow, O, sole surviving image of my own Astyanax ! Those eyes are his eyes,
those hands his hands, that face his face, and he would
now be growing to manhood by your side, in bloom like
yours ! " Tears started forth, as I addressed my parting words
to the royal pair: ' Live long and happily, as those should
for whom the book of Fortune is closed. We, alas ! are still
called to turn page after page. You have won your rest :
you have no expanse of sea to plough, no Ausonian fields to
chase, still retiring as you advance. Your eyes look upon a
copy of the old Xanthus, upon a Troy which your own hands
have made—made, I would hope and pray, with happier
auspices, and with less peril of a visit from Greece. If the
day ever arrive when I shall enter Tiber and the fields that
neighbour Tiber, and look on the walls which Fate has made
over to my people, then we will have our two kindred cities,
our two fraternal nations—the one in Epirus, the other in

Hesperia, with a common founder, Dardanus, and a common history—animated by one heart, till they come to be one Troy. Be this the destined care of our posterity!"

'We push on over the sea under Ceraunia's neighbouring range, whence there is a way to Italy, the shortest course through the water. Meantime the sun drops, and the mountains are veiled in shadow. We stretch ourselves gladly on the lap of earth by the water's side, having cast lots for the oars, and take our ease dispersedly along the dry beach. Sleep's dew sprinkles our wearied limbs. Not yet was night's car, entering the middle of its circle, drawn by the unflagging hours, when Palinurus, with no thought of sloth, springs from his bed, explores every wind, and catches with his ears the voices of the air. All the stars he notes, as they swim through the silent sky, looking round on Arcturus, and the showery Hyades, and the twin Bears, and Orion in his panoply of gold. Soon as he sees them all set in a heaven of calm, he gives a clear signal from the stern. We break up our quarters, essay our flight, and spread the wings of our sails. And now the stars were fled, and Aurora was just reddening in the sky, when in the distance we see the dim hills and low plains of Italy. "Italy!" Achates was the first to cry. Italy, our crews welcome with a shout of rapture. Then my father, Anchises, wreathed a mighty bowl with a garland, and filled it with wine, and called on the gods, standing upon the tall stern: "Ye powers that rule sea and land and weather, waft us a fair wind and a smooth passage, and breathe auspiciously!" The breeze we wished for freshens; the harbour opens as we near it, and the temple of Minerva is seen crowning the height. The crews furl the sails, and turn their prows coastward. The harbour is curved into an arch by the easterly waves; a barrier of cliffs on each side foams again with the briny spray; between them the haven lies concealed; the towery rocks let down their arms like two walls, and the temple retires from the shore. Here on the grass I saw four horses, the first token of heaven's will, browsing the meadow at large, of snowy whiteness. And Anchises, my father, breaks forth: "War is on thy front, land of the stranger; for war thy horses are prepared; war is threatened by the cattle we see. Still, these beasts no less are trained one day to stoop to the car, and carry harness and curb in harmony with the yoke; yes," cries he, "there is hope of peace, too." With that we make our prayers to the sacred majesty of Pallas, queen of clanging arms, the first to welcome us in the hour of our joy; and, according to Helenus' order, that order which he gave so earnestly, we duly solemnise to Juno of Argos the prescribed honours. Then, without dallying, soon as our vows were paid in course, we turn landward the horns of our covered sailyards, and leave the homes of the sons of Greece, and the fields we could not trust. Next we sight the bay of Tarentum, the city, if legend say true, of Hercules; right against us rises the goddess of Lacinium, and the towers of Caulon, and Scylaceum, wrecker of ships. Then, in the distance, from the surge is seen Trinacrian Ætna; and the heavy groaning of the sea and the beating of the rocks is heard from afar, and broken voices on the beach, and the depths leap up to sight, and the sands are in a turmoil with the surge. Then, my father, Anchises: "No doubt this is that Charybdis; these the cliffs, these the frightful rocks of Helenus' song. Snatch us from them, comrades; rise on your oars as one man." They do no less than bidden; first of all Palinurus turned the plashing prow to the waters on the left; for the left makes the whole fleet, oars, winds, and all. Up we go to heaven on the arched back of the wave; down again, as the water gives way under us, we sink to the place of death below. Thrice the rocks shouted in our ears deep in their stony hollows; twice we saw the foam dashed up, and the stars all dripping. Meanwhile, tired and spent, we lose wind and sunlight at once, and, in our ignorance of the way, float to the land of the Cyclops.

'There is a haven, sheltered from the approach of the winds, and spacious, were that all; but Ætna is near, thundering with appalling crashes; at one time it hurls to the sky a black cloud, a smoky whirlwind of soot and glowing ashes, and upheaves balls of fire, and licks the stars; at another it raises rocks, torn from the mountain's bowels, and whirls heaps of molten stones into the air with a groan, and boils up from its very foundations. The legend is, that the body of Enceladus, blasted by lightning, is kept down by this mighty weight, and that the giant bulk of Ætna, piled on him, breathes forth penal fire through passages which that fire has burst; and ever, as he shifts his side from weariness, all Trinacria quakes and groans, and draws up a curtain of smoke over the sky. That night, in the shelter of the woods, we endure the visitation of monstrous portents, yet see not what cause produces the sound. For there was no starlight, no sky, bright with a heaven of constellations, but the firmament was dim and murky, and dead night was keeping the moon in a prison of storm-clouds.

'And now the next day was breaking in early dawn, and Aurora had drawn off the dewy shadow from the sky, when suddenly from the woods comes forth the strange figure of a man unknown, in piteous trim—a picture completed by Famine's master-stroke, and stretches his hands in sup-plication to the shore. We look back: there was filth to make us shudder, a length of beard, a covering fastened with thorns; yet the rest betokened a Greek, who had once been sent to Troy in the army of his nation. As for him, when he saw from afar the dress of Dardan land and the arms of Troy, for a moment he faltered, scared by the sight, and checked his steps; soon he ran headlong to the shore, crying and praying: "By the stars I adjure you, by the powers above, by this blessed light of heaven we breathe, take me with you, Teucrians; carry me off to any land you will; this will be enough. I know I am one of the Danaan crews; I own that I carried war into your Trojan homes; for which, if the guilt of my crime is so black, fling me piece-meal to the waves, drown me deep in the great sea. If I am to die, there will be pleasure in dying by the hands of men." His speech was over, and he was clinging about us, clasping our knees, and writhing round them. We encourage him to tell us who he is, of what race sprung, to reveal what fortune has since made him its sport. My father, Anchises, after no long pause, himself gives his hand to the youth, and reassures him by the powerful pledge. He at length lays aside his fear, and speaks as follows :—

' " I come from Ithaca, a comrade of the ill-starred Ulysses, my name Achemenides. I went to Troy, leaving my father, Adamastus, who was poor. Would that his lot had remained mine! Here, in their hurry to leave the door of the slaughterhouse, my comrades forgot me, and so left me behind in the Cyclops' enormous den. It is a house of gore and bloody feasting, deep, and dark, and huge; its master towers aloft, and strikes the stars on high (ye gods, remove from the earth a plague like this!), whom no eye rests on with pleasure, no tongue dare accost. The flesh of wretched men and their black blood are the food he feeds on. These eyes saw, when two bodies from our company, caught by his huge hand, as he threw back his head in the midst of the den, were being brained against the rock, and the floor was plashed and swimming with blood—they saw, when he was crunching their limbs, dripping with black gore, and the warm joints were quivering under his teeth. He did it, but not unpunished. Ulysses was not the man to brook a deed like this; the brain of Ithaca was not wanting to itself when the need was so great. For soon as, gorged with his food and buried in wine, he bent and dropped his neck, and lay all along the den in unmeasured length, belching out gore in his sleep, and gobbets mixed with bloody wine; then we, having made our prayer to the great gods and drawn our places by lot, surround him on all sides as one man, and with a sharp weapon bore out his eye, that vast eye, which used to lie single and sunk under his grim brow,[1] and thus at last take triumphant vengeance for our comrades' shades. But fly, unhappy men, fly, and tear your cable from the shore. For hideous and huge as is Polyphemus, folding in his den his woolly flocks and pressing their udders, as hideous and huge are a hundred others that dwell everywhere along this coast, monster Cyclops, and stalk over the tall mountains. It is now the third moon, whose horns are filling out with light, that I am dragging along my life in the woods, among the lonely lairs where wild beasts dwell, and looking forth on the huge Cyclops as they stalk from rock to rock, and trembling at their tread and at the sound of their voices. My wretched fare, berries and stony cornels, is supplied by the boughs, and herbage uprooted yields me food. As I turned my eyes all about, this fleet of yours at last I saw advancing to the shore; with this, prove it what might, I cast in my lot; it is enough to have escaped this race of monsters. Sooner do you destroy this life by any death you please."

'Scarce had he ended, when on the mountain-top we see the giant himself, moving along with his enormous bulk among his cattle, and making for the well-known shore—a monster dreadful, hideous, huge, with his eye extinguished.

---

[1] Another line omitted in the translation.—[ED.]

A pine, lopped by his own hand, guides him and steadies his footsteps. His woolly sheep accompany him—there is his sole pleasure, the solace of his suffering. After he had touched the waves of the deep and come to the sea, he washes with its water the gore that trickles from his scooped-out eye, gnashing his teeth with a groan; and he steps through the sea, now at main height, while the wave has not yet wetted his tall sides. We, in alarm, hasten our flight from the place, taking on board the suppliant, who had thus made good his claim, and silently cut the cable; then throw ourselves forward, and with emulous oars sweep along the sea. He perceived it, and turned his steps towards the noise he heard. But when he finds he has no means of grasping at us with his hand, no power of keeping pace with the Ionian waves in pursuit, he raises a gigantic roar, at which the sea and all its waters trembled inwardly, and the land of Italy shuddered to its core, and Ætna bellowed through her winding caverns. But the tribe of the Cyclops, startled from wood and lofty mountain, rush to the haven and fill the shore. There we see them standing, each with the empty menace of his grim eye, the brethren of Ætna, lifting their tall heads to heaven, a dire assemblage— like as on some tall peak, skiey oaks or cone-bearing cypresses stand together, a lofty forest of Jupiter, or a grove of Diana. Headlong our crews are driven by keen terror to fling out the ropes anywhither, and stretch their sails to the winds that would catch them. On the other hand, Helenus' warning bids them not to hold on their way between Scylla and Charybdis, a passage on either side removed but a hair's breadth from death; so our purpose stands to spread our sails backward. When lo ! the north wind is upon us, sped from Pelorus' narrow strait. On I fly, past Pantagia's mouth of living rock, and the bay of Megara, and low-lying Thapsus. Such were the coasts named to us by Achemenides, as he retraced his former wanderings—Achemenides, comrade of the ill-starred Ulysses.

'Stretched before the Sicanian bay lies an island, over against Plemyrium the billowy—former ages named it Ortygia. Hither, the legend is, Alpheus, the river of Elis, made himself a secret passage under the sea; and he now, through thy mouth, Arethusa, blends with the waters of Sicily. Obedient to command, we worship the mighty gods of the place; and from thence I pass the over-rich soil of Helorus the marshy. Hence we skirt the tall crags and jutting rocks of Pachynus, and Camarina is seen in the distance. Camarina, which the oracle gave no man leave to disturb, and the plains of Gela, and Gela itself, mighty city, called from the stream that laves it. Next Acragas the craggy displays from afar its lofty walls, one day the breeder of generous steeds. Thee, too, I leave, by favour of the winds, palmy Selinus, and pick my way through the sunk rocks that make Lilybeium's waters perilous. Hence Drepanum receives me, with its haven and its joyless coast. Here, after so many storms on the sea had done their worst, woe is me! I lose him that had made every care and danger light, my father, Anchises. Here, best of sires, you leave your son, lone and weary, you, who had been snatched from those fearful dangers, alas! in vain. Helenus, the seer, among the thousand horrors he foretold, warned me not of this agony; no, nor dread Celæno. This was my last suffering, this the goal of my long journeyings. It was on parting hence that Heaven drove me on your coast.'

Thus father Æneas, alone, amid the hush of all around, was recounting Heaven's destined dealings, and telling of his voyages; and now, at length, he was silent, made an end, and took his rest.

BOOK IV.

BUT the queen, pierced long since by love's cruel shaft, is feeding the wound with her life-blood, and wasting under a hidden fire. Many times the hero's own worth comes back to her mind, many times the glory of his race ; his every look remains imprinted on her breast, and his every word, nor will trouble let soothing sleep have access to her frame.

The dawn-goddess of the morrow was surveying the earth with Phœbus' torch in her hand, and had already withdrawn the dewy shadow from the sky, when she, sick of soul, thus bespoke the sister whose heart was one with hers :—' Anna, my sister, what dreams are these that confound and appal me ! Who is this new guest that has entered our door ! What a face and carriage ! What strength of breast and shoulders ! I do believe—it is no mere fancy—that he has the blood of gods in his veins. An ignoble soul is known by the coward's brand. Ah ! by what fates he has been tossed ! What wars he was recounting, every pang of them borne by himself ! Were it not the fixed, immovable purpose of my mind never to consent to join myself with any in wedlock's bands, since my first love played me false and made me the dupe of death—had I not been weary of bridal bed and nuptial torch, perchance I might have stooped to this one reproach. Anna —for I will own the truth—since the fate of Sychæus, my poor husband—since the sprinkling of the gods of my home with the blood my brother shed, he and he only has touched my heart and shaken my resolution till it totters. I recognise the traces of the old flame. But first I would pray that earth may yawn for me from her foundations, or the all-powerful sire hurl me thunder-stricken to the shades, to the wan shades of Erebus and abysmal night, ere I violate thee, my woman's honour, or unknit the bonds thou tiest. He who first wedded me, he has carried off my heart—let him keep it all his own, and retain it in his grave.' Thus having said, she deluged her bosom with a burst of tears.

Anna replies :—' Sweet love, dearer than the light to your sister's eye, are you to pine and grieve in loneliness through life's long spring, nor know aught of a mother's joy in her children, nor of the prizes Venus gives ? Think you that dead ashes and ghosts low in the grave take this to heart ? Grant that no husbands have touched your bleeding heart in times gone by, none now in Libya, none before in Tyre ; yes, Iarbas has been slighted, and the other chieftains whom Afric, rich in triumphs, rears as its own—will you fight against a welcome, no less than an unwelcome passion ? Nor does it cross your mind in whose territories you are settled ? On one side the cities of the Gætulians, a race invincible in war, and the Numidians environ you, unbridled as their steeds, and the inhospitable Syrtis ; on another, a region unpeopled by drought, and the widespread barbarism of the nation of Barce. What need to talk of the war-cloud threatening from Tyre, and the menaces of our brother ? It is under Heaven's auspices, I deem, and by Juno's blessing, that the vessels of Ilion have made this voyage hither. What a city, my sister, will ours become before your eyes ! what an empire will grow out of a marriage like this ! With the arms of the Teucrians at its back, to what a height will the glory of Carthage soar ! Only be it yours to implore the favour of Heaven, and having won its acceptance, give free course to hospitality and weave a chain of pleas for delay, while the tempest is raging its full on the sea, and Orion, the star of rain, while his ships are still battered, and the rigour of the sky still unyielding.' By these words she added fresh fuel to the fire of love, gave confidence to her wavering mind, and loosed the ties of woman's honour.

First they approach the temples and inquire for pardon from altar to altar; duly they slaughter chosen sheep to Ceres the lawgiver, to Phœbus, and to father Lyæus—above all to Juno, who makes marriage bonds her care. Dido herself, in all her beauty, takes a goblet in her hand, and pours it out full between the horns of a heifer of gleaming white, or moves majestic in the presence of the gods towards the richly-laden altars, and solemnises the day with offerings, and gazing greedily on the victims' opened breasts, consults the entrails yet quivering with life. Alas! how blind are the eyes of seers! What can vows, what can temples do for the madness of love? All the while a flame is preying on the very marrow of her bones, and deep in her breast a wound keeps noiselessly alive. She is on fire, the ill-fated Dido, and in her madness ranges the whole city through, like a doe from an arrow-shot, whom, unguarded in the thick of the Cretan woods, a shepherd, chasing her with his darts, has pierced from a distance, and left the flying steel in the wound, unknowing of his prize; she at full speed scours the forests and lawns of Dicte; the deadly reed still sticks in her side. Now she leads Æneas with her through the heart of the town, and displays the wealth of Sidon, and the city built to dwell in. She begins to speak, and stops midway in the utterance. Now, as the day fades, she seeks again the banquet of yesterday, and once more in frenzy asks to hear of the agonies of Troy, and hangs once more on his lips as he tells the tale. After-wards, when the guests are gone, and the dim moon in turn is hiding her light, and the setting stars invite to slumber, alone she mourns in the empty hall, and presses the couch he has just left; him far away she sees and hears, herself far away; or holds Ascanius long in her lap, spellbound by his father's image, to cheat, if she can, her ungovernable passion. The towers that were rising rise no longer; the youth ceases to practise arms, or to make ready havens and bulwarks for safety in war; the works are broken and suspended, the giant frowning of the walls, and the engine level with the sky.

Soon as Jove's loved wife saw that she was so mastered by the plague, and that good name could not stand in the face of passion, she, the daughter of Saturn, bespeaks Venus thus: —'Brilliant truly is the praise, ample the spoils you are carrying off, you and your boy—great and memorable the fame, if the plots of two gods have really conquered one woman. No; I am not so blind either to your fears of my city, to your suspicions of the open doors of my stately Carthage. But when is this to end? or what calls now for such terrible contention? Suppose for a change we establish perpetual peace and a firm marriage bond. You have gained what your whole heart went to seek. Dido is ablaze with love, and the madness is coursing through her frame. Jointly then let us rule this nation, each with full sovereignty; let her stoop to be the slave of a Phrygian husband, and make over her Tyrians in place of dowry to your control.'

To her—for she saw that she had spoken with a feigned intent, meaning to divert the Italian empire to the coast of Libya—Venus thus replied:—'Who would be so mad as to spurn offers like these, and prefer your enmity to your friendship, were it but certain that the issue you name would bring good fortune in its train? But I am groping blindly after destiny—whether it be Jupiter's will

that the Tyrians and the voyagers from Troy should have one
city—whether he would have the two nations blended and a
league made between them. You are his wife; it is your
place to approach him by entreaty. Go on, I will follow.'
Imperial Juno rejoined thus :—'That task shall rest with me.
Now, in what way our present purpose can be contrived, lend
me your attention, and I will explain in brief. Æneas and
Dido, poor sufferer! are proposing to go hunting in the forest,
when first to-morrow's sun displays his rising, and with his
beams uncurtains the globe. On them I will pour from above
a black storm of mingled rain and hail, just when the horsemen are all astir, and spreading their toils before the wood-
walks, and the whole heaven shall be convulsed with thunder.
The train shall fly here and there, and be lost in the thick
darkness. Dido and the Trojan chief shall find themselves in
the same cave. I will be there, and, if I may count on your
sanction, will unite her to him in lasting wedlock, and consecrate her his for life. Thus shall Hymen give us his presence.'
The Queen of Cythera makes no demur, but nods assent,
smiling at the trick she has found out.

Meanwhile Aurora has risen, and left the ocean. Rising
with the day-star, the chivalry of Carthage streams through
the gates, their woven toils, and nets, and hunting-spears
tipped with broad iron, and Massylian horsemen hurry along,
and a force of keen-scented hounds. There are the Punic
princes, waiting for the queen, who still lingers in her
chamber ; there stands her palfrey, conspicuous in purple and
gold, fiercely champing the foaming bit. At length she comes
forth, with a mighty train attending, a Tyrian scarf round
her, itself surrounded by an embroidered border ; her quiver
of gold, her hair knotted up with gold, her purple robe
fastened with a golden clasp. The Phrygian train, too, are
in motion, and Iulus, all exultation. Æneas himself, comely

beyond all the rest, adds his presence to theirs, and joins the procession; like Apollo, when he leaves his Lycian winter-seat and the stream of Xanthus, and visits Delos, his mother's isle, and renews the dance; while with mingled voices round the altar shout Cretans and Dryopians, and tattooed Agathyrsians. The god in majesty walks on the heights of Cynthus, training his luxuriant hair with the soft pressure of a wreath of leaves, and twining it with gold; his arrows rattle on his shoulders. Not with less ease than he moved Æneas; such the beauty that sparkles in that peerless countenance. When they reach the high mountains and the pathless coverts, see! the wild goats, dropping from the tops of the crags, have run down the slopes; in another quarter the deer are scouring the open plains, massing their herds as they fly in a whirlwind of dust, and leaving the mountains. But young Ascanius is in the heart of the glens, exulting in his fiery courser. Now he passes one, now another of his comrades at full speed, and prays that in the midst of such spiritless game he may be blest with the sight of a foaming boar, or that a tawny lion may come down the hill. Meantime the sky begins to be convulsed with a mighty turmoil; a storm-cloud follows of mingled rain and hail. The Tyrian train, all in confusion, and the chivalry of Troy, and the hope of Dardania, Venus' grandson, have sought shelter in their terror up and down the country, some here, some there. The streams run in torrents down the hills. Dido and the Trojan chief find themselves in the same cave. Earth, the mother of all, and Juno give the sign.

Lightnings blaze, and heaven flashes in sympathy with the bridal; and from mountain-tops the nymphs give the nuptial shout. That day was the birthday of death, the birthday of woe. Henceforth she has no thought for the common eye or the common tongue; it is not a stolen passion that Dido has now in her mind—no, she calls it marriage; that name is the screen of her sin.

Instantly Fame takes her journey through Libya's great cities—Fame, a monster surpassed in speed by none; her nimbleness lends her life, and she gains strength as she goes. At first fear keeps her low; soon she rears herself skyward, and treads on the ground, while her head is hidden among the clouds. Earth, her parent, provoked to anger against the gods, brought her forth, they say, the youngest of the family of Cœus and Enceladus—swift of foot and untiring of wing, a portent terrible and vast—who, for every feather on her body has an ever-wakeful eye beneath, marvellous to tell, for every eye a loud tongue and mouth, and a pricked-up ear. At night she flies midway between heaven and earth, hissing through the darkness, nor ever yields her eyes to the sweets of sleep. In the daylight she sits sentinel on a high house-top, or on a lofty turret, and makes great cities afraid; as apt to cling to falsehood and wrong as to proclaim the truth. So then she was filling the public ear with a thousand tales —things done and things never done alike the burden of her song—how that Æneas, a prince of Trojan blood, had arrived at Carthage, a hero whom lovely Dido deigned to make her husband, and now in luxurious ease they were wearing away the length of winter together, forgetful of the crowns they wore or hoped to wear, and enthralled by unworthy passion. Such are the tales the fiendlike goddess spreads from tongue to tongue. Then, in due course, she turns her steps to King Iarbas, and inflames him with her rumours, and piles his indignation high. He, the son of Ammon, from the ravished embrace of a Garamantian nymph, built within his broad realms a hundred temples to Jove, and in each temple an altar; there he had consecrated an ever-wakeful fire, the god's unsleeping sentry, a floor thick with victims' blood, and doors

wreathed with particoloured garlands. And he, frenzied in
soul, and stung by the bitter tidings, is said, as he stood
before the altars, with the majesty of Heaven all around him,
to have prayed long and earnestly to Jove with upturned
hands :—'Jove, the Almighty, to whom in this my reign the
Moorish race, feasting on embroidered couches, pour out the
offering of the vintage, seest thou this? or is our dread of
thee, Father, when thou hurlest thy lightnings, an idle panic?
are those aimless fires in the clouds that appal us? have their
confused rumblings no meaning? See here : a woman, who,
wandering in our territories, bought leave to build a petty
town, to whom we made over a strip of land for tillage, with
its rights of lordship, she has rejected an alliance with us,
and received Æneas into her kingdom, to be its lord and hers.
And now that second Paris, with his emasculate following,
a Mæonian cap supporting his chin and his essenced hair,
is enjoying his prize, while we, forsooth, are making offerings
to temples of thine, and keeping alive an idle rumour.'
  Thus as he prayed, his hands grasping the altar, the
almighty one heard him, and turned his eyes to the queenly
city and the guilty pair, lost to their better fame. Then
thus he bespeaks Mercury, and gives him a charge like this :
—'Go, haste, my son, summon the Zephyrs, and float on thy
wings ; address the Dardan chief, who is now dallying in
Tyrian Carthage, and giving no thought to the city which
Destiny makes his own ; carry him my commands through
the flying air. It was not a man like that whom his beauteous mother promised us in him, and on the strength of her
word twice rescued him from the sword of Greece. No, he
was to be one who should govern Italy—Italy, with its brood
of unborn empires, and the war-cry bursting from its heart—
who should carry down a line sprung from the grand fountain-
head of Teucer's blood, and should force the whole world to

N

bow to the laws he makes. If he is fired by no spark of ambition for greatness like this, and will not rear a toilsome fabric for his own praise, is it a father's heart that grudges Ascanius the hills of Rome? What is he building? What does he look to in lingering on among a nation of enemies, with no thought for the great Ausonian family, or for the fields of Lavinium? Away with him to sea! This is our sentence; thus far be our messenger.'

Jove had spoken, and Mercury was preparing to execute the great sire's command: first he binds to his feet his sandals, all of gold, which carry him, uplifted by their pinions, over sea no less than land, with the swiftness of the wind that wafts him. Then he takes his rod—the rod with which he is wont to call up pale spectres from the place of death—to send others on their melancholy way to Tartarus, to give sleep or take it away, and to open the eyes when death is past. With this in hand, he drives the winds before him, and makes a path through the sea of clouds. And now in his flight he espies the crest and the tall sides of Atlas the rugged, who with his top supports the sky—Atlas, whose pine-crowned head, ever wreathed with dark clouds, is buffeted by wind and rain. A mantle of snow wraps his shoulders; rivers tumble from his hoary chin, and his grisly beard is stiff with ice. Here first Cyllene's god poised himself on his wings and rested; then from his stand stooping his whole body, he sent himself headlong to the sea, like a bird which haunting the coast and the fishy rocks flies low, close to the water. Even so was he flying between earth and heaven, between Libya's sandy coast and the winds that swept it, leaving his mother's father behind, himself Cyllene's progeny.

Soon as his winged feet alit among the huts of Carthage, he sees Æneas founding towers and making houses new. A sword was at his side, starred with yellow jaspers, and a

mantle drooped from his shoulders, ablaze with Tyrian purple
—a costly gift which Dido had made, varying the web with
threads of gold. Instantly he assails him :—' And are you at
a time like this laying the foundations of stately Carthage,
and building, like a fond husband, your wife's goodly city, forgetting, alas ! your own kingdom and the cares that should be
yours ? It is no less than the ruler of the gods who sends me
down to you from his bright Olympus—he whose nod sways
heaven and earth; it is he that bids me carry his commands
through the flying air. What are you building ? what do you
look to in squandering your leisure in Libyan land ? If you
are fired by no spark of ambition for the greatness in your view,
and will not rear a toilsome fabric for your own praise, think
of Ascanius rising into youth, think of Iulus, your heir and
your hope, to whom you owe the crown of Italy and the realm
of Rome.' With these words Cyllene's god quitted mortal
sight ere he had well ceased to speak, and vanished away from
the eye into unsubstantial air.

The sight left Æneas dumb and aghast indeed; his hair
stood shudderingly erect ; his speech clave to his throat. He
burns to take flight and leave the land of pleasure, as his ears
ring with the thunder of Heaven's imperious warning. What
—ah ! what is he to do ? with what address can he now dare to
approach the impassioned queen ? what first advances can he
employ ? And thus he despatches his rapid thought hither and
thither, hurrying it east and west, and sweeping every corner of
the field. So balancing, at last he thought this judgment the
best. He calls Mnestheus and Sergestus and brave Serestus ;
bids them quietly get ready the fleet, muster the crews on
the shore, with their arms in their hands, hiding the reason
for so sudden a change. Meantime he, while Dido, kindest
of friends, is in ignorance, deeming love's chain too strong to
be snapped, will feel his way, and find what are the happiest

moments for speech, what the right hold to take of circumstance. At once all gladly obey his command, and are busy on the tasks enjoined.

But the queen (who can cheat a lover's senses?) scented the plot, and caught the first sound of the coming stir, alive to fear in the midst of safety. Fame, as before, the same baleful fiend, whispered in her frenzied ear that the fleet was being equipped and the voyage got ready. She storms in impotence of soul, and, all on fire, goes raving through the city, like a Mænad starting up at the rattle of the sacred emblems, when the triennial orgies lash her with the cry of Bacchus, and Cithæron's yell calls her into the night. At length she thus bespeaks Æneas, unaddressed by him :—

'To hide, yes, hide your enormous crime, perfidious wretch, did you hope *that* might be done—to steal away in silence from my realm? Has our love no power to keep you? has our troth, once plighted, none, nor she whom you doom to a cruel death, your Dido? Nay, are you fitting out your fleet with winter's sky overhead, and hastening to cross the deep in the face of all the northern winds, hard-hearted as you are? Why, suppose you were not seeking a strange clime and a home you know not—suppose old Troy were still standing —would even Troy draw you to seek her across a billowy sea? Flying, and from me! By the tears I shed, and by your plighted hand, since my own act, alas! has left me nought else to plead—by our union—by the nuptial rites thus prefaced—if I have ever deserved well of you, or aught of mine ever gave you pleasure—have pity on a falling house, and strip off, I conjure you, if prayer be not too late, the mind that clothes you. It is owing to you that the Libyan tribes and the Nomad chiefs hate me, that my own Tyrians are estranged; owing to you, yes, you, that my woman's honour has been put out, and that which was my one passport to immortality, my former fame. To whom are you abandoning a dying woman, my guest?—since the name of husband has dwindled to that. Why do I live any longer?—to give my brother Pygmalion time to batter down my walls, or Iarbas the Moor to carry me away captive? Had I but borne any offspring of you before your flight, were there some tiny Æneas to play in my hall, and remind me of you, though but in look, I should not then feel utterly captive and forlorn.'

She ceased. He all the while, at Jove's command, was keeping his eyes unmoved, and shutting up in his heart his great love. At length he answers in brief:—'Fair queen, name all the claims to gratitude you can. I shall never gainsay one, nor will the thought of Elissa ever be unwelcome while memory lasts, while breath animates this frame. A few words I will say, as the case admits. I never counted— do not dream it—on stealthily concealing my flight. I never came with a bridegroom's torch in my hand, nor was this the alliance to which I agreed. For me, were the Fates to suffer me to live under a star of my own choosing, and to make with care the terms I would, the city of Troy, first of all the dear remains of what was mine, would claim my tendance. Priam's tall roof-tree would still be standing, and my hand would have built a restored Pergamus, to solace the vanquished. But now to princely Italy Grynean Apollo, to Italy his Lycian oracles bid me repair. There is my heart, there my fatherland. If you are riveted here by the sight of your stately Carthage, a daughter of Phœnicia by a Libyan town, why, I would ask, should jealousy forbid Teucrians to settle in Ausonian land? We, like you, have the right of looking for a foreign realm. There is my father Anchises, oft as night's dewy shades invest the earth, oft as the fiery stars arise, warning me in dreams and appalling me by his troubled presence. There is my son Ascanius, and the wrongs heaped on his dear head every day that I rob him of the crown of Hesperia, and of the land that fate makes his. Now, too, the messenger of the gods, sent down from Jove himself (I swear by both our lives) has brought me orders through the flying air. With my own eyes I saw the god in clear daylight entering the walls, and took in his words with the ears that hear you now. Cease then to harrow up both our souls by your reproaches : my quest of Italy is not of my own motion.'

Long ere he had done this speech she was glaring at him askance, rolling her eyes this way and that, and scanning the whole man with her silent glances, and thus she bursts forth all ablaze :—' No goddess was mother of yours, no Dardanus the head of your line, perfidious wretch !—no, your parent was Caucasus, rugged and craggy, and Hyrcanian tigresses put their breasts to your lips. For why should I suppress aught ? or for what worse evil hold myself in reserve ? Did he groan when I wept ? did he move those hard eyes ? did he yield and shed tears, or pity her that loved him ? What first ? what last ? Now, neither Juno, queen of all, nor Jove, the almighty Father, eyes us with impartial regard. Nowhere is there aught to trust—nowhere. A shipwrecked beggar, I welcomed him, and madly gave him a share of my realm ; his lost fleet, his crews, I brought back from death's door. Ah ! Fury sets me on fire, and whirls me round ! Now, prophet Apollo, now the Lycian oracles. Now the messenger of the gods, sent down by Jove himself, bears his grim bidding through the air ! Aye, of course, that is the employment of the powers above, those the cares that break their repose ! I retain not your person, nor refute your talk. Go, chase Italy with the winds at your back ; look for realms with the whole sea between you. I have hope that on the rocks midway, if the gods are as power- ful as they are good, you will drain the cup of punishment, with Dido's name ever on your lips. I will follow you with

murky fires when I am far away ; and when cold death shall
have parted soul and body, my shade shall haunt you everywhere. Yes, wretch, you shall suffer. I shall hear it—the
news will reach me down among the dead.' So saying, she
snaps short her speech, and flies with loathing from the daylight, and breaks and rushes from his sight, leaving him
hesitating, and fearing, and thinking of a thousand things to
say. Her maidens support her, and carry her sinking frame
into her marble chamber, and lay her on her bed.

But good Æneas, though yearning to solace and soothe her
agonised spirit, and by his words to check the onset of
sorrow, with many a groan, his whole soul upheaved by
the force of love, goes nevertheless about the commands of
Heaven, and repairs to his fleet. The Teucrians redouble
their efforts, and along the whole range of the shore drag
their tall ships down. The keels are careened and floated.
They carry oars with their leaves still on, and timber un-
fashioned as it stood in the woods, so strong their eagerness to fly. You may see them all in motion, streaming
from every part of the city. Even as ants when they are
sacking a huge heap of wheat, provident of winter days, and
laying up the plunder in their stores ; a black column is seen
moving through the plain, and they convey their booty along
the grass in a narrow path : some are putting their shoulders
to the big grains, and pushing them along ; others are rallying
the force and punishing the stragglers ; the whole track is in
a glow of work. What were your feelings then, poor Dido,
at a sight like this ! How deep the groans you heaved, when
you looked out from your lofty tower on a beach all seething
and swarming, and saw the whole sea before you deafened
with that hubbub of voices ! Tyrant love ! what force dost
thou not put on human hearts ? Again she has to condescend
to tears, again to use the weapons of entreaty, and bow her

spirit in suppliance under love's yoke, lest she should have left aught untried, and be rushing on a needless death.

'Anna, you see there is hurrying all over the shore—they are met from every side; the canvas is already wooing the gale, and the joyful sailors have wreathed the sterns. If I have had the foresight to anticipate so heavy a blow, I shall have the power to bear it too, my sister. Yet, Anna, in my misery, perform me this one service. You, and you only, the perfidious man was wont to make his friend—aye, even to trust you with his secret thoughts. You, and you only, know the subtle approaches to his heart, and the times of essaying them. Go, then, my sister, and supplicate our haughty foe. Tell him I was no party to the Danaan league at Aulis to destroy the Trojan nation; I sent no ships to Pergamus; I never disinterred his father Anchises, his dust or his spirit. Why will he not let my words sink down into his obdurate ears? Whither is he hurrying? Let him grant this last boon to her who loves him so wildly; let him wait till the way is smoothed for his flight, and there are winds to waft him. I am not asking him now to renew our old vows which he has forsworn. I am not asking him to forego his fair Latium, and resign his crown. I entreat but a few vacant hours, a respite and breathing-space for my passion, till my fortune shall have taught baffled love how to grieve. This is my last request of you. Oh, pity your poor sister!— a request which when granted shall be returned with interest in death.'

Such was her appeal—such the wailing which her afflicted sister bears to him, and bears again; but no wailing moves him, no words find him a gentle listener. Fate bars the way, and Heaven closes the hero's relenting ears. Even as an aged oak, still hale and strong, which Alpine winds, blowing now here, now there, strive emulously to uproot—a loud noise is

heard, and, as the stem rocks, heaps of leaves pile the ground;
but the tree cleaves firmly to the cliff; high as its head
strikes into the air, so deep its root strikes down to the abyss—
even thus the hero is assailed on all sides by a storm of words:
his mighty breast thrills through and through with agony; but
his mind is unshaken, and tears are showered in vain.

Then at last, maddened by her destiny, poor Dido prays
for death: heaven's vault is a weariness to look on. To confirm her in pursuing her intent, and closing her eyes on the
sun, she saw, as she was laying her offerings on the incense-
steaming altars—horrible to tell—the sacred liquor turn
black, and the streams of wine curdle into loathly gore. This
appearance she told to none, not even to her sister. Moreover, there was in her palace a marble chapel to her former
husband, to which she used to pay singular honours, wreathing it with snowy fillets and festal boughs; from it she
thought she heard a voice, the accents of the dead man calling her, when the darkness of night was shrouding the earth;
and on the roof a lonely owl in funereal tones kept complaining again and again, and drawing out wailingly its
protracted notes; and a thousand predictions of seers of
other days come back on her, terrifying her with their awful
warnings. When she dreams, there is Æneas himself driving
her in furious chase: she seems always being left alone to
herself, always pacing companionless on a never-ending road,
and looking for her Tyrians in a realm without inhabitants—
like Pentheus, when in frenzy he sees troops of Furies, and
two suns, and a double Thebes rising round him; or Agamemnon's Orestes rushing over the stage, as he flies from his
mother, who is armed with torches and deadly snakes, while
the avenging fiends sit couched on the threshold.

So when, spent with agony, she gave conception to the
demon, and resolved on death, she settled with herself time

and means, and thus bespoke her grieving sister, her face
disguising her intent, and hope smiling on her brow :—
' Dearest, I have found a way—wish me joy, as a sister
should—to bring him back to me, or to loose me from the
love which binds me to him. Hard by the bound of ocean
and the setting sun lies the extreme Ethiopian clime, where
mighty Atlas turns round on his shoulders the pole, studded
with burning stars. From that clime, I have heard of a
priestess of the Massylian race, once guardian of the temple
of the Hesperides, who used to give the dragon his food, and
so preserve the sacred boughs on the tree, sprinkling for him
moist honey and drowsy poppy-seed. She, by her spells,
undertakes to release souls at her pleasure, while into others
she shoots cruel pangs ; she stops the water in the river-bed,
and turns back the stars in their courses, and calls ghosts
from realms of night. You will see the earth bellowing
under you, and the ashes coming down from the mountain-
top. By the gods I swear, dearest sister, by you and your
dear life, that unwillingly I gird on the weapons of magic.
Do you, in the privacy of the inner court, build a pile to the
open sky ; lay on it the arms which that godless man left
hanging in the chamber, and all his doffed apparel, and the
nuptial bed which was my undoing. To destroy every
memorial of the hateful wretch is my pleasure, and the
priestess' bidding.' This said, she is silent—paleness over-
spreads her face. Yet Anna does not dream that these strange
rites are a veil to hide her sister's death : she cannot grasp
frenzy like that ; she fears no darker day than that of their
mourning for Sychæus, and so she does her bidding.

But the queen, when the pile had been built in the heart
of the palace to the open sky, a giant mass of pine-wood and
hewn oak, spans the place with garlands, and crowns it with
funeral boughs. High above it on the couch she sets the

doffed apparel, and the sword that had been left, and the image of the false lover, knowing too well what was to come. Altars rise here and there; the priestess, with hair dishevelled, thunders out the roll of three hundred gods, Erebus and Chaos, and Hecate with her triple form—the three faces borne by maiden Dian. See! she has sprinkled water, brought, so she feigns, from Avernus' spring, and she is getting green downy herbs, cropped by moonlight with brazen shears, whose sap is the milk of deadly poison, and the love-charm, torn from the brow of the new-born foal, ere the mother could snatch it. Dido herself, with salted cake and pure hands at the altars, one foot unshod, her vest ungirdled, makes her dying appeal to the gods and to the stars who share Fate's counsels, begging the powers, if any there be, that watch, righteous and unforgetting, over ill-yoked lovers, to hear her prayer.

It was night, and overtoiled mortality throughout the earth was enjoying peaceful slumber; the woods were at rest, and the raging waves—the hour when the stars are rolling midway in their smooth courses, when all the land is hushed, cattle, and gay-plumed birds, haunters far and wide of clear waters and rough forest-ground, lapped in sleep with stilly night overhead, their troubles assuaged, their hearts dead to care. Not so the vexed spirit of Phœnicia's daughter; she never relaxes into slumber, or welcomes the night to eye or bosom; sorrow doubles peal on peal; once more love swells, and storms, and surges, with a mighty tempest of passion. Thus, then, she plunges into speech, and whirls her thoughts about thus in the depth of her soul:—'What am I about? Am I to make fresh proof of my former suitors, with scorn before me? Must I stoop to court Nomad bridegrooms, whose offered hand I have spurned so often? Well, then, shall I follow the fleet of Ilion, and be at the beck and call of Teucrian masters?

Is it that they think with pleasure on the succour once rendered them? that gratitude for past kindness yet lives in their memory? But even if I wished it, who will give me leave, or admit the unwelcome guest to his haughty ships? Are you so ignorant, poor wretch? Do you not yet understand the perjury of the race of Laomedon? What then? Shall I fly alone, and swell the triumph of their crews? or shall I put to sea, with the Tyrians and the whole force of my people at my back, dragging those whom it was so hard to uproot from their Sidonian home again into the deep, and bidding them spread sail to the winds? No!—die the death you have merited, and let the sword put your sorrow to flight. You, sister, are the cause; overmastered by my tears, you heap this deadly fuel on my flame, and fling me upon my enemy. Why could I not forswear wedlock, and live an unblamed life in savage freedom, nor meddle with troubles like these? Why did I not keep the faith I vowed to the ashes of Sychæus?' Such were the reproaches that broke from that bursting heart.

Meanwhile Æneas, resolved on his journey, was slumbering in his vessel's tall stern, all being now in readiness. To him a vision of the god appearing again with the same countenance, presented itself as he slept, and seemed to give this second warning—the perfect picture of Mercury, his voice, his blooming hue, his yellow locks, and the youthful grace of his frame: —'Goddess-born, at a crisis like this can you slumber on? Do you not see the wall of danger which is fast rising round you, infatuate that you are, nor hear the favouring whisper of the western gale? She is revolving in her bosom thoughts of craft and cruelty, resolved on death, and surging with a changeful tempest of passion. Will you not haste away while haste is in your power? You will look on a sea convulsed with ships, an array of fierce torch-fires, a coast glowing with flame, if the dawn-goddess shall have found you loitering here on land. Quick !—burst through delay. A thing of moods and changes is woman ever.' He said, and was lost in the darkness of night.

At once Æneas, scared by the sudden apparition, springs up from sleep, and rouses his comrades. 'Wake in a moment, my friends, and seat you on the benches. Unfurl the sails with all speed. See ! here is a god sent down from heaven on high, urging us again to hasten our flight, and cut the twisted cables. Yes ! sacred power, we follow thee, whoever thou art, and a second time with joy obey thy behest. Be thou with us, and graciously aid us, and let propitious stars be ascendant in the sky.' So saying, he snatches from the scabbard his flashing sword, and with the drawn blade cuts the hawsers. The spark flies from man to man ; they scour, they scud, they have left the shore behind ; you cannot see the water for ships. With strong strokes they dash the foam, and sweep the blue.

And now Aurora was beginning to sprinkle the earth with fresh light, rising from Tithonus' saffron couch. Soon as the queen from her watch-tower saw the grey dawn brighten, and · the fleet moving on with even canvas, and coast and haven forsaken, with never an oar left, thrice and again smiting her beauteous breast with her hands, and rending her golden locks, 'Great Jupiter !' cries she, 'shall he go ? Shall a chance-comer boast of having flouted our realm ? Will they not get their arms at once, and give chase from all the town, and pull, some of them, the ships from the docks ? Away ! bring fire ; quick ! get darts, ply oars ! What am I saying ? Where am I ? What madness turns my brain ? Wretched Dido ! do your sins sting you now ? They should have done so then, when you were giving your crown away. What truth ! what fealty !—the man who, they say, carries about with him the gods of his country, and took up on his shoulders his old worn-out father! Might I not have caught and torn him piecemeal, and scattered him to the waves?—destroyed his friends, aye, and his own Ascanius, and served up the boy for his father's meal? But the chance of a battle would have been doubtful. Let it have been. I was to die, and whom had I to fear? I would have flung torches into his camp, filled his decks with flame, consumed son and sire and the whole line, and leapt myself upon the pile. Sun, whose torch shows thee all that is done on earth, and thou, Juno, revealer and witness of these stirrings of the heart, and Hecate, whose name is yelled in civic crossways by night, avenging fiends, and gods of dying Elissa, listen to this! Let your power stoop to ills that call for it, and hear what I now pray! If it must needs be that the accursed wretch gain the haven and float to shore—if such the requirement of Jove's destiny, such the fixed goal—yet grant that, harassed by the sword and battle of a warlike nation, a wanderer from his own confines, torn from his Iulus' arms, he may pray for succour, and see his friends dying miserably round him! Nor when he has yielded to the terms of an unjust peace, may he enjoy his crown, or the life he loves; but may he fall before his time, and lie unburied in the midst of the plain! This is my prayer—these the last accents that flow from me with my life-blood. And you, my Tyrians, let your hatred persecute the race and people for all time to come. Be this the offering you send down to my ashes: never be there love or league between nation and nation. Arise from my bones, my unknown avenger, destined with fire and sword to pursue the Dardanian settlers, now or in after-days, whenever strength shall be given! Let coast be at war with coast, water with wave, army with army; fight they, and their sons, and their sons' sons!'

Thus she said, as she whirled her thought to this side and

that, seeking at once to cut short the life she now abhorred. Then briefly she spoke to Barce, Sychæus' nurse, for her own was left in her old country, in the black ashes of the grave : —'Fetch me here, dear nurse, my sister Anna. Bid her hasten to sprinkle herself with water from the stream, and bring with her the cattle and the atoning offerings prescribed. Let her come with these; and do you cover your brow with the holy fillet. The sacrifice to Stygian Jove, which I have duly commenced and made ready, I wish now to accomplish, and with it the end of my sorrows, giving to the flame the pile that pillows the Dardan head !' She said : the nurse began to quicken her pace with an old wife's zeal.

But Dido, wildered and maddened by her enormous resolve, rolling her bloodshot eye, her quivering cheeks stained with fiery streaks, and pale with the shadow of death, bursts the door of the inner palace, and frantically climbs the tall pile, and unsheathes the Dardan sword, a gift procured for a far different end. Then, after surveying the Trojan garments and the bed, too well known, and pausing awhile to weep and think, she pressed her bosom to the couch, and uttered her last words :—

'Relics, once darlings of mine, while Fate and Heaven gave leave, receive this my soul, and release me from these my sorrows. I have lived my life—the course assigned me by Fortune is run, and now the august phantom of Dido shall pass underground. I have built a splendid city. I have seen my walls completed. In vengeance for a husband, I have punished a brother that hated me—blest, ah ! blest beyond human bliss, if only Dardan ships had never touched coast of ours !' She spoke—and kissing the couch : 'Is it to be death without revenge ? But be it death,' she cries—'this, this is the road by which I love to pass to the shades. Let the heartless Dardanian's eyes drink in this flame from the deep, and let him carry with him the presage of my death.'

She spoke, and even while she was yet speaking, her attendants see her fallen on the sword, the blade spouting blood,
and her hands dabbled in it. Their shrieks rise to the lofty
roof; Fame runs wild through the convulsed city. With
wailing and groaning, and screams of women, the palace rings;
the sky resounds with mighty cries and beating of breasts—
even as if the foe were to burst the gates and topple down
Carthage or ancient Tyre, and the infuriate flame were leaping
from roof to roof among the dwellings of men and gods.

Her sister heard it. Breathless and frantic, with wild speed,
disfiguring her cheeks with her nails, her bosom with her fists,
she bursts through the press, and calls by name on the dying
queen:—'Was this your secret, sister? Were you plotting
to cheat me? Was this what your pile was preparing for me,
your fires, and your altars? What should a lone heart grieve
for first? Did you disdain your sister's company in death?
You should have called me to share your fate—the same keen
sword-pang, the same hour, should have been the end of both.
And did these hands build the pile, this voice call on the gods
of our house, that you might lie there, while I, hard-hearted
wretch, was away? Yes, sister, you have destroyed yourself
and me, the people and the elders of Sidon, and your own fair
city. Let in the water to the wounds; let me cleanse them,
and if any remains of breath be still flickering, catch them in
my mouth!' As she·thus spoke, she was at the top of the
lofty steps, and was embracing and fondling in her bosom her
dying sister, and stanching with her robe the black streams of
blood. Dido strives to raise her heavy eyes, and sinks down
again, the deep stab gurgles in her breast. Thrice, with an
effort, she lifted and reared herself up on her elbow; thrice, she
fell back on the couch, and with helpless wandering eyes aloft
in the sky, sought for the light and groaned when she found it.

Then Juno almighty, in compassion for her lengthened agony

and her trouble in dying, sent down Iris from Olympus to part the struggling soul and its prison of flesh. For, as she was dying, not in the course of fate, nor for any crime of hers, but in mere misery, before her time, the victim of sudden frenzy, not yet had Proserpine carried off a lock of her yellow hair, and thus doomed her head to Styx and the place of death. So then Iris glides down the sky with saffron wings dew-besprent, trailing a thousand various colours in the face of the sun, and alights above her head. ' This I am bidden to bear away as an offering to Pluto, and hereby set you free from the body.' So saying, she stretches her hand and cuts the lock : at once all heat parts from the frame, and the life has passed into air.

BOOK V.

ÆNEAS, meantime, was well on his road, holding with set purpose on the watery way, and cutting through billows gloomed by the North wind, with eyes ever and anon turned back to the city, which poor Elissa's funeral flame now began to illumine. What cause has lit up a blaze so mighty they cannot tell; but as they think of the cruel pangs which follow outrage done on great love, and their knowledge what a frantic woman can do, the Teucrian hearts are swept through a train of dismal presage.

Soon as the ships gained the mid-ocean, and no land met the view any more—waters everywhere and everywhere skies—a dark rain-cloud arose and stood over the hero's head, charged with night and winter tempest, and darkness ruffled the billow's crest. Palinurus himself, the pilot, was heard from the lofty stern :—'Ah ! why has such an army of storms encompassed the heaven? What hast thou for us now, old Father Neptune?' No sooner said than he bids them gather up the tackle and ply the lusty oar, and shifts the sheet to the wind, and speaks thus :—'Noble Æneas, though Jove himself were to pledge me his faith, I could not hope to reach Italy with a sky like this. The winds shift and storm cross-wise, ever rising from the blackening West, and the mist is being massed into clouds. We cannot make head against them, or struggle as we should. Well, since Fortune exerts her tyranny, let us follow, and turn our faces as she pulls the

rein. I take it, too, we are not far from the friendly brother-
coast of your Eryx, and the havens of Sicania, if my memory
serves me as I retrace the stars I watched long ago.' To him
good Æneas :—'I have seen myself this long time that such
is the winds' will, and all your counter-efforts vain. Turn
sail and ship. Could any land indeed be welcomer, any that
I would sooner choose to harbour my weary ships, than the
land which keeps for me above ground the Dardan Acestes,
and laps in its breast the bones of my sire Anchises?' This
said, they make for the haven ; favouring zephyrs swell their
sail, the fleet rides swiftly over the flood, and at last they
touch with joy the strand they know so well.

From a hill's tall top Acestes had marked with wonder afar
off the new arrival, and the friendly vessels ; up he runs, all
in the savage trim of hunting-spear and Libyan bearskin—
Acestes, son of a Trojan mother by the river Crimisus. The
ancestral blood quickens in his veins as he gives them joy of
their safe arrival, welcomes them with the plenty of rustic
royalty, and soothes their weariness with every kind appliance.

On the morrow, when the first dawn of the bright day-
spring had put the stars to flight, Æneas calls his comrades
to a gathering from all the shore, and standing on a heaped
mound bespeaks them thus :—'Mighty sons of Dardanus,
race of Heaven's high parentage, the months are all past and
the year has fulfilled its cycle, since we gave to the earth the
earthly relics, the ashes of my deified sire, and consecrated
the altars of mourning. And now, if I err not, the very day
is here—that day which for me shall ever be a day of weeping,
ever a day of honour, since you, ye gods, have willed it so.
Though this day were to find me among the Gætulian Syrtes,
a homeless wanderer—were it to surprise me in the Argive
main or in the streets of Mycenæ—still would I pay my
yearly vows and the pomp of solemn observance, and would

pile the altars with their proper gifts. And now, behold, by an unsought chance we are standing—not in truth I deem without the providence, the beckoning hand of Heaven—at the very grave, the buried ashes of my sire, driven as we are into this friendly haven. Come, then, solemnise we all the glad celebration; pray we for winds, and may He be pleased that I should offer these rites yearly in a city of my own building, in a temple dedicated to himself. Two heads of oxen Acestes, like a true son of Troy, gives you for each ship; call to the feasts the gods of the hearth, both those of our fathers and those worshipped by Acestes our host. Furthermore, if the ninth day hence the dawn-goddess restore to mortals the genial light, and make the world visible with sunshine, I will set up, first of all, for all Teucrian comers, a match among our swift fleet; then let him that is light of foot, and him that, glorying in his strength, bears himself more proudly with the dart and the flying arrow, or has confidence to join battle in gauntlets of raw hide, let one and all be here, and look for the prizes that victory earns. Give me your auspicious voices, and bind your brows with green.'

This spoken, he shrouds his own brows with his mother's myrtle. So does Helymus, so does veteran Acestes, so young Ascanius—so the whole multitude of warriors. He was already on his way from the council to the tomb with many thousands round him, the centre of a great company. Here in due libation he pours on the ground two bowls of the wine-god's pure juice, two of new milk, two of sacrificial blood; he flings bright flowers, and makes this utterance :—' Hail to thee, blessed sire, once more! hail to you, ashes of one rescued in vain, spirit and shade of my father! It was not in Fate that thou shouldst journey with me to the Italian frontier and the fields of Destiny, or see the Ausonian Tiber, whatever that name may import.' He had said this, when from the

depth of the grave a smooth shining serpent trailed along seven
spires, seven volumes of giant length, coiling peacefully round
the tomb and gliding between the altars : dark green flecks
were on its back ; its scales were all ablaze with spots of golden
lustre, even as the bow in the clouds showers a thousand various
colours in the face of the sun. Æneas stood wonder-struck :
the creature, winding its long column among the dishes and
the polished goblets, tasted of the viands, and then, innocent
of harm, re-entered the tomb at its base, leaving the altars
where its mouth had been. Quickened by this, the hero
resumes the work of homage to his sire, not knowing whether
to think this the genius of the spot or his father's menial spirit:
duly he slays two young sheep, two swine, two black-skinned
bullocks ; again and again he pours goblets of wine, again
and again he calls on the soul of great Anchises and the shade
loosed from Acheron's prison. His comrades, too, each according to his means, give glad offerings—they pile the altars,
they slay the bullocks ; others in their function set on the
cauldrons, and, stretched along the grass, hold the spits over
the embers and roast the flesh.

And now the expected day was come ; the steeds of Phaethon
were ushering in the goddess of the ninth dawn through a
heaven of clear light ; the rumoured spectacle and the great
name of Acestes had brought the neighbouring people from
their homes ; the holiday crowd was flooding the shore, to
gaze on the family of Æneas, and some too ready to dispute
the prizes. First, in sight of all, the gifts are bestowed in the
midst of the ring—hallowed tripods and verdant chaplets, and
palms, the conquerors' special guerdon—armour and raiment
of purple dye—a talent's weight of silver and gold ; and from
a mound in the centre the shrill trumpet proclaims the
sports begun. The first contest, waged with labouring oars, is
entered by four ships, the flower of the entire fleet. There is

Mnestheus, with his fiery crew, speeding along the swift Shark —Mnestheus, hereafter a prince of Italy, who gives his name to the Memmian line; there is Gyas with his monster Chimæra, that monster mass [1] which three tiers of stout Dardans are pulling on, the oars rising in a triple bank; Sergestus, from whom the Sergian house gains the name it keeps, sails in the mighty Centaur; and in the sea-green Scylla Cloanthus, your great forefather, Cluentius of Rome.

At a distance in the sea is a rock, over against the spray-washed shore—sometimes covered by the swelling waves that beat on it, when the wintry north winds hide the stars from view—in a calm it rests in peace, and rises over the unruffled waters, a broad table-land, a welcome basking-ground for the sea-bird. Here Æneas set up a green stem of leafy oak with his own royal hand—a sign for the sailors, that they might know whence to begin their return, and where to double round their long voyage. Then they choose their places by lot: there are the captains on the sterns, a glorious sight, gleaming far with gold and purple; the crews are crowned with thick poplar leaves, and their bare shoulders shine with the oil that has rubbed them. They seat them on the benches, every arm is strained on the oar—straining they expect the signal, and their beating hearts are drained at each stroke by panting fear and high-strung ambition. Then, when the shrill trumpet has uttered its voice, all in a moment dart forward from their bounds, the seaman's shout pierces the sky; the upturned seas foam as the arm is drawn back to the chest. With measured strokes they plough their furrows; the water is one yawning chasm, rent asunder by the oar and the pointed beak. Not such the headlong speed when in two-horse race the chariots dash into the plain and pour along from their floodgates, or when the drivers shake the streaming

---

[1] A caret in the MS. notes the omission of *Urbis opus.*—[ED.]

reins over their flying steeds, and hang floating over the lash. Then plaudits, and shouts of manly voices, and the clamorous fervour of the backers, make the whole woodland ring ; the pent-up shores keep the sound rolling ; the hills send back the blows of the noise. See ! flying ahead of the rest, gliding over the first water in the midst of crowd and hubbub, is Gyas ; next him comes Cloanthus, with better oars, but the slow pinewood's weight keeps him back. After them at equal distance the Shark and the Centaur strive to win precedence. And now the Shark has it. Now she is beaten and passed by the Centaur. Now the two ride abreast stem to stem, cutting with their long keels the salt waves. And now they were nearing the rock, and the goal was just in their grasp, when Gyas, the leader, the victor of the halfway-passage, calls aloud to his ship's pilot Mencetes :—'Whither away so far to my right ? Steer us hither ; hug the shore ; let the oar-blade graze the cliffs on the left ; leave the deep to others.' Thus he ; but Mencetes, afraid of hidden rocks, keeps turning the prow well towards the sea. 'Whither away from the right course ? Make for the rocks, Mencetes !' shouted Gyas again ; and see ! looking back, he perceives Cloanthus gaining on him close behind. Between Gyas' ship and the sounding rocks he threads his way to the left, steering inward, and in an instant passes the winner, leaves the goal behind, and gains the smooth open sea. Grief turned the youth's very marrow to flame, nor were his cheeks free from tears ; he seizes the slow Mencetes, forgetting at once his own decency and his crew's safety, and flings him headlong from the lofty stern into the sea. Himself becomes their guide at the helm, himself their pilot, cheering on the rowers, and turning the rudder to the shore. But Mencetes, when at last disgorged from the bottom of the sea, heavy with age, and with his dripping clothes all hanging about him, climbs the cliff-top, and seats himself on a dry rock. The Teucrians laughed as he was falling, laughed as he was swimming, and now they laugh as he discharges from his chest the draught of brine. Then sprung up an ecstatic hope in the two last, Sergestus and Mnestheus, of passing the lagging Gyas. Sergestus gets the choice of water and comes nearer the rock—not first, however, he by a whole vessel's length—half his ship is ahead, half is overlapped by the beak of his rival, the Shark. Mnestheus walks through the ship among the crew and cheers them on. 'Now, now rise to your oars, old Hector's men, whom I chose to follow me at Troy's last gasp; now put out the strength, the spirit I saw you exert in the Gætulian Syrtes, the Ionian Sea, the entangling waves of Malea. It is not the first place I look for. I am not the man; this is no struggle for victory—yet might it be!—but conquest is for them, Neptune, to whom thou givest it. Let our shame be to come in last; be this your victory, friends, to keep off disgrace.' Straining every nerve, they throw themselves forward; their mighty strokes make the brazen keel quiver, the ground flies from under them; thick panting shakes their limbs, their parched throats; sweat flows down in streams.

A mere chance gave them the wished pre-eminence; for while Sergestus, blind with passion, keeps driving his prow towards the rock nearer and nearer, and pressing through the narrow passage, his ill star entangled him with a projecting crag. The cliffs were jarred, the oars cracked as they met the sharp flint, and the prow hung where it had lodged. Up spring the sailors with loud shout, while the ship stands still. They bring out their iron-shod poles and pointed boat-hooks, and pick up the broken oars in the water. But Mnestheus, rejoicing, and keener for success, with quick plashing oars, and the winds at his call, makes for the seas that shelve to the coast and speeds along the clear expanse. Like as a dove, suddenly startled in a cave, where in the hollow of the rock are her home and her loved nestlings, issues out to fly over the plain, clapping loud her pinions in terror in the cell—then, gliding smooth through the tranquil air, she winnows her liquid way without a motion of her rapid wings—so with Mnestheus, so the Shark, flying of herself, cuts through the last water of the course, so the mere impulse bears her speeding on. First he takes leave of Sergestus, struggling with the tall rock and the shallow water, and in vain calling for help, and learning to run along with broken oars. Then he comes up with Gyas and the great monster Chimæra itself; she yields, because deprived of her pilot. And now there remains Cloanthus alone, just at the very end of the race; him he makes for, and presses on him with all the force of effort. Then, indeed, the shouting redoubles—all lend their goodwill to spur on the second man, and the sky echoes with the din. These think it shame to lose the glory that they have won, the prize that is already their own, and would fain barter life for renown; these are feeding on success, they feel strong because they feel that they are thought strong. And perhaps their beaks would have been even and the prize divided, had not Cloanthus, stretching out both hands over the deep, breathed a prayer and called the gods to hear his vow :—' Powers whose is the rule of ocean, whose waters I ride, for you with glad heart will I lead to your altars on this shore a snow-white bull, as a debtor should ; I will throw the entrails afar into the salt waves, and pour out a clear stream of wine.' He said, and deep down among the billows there heard him all the Nereids and Phorcus' train, and maiden Panopea, and father Portunus himself, with his own great hand, pushed the ship as she moved ; fleeter than southwind or winged arrow he flies to the land and is lodged already deep in the haven.

Then Anchises' son, duly summoning the whole company,
proclaims by a loud-voiced herald Cloanthus conqueror, and
drapes his brow with green bay; he gives each crew a gift
at its choice, three bullocks, and wine, and the present of
a great talent of silver. To the captains themselves he
further gives especial honours, to the conqueror a gold-
broïdered scarf, round which runs a length of Melibœan
purple with a double Mæander; enwoven therein is the royal
boy on leafy Ida, plying the swift stag with the javelin
and the chase, keen of eye, his chest seeming to heave;
then, swooping down from Ida, the bearer of Jove's armour
has snatched him up aloft in his crooked talons, while his
aged guardians are stretching in vain their hands to heaven,
and the barking of the hounds streams furious to the sky.
But for him whose prowess gained him the second place
there is a cuirass of linked chain mail, three-threaded with
gold, which the hero himself had stripped with a conqueror's
hand from Demoleos on swift Simois' bank under the shadow
of Troy; this he gives the warrior for his own, a glory and
a defence in the battle. Scarce could the two servants,
Phegeus and Sagaris, support its many folds, pushing shoulder
to shoulder; yet Demoleos, in his day, with it on his breast,
used to drive the Trojans in flight before him. The third
present he makes a pair of brazen cauldrons, and two cups of
wrought silver, rough with fretwork.

And now all had received their presents, and each, glorying
in his treasure, was walking along with purple festooning
round his brows, when Sergestus, at last with great pain dis-
lodged from the cruel rock, his oars lost and one whole side
crippled, was seen propelling among jeers his inglorious vessel.
Like as a serpent surprised on the highway, whom a brazen
wheel has driven across, or a traveller, heavy of hand, has left
half dead and mangled by a stone, writhes its long body in

ineffectual flight, its upper part all fury, its eyes blazing, its hissing throat reared aloft, the lower part, disabled by the wound, clogs it as it wreaths its spires and doubles upon its own joints. Such was the oarage with which the ship pushed herself slowly along : she makes sail, however, and enters the haven with canvas flying. To Sergestus Æneas gives the present he had promised, delighted to see the ship rescued and the crew brought back. His prize is a slave, not unversed in Pallas' labours, Pholœ, Cretan born, with twin sons at her breast.

This match dismissed, good Æneas takes his way to a grassy plain, surrounded on all sides with woods and sloping hills : in the middle of the valley was a circle, as of a theatre ; thither it was that the hero repaired with many thousands, the centre of a vast assembly, and sat on a raised throne. Then he invites, with hope of reward, the bold spirits who may wish to contend in the swift foot-race, and sets up the prizes. Candidates flock from all sides, Teucrian and Sicanian mixed. Nisus and Euryalus the foremost. Euryalus conspicuous for beauty and blooming youth, Nisus for the pure love he bore the boy ; following them came Diores, a royal scion of Priam's illustrious stock ; then Salius and Patron together, one from Acarnania, the other from Tegea, an Arcadian by blood ; next two Trinacrian youths, Helymus and Panopes, trained foresters, comrades of their elder friend, Acestes, and many others, whom dim tradition leaves in darkness. As they crowd round him, Æneas bespeaks them thus :—' Hear what I have to say, and give the heed of a glad heart. No one of this company shall go away unguerdoned by me. I will give a pair of Gnossian darts, shining with polished steel, and an axe chased with silver for the hand to wield. This honour all shall obtain alike. The three first shall receive prizes, and shall wear also wreaths of yellow-green olive. Let the first, as

conqueror, have a horse, full decorated with trappings; the
second an Amazonian quiver, full of Thracian shafts, with a
belt of broad gold to encompass it, and a buckle of a polished
jewel to fasten it; let the third go away content with this
Argive helmet.' This said, they take their places, and suddenly, on hearing the signal, dash into the course, and leave
the barrier behind, pouring on like a burst of rain, their
eyes fixed on the goal. First of all, away goes Nisus, his
limbs flying far before all the rest, swifter than wind and
winged thunderbolt; next to him, but next at a long distance,
follows Salius; then, at a shorter space, Euryalus third.
After Euryalus comes Helymus; close on him, see! flies
Diores, heel touching heel and shoulder shoulder: were the
course but longer, he would be shooting on and darting beyond
him, and turning a doubtful race to a victory.

Now they were just at the end of the course, all panting
as they reached the goal, when Nisus, the ill-starred, slides in
a puddle of blood, which lay there just as it had been spilt
after a sacrifice of bullocks, soaking the ground and the growing grass. Poor youth! just in the moment of triumph,
he could not keep his sliddery footing on the soil he trod,
but fell flat in' the very middle of unclean ordure and sacrificial gore. But he forgot not Euryalus—forgot not his love
—no! he threw himself in Salius' way, rising in that slippery place—and Salius lay there too, flung on the puddled
floor. Forth darts Euryalus, and gains the first place, a
winner, thanks to his friend, cheered in his flight by plaudit
and shouting. Next comes in Helymus and Diores, thus made
the third prize. But now Salius is heard, deafening with his
clamour the whole company in the ring and the seniors in the
first rank, and insisting that the prize, which he had lost by a
trick, be restored him. Euryalus is supported by the popular
voice, by the tears he sheds so gracefully, and the greater

loveliness of worth when seen in a beauteous form. Diores backs his claim with loud appealing shouts; he had just won the prize, and his attainment of the third place was all for nothing if the first reward were to be given to Salius. To whom father Æneas:—'Your rewards, boys, remain fixed as they ever were; no one disturbs the palm once arranged: suffer me to show pity to a friend's undeserved misfortune.' So saying, he gives Salius the enormous hide of a Gætulian lion, loaded with shaggy hair and talons of gold. On which Nisus:—'If the vanquished are rewarded so largely—if you can feel for tumblers—what prize will be great enough for Nisus' claims? My prowess had earned me the first chaplet, had not unkind Fortune played me foul, as she played Salius;' and with these words he displayed his features and his limbs, all dishonoured by slime and ordure. The gracious prince smiled at him,.and bade them bring out a shield of Didymaon's workmanship, once wrested by the Danaans from Neptune's hallowed gate, and with this signal present he endows the illustrious youth.

Next, when the race was finished, and the prizes duly given :—'Now, whoever has courage, and a vigorous collected mind in his breast, let him come forward, bind on the gloves, and lift his arms.' Thus speaks Æneas, and sets forth two prizes for the contest: for the conqueror, a bullock with gilded horns and fillet festoons; a sword and a splendid helmet, as a consolation to the vanquished. In a moment, with all the thews of a giant, rises Dares, uprearing himself amid a loud hum of applause—the sole champion who used to enter the lists with Paris: once at the tomb where mighty Hector lies buried, he encountered the great conqueror Butes, who carried his enormous bulk to the field with all the pride of Amycus' Bebrycian blood—struck him down, and stretched him in death on the yellow sand. Such are Dares' powers, as he lifts high his crest for the battle, displays his broad shoulders, throws out his arms alternately, and strikes the air with his blows.   How to find his match is the cry; no one of all that company dares to confront such a champion, and draw on the gauntlets.   So, with confident action, thinking that all were retiring from the prize, he stands before Æneas, and without further prelude grasps with his left hand the bull by the horn, and bespeaks him thus :—' Goddess-born, if no one dares to take the risk of the fight, how long are we to stand still ?   How long is it seemly to keep me waiting ?   Give the word for me to carry off the prize.' A simultaneous shout broke from the sons of Dardanus, all voting that their champion should have the promised gift made good.

On this Acestes, with grave severity of speech, rebukes Entellus, just as he chanced to be seated next him on the verdant grassy couch.   ' Entellus, once known as the bravest of heroes, and all for nought, will you brook so calmly that a prize so great be carried off without a blow ?   Where are we now to look for that mighty deity your master, Eryx, vaunted so often and so idly ?   Where is that glory which spread all Trinacria through, and those spoils that hang from your roof ?'   He replied : ' It is not the love of praise, not ambition, that has died out, extinguished by fear.   No, indeed ; but my blood is dulled and chilled by the frost of age, and the strength in my limbs withered and ice-bound. Had I now what I once had, what is now the glory and the boast of that loud braggart there ; had I but the treasure of youth, I should not have needed the reward and the goodly bullock to bring me into the field ; nor are gifts what I care for.'   So saying, he flung into the midst a pair of gauntlets of enormous weight, with which the fiery Eryx was wont to deal his blows in combat, stringing his arms with the tough hide. Every heart was amazed, so vast were the seven huge bull-hides, hardened with patches of lead and iron. More than all the rest Dares is astonished, and recoils many paces; and the hero himself, Anchises' son, stands turning in his hands the massive weight and the enormous wrappers of twisted thong. Then the old man fetched from his heart words like these :—' What if any one here had seen those mightier weapons, Hercules' own gauntlets, and the fatal combat on this very strand? These are the arms that Eryx, your brother, once wielded; you see on them still the stains of blood and sprinkled brains. With these he stood up against the great Alcides. These I was trained to use while fresher blood inspired me with strength, and the snows of age, my jealous rival, were not yet sprinkled on my brows. But if Dares the Trojan refuses our Sicilian weapons, and that is good Æneas' fixed wish, approved by Acestes, my backer in the fight, make we the contest even. I spare you the bull-hides of Eryx—never fear—and do you put off your Trojan gauntlets.' So saying, he flung off from his shoulders his double garment, and displays the giant joints of his limbs, the giant bone-work of his arms, and stands, a mighty frame, in the midst of the sand.

Then Anchises' son brought out with his royal hand two pairs of equal gauntlets, and bound round the fists of the twain weapons of even force. At once each rose on tiptoe, and raised his arms undaunted to the air of heaven. They draw back their towering heads out of the reach of blows, and make their fists meet in the melée, and provoke the battle. The one is better in quick movement of the foot, and youth lends him confidence; the other's strength is in brawny limbs and giant bulk, but his knees are heavy and unstable, and a troubled panting shakes that vast frame. Many the blows that the champions hail on each other in

vain ; many are showered on the hollow side, and draw loud
echoes from the chest. The fist keeps playing round ear and
temple ; the teeth chatter under the cruel blow. Heavily
stands Entellus, unmoved, in the same strained posture ; his
bending body and watchful eye alone withdraw him from the
volley. His rival, like a general who throws up mounds
round a high-walled town, or sits down with his army before
a mountain fort, tries now this approach, now that, recon-
noitres the whole stronghold, and plies him with manifold
assaults, baffled in each. Rising to the stroke, Entellus put
forth his right hand, and raised it aloft ; the other's quick
eye foresaw the downcoming blow, and his lithe frame darts
beyond its range. Entellus has flung his whole force on air ;
at once, untouched by his foe, the heavy giant, with heavy
giant weight, falls to earth, even as one day falls hollow-
hearted with hollow crash on Erymanthus or lofty Ida, up-
torn by the roots, a mighty pine. Eagerly start up at once
the Teucrian and Trinacrian chivalry ; up soars a shout to
heaven ; and first runs up Acestes, and soothingly raises from
the ground his friend, aged as he. But not slackened by his
overthrow, nor daunted, the hero comes back fiercer to the
field, with anger goading force ; that mass of strength is
enkindled at last by shame and conscious prowess. All on
fire, he drives Dares headlong over the whole plain, now with
his right hand showering blows, now with his giant left. No
stint, no stay ; thick as the hail with which the storm-clouds
rattle on the roof, so thick the blows with which the hero,
crowding on with both hands, is battering and whirling Dares.
Then father Æneas thought fit to stem the tide of fury, nor
suffered Entellus' wounded spirit to glut its rage further, but
put an end to the fray, and rescued the gasping Dares with
soothing words, and bespeaks him thus :—'My poor friend !
what monstrous madness has seized you ? See you not that

strength has passed over—that the gods have changed their sides? Give way to Heaven.' He said, and his word closed the fight. But Dares is in the hands of his faithful comrades, dragging after him his feeble knees, dropping his head on this side and on that, discharging from his mouth clotted gore, teeth and blood together. Thus they lead him to the ships ; summoned, they receive for him the helmet and the sword ; the palm and the bull they leave to Entellus. Hereon the conqueror, towering in pride of soul, and exulting in his prize, the bull : ' Goddess-born,' cries he, ' and you, Teucrians, take measure at once of the strength which dwelt in my frame, while that frame was young, and the death from whose door you have called back, and are still keeping, your Dares.' So saying, he took his stand full before the face of the bullock, which was there as the prize of the fray, and with arm drawn back, swung the iron gauntlet right between the horns, rising to his full height, crashed down on the bone, and shattered the brain. Prostrated, breathless, and quivering, on earth lies the bull. He from his bosom's depth speaks thus over the dead :—' This life, Eryx, I render to thee—a better substitute for Dares' death ; here, as a conqueror may, I resign the gauntlets and the game.'

Next Æneas invites those who may care to vie in shooting the fleet arrow, and sets forth the prizes. With his own giant hand he rears upright the mast from Serestus' ship, and from its lofty summit ties a fluttering dove with a cord passed round the mast—a mark for aiming the steel. The archers are met ; the lot has been thrown and received by the brazen helmet. See ! first, among the shouts of his friends, comes out before all the place of Hyrtacus' son, Hippocoon, who is followed by Mnestheus, late conqueror in the ship-race —Mnestheus, crowned with the green olive-wreath. Third comes Eurytion, thy brother, thrice glorious Pandarus, who in

P

elder days, bidden to destroy the truce, was the first to wing thy weapon into the Achæan ranks. Last is Acestes, sunk at the bottom of the helm, the old man's spirit nerving his arm to essay the task of the young. And now, with stern strength, they bend and arch their bows, each hero his own, and draw forth the shaft from the quiver. First through heaven from the twanging string the arrow of Hyrtacus' youthful son pierces sharp and shrill the flying air: it hits—it is lodged full in the mast-tree. After him stood keen Mnestheus, his bowstring drawn to his breast, his bow pointing upwards, eye and shaft levelled at once. But the bird itself, hapless man! his arrow had not power to touch that: it cut the knot and the hempen fastening by which she hung, tied by the foot, from the mast's top. Away she flew, all among the south-winds and their murky clouds. Then, quick as thought, his bow long since ready, and his shaft poised on the string, Eurytion breathed a vow to his brother, fixing his eye on her in the moment of her triumph high up in the open sky, and as she claps her wings, pierces the dark cloudy covert, and strikes the dove. Down she drops unnerved, leaving her life among the stars of ether, and as she tumbles to earth, brings back the arrow in her breast. Acestes remained alone, a champion with no prize to gain; yet he shot his weapon into the air aloft, displaying at once his veteran skill and the force of his twanging bow. And now their eyes are met by a sudden portent, drawing a mighty augury in its train. In after days the vast issue told the tale, and terror-striking seers shrieked their omens too late. For as it flew in the clouds of heaven, the reed took fire, and marked its way with a trail of flame, and wasted and vanished wholly into unsubstantial air; even as stars unfastened from the firmament oft sweep across and drag their blazing hair as they fly. Fixed aghast to the spot, in prayer to Heaven, hung the stout sons of Trinacria and Troy; nor does Æneas' sovran judgment reject the omen. He clasps the glad Acestes to his heart, loads him with costly gifts, and bespeaks him thus :—'Take them, my father; for Olympus' mighty monarch has said by the voice of these omens that yours is to be a prize drawn without a lot. From Anchises the aged himself comes the present I now bestow—a bowl embossed with figures, which in old days Cisseus gave to my sire Anchises in royal bounty, a standing remembrance of himself and a testimony of his love.' So saying, he crowns his brow with verdant bays, and proclaims, first of all, the conquering name of Acestes. Nor did good Eurytion grudge the pre-eminence, though he and none but he brought down the bird from the sky. Next steps into the prize he who cut the cord; last, he whose quivering arrow nailed the mast.

But father Æneas, ere the match was over, calls to his side the guardian and companion of Iulus' tender years, Epytides, and thus speaks into his ear in secret :—'Go now and tell Ascanius, if his company of boys is ready, and the movements of his young cavalry duly marshalled, to bring them into the field in his grandsire's honour, and show himself in arms.' He, by his own voice, bids the whole surging crowd retire from the length of the circus, and leave the field clear. The boys come prancing in on well-reined steeds, in even lines of light brightening their parents' eyes; and as they pass, an admiring shout breaks from the gathered chivalry of Sicily and Troy. All alike have their flowing hair, duly cinctured with stripped leaves; each bears two cornel javelins tipped with steel; some have polished quivers at their backs; round the top of the chest goes a pliant chain of twisted gold circling the neck. Three are the companies of horse, three the leaders that scour the plain; twelve boys follow each, a glittering show, in equal divisions and commanded alike. The first of the youthful bands is led as to victory by a young Priam, who revives his grandsire's name, thy princely offspring, Polites, destined to people Italy; him a Thracian steed carries, dappled with spots of white, with white on the extremes of his prancing feet, and white on his towering brow. Next is Atys, whence comes the house of Roman Atii—Atys the young, the boyish friend of the boy Iulus. Last of all, and excelling all in beauty, Iulus rides in on a Sidonian steed, bestowed on him by Dido the fair, in remembrance of herself, and in testimony of her love. The remaining youth are borne on Trinacrian horses from old Acestes' stalls. The Dardans welcome them with reassuring plaudits, and gaze on them with rapture, and trace in their young faces the features of their old sires. Soon as the riders have made their joyous survey of the whole gazing crowd and of their friends' loving eyes, Epytides gives the expected signal with far-reaching shout and loud cracking whip. In regular order they gallop asunder, the three companies breaking and parting right and left; and again, at the word of command, they wheel round, and charge each other with levelled lances. Then they essay other advances and other retreats in quarters still opposite, each entangling each in circles within circles, and in their real armour raise an image of battle. Now they expose their backs in flight, now they turn their spear-points in charge, now as in truce they ride along side by side. Even as men tell of that old labyrinth in lofty Crete, its way cunningly woven with blind high walls, and the ambiguous mystery of its thousand paths, winding till the pursuer's every trace was baffled by a maze without solution and without return, not unlike are the courses in which these sons of the Teucrians interlace their movements—a gamesome tangle of flying and fighting, as it were dolphins that swimming the watery seas dart through the Carpathian and the Libyan, and sport along the billows. Such was the form of exercise, and such the game that Ascanius, when he built the cincturing walls of Alba the Long, was the first to revive, and taught the early Latians to celebrate it as he had done in his boyhood, he and the youth of Troy with him ; the men of Alba taught their sons ; from them mighty Rome received the tradition and maintained the observance of her sires ; and the boys still bear the name of Troy, and their band is styled the band of Troy. Thus far went the solemn games in honour of the deified sire.

Now it was that Fortune exchanged her old faith for new. While they are rendering to the tomb the due solemnities of the varied games, Juno, Saturn's daughter, has sped down Iris from heaven to the feet of Ilion, with breath of winds to waft her on her way—Juno, deep-brooding over many thoughts, her ancient wrath yet unsated. Speeding along her many-coloured bow, seen of none, runs swiftly down the celestial maid. She beholds that mighty concourse ; she looks round on the coast, and sees harbour abandoned and fleet forsaken. Far away, in the privacy of a solitary beach, the Trojan dames were weeping for lost Anchises, and, as they wept, were gazing, one and all, wistfully on the great deep. Alas, that wearied souls should still have those many waters to pass, and that vast breadth of sea ! Such the one cry of every heart. Oh for a city ! the toils of the main are a weariness to bear ! So, then, in the midst of them, she suddenly alights—no novice in the ways of doing hurt— and lays by her heavenly form and heavenly raiment. She takes the shape of Beroe, the aged wife of Doryclus of Tmaros, a dame who once had had race and name and children, and in this guise stands in the midst of the Dardan matrons. 'Wretched women,' cries she, 'not to have been dragged to the death of battle by the force of Achaia under our country's walls! Hapless nation! What worse than death has Fortune in store for you? Here is the seventh summer rolling on since Troy's overthrow, and all the while we are being driven, land and ocean over, among all the rocks of an unfriendly sea, under all the stars of heaven, as through the great deep ,we follow after retreating Italy, and are tossed from wave to wave. Here is the brother-land of Eryx; here is Acestes, our ancient friend. Who shall gainsay digging a foundation, and giving a people the city they crave? O my country! O gods of our homes, snatched in vain from the foe! Shall there never be walls named with the name of Troy? Shall I never on earth see the streams that Hector loved—his Xanthus and his Simois? Come, join me in burning up these accursed ships. For in my sleep methought the likeness of Cassandra the seer put blazing torches into my hands. Here,' she said, 'and here only, look for Troy: here, and here only, is your home. The hour for action is come. Heaven's wonders brook not man's delay. See here! four altars to Neptune. The god himself gives us the fire and the will.'

So saying, she is the first to snatch the baleful brand— swinging back her hand on high; with strong effort she whirls and flings it. The dames of Ilion gaze with straining mind and wildered brain. Then one of the crowd, the eldest of all, Pyrgo, the royal nurse of Priam's many sons : ' No Beroe have you here, matrons—this is not Doryclus' wife, of Rhoeteum—mark those signs of heavenly beauty, those glowing eyes—what a presence is there—what features—what a tone in her voice—what majesty in her gait! Beroe, I myself parted from but now, and left her sick and sullen to think that she alone should fail at this observance, nor pay Anchises the honour that is his due.' Such were her words, while the matrons, doubtful at first, were looking on the ships with evil eyes, distracted between their fatal yearning for a country

now theirs, and the voice of destiny from realms beyond the
sea—when the goddess, spreading her two wings, soared up
into the sky and severed the clouds as she flew with the
giant span of her bow. Then indeed, maddened by the portent,
goaded by frenzy, they shriek one and all, and snatch fire from
house and hearth—some strip the altars, and fling on the vessels
leaf and bough and brand. The fire-god revels in full career
along bench and oar, and painted pine-wood stern. The
news of the fleet on fire is carried by Eumelus to Anchises'
tomb, and the seats in the circus. They look back, and with
their own eyes see sparks and smoke in a black flickering
cloud. First of all Ascanius, riding in triumph at the head of
his cavalry, spurred his horse just as he was to the wildering
camp, while his breathless guardians strive in vain to stay him.
'What strange madness this? whither now, whither would ye
go,' cries he, 'my poor countrywomen? It is not the Argive
foe and his hated camp—it is your own hopes that you are
burning. See, I am your own Ascanius'—at his feet he flung
his empty helmet which he was wearing in sport as he helped
to raise the image of war. Quick follows Æneas, quick the
Teucrian host at his heels. But the matrons are flying in
panic along the coast, now here, now there, stealing to the
thickest woods and the deepest caves. They loathe the deed
and the daylight. Sobered, they know their friends again, and
Juno is exorcised from their souls. But not for all this will
blaze and burning resign their unslaked powers: deep
among the moistened timber smoulders the quick tow, discharging a slow lazy smoke: the crawling heat preys on the keels,
and the plague sinks down into the vessel's every limb, and
strength of giant warriors and streaming water-floods are all of
no avail. Then good Æneas began to tear his raiment from
his back and call the gods for aid, and raise his hands in
prayer: 'Jove Almighty, if thy hate would not yet sweep off

the whole Trojan race to a man, if thy ancient goodness has
yet any regard for human suffering, grant the fleet to escape
from flame now, Father, even now, and rescue from death the
shattered commonweal of Troy. Or else do thou with thy
wrathful bolt send down this poor remnant to the grave, if
that is my fit reward, and here with thy own right hand over-
whelm us all.' Scarce had the words been breathed, when a
black tempest is set loose, raging with fierce bursts of rain :
the thunder-peals thrill through highland and lowland—down
from the whole sky pours a torrent of blinding water, thickened
to blackness by the southern winds—the ships are filled, the
smouldering timbers soaked—till every spark is quenched at
last, and all the vessels, with the loss of four, rescued from
the deadly plague.

But father Æneas, staggering under this cruel blow, began
to shift from side to side a vast burden of care, as he pondered
should he settle in the plains of Sicily, shutting his ears to
Fate's voice, or still make for the shores of Italy. Then
Nautes the aged—whom Tritonian Pallas singled from his
kind, to teach her lore and dower him with the fame of abundant wisdom—hers the oracular utterances which told what
Heaven's awful wrath portended, or what the stern sequence
of destiny required—he it was that addressed Æneas thus in
words of comfort : 'Goddess-born, be it ours to follow as Fate
pulls us to or fro ; come what may, there is no conquering
fortune but by endurance. Here you have Acestes, the blood
of Dardanus and of gods mingling in his veins—make him
the partner of your thoughts, and invite the aid he will gladly
give. Consign to him the crews whom your missing ships
have left homeless, and those who are tired of high emprize
and of following your fortunes—the old, old men, and the
matrons, weary of ocean, and whatever you have that is weak
and timorsome—set these apart, and suffer them to have in

this land a city of rest. The town's name, with leave given, they shall call Acesta.'

The fire thus kindled by the words of his aged friend, now indeed the thoughts of his mind distract him utterly. An'. now black Night, car-borne, was mounting the sky, when the semblance of his sire Anchises, gliding from heaven, seemed to break on his musings in words like these : ' My son, dearer to me of old than life, while life was yet mine—my son, trained in the school of Troy's destiny, I come hither at the command of Jove—of him who chased the fire from your ships, and looked down on your need in pity from on high. Obey the counsel which Nautes the aged now so wisely gives you. The flower of your youth, the stoutest hearts you have, let these and these only follow you to Italy—hard and of iron grain is the race you have to war down in Latium. Still, ere you go there, come to the infernal halls of Dis, and travel through Avernus' deep shades till you meet your father. No, my son, godless Tartarus and its spectres of sorrow have no hold on me—the company of the good is my loved resort and Elysium my dwelling. The virgin Sibyl shall point you the way, and the streaming blood of black cattle unlock the gate. There you shall hear of your whole posterity, and the city that Fate has in store. And now farewell, dark Night has reached the midst of her swift career, and the relentless Day-star has touched me with the breath of his panting steeds.' He said, and vanished, like smoke, into unsubstantial air. ' Whither away now ?' cries Æneas; ' whither in such haste ? from whom are you flying ? what power withholds you from my embrace ?' With these words he wakes to life the embers and their slumbering flame, and in suppliance worships the god of Pergamus and hoary Vesta's shrine with duteous meal and a full-charged censer.

At once he calls his friends to his side, and Acestes, first of all, shows to them the command of Jove, and his loved father's precept, and what is now the settled judgment of his mind. Brief is the parley, nor does Acestes gainsay his bidding. They remove the matrons to the new city's roll, and disembark a willing crew of hearts that need not the stir of great renown. For themselves they repair the benches and restore the vessels' half-burnt timber, shape the oars and fit the ropes, a little band, but a living well-spring of martial worth. Æneas, meanwhile, is marking out the city with the plough, and assigning the dwellings by lot, creating an Ilium here, and there a Troy. Acestes, true Trojan, wields with joy his new sceptre, and proclaims a court, and gives laws to his assembled senate.[1]

And now the whole nation had enjoyed a nine days' banquet, and the altars had received due observance; the sleeping winds have lulled the waves, and the repeated whispers of the south invite to the deep once more. Uprises along the winding shore a mighty sound of weeping; prolonged embraces make day and night move slow. Even the matrons, even the weaklings, who so lately shuddered at the look of the sea, and could not bear its name, would now fain go and endure all the weariness of the journey. Them the good Æneas cheers with words of kindness, and tearfully commends them to Acestes, his kinsman and theirs. Then he bids slay three calves to Eryx, and a ewe-lamb to the weather gods, and in due course has the cable cut, while he, his head wreathed with stript olive leaves, stands aloft in the prow with a charger in hand, and far into the briny waves flings the entrails, and pours the sparkling wine. A wind gets up from the stern, and escorts them on their way. Each vying with each, the crews strike the water, and sweep the marble surface.

Meanwhile Venus, harassed with care, bespeaks Neptune,

---

[1] Three lines omitted in the MS.—[ED.]

and utters from her heart plaints like these : 'The fell wrath of Juno's bottomless heart constrains me, Neptune, to stoop to all the abasement of prayer—wrath that no length of time softens, no piety of man, unconquered and unsilenced by Jove's behest, by destiny itself. It is not enough that her monstrous malice has torn the heart from the breast of Phrygia, and dragged a city through an infinity of vengeance—the remnants of Troy, the very ashes and bones of the slain— these she pursues ; rage so fiendish let *her* trace to its source. Thou thyself canst bear me witness but now in the Libyan waters, what mountains she raised all in a moment—all ocean she confounded with heaven, blindly relying on Æolus' storms to convulse a realm where thou art master. See now—goading the matrons of Troy to crime, she has basely burnt their ships, and driven them in the ruins of their fleet to leave their mates to a home on an unknown shore. These poor relics, then, let *them*, I beg, spread the sail in safety along thy waters ; let them touch the mouth of Laurentian Tiber, if my prayer is lawful, if that city is granted them of Fate.'

Then thus spake Saturn's son, lord of the ocean deep : ' All right hast thou, queen of Cythera, to place thy trust in these realms of mine, whence thou drawest thy birth. And I have earned it too—often have I checked the madness, the mighty raving of sky and sea ; nor less on earth (bear witness Xanthus and Simois !) has thy Æneas known my care. When Achilles was chasing Troy's gasping bands, forcing them against their own ramparts, and offering whole hecatombs to Death, till the choked rivers groaned again, and Xanthus could not thread his way, or roll himself into the sea—in that day, as Æneas confronted Peleus' mighty son with weaker arm and weaker aid from heaven, I snatched him away in a circling cloud even while my whole heart was bent on overthrowing from their base the buildings of my own hand, the walls of perjured

Troy. As my mind was then, it abides now. Banish thy fears ; safely, according to thy prayer, he shall reach Avernus haven. One there shall be, and one only, whom thou shalt ask in vain from the engulfing surge—one life, and one only, shall be given for thousands.'

With these words, having soothed to joy the goddess' heart, the august Father yokes his steeds with a yoke of gold, and puts to their fierce mouth the foaming bit, and gives full course to his flowing reins. The azure car glides lightly over the water's surface—the waves sink down, the swelling sea stills its waters under the wheels of thunder—the storm-clouds fly away over the wide waste of heaven. Then come the hundred shapes of attendant powers : enormous whales and Glaucus' aged train, and Ino's young Palæmon, and rapid Tritons, and the whole host that Phorcus leads; on the left are Thetis, and Melite, and maiden Panopea, Nesæe, and Spio, and Thalia, and Cymodoce.

And now father Æneas feels a soft thrill of succeeding joy shoot through his anxious bosom ; at once he bids every mast be reared, every sail stretched on its yard-arm. One and all strain the rope and loosen the sheet, now right, now left— one and all turn to and fro the sailyard's lofty horns ; the fleet is wafted by the gales it loves. First, before all, Palinurus led the crowding ranks; after him the rest, as bidden, shaped their course. And now dewy Night had well-nigh reached the cope of heaven's arch—in calm repose the sailors were relaxing their limbs, stretched each by his oar along the hard benches—when Sleep's power, dropping lightly down from the stars of heaven, parted the dusky air, and swam through the night, in quest of you, poor Palinurus, with a fatal freight of dreams for your guiltless head. The god has sat down high on the stern, in the likeness of Phorbas, and these are the words he utters : ' Son of Iasus, Palinurus,

the sea itself is steering the fleet ; the winds breathe evenly
and fully ; it is slumber's own hour ; come, relax that strained
head, and let those weary eyes play truant from their toil.
I myself will undertake your functions awhile in your stead.'
Hardly raising his eyes, Palinurus answered him thus :—'*I*
blind myself to smiling seas and sleeping waves : is that your
will ? *I* place my faith on this fickle monster ? What ? trust
Æneas to lying gales and fair skies, whose fraud I have rued
so often ? ' So he said, and went on cleaving and clinging,
never dropping his hand from the rudder, nor his eye from
the stars.   When lo ! the god waves over his two temples
a bough dripping with Lethe's dews, and drugged by the
charms of Styx, and in his own despite closes his swimming eyes.   Scarce had sudden slumber begun to unstring
his limbs, when the power, leaning over him, hurled him
headlong into the streaming waves, tearing away part of the
vessel's stern and the rudder as he fell, with many a cry for
help that never came, while Sleep himself soared high on his
wings into the yielding air.   Safely, nevertheless, rides the
fleet over the water, travelling undaunted in the strength of
Neptune's royal promise.   And now it was nearing the cliffs
of the Sirens' isle, cliffs unfriendly in days of old, and white
with .many a seaman's bones, and the rocks were sounding
hollow from afar with the untiring surge, when the great
Father perceived the unsteady reel of the masterless ship, and
guided it himself through the night of waters, groaning oft,
and staggering under the loss of his friend : ' Victim of faith
in the calm of sky and sea, you will lie, Palinurus, a naked
corpse on a strand unknown.'

BOOK VI.

So saying and weeping, he gives rope to his fleet, and in due time is wafted smoothly to Cumæ's shores of Eubœan fame. They turn their prows seaward : then the anchor with griping fang began to moor vessel after vessel, and crooked keels fringe all the coast. With fiery zeal the crews leap out on the Hesperian shore : some look for the seed of fire where it lies deep down in the veins of flint : some strip the woods, the wild beast's shaggy covert, and point with joy to the streams they find. But good Æneas repairs to the heights on which Apollo sits exalted, and the privacy of the dread Sibyl, stretching far away into a vast cavern—the Sibyl, into whose breast the prophet that speaks at Delos breathes his own mighty mind and soul, and opens the future to her eye. And now they are entering the groves of the Trivian goddess and the golden palace.

Dædalus, so runs the legend, flying from Minos' sceptre, dared to trust himself in air on swift wings of his own workmanship, sailed to the cold north along an unwonted way, and at last stood buoyant on the top of this Eubœan hill. Grateful to the land that first received him, he dedicated to thee, Phœbus, his feathery oarage, and raised a mighty temple. On the doors was seen Androgeos' death : there too were the sons of Cecrops, constrained—O cruel woe !—to pay in penalty the yearly tale of seven of their sons' lives : the urn is standing, and the lots drawn out. On the other side,

breasting the wave, the Gnossian land frowns responsive.
There is Pasiphäe's tragic passion for the bull, and the mingled
birth, the Minotaur, half man, half brute, a monument of
monstrous love. There is the edifice, that marvel of toiling
skill, and its inextricable maze—inextricable, had not Dædalus in pity for the enthralling passion of the royal princess,
himself unravelled the craft and mystery of those chambers,
guiding the lover's dark steps with a clue of thread. You too,
poor Icarus, had borne no mean part in that splendid portraiture, would grief have given art its way. Twice the artist
essayed to represent the tragedy in gold : twice the father's
hands dropped down palsied. So they would have gone on
scanning all in succession, had not Achates returned from his
errand, and with him the priestess of Phœbus and Diana,
Deiphobe, Glaucus' daughter, who thus bespeaks the king :
'Not this the time for shows like these ; your present work
is to sacrifice seven bullocks untouched by the yoke, seven
sheep duly chosen.'

This said to Æneas, whose followers swiftly perform the
prescribed rites, she summons the Teucrians into the lofty
temple, herself its priestess. One huge side of the Eubœan
cliff has been hollowed into a cave, approached by a hundred
broad avenues, a hundred mouths—from these a hundred
voices are poured, the responses of the Sibyl. Just as they
were on the threshold, 'It is the moment to pray for the
oracle,' cries the maiden ; 'the god, the god is here.' Thus
as she spoke at the gate, her visage, her hue changed suddenly
—her hair started from its braid—her bosom heaves and
pants, her wild soul swells with frenzy—she grows larger to
the view, and her tones are not of earth, as the breath of
the divine presence comes on her nearer and nearer. 'What !
a laggard at vows and prayers ? Æneas of Troy a laggard ?
for that is the only spell to part asunder the great closed lips

of the terror-smitten shrine.' She said, and was mute. A cold shudder runs through the Teucrians' iron frames, and their king pours out his very soul in prayer: 'Phœbus, ever Troy's pitying friend in her cruel agonies—thou who didst level Paris' Dardan bow and string his Dardan arm against the vast frame of Æacides—by thy guidance I have penetrated all these unknown seas that swathe mighty continents. The Massylian tribes, thrust away by Nature out of view, and the quicksands that environ their coasts—now at last our hands are on the flying skirts of Italy. Oh, let it suffice Troy's fortune to have followed us thus far! Ye too may now justly spare our nation of Pergamus, gods and goddesses all, whose eyes were affronted by Troy and the great glories of Dardan land. And thou, most holy prophetess, that canst read the future as the present, grant me —I am asking for no crown that Fate does not owe me— grant a settlement in Latium to the Teucrians, their wandering gods, even the travel-tost deities of Troy. Then to Phœbus and his Trivian sister I will set up a temple of solid marble, and appoint feast-days in Phœbus' name. For thee too an august shrine is in store in that our future realm. For there I will lodge thy oracles and the secret words of destiny which thou shalt speak to my nation, and consecrate chosen men to thy gracious service. Only commit not thy strains to leaves, lest they float all confusedly the sport of the whirling winds. Utter them with thine own mouth, I implore thee.' So his prayer ended.

But the prophetess, not yet Phœbus' willing slave, is storming with giant frenzy in her cavern, as though she hoped to unseat from her bosom the mighty god. All the more sharply he plies her mouth with his bit till its fury flags, tames her savage soul, and moulds her to his will by strong constraint. And now the hundred mighty doors of the chamber have flown

open of their own accord, and are wafting through the air the
voice of prophecy: ' O you whose vast perils by sea are over
at length ! but on land there are heavier yet in store. The
sons of Dardanus shall come to the realm of Lavinium—from
this care set your mind at rest—but think not that they shall
also have joy of their coming. War, savage war, and the
Tiber foaming with surges of blood, is the vision I see. No
lack for you of Simois, or Xanthus, or a Dorian camp. Another
Achilles is reserved for Latium, he too goddess-born—nor will
Juno ever be seen to quit her fastened hold on Troy—while
you, a needy suppliant—what nation, what city in Italy will
not have had you knocking at its gates ! Once more will an
alien bride bring on the Teucrians all this woe—once more a
foreign bed. But you, yield not to affliction, but go forth all
the bolder to meet it, so far as your destiny gives you leave.
The first glimpse of safety, little as you dream it, shall dawn
on you from a Grecian town.'

Such are the words with which Cumæ's Sibyl from her cell
shrills forth awful mysteries and booms again from the cavern,
robing her truth in darkness—such the violence with which
Apollo shakes the bridle in her frenzied mouth and plies her
bosom with his goad. Soon as her frenzy abated and the madness of her lips grew calm, Æneas the hero began : ' No feature,
awful maiden, that suffering can show rises on my sight new
or unlooked-for—I have foreseen all and scanned all in fancy
already. I have but one prayer to make : since here it is that
Fame tells of the gate of the infernal monarch, and the murky
pool of Acheron's overflow, grant me to pass to the sight, to
the presence of my loved father—teach the way, and unlock
the sacred doors. Him I bore away through flames and a
driving tempest of darts on these my shoulders and rescued
him from the midst of the foe : he was the companion of my
journey, and encountered with me all the waves of ocean, all

Q

the terrors of sea and sky in his own feeble frame, beyond the strength and the day of old age. Nay more—that I would kneel to thee and approach thy dwelling—this was his charge, his oft-repeated prayer. Oh, of thy grace, pity the son and the sire; for thou art all-powerful, nor is it for nought that Hecate has set thee over the groves of Avernus. If Orpheus had the power to fetch back the shade of his wife, by the help of his Thracian lyre and its sounding strings—if Pollux redeemed his brother by dying in turn with him, and went and returned on the path those many times—why talk of Theseus, why of great Alcides ? my line, like theirs, is from Jove most high.'

Such were his prayers, while his hands clasped the altar, when thus the prophetess began : 'Heir of the blood of gods, son of Anchises of Troy, easy is the going down to Avernus— all night and all day the gate of gloomy Pluto stands unbarred ; but to retrace your footsteps, and win your way back to the upper air, that is the labour, that the task. There have been a few, favourites of gracious Jove, or exalted to heaven by the blaze of inborn worth, themselves sprung from the gods, who have had the power. The whole intervening space is possessed by woods, and lapped round by the black windings of Cocytus' stream. And now, if your heart's yearning is so great, your passion so strong, twice to stem the Stygian pool, twice to gaze on the night of Tartarus—if it be your joy to give scope to a madman's striving—hear what must first be done. Deep in the shade of a tree lurks a branch, all of gold, foliage alike and limber twig, dedicated to the service of the Juno of the shades ; it is shrouded by the whole labyrinth of the forest, closed in by the boskage that darkens the glens. Yet none may pierce the subterranean mystery, till a man have gathered from the tree that leafy sprout of gold, for this it is that fair Proserpine has ordained to be brought her as her own proper tribute. Pluck off one, another is there unfailingly, of gold

as pure, a twig burgeoning with as fine an ore. Let then your
eye be keen to explore it, your hand quick to pluck it when
duly found, for it will follow the touch with willingness and
ease, if you have a call from Fate ; if not, no strength of yours
will overcome it, no force of steel tear it away. But, besides
this, you have the breathless corpse of a friend lying unburied
—alas ! you know it not—tainting your whole fleet with the
air of death, while you are asking Heaven's will, and lingering on this our threshold. Him first consign to his proper
place, and hide him in the grave. Lead black cattle to the
altar : be this the expiation to pave your way. Thus at last
you shall look on the groves of Styx and the realms untrodden
of the living.' She said, and closed her lips in silence.

Æneas, with saddened face and steadfast eye, moves on,
leaving the cave behind, and revolves in his mind the secrets
of the future. Achates, ever faithful, walks at his side, and
plants his foot with no less consciousness of care. Many were
the things exchanged in their ranging talk—who could be the
dead comrade that the priestess spoke of, what the corpse that
needed burial. And lo ! Misenus, soon as they came, there
on the dry beach they see him, snatched by death that should
have spared him—Misenus, son of Æolus, than whom none
was mightier to stir men's hearts with his clarion, and kindle
with music the war-god's flame. Hector the great had been
his chief : in Hector's service he performed a warrior's part,
famous alike with the trumpet and the spear. But after the
conquering arm of Achilles robbed his master of life, valiant
hero, he made himself the comrade of the Dardan Æneas, nor
found the standard he followed meaner than of old. But in
those days, as he was making his hollow shell ring over the
waters, infatuate mortal, challenging the gods to compete,
Triton, roused to jealousy, seized him, if the story be true,
and plunged him in a moment in the billow that laps among

the rocks. So they all stood round, uttering loud shrieks; louder than the rest Æneas the good. And then without delay they set about the Sibyl's bidding, weeping sore, and in mournful rivalry heap up the funeral pyre with trees, and carry it into the sky.

Away they go to an ancient wood, the wild beast's tall covert—down go the pitch-trees; the holm-oak rings with the axe's blows, and so do the ashen beams; the wedge cleaves through the fissile oak; they roll down from the heights huge mountain ashes. There is Æneas, in this, as in other labours, the first to cheer on his comrades, and wielding a weapon like theirs; and thus he ponders in the sad silence of his own breast, looking at the immeasurable wood, and , thus gives utterance to his prayer: 'Oh that at this moment that golden branch on the tree would reveal itself to our sight in all this depth of forest! for I see that in all things the prophetess has told us of you, Misenus, alas! too truly!' Scarce had he spoken, when, as by chance, a pair of doves come flying along the sky, under the hero's very eyes, and settle on the turf at his feet. At once the mighty chief recognises his mother's birds, and gladly breathes a second prayer: 'Oh guide us on our way, wherever it be, and as ye fly direct our steps into the grove where the precious branch casts its shade on the rich ground! Thou too forsake not our perplexity, O goddess mother!' ·Thus much he said, and checked his advancing foot, watching to see what prognostics they bring, whither they aim their onward course. They, as they graze, go ever forward on the wing, as far as the eyes of the travellers can keep them in view. Then when they come to Avernus' noisesome jaws, swiftly they soar aloft, and gliding through the clear sky settle twain on the same tree, their chosen seat, whence there flashed through the branches the contrasted gleam of gold. Even as in the woods, in the cold of mid-

winter, the mistletoe is wont to put forth new leaves, a veget-
able growth, but of no parent tree, and with its yellow produce
to surround the tapering boles, so looked the leafy gold among
the holm-oak's dark shade—so in the light breeze tinkled the
foil. Æneas snatches it at once, plucks it off with eagerness
overpowering its delay, and carries it to the home of the
prophetic Sibyl.

Meantime, with not less zeal, the Teucrians on the shore
were mourning for Misenus, and paying the last honour to the
thankless ashes. First they raised a pile, unctuous with pine-
wood, and high-heaped with planks of oak : they wreath its
sides with gloomy foliage, and set up before it funeral cypresses,
and adorn it with a covering of refulgent armour. Some
make ready heated water and cauldrons bubbling over the
fire, and wash and anoint the cold corpse. Loud rings the
wail : then, the dirge over, they place the limbs on the couch
that claims them, and fling over them purple garments, the
dead men's usual covering. Some put their shoulders to the
heavy bier in melancholy service, and after ancestral fashion,
with averted eyes, apply the torch from under. The rich
heap is ablaze—offerings of incense, sacrificial viands, oil
streaming from the bowl. After that the ashes were fallen in
and the blaze was lulled, they drenched with wine the relics
and the thirsty embers on the pyre, and Corynæus gathered
up the bones, and stored them in a brazen urn. He, too,
carried round pure water, and sprinkled thrice the comrades
of the dead, scattering the thin drops with a branch of fruitful
olive—so he expiated the company, and spoke the last solemn
words. But good Æneas raises over the dead a monument of
massive size, setting up for the hero his own proper arms, the
oar and the trumpet, under a skiey mountain, which is now
from him called Misenus, and retains from age to age the
everlasting name.

This done, he hastens to execute the Sibyl's bidding. A deep cave there was, yawning wide with giant throat, rough and shingly, shadowed by the black pool and the gloom of the forest—a cave, over whose mouth no winged thing could fly unharmed, so poisonous the breath that exhaling from its pitchy jaws steamed up to the sky—whence Greece has given the spot the name *Aornos.* Here first the priestess places in sacrificial station four black-skinned bullocks, and empties wine over their brows, and plucking from between their horns the hairs of the crown, throws them into the hallowed flame, as the firstfruits of worship, with loud cries on Hecate, queen in heaven, and Erebus both. Others put the knife to the throat, and catch in chargers the steaming blood. With his own sword Æneas strikes down a lamb of sable fleece, for the Furies' mother and her mighty sister, and a barren heifer for thee, dread Proserpine. Then to the Stygian monarch he rears altars, blazing through the darkness, and piles on the flame the bulls' carcases entire, pouring fat oil on the entrails all aglow. When, hark! as the sun began to glimmer and dawn, the ground is bellowing under their feet, and the wood-crowned heights are nodding, and the baying of dogs sounds through the gloom, for the goddess is at hand. 'Hence, hence with your unhallowed feet!' clamours the prophetess, 'and rid the whole grove of your presence. And you—strike into the road, and pluck your sword from his scabbard—now is the hour for courage, Æneas, now for a stout heart.' No more she said, but flung herself wildly into the cavern's mouth; and he, with no faltering step, keeps pace with his guide.

Ye gods, whose empire is the shades—spirits of silence, Chaos and Phlegethon, stretching wide in the stillness of night, suffer me to tell what has reached my ears; grant me your aid to reveal things buried underground, deep and dark.

On they went, darkling in solitary night, far into the
gloom, through Pluto's void halls and ghostly realms—like a
journey in a wood under the niggard beams of a doubtful
moon, when Jupiter has shrouded heaven in shadow, and
black Night has stolen the colour from Nature's face. There
before the threshold, in the very mouth of Hell, Agony and
the fiends of Remorse have made their lair : there dwell
wan Diseases, and woful Age, and Terror, and Hunger that
prompts to Sin, and loathly Want—shapes of hideous view—
and Death, and Suffering ; then comes Sleep, Death's blood-
brother, and the soul's guilty joys, and deadly War couched in
the gate, and the Furies' iron chambers, and frantic Strife,
with bloody fillets wreathed in her snaky hair.

In the midst there stands, with boughs and aged arms out-
spread, a massive elm, of broad shade, the chosen seat, so
Rumour tells, of bodiless dreams, which cling close to its
every leaf. There, too, are a hundred monstrous shapes of
wild beasts of divers kinds, Centaurs stalled in the entrance
and two-formed Scyllas, and Briareus, the hundred-handed,
and the portent of Lerna, hissing fearfully, and Chimæra in
her panoply of flames, Gorgons, and Harpies, and the semblance of the three-bodied spectre. At once Æneas grasps
his sword, in the haste of sudden alarm, and meets their
advance with its drawn blade ; and did not his companion
warn him, of her own knowledge, that they are but thin
unbodied spirits flitting in a hollow mask of substance, he
would be rushing among them, and slashing shadows asunder
with the steel's unavailing blows.

Hence runs the road that leads to the waters of Tartarean
Acheron, whose gulfy stream, churning mud in its monstrous
depths, is all aglow, and disgorges into Cocytus the whole of
its sand. These waters are guarded by a grisly ferryman,
frightful and foul—Charon ; his chin an uncleared forest of

hoary hair; his eyes a mass of flame; while his uncleanly garb hangs from his shoulders, gathered into a knot. With his own hand he pushes on the craft with a pole, and trims the sails, and moves the dead heavily along in his boat of iron-grey, himself already in years; but a god's old age is green and vigorous. Towards him the whole crowd was pouring to the bank : matrons and warriors, and bodies of mighty heroes discharged of life, boys and unwedded maidens, and youths laid on the pile of death in their parents' eyes—many as are the leaves that drop and fall in the woods in autumn's early cold, or many as are the birds that flock massed together from the deep to the land, when the wintry year drives them over sea to tenant a sunnier clime. There they stood, each praying that he might be the first to cross, with hands yearningly out-stretched towards the further shore; but the grim boatman takes on board now these, now those, while others he drives away, and bars them from the river's brink. Æneas cries as a man perplexed and startled by the tumult : ' Tell me, dread maiden, what means this concourse to the stream ? Of what are these spirits in quest ? What choice decides that these shall retire from the shore, while those are rowing through that leaden pool ?' To him in brief returned the aged priestess : ' Son of Anchises, Heaven's undoubted offspring, before you are Cocytus' depths and the marshy flood of Styx, that power by whose name the gods fear to swear in vain. The whole multitude you see here is helpless and tombless; Charon is the ferryman ; those who ride the wave are the buried. He may not ferry them from the dreadful banks across that noisy current till their bones have found a place of rest. A hundred years they wander hovering about these shores ; then at last they embark, and see again the flood of their longing.' Anchises' son stood and paused, musing deeply, and pitying at his heart a lot so unkind. Yes, there he sees, sadly wandering without death's last tribute, Leucaspis and Orontes, the captain of Lycia's fleet: both had sailed with him from Troy over the stormy water, and the south wind whelmed them both, engulfing the vessel and its crew.

Lo! he sees his pilot, Palinurus, moving along—Palinurus, who but now, while voyaging from Libya, his eyes bent on the stars, had fallen from the stern, flung out into the wide waste of waters. So when he had at last taken knowledge of his features, now saddened, in the deep gloom, he thus accosts him first: 'Who was it, Palinurus, of all the gods, that tore you from us, and whelmed you in the wide sea? Tell me who. Till now I never found him false; but in this one response Apollo has proved a cheat, foretelling that you would be unharmed on the deep, and win your way to the Ausonian frontier, and thus it is that he keeps his word!' 'Nay,' returned he, 'my chief, Anchises' son, Phœbus' tripod has told you no lie, nor did any god whelm me in the sea. No, I chanced to fall, tearing away by main force the rudder, to which I was clinging like sentry to his post, as I guided your course, and dragging it with me in my headlong whirl. Witness those cruel waters, I felt no fear for my own life like that which seized me for your ship, lest, disarmed and disabled, shaken loose from her ruler's hand, she should give way under the great sea that was rising then. Three long nights of storm the south wind swept me over the vast wilderness of convulsed ocean. Hardly at last, at the fourth dawn, I looked out aloft upon Italy from the crest of the wave. Stroke by stroke I was swimming to shore; and now I was just laying hold on safety, had not the savage natives come on me, sword in hand, clogged as I was with my dripping clothes, and clutching with talon fingers the steep mountain-top, and deemed blindly they had found a prize. Now the wave is my home, and the winds keep

tossing me on the beach. Oh, by heaven's pleasant sunshine
and bright sky ; by your father, I adjure you ; by the promise growing up with your Iulus, rescue me with that unconquered arm from this cruel fate: be yourself, and either
spread earth upon me, for that you can surely do, and put
back to Velia's haven ; or, if any way there be, any that your
goddess mother can reveal—for well I ween it is not without
Heaven's leave that you purpose to stem these fearful tides
and the reluctant pool of Styx—stretch your hand to your
poor friend, and take me with you over the water, that at
least I may find in death a place of rest and peace.' So had
he spoken, when thus the priestess begins : ' What demon,
Palinurus, has set on you so monstrous a desire ? You, unburied, look on the Stygian water, and the dread river of
the furies ? You set foot on the bank unbidden ? Cease to
dream that Heaven's destiny can be swayed by prayer. Yet
hear and retain a word which may console your hard lot.
For know that the dwellers in that fatal border, goaded far
and wide through their cities by prodigies from heaven, shall
propitiate your dust: they shall erect a tomb, and through
that tomb send down your funeral dues, and the spot shall
bear for ever the name of Palinurus.' These words allayed
his cares, and banished for awhile grief from that sad bosom :
his heart leaps to the land that is called by his name.

They accordingly continue their journey, and approach the
river. Soon as the boatman saw them, at the moment, from
the wave of Styx, moving through the stilly forest, and turning their steps to the bank, he first bespeaks them thus, and
assails them unaccosted : ' You, whoever you are, that are
making for these waters of ours in warlike trim, speak your
errand from the spot where you are, and come no nearer. This
is the place for the shadows, for Sleep and slumberous Night.
The bodies of the living may not be ferried in my Stygian

barque. Nay, it was not to my joy that I gave Alcides a
passage over the lake, nor Theseus and Pirithous, born of
gods, though they were, and of strength unsubdued. The one
laid a jailer's hand on the warder of Tartarus, even at the foot
of the king's own throne, and dragged him trembling along :
the others essayed to carry off the queen from Pluto's bridal
chamber.' To which the Amphrysian priestess replied in
brief : 'Here there are no stratagems like those ; be not
discomposed ; these weapons are not borne for violence ; the
monstrous guardian of your gate is free to terrify the bloodless spectres from his den with his unending bark ; Proserpine
is free to keep her uncle's home as faithful wife should.
This is Æneas of Troy, renowned for piety and arms alike :
it is to see his father that he is going down to Erebus' lowest
depth of gloom. If thou art moved in nought by the spectacle of piety so signal, yet let this branch '—she uncovered
the branch which was concealed in her robe—'claim recogni-
tion.' At once the angry swell subsides, and the breast is
calm. No further parley. Gazing in wonder at the sacred
offering of the fated bough, last seen so long ago, he turns to
them the sea-green * boat, and draws near the bank. Then he
dislodges other ghostly passengers who were sitting along the
benches, and clears the gangways, while he takes into the
vessel's hollow the mighty Æneas. The sutures of the boat
cracked beneath the weight, as through its rents it drew in
large draughts of marsh-water. At length priestess and prince
are safe across the flood, set down amid featureless mud and
blue-green rushes.

Cerberus, the monster, makes the whole realm ring with his
three barking throats, as he lies in giant length fronting them

---

* So the MS. reads as a translation of *Cæruleam* which, in his note on
this passage, Mr. Conington explains as the same as *ferrugineam*, translated 'iron-grey' above.—[ED.]

in his den's mouth. The priestess, seeing the snakes already
bristling on his neck, throws him a morsel steeped in the
slumber of honey and medicated meal. He, in the frenzy of
hunger, opens his triple jaws to catch it as it comes, and
stretches his enormous back at length on the ground, till
his huge bulk covers the den. Æneas masters the approach
while the warder sleeps, and swiftly passes from the bank of
the river without return.

At once there breaks on his ear a voice of mighty wailing,
infant spirits sobbing and crying on the threshold, babes that,
portionless of the sweets of life, were snatched from the breast
by the black death-day's tyranny, and whelmed in untimely
night. Next to them are those who were done to death by
false accusation. Yet let none think that the lot of award
or the judge's sentence are wanting here. There sits Minos,
the president, urn in hand: he summons an assembly of
the speechless, and takes cognisance of earthly lives and
earthly sins.

Next to them comes the dwelling-place of the sons of sorrow,
who, though guiltless, procured their own death by violence,
and, for mere hatred of the sunshine, flung their lives away.
Oh, how gladly would they now, in the air above, bear to the
end the load of poverty and the full extremity of toil! But
Fate bars the way: the unlovely pool swathes them round
in her doleful waters, and Styx, with her ninefold windings,
keeps them fast.

Not far hence the traveller's eye sees stretching on every
side the Mourning Fields: such the name they bear. Here
dwell those whom cruel Love's consuming tooth has eaten to
the heart, in the privacy of hidden walks and an enshrouding
myrtle wood: their tender sorrows quit them not even in
death. In this region he sees Phædra and Procris, and sad
Eriphyle, pointing to the wounds of her ruthless son, and

Evadne, and Pasiphæ : along with them moves Laodamia, and Cæneus, once a man, now a woman, brought back by the turn of fate to her former self. Among these was Phœnicia's daughter, Dido, fresh from her death-wound, wandering in that mighty wood : soon as the Trojan hero stood at her side, and knew her, looming dimly through the dusk—as a man sees or thinks he sees through the clouds, when the month is young, the rising moon—his tears broke forth, and he addressed her tenderly and lovingly. 'Unhappy Dido ! and was it then a true messenger that reached me with the tale that you were dead : that the sword had done its worst ? Was it, alas, to a grave that I brought you ? By the stars of heaven I swear, by the powers above, by all that is most sacred here underground, against my will, fair queen, I quitted your coast. No; it was the command of the gods ; the same stern force which compels me now to pass through this realm of shade, this wilderness of squalor and abysmal night ; it was that which drove me by its uttered will : nor could I have thought that my departure would bring on you such violence of grief. Stay your step, and withdraw not from the look I bend on you. Whom would you shun ? the last word which fate suffers me to address you is this.' With words like these, Æneas kept soothing the soul that blazed forth through those scowling eyes, and moving himself to tears. She stood with averted head and eyes on the ground, her features as little moved by the speech he essayed as if she held the station of a stubborn flint, or a crag of Marpessa. At length she flung herself away, and, unforgiving still, fled into the shadow of the wood, where her former lord, Sychæus, answers her sorrows with his, and gives her full measure for her love. Yet, none the less, Æneas, thrilled through and through by her cruel fate, follows far on her track with tears, and sends his pity along with her.

Thence he turns, to encounter the appointed way. And now they were already in the furthest region, the separate place tenanted by the great heroes of war. Here there meets him Tydeus, here Parthenopæus, illustrious in arms, and the spectre of pale Adrastus. Here are chiefs of Dardan line, wailed long and loudly in the upper air as they lay low in fight: as he saw them all in long array, he groaned heavily. Glaucus and Medon, and Thersilochus, the three sons of Antenor, and Polyphœtes, Ceres' priest, and Idæus, with his hand still on the car, still on the armour. They surround him, right and left, the ghostly crowd; one look is not sufficient: they would fain linger on and on, and step side by side with him, and learn the cause of his coming. But the nobles of the Danaans, and the flower of Agamemnon's bands, when they saw the hero and his armour gleaming through the shade, were smitten with strange alarm: some turn their backs in flight, as erst they fled to the ships: others raise a feeble war-shout. The cry they essay mocks their straining throats.

Here it is that he sees Priam's son, mangled all over, Deiphobus, his face cruelly marred—face and both hands— his temples despoiled of his ears, and his nose lopped by unseemly carnage. Scarce, in truth, he recognised him, trembling as he was, and trying to hide the terrible vengeance wreaked on him: unaccosted, he addresses him in the tones he knew of old: ' Deiphobus, mighty warrior, scion of Teucer's illustrious stock, who has had the ambition to avenge himself so cruelly? who has had his will of you thus? For me, Rumour told me on that fatal night that you had sunk down, tired with the work of slaughtering the Greeks, on a heap of undistinguished carnage. Then with my own hand, I set up an empty tomb on the Rhœtean shore, and thrice with a loud voice invoked your spirit. There are your name and your arms to keep the spot in memory: your self, dear friend, I could not see, so as to give you repose in the fatherland I was leaving.' To whom the son of Priam : 'Dear friend, you have failed in nought : all that Deiphobus could claim has been paid by you to him and to his shade. No ; it was my own destiny and the deadly wickedness of the Spartan woman that plunged me thus deep in ill : these tokens are of her leaving. How we spent that fatal night in treacherous joyance you know well : too good cause is there to bear it in mind. When the fateful horse at one bound surmounted the height of Pergamus, and brought a mailclad infantry in its laden womb, she feigned a solemn dance, and led round the city Phrygian dames in Bacchic ecstasy ; herself in their midst raising a mighty torch aloft, and calling to the Danaans from the top of the citadel. That hour I spent with care, and over-borne with sleep, was in the hold of our ill-starred bridal chamber, weighed down as I lay, by slumber sweet and sound, the very image of the deep calm of death. Meantime, my peerless helpmate removes from the house arms of every sort : yes, my trusty sword she had withdrawn from my pillow, and now she calls Menelaus to come in, and throws wide the door, hoping, I doubt not, that the greatness of the boon would soften her lover's heart, and that the memory of her crime of old could thus be wiped from men's minds. Why make the story long ? They burst into the chamber, along with them that child of Æolus, then as ever the counsellor of evil. Recompense, ye gods, the Greeks in kind, if these lips, that ask for retribution, are pure and loyal. But you ; what chance has brought you here in your lifetime, let me ask in turn ? Are you come under the spell of ocean-wandering, or by the command of heaven ? or what tyranny of fortune constrains you to visit these sad, sunless dwellings, the abode of confusion ? '

In this interchange of talk, the Dawn-goddess in her flushing car, careering through the sky, had well passed the summit of the arch ; and perchance they had spent all their allotted time in converse like this, had not the Sibyl warned her companion with brief address : ' Night is hastening, Æneas ; and we, as we weep, are making hours pass. This is the spot where the road parts in twain. The right, which goes under the palace-wall of mighty Dis—there lies our way to Elysium ; the left puts in motion the tortures of the wicked, and sends them to Tartarus, the home of crime.' Deiphobus replied : 'Frown not, dread priestess, I depart, to make the ghostly number complete, and plunge again in darkness. Go on your way, our nation's glory, go : may your experience of fate be more blest.' He said, and, while yet speaking, turned away.

Suddenly, Æneas looks back, and, under a rock on the left, sees a broad stronghold, girt by a triple.wall ; a fierce stream surrounds it with surges of fire, Tartarean Phlegethon, and tosses craggy fragments in thunder. Full in front is a vast gate, its pillars of solid adamant. No force of man, not even the embattled powers of heaven,. could break it down. Rising in air is a turret of iron, and Tisiphone, with a gory robe girt round her, sits at the vestibule with sleepless vigilance night and day. Hence sounds of wailing meet the ear, and the crack of remorseless whips ; the clank of steel follows, and the trailing of the chain. Æneas stood still, riveted by the terror of the noise. 'What shapes is guilt wearing now ? tell me, dread maiden. What are the torments that lie on it so hard ? what mean these loud upsoaring shrieks ? ' The priestess returned : ' Noble leader of the Teucrians, no innocent foot may tread that guilty threshold ; but the day when Hecate set me over the groves of Avernus, she taught me from her own lips the punishments of Heaven, and led me through from end to end. Here rules Gnosian Rhadamanthus, a reign of iron—avenger, at once, and judge of cowering guilt, he compels a confession of what crimes soever men in upper air, blindly rejoicing in the cheat, have kept secret till the hour of death, to be expiated then. In a moment, Tisiphone the torturer, with uplifted scourge, lashes from side to side the spurned and guilty soul : and brandishing in her left grim knots of serpents, summons her unpitying sisterhood. Then at last, grating on their dread-sounding hinge, the awful gates are opened. See you what manner of sentry is seated at the entrance ? what a presence is guarding the threshold ? Know that a Hydra fiercer yet with fifty monstrous throats, each a yawning pit, holds her seat within. Then there is the abyss of Tartarus in sheer descent, extending under the shades, twice as far as man's skyward gaze from earth to the heaven of Olympus. Here are earth's ancient progeny, the Titan brood, hurled down by the thunderbolt to wallow in the depths of the gulf. Here too saw I the twin sons of Aloeus, frames of giant bulk, who essayed by force of hand to pluck down the mighty heavens, and dislodge Jove from his realm in the sky. I saw too Salmoneus, smitten with cruel vengeance, while mimicking the fires of Jove and the rumblings of Olympus. Borne in a four-horse car, a flaring torch in hand, he was making his triumphal progress through the tribes of Greece, and the midst of Elis' city, and bidding men accord him a god's homage. Madman ! to counterfeit the storm-cloud and the unrivalled thunder-bolt with the rattle of brass and the beat of horses' horny hoofs. But the almighty sire from the depth of his cloudy dwelling, hurled his weapon—no futile firebrand his, no pinewood's smoky glare—and dashed him headlong down with that tremendous blast. Tityos, too, the foster-child of Earth's common breast, it was mine to see : his body lies extended over nine whole acres, and there is a monstrous vulture with hooked beak shearing away his imperishable liver, and reaping a harvest of suffering from his vitals, as it digs deep for its meal, and burrows in the cavern of his breast, nor gives the new-growing filaments rest or respite. What need to tell of the Lapithæ, of Ixion and Pirithous— men who live under a black crag, ever falling, and just in act to drop? The lofty couch is spread for the banquet, and the pillar of gold gleams underneath : the feast is before them, served in kingly luxury; but the eldest of the Furies is couched at their side : she will not let them stretch a hand to the board : she starts up with torch uplifted and thunder in her tones. Here are they who lived in hatred with their brethren while life yet was ; who smote a parent or wove for a client the web of fraud ; who gained a treasure and brooded over it alone, and never shared it with their kin—a mighty number these—adulterers, who were slain for their crime ; citizens who followed the standard of treason ; slaves who shrunk not from breaking their troth to their lords : all in prison awaiting their doom. Ask not *what* doom is theirs, what phase, what fate has whelmed them so deep. Others roll the huge stone up the hill, or hang dispread from the spokes of the wheel : there sits, as he will sit for evermore, unhappy Theseus : and Phlegyas, from the depth of his agony, keeps warning all, and proclaiming with a voice of terror through the shades : "Learn hereby to be righteous, and not to scorn the gods." This sold his country for gold, and saddled her with a tyrant ; for gain he made and unmade laws : this assailed his daughter's bed, and essayed a forbidden union : all dared some monstrous crime, and enjoyed their daring. No ; had I even a hundred tongues, and a hundred mouths, and lungs of iron, not then could I embrace all the types of crime, or rehearse the whole muster-roll of vengeance.'

So spoke Apollo's aged priestess ; and then resuming : 'But come,' she cries, 'speed on your way, and fulfil the duty you have essayed : quicken we our pace. I see the walls which the Cyclopian forge raised in air, and the arched gates con-

fronting us, where sacred rule bids us set down our offering.'
As she spoke, they step side by side through the dusky ways,
dispatch the interval of distance, and draw near the gate.
Æneas masters the approach, sprinkles his body with pure
spring water, and fixes the branch on the portal's front.

And now these things done at length, and the offering to
the goddess accomplished, they have reached the regions of
bliss, green pleasaunces of happy groves, and the abodes of the
blest. Here ether clothes the plains with an ampler pleni-
tude and a dazzling lustre; and the eye beholds a sun and
stars of its own. There are some, plying their limbs on the
grassy wrestling-ground, conflicting in sport, and grappling
each other on the yellow sand: some are beating their feet
in the dance, and chanting songs. There, too, is the Thracian
priest in his flowing robe, singing the seven notes in unison
with the dancer's measure, and striking them now with his
fingers, now with the quill of ivory. Here are the old race
of Teucer, a goodly family, heroes of lofty soul, born in
earth's better days, Ilus and Assaracus, and Dardanus, founder
of Troy. From afar he gazes wonderingly on their warrior
arms and their ghostly chariots. Their spears stand rooted
in the ground, and their unyoked steeds graze dispersedly
over the meadow. All the delight they took when alive in
chariots and armour, all their pride in grooming and feeding
their horses, goes with them underground, and animates them
there. See, too, his eye rests on others regaling on either
hand upon the grass, and singing in chorus a joyous pæan, all
in a fragrant grove of bay, the source whence welling forth
into the upper world, Eridanus flows in broad current between
his wooded banks. Here is a noble company who braved
wounds in fight for fatherland; all the priests who kept their
purity while life was; all the poets whose hearts were clean,
and their songs worthy Phœbus' ear; all who by cunning

inventions gave a grace to life, and whose worthy deeds made their fellows think of them with love : each has his brow cinctured with a snow-white fillet. Looking on the multitude as it streamed around, the Sibyl bespoke them thus—Musæus before all ; for he stands the centre of that vast crowd, which looks up to him, as with rising shoulders he towers above them : 'Tell us, happy spirits, and you, best of bards, which is Anchises' haunt ? which his home ? for it is to see him that we have come hither, and won our way over the mighty river of Erebus.' Instant the hero replied in brief : 'Here there are no fixed abodes : our dwellings are in shadowy groves : our settlements on the velvet slope of banks and meadows fresh with running streams. But come, if you will, climb this hill with me, and I will set your feet at once on a road that will lead you.' So saying, he moves on before, and from the top of the ridge points to broad fields of light, while they descend from the summit.

But father Anchises, down in the depth of the green dell, was surveying with fond observance the spirits now confined there, but hereafter to pass into the light of day, and scanning, as chance would have it, the whole multitude of his people, even his loved posterity, their destinies, their warrior deeds, their ways and their works. Soon as he saw Æneas advancing through the grass to meet him, he stretched out both his hands with eager movement, tears gushed over his cheeks, and words escaped his lips : 'And are you come at last ? has love fulfilled a father's hopes and surmounted the perils of the way ? is it mine to look on your face, my son, and listen and reply as we talked of old ? Yes ; I was even thinking so in my own mind. I was reckoning that it would be, counting over the days. Nor has my longing played me false. Oh, the lands and the mighty seas from which you have come to my presence ! the dangers, my son, that have tossed and smitten you ! Oh, how I have feared lest you should come to harm in that realm of Libya !' The son replied : ' Your shade it was, father, your melancholy shade, that, coming to me oft and oft, constrained me to knock at these doors : here, in the Tyrrhene deep my ships are riding at anchor. Let us grasp hand in hand : let us, my father ! Oh, withdraw not from my embrace !' As he spoke, the streaming tears rolled down his face. Thrice, as he stood, he essayed to fling his arms round that dear neck : thrice the phantom escaped the hands that caught at it in vain, impalpable as the wind, fleeting as the wings of sleep.

Meanwhile Æneas sees in the retired vale a secluded grove' with brakes and rustling woods, and the river of Lethe, which floats along by those abodes of peace. Round it were flying races and tribes untold : even as in the meadows when bees in calm summer-tide settle on flower after flower, and stream over the milk-white lilies, the humming fills the plain. Startled at the sudden sight, Æneas wonderingly inquires what it means, what are those waters in the distance, or who the men that are thronging the banks in crowds so vast. To him his father Anchises : ' They are spirits to whom Destiny has promised new bodies, there at the side of Lethe's water, drinking the wave of carelessness, and the long draught of oblivion. In truth I have long wished to tell you of them and show them before you, to recount the long line of my kindred, that you may rejoice with me now that Italy is found.' ' Oh, my father ! and must we think that there are souls that fly hence aloft into the upper air, and thus return to the sluggish fellowship of the body ? can their longing for light be so mad as this ?' ' I will tell you, my son, nor hold you longer in doubt.' So replies Anchises, and unfolds the story in order.

' Know, first, that heaven and earth, and the watery plains,

and the Moon's lucid ball, and Titan's starry fires are kept
alive by a spirit within : a mind pervading each limb stirs the
whole frame and mingles with the mighty mass. Hence
spring the races of men and beasts, and living things with
wings, and the strange forms that Ocean carries beneath his
marble surface. These particles have a fiery glow, a heavenly
nature, struggling against the clogs of corrupting flesh, the
dullness of limbs of clay and bodies ready to die. Hence
come their fears and lusts, their joys and griefs : nor can
they discern the heavenly light, prisoned as they are in
night and blind dungeon walls. Nay, when life's last ray
has faded from them, not even then, poor wretches, are they
wholly freed from ill, freed from every plague of the flesh :
those many taints must needs be ingrained strangely in the
being, so long as they have grown with it. So they are
schooled with punishment, and pay in suffering for ancient
ill : some are hung up and dispread to the piercing winds :
others have the stain of wickedness washed out under the
whelming gulf, or burnt out with fire : each is chastised in
his own spirit : then we are sped through the breadth of
Elysium, while some few remain to inhabit these happy plains,
till the lapse of ages, when time's cycle. is complete, has
cleansed the ingrained blot and left a pure residue of heavenly
intelligence, the flame of essential ether. All of these, when
they have rounded the circle of a thousand years, Heaven
summons to the stream of Lethe, a mighty concourse, to the
end that with memory effaced they may return to the vault
of the sky, and learn to wish for a new union with the body.'

Anchises ended : he draws his son and the Sibyl with
him into the midst of the assemblage, the heart of that buzzing
crowd, and mounts an eminence, whence he might see face
to face the whole of the long procession, and learn each
comer's looks.

'Now then, for the glories of the Dardan race from this time onward, the posterity reserved for you in the Italian line, noble spirits, the ordained heirs of our proud name : of these I will tell you, and inform you of your destiny.

'He whom you see there, the youth leaning on the pointless spear, his lot is to fill the next place in light : he will be first to rise to upper day, born from the admixture of Italian blood, Silvius, that great Alban name, your latest offspring, whom in your old age at set of life your spouse Lavinia will bear you in the woods, himself a king and the father of kings to be : from him it is that our race shall rule over Alba the Long. Next comes mighty Procas, the pride of the people of Troy, and Capys, and Numitor, and a second bearer of your name, Silvius Æneas, himself renowned alike for piety and for valour, if ever he should come to the throne of Alba. What glorious youths ! look what strength they carry in their port, while their brows are shaded by the civic oak ! These shall uprear for you, high on the mountains, Nomentum, and Gabii, and Fidenæ's town, and the towers of Collatia, Pometii and Inuus' camp, and Bola, and Cora ; names which shall one day be named : now they are mere nameless lands. Romulus, too, the child of Mars, shall come along with his grandsire. Romulus, whom a mother, bearing Ilium's name, shall produce from the blood of Assaracus. See you the two plumes standing on his crest, how his sire marks him even now for the upper world by his own token of honour ? Yes, my son, it is by his auspices that our glorious Rome shall extend her empire to earth's end, her ambition to the skies, and embrace seven hills with the wall of a single city, blest parent of a warrior brood : even as the mighty Berecyntian mother rides tower-crowned through the towns of Phrygia, proud of the gods that have sprung from her, a hundred grand-children at her knee, all dwellers in heaven, all lords of the lofty sky.

Hither now turn your two rays of vision : look at this family,
at Romans of your own.　Heré is Cæsar : here the whole progeny of Iulus, as it will pass one day under heaven's mighty
cope.　This, this is he, the man promised to you so often,
Augustus Cæsar, true child of a god, who shall establish again
for Latium a golden age in that very region where Saturn
once reigned, while he stretches his sway alike beyond Garamantian and Indian.　See, the land is lying outside the stars,
outside the sun's yearly path, where heaven-carrier Atlas
turns round on his shoulder the pole, studded with burning
constellations.　In view of his approach, a shiver runs already
by oracular warning through Caspian realms and Mæotian
land, and there is stir and confusion at the mouths of seven-
fold Nile.　Nay, even Alcides traversed no such length of
earth, though he stalked the brazen-footed deer, or tamed
Erymanthus' savage wilds, and appalled Lerna with his arrows :
no, nor he who guides his triumphal car with reins of ivy-leaf,
Bacchus, driving his tigers down from Nysa's lofty top.　And
do we still hesitate to let prowess give scope to power, or does
fear prevent our setting foot on Ausonian soil ?　But who is
he in the distance, conspicuous with a wreath of olive, with
sacred vessels in his hand ?　Ah ! I know the hoary hair and
beard of the king of Rome, who shall give the infant city the
support of law, sent from his homely Cures and a land of
poverty into a mighty empire.　Next shall come one doomed
to break his country's peace, and stir up with the war-cry
of his name, Tullus, warriors rusting in ease and squadrons
that have forgotten their triumphs.　Ancus follows, a greater
boaster, even now too ready to catch the breath of a popular
cheer.　Would you look too at the kings of Tarquin's house,
at the haughty spirit of Brutus the avenger, and the fasces
retrieved ?　He shall be the first to take the consul's power
and the axes of doom : the father will bring his rebel sons

to death, all for fair freedom's sake. Unhappy man! let
after ages speak of that deed as they will, strong over all
will be patriot passion and unmeasured thirst of praise. Look,
there are the Drusi and the Decii, and Torquatus with his
unpitying axe, and Camillus the restorer of the standards.
But those whom you see there, dressed alike in gleaming
armour—spirits at harmony now and so long as they are confined in darkness—alas! how vast a war will they wage, each
with each, if they shall attain the light of day, what arraying
of hosts, what carnage will there be! Father-in-law and son-
in-law, the one coming down from Alpine ramparts and the
stronghold of Monœcus: the other drawn up against him with
the forces of the east. Do not, do not, my children, make
wars like these familiar to your spirits: turn not your country's
valour against your country's vitals: and you, restrain yourself
the first: you, whose lineage is from heaven, drop the steel
from your grasp, heir of Anchises' blood. See here, a conqueror who shall drive to the lofty Capitol the car of triumph
over Corinth, glorious from Achæan slaughter: here one who
shall lay Argos in dust, and Agamemnon's own Mycenæ, ay,
and the heir of Æacus, with Achilles' martial blood in his
veins: a Roman's vengeance for his Trojan grandsires, and
for Pallas' insulted fame. What tongue would leave you
unpraised, great Cato, or Cossus, you? or the race of the
Gracchi, or those twin thunderbolts of war, the Scipios, Libya's
ruin, or Fabricius, princely in his poverty, or you, Serranus,
sowing your own ploughed fields? When, ye Fabii, will
panting praise overtake you? You are in truth our greatest,
the single saviour of our state by delay. Others, I doubt not,
will mould the breathing brass to more flesh-like softness, and
spread over marble the look of life. Others will plead better
at the bar, will trace with the rod the courses of heaven, and
foretell the risings of the stars. Yours, Roman, be the lesson

to govern the nations as their lord : this is your destined culture, to impose the settled rule of peace, to spare the humbled,
and to crush the proud.'

Father Anchises paused ; and, as they wondered, went on
to say : 'See how Marcellus advances in the glory of the
general's spoils, towering with conqueror's majesty over all the
warriors near ! When the state of Rome reels under the
invader's shock, he shall stay it; his horse's hoofs shall trample
the Carthaginian and the revolted Gaul ; and he shall dedicate
the third suit of armour to Quirinus the sire.' Hereupon
Æneas, for he saw walking at Marcellus' side a youth of goodly
presence and in gleaming armour, but with little joy on his brow
and downcast eyes : 'Who, my father, is he that thus attends
the warrior's march ? his son, or one of the glorious line of his
posterity ? What a hum runs through the attendant train !
how lofty his own mien ! but the shadow of gloomy night
hovers saddening round his head.' Father Anchises began, tears
gushing forth the while : 'Alas, my son ! ask not of the heavy
grief that those of your blood must bear. Of him the fates
shall give but a glimpse to earth, nor suffer him to continue
longer. Yes, powers of the sky ! Rome's race would have been
in your eyes too strong, had a boon like this been its own for
ever. What groanings of the brave shall be wafted from
Mars' broad field to Mars' mighty town ! What a funeral,
father Tiber, shall thine eyes behold, as thou flowest past
that new-built sepulchre ! No child of the stock of Ilion shall
raise his Latian ancestors to such heights of hope : never
while time lasts shall the land of Romulus take such pride
in any that she has reared. Woe for the piety, for the
ancient faith, for the arm unconquered in battle ! Never
would foeman have met that armed presence unscathed,
marched he on foot into the field or tore with bloody spur
the flank of his foaming steed. Child of a nation's sorrow !

were there hope of thy breaking the tyranny of fate, thou shalt be Marcellus. Bring me handfuls of lilies, that I may strew the grave with their dazzling hues, and crown, if only with these gifts, my young descendant's shade, and perform the vain service of sorrow.' Thus they wander here and there through the whole expanse in the broad fields of shadow and take note of all. Soon as Anchises had taken his son from end to end, and fired his mind with the prospect of that glorious history, he then tells the warrior of the battles that he must fight at once, and informs him of the Laurentian tribes and Latinus' town, and how to shun or stand the shock of every peril.

There are two gates of Sleep: the one, as story tells, of horn, supplying a ready exit for true spirits : the other gleaming with the polish of dazzling ivory, but through it the powers below send false dreams to the world above. Thither Anchises, talking thus, conducts his son and the Sibyl, and dismisses them by the gate of ivory. Æneas traces his way to the fleet and returns to his comrades ; then sails along the shore for Caieta's haven. The anchor is cast from the prow : the keels are ranged on the beach.

BOOK VII.

AND thou, too, in thy death, Caieta, nurse of Æneas, hast left to our coast the heritage of an ever-living fame; still in this later day thy glory hovers over thy resting-place, and a name on Hesperia's mighty seaboard is thy monument, if that be renown. So when good Æneas had paid the last dues and raised a funeral mound, and had waited for the calming of the deep, he spreads sail and leaves the harbour. Nightward the breezes blow, nor does the fair Moon scorn to show the way: her rippling light makes the sea shine again. The next land they skirt is the coast of Circe's realm, where in queenly state the daughter of the Sun thrills her forest fastness with never-ending song, and in her haughty mansion burns fragrant cedar to give light by night, as she draws her shrill comb over the delicate warp. From the shore they heard the growling noise of lions in wrath, disdaining their bonds and roaring in midnight hour, bristly boars and caged bears venting their rage, and shapes of huge wolves fiercely howling: things which Circe, fell goddess, had transformed by her magic drugs from the mien of man to a beast's visage and a beast's hide. So, lest the pious race of Troy should suffer such monstrous change, were they to seek harbour there or approach the perilous shore, Neptune filled their sails with favouring breezes, sped their flight along, and wafted them past the seething waters.

The sea was just reddening in the dawn, and Aurora was shining down from heaven's height in saffron robe and rosy

car when all at once the winds were laid, and every breath
sank in sudden sleep, and the oars pull slowly against the
smooth unmoving wave. In the same moment Æneas, looking
out from the sea, beholds a mighty forest. Among the trees
Tiber, that beauteous river, with his gulfy rapids and the
burden of his yellow sand, breaks into the main. Around
and above, birds of all plumes, the constant tenants of bank and
stream, were lulling the air with their notes and flying among
the woods. He bids his comrades turn aside and set their prows
landward, and enters with joy the river's shadowed bed.

Now be with me Erato, and I will unfold who were the
kings, what the stage of circumstance, what the condition
of ancient Latium, when the stranger host first landed on
Ausonian shores, and will recall how the first blood was
drawn. Thou, goddess, thou prompt thy poet's memory.
Mine is a tale of grisly war, of battle array, and princes in
their fury rushing on carnage—of Tyrrhenian ranks, and all
Hesperia mustered in arms. Grander is the pile of events
that rises on my view, grander the task I essay. It was
the time when king Latinus, now stricken in age, was ruling
country and city in the calm of years of peace. He, as story
tells us, was the son of Faunus and a Laurentine nymph, Marica.
Faunus' father was Picus, who owes his birth to thee, great
Saturn: thou art the first founder of the line. No son, no
male progeny, so Heaven willed, had Latinus now; just as it
was budding into youth, the branch was cut off. The sole
maintainer of the race, the sole guardian of that princely house
was a daughter, already ripe for wedlock, already arrived at
full-blown womanhood. Many were her wooers from mighty
Latium, nay, from all Ausonia. One wooer there was in
beauty passing others, Turnus, strong in the glory of sires and
grandsires: his alliance the queen with intense yearning was
seeking to compass; but heavenly portents bar the way with

manifold alarm. There was a laurel in the middle of the palace, in the very heart of royal privacy, sacred in its every leaf, cherished by the awful observance of many years; men said that father Latinus himself found it there when he first laid the foundation of the tower, dedicated it to Phœbus, and thence gave his new people the name of Laurentines. On the top of this tree lodged a dense swarm of bees, marvellous to tell, sailing thither with loud humming noise across the liquid air, and twining their legs together, the cluster in a moment was seen to hang from the leafy bough. At once spoke a prophet: 'There is a stranger approaching: I see him now; along this self-same path a troop is moving hitherward, and commanding the height of the citadel.' Moreover, while Lavinia is applying the hallowed torch to the altars, as she stands in maiden purity at her father's side, she was seen, oh, monstrous sight! to catch the fire with her long tresses, all her headgear consuming in the crackling flame, her queenly hair, her jewelled coronal all ablaze, till at last she was wrapt in smoke and yellow glare, and scattered the fire-god's sparks the whole palace through. There indeed was a tale of horror, a marvel and a portent; for, said the wise men, she will herself be illustrious in fame and fortune, but to the nation she bodes tremendous war. Troubled by these prodigies, the king repairs to the oracle of Faunus, his prophetic sire, to question at the groves beneath Albunea's shade—that queen of forests, ever vocal with the sacred waters, ever breathing from its dark heart deadly vaporous steam. It is here that the tribes of Italy and all Œnotrian land seek answers in their perplexity; hither the priestess brings the enquirer's offering, lies in the still of night on a couch of slaughtered sheep's skins, and turns to sleep, when she sees many phantoms flitting in marvellous fashion, and hears divers voices, and enjoys communion with the gods, and holds converse with Acheron down in Avernus' deep.

Here also king Latinus, in quest of an answer, was sacrificing duly a hundred sheep of the second year, and was lying on their skins, a fleecy bed, when sudden from the depth of the grove an utterance was heard: 'Look not to ally your daughter in wedlock of Latium, O my son; put not faith in marriage chambers dressed and ready; there are sons-in-law from a far country now on their way, men destined by mixing their blood with ours to exalt our name to the spheres—men whose lineal posterity shall one day look down and see under their feet the whole world, far as the two oceans which the sun surveys in his daily round, revolving beneath them and wielded by their control.' Such was the response of father Faunus, the counsel given at still of night: nor does Latinus hold it shut in the prison of his own lips; but Fame had flown with the rumour through Ausonia far and wide from city to city, when the young chivalry of old Laomedon anchored their ships on the river's grassy bank.

Æneas and his chief captains, and Iulus young and fair, lay their limbs to rest under the boughs of a lofty tree; there they spread the banquet, putting cakes of flour along the sward to support the food—such was Jove's high inspiration—and rearing on the wheaten foundation a pile of wilding fruits. It chanced that when the rest was eaten, the want of meat forced them to ply their tooth on those scanty gifts of Ceres—to profane with venturous hand and mouth the sanctity of the cake's fated circle, nor respect the square impressed on its surface. 'What! eating our tables as well?' cries Iulus, in his merry vein; that and no more. That utterance first told the hearers that their toils were over: even as it fell from the boy's mouth his father caught it up and broke it short, wondering in himself at the power of Heaven. Then anon: 'Hail to thee, promised land of my destiny! hail to you,' he cries, 'Troy's faithful gods! Yes, here is our home—this our country. It was my father—these, I remember, were the mystic words of fate he left me: My son, whenever you are wafted to an unknown coast, and hunger drives you, failing food, to eat your tables, then remember my saying, there look for a home of rest, set up your first roof-tree and strengthen it with mound and rampart. This was the hunger he meant. This was the last strait in store for us, not the beginning but the end of death. Come then, take heart, and with the morrow's earliest light explore we what is the place, who its dwellers, where the city of the nation, making from the haven in different ways. Meanwhile pour libations to Jove, invoke in prayer my sire Anchises, and set again the wine on the board. So having said, he wreathes his brow with the leafy spray, and offers prayer to the genius of the spot; to Earth the eldest of the gods; to the nymphs and the streams yet unknown by name: after that, to Night and Night's new-born stars and Ida's Jove, and Phrygia's mighty mother, invoking each in turn, and his own two parents in the upper and the nether world. Just then the Almighty Father thundered thrice aloft in a clear sky, and with his own right hand flashed in open view from on high a cloud ablaze with rays of golden light. At once the news spreads among the Trojan ranks that the day has arrived when they are to build their promised city. With emulous haste they celebrate the banquet, and in the power of the august presage set on the bowls exultingly, and wreathe the wine.

Soon as on the morrow the risen day began to illumine the earth with the first sparkle of her torch, some here, some there, they set about exploring the city, the frontiers, the seaboard of the country. This, they learn, is the spring of Numicius, this the river Tiber, this the home of the brave Latian race. Thereupon Anchises' son commands an embassy of a hundred, chosen from all classes alike, to go to the monarch's royal city, all of them with wreathed boughs from Pallas' tree, to carry presents for his honoured hand, and entreat his friendship for the Teucrians. They delay not, but hasten at his bidding, moving with rapid pace, while he is marking out the city with a shallow trench, preparing the ground, and surrounding this their first settlement on the coast, camp-fashion, with battlements and earthworks. Meanwhile the missioned band had performed their journey, and were in sight of the towers and stately homes of Latium, and passing under the city wall. In a space before the town, boys and youths in their prime are exercising on horseback, and breaking in their harnessed cars among clouds of dust, or bending the sharp-springing bow, or hurling from the arm the quivering javelin, or vying on foot or with the gloves, when galloping up, a messenger announces, in the aged monarch's ears, that mighty men have arrived in strange attire. The king bids him summon them into the presence-hall, and takes his seat in the midst on his ancestral throne. It was a reverend pile, of vast proportions, raised high upon a hundred pillars, on the city's topmost ground, the palace of Picus the Laurentine, clothed in the terror of waving woods and hereditary awe. Here it was held to be of auspicious presage that kings should first take in hand the sceptre, and lift up the fasces : this temple was their senate-house, the hall for their sacrificial feasts : here, when a ram was slain, the seniors were wont to banquet down long lines of tables. Here, too, in succession were the effigies of past generations, carved from ancient cedar. Italus and father Sabinus, planter of the vine, preserving in that mimic form his curved hook, and hoary Saturn, and the image of two-faced Janus, all standing in the vestibule, and other kings from the earliest days, and heroes who had sustained the war-god's wounds in fighting for their country. Moreover, there was hanging

s

on the sacred doors abundance of armour, captive chariots, crooked axe-heads, helmet-crests, ponderous gates, javelins, and shields, and beaks torn from vessels. There, as in life, was sitting, decked with Quirinal staff and robe of scanty border, in his left hand the sacred shield, Picus, tamer of the steed, he whom, in her bridal jealousy, Circe, by a stroke of her golden rod and the witchery of her drugs, transformed to a bird, and scattered spots over his wings. Such was the temple where Latinus, seated on his ancestral throne, summoned the Teucrians to his presence within, and on their entry with placid mien bespoke them thus :—

'Tell me, sons of Dardanus—for we know your city and your race, and your coming over the deep has reached our ears—what is your errand? what cause or what necessity has wafted your ships to our Ausonian coast through those many leagues of blue water? Be it from ignorance of the way or stress of weather, or any of the thousand chances that happen to seamen on the main, that you have passed between our river's banks, and are resting in the haven, shrink not from our welcome, but know in the Latian race the true people of Saturn, kept in righteousness by no band of law, but by our own instinct and the rule of our parent-god. And now I remember, though years have dulled the freshness of the tale, that aged Auruncans used to tell how in this land Dardanus saw the light, and hence he won his way to the towns of Phrygian Ida and Thracian Samos, which men now call Samothrace. Ay, it was from the house of Tuscan Corythus he went, and now the golden palace of starry heaven seats him on a throne, and among the altars of the gods makes room for him.'

He ended; and Ilioneus followed thus: 'Great king, illustrious son of Faunus, no stress of gloomy storm has made us the sport of the waves and driven us on your coast, no sky or land misread has beguiled us of our track : of set purpose, with full intent, we are arrived one and all at your city, driven from a realm once the greatest which the sun surveyed in his course from end to end of heaven. From Jove is the origin of our race ; in Jove, as their ancestor, the sons of Dardanus glory ; our monarch himself, sprung of Jove's own pure blood, Æneas of Troy, has sent us to your doors. How dire a hurricane, launched from fell Mycenæ, swept over Ida's plains—how the two worlds of Europe and Asia, fate driving each, met and crashed together—has reached the ears of the man, if such there be, whom earth's last corner withdraws from the wash of ocean, and his too who is parted from his fellows by the zone that lies midmost among the four, the zone of the tyrannous sun. From the jaws of that deluge flying over many and mighty waters, we ask of you for our country's gods a narrow resting-place—the harmless privilege of the coast, and the common liberty of water and air. We shall be no disgrace to your kingdom, nor light shall be the fame that men will blaze of you, nor shall gratitude for your great bounty grow old, nor shall Ausonia mourn the day when she welcomed Troy to her heart. I swear by Æneas' star, by his strong right hand, known as such by all who have proved it in friendship or in war, many have been the peoples, many the nations—nay, scorn us not for that we accost you with fillets of suppliance and words of prayer—who have sued for our company and wished to make us one with them. But the oracles of heaven, speaking as they only can, have driven us to search out your realms. Hence sprang Dardanus ; hither Apollo bids us return, with the instance of high command, even to Tuscan Tiber and the sacred waters of Numicius' spring. Moreover here are presents from Æneas, the scanty offerings of past prosperity, relics snatched from the flames of Troy. From this gold his father, Anchises, poured libations at the altar; this was Priam's royal accoutrement, when he gave laws in kingly fashion to the assembled people; this sceptre, this sacred diadem, these robes, the work of Trojan dames.'

Thus, as Ilioneus is speaking, Latinus holds his countenance in set downcast gaze, and sits rooted to his throne, turning his eyes in intense thought. Nor does the broidered purple stir his princely mind; no, nor the sceptre of Priam, so deeply as he ponders on the wedlock, the bridal bed of his daughter, revolving in his breast old Faunus' oracle. This must be that predicted son-in-law, arrived from a foreign home, destined to reign in joint sovereignty with himself; thence must be born that glorious progeny, whose prowess is to master the world. At length he breaks out in glad tones: 'May the gods prosper our intent and ratify their own presage! Yes, Trojan, you shall have your prayer, nor do I reject your presents. Long as Latinus shall reign, you shall not lack the bounty of a fruitful soil, nor miss the wealth of Troy. Let but Æneas himself, if his desire of us is so great, if he covets the tie of hospitality and the style of alliance, come to our presence, nor shrink from eyes that will view him kindly. Peace will be incomplete till I have touched your monarch's hand. And now do you take back to your king this my message: I have a daughter, whose marriage with a husband of our nation is forbidden by voices from my father's shrine, by countless prodigies from heaven; sons-in-law are to arrive from foreign climes —such, they say, is Fate's will for Latium—who by mixing their blood with ours are to exalt our name to the spheres. That he is this chosen one of destiny is my belief, and, if my mind reads the future true, my award.' With these words the old king makes choice of horses from the multitude he possessed. Three hundred there were, sleek-coated, standing in their lofty stalls. At once he bids his servants bring for each of the Teucrians a fleet-foot with housings of embroidered purple; golden poitrels hang down to the chest of each; there is gold on their coverings; yellow gold under their champing teeth. For the absent Æneas he orders a car and two coursers of ethereal seed, snorting fire from their nostrils, sprung of that brood which artful Circe raised up fraudfully to her father the Sun, a spurious race, from the womb of a mortal dam. Thus graced with gifts and kind speeches, the children of Æneas journey homeward on their tall steeds, and carry tidings of peace.

Meanwhile, there was Jove's relentless spouse travelling back from her own Argos, city of Inachus, and already launched on mid air; looking from the sky over Sicilian Pachynus, she beheld in distant prospect Æneas in his hour of joy and the Dardan fleet. Already she sees him building his home; already he has made the soil his friend, and has parted from his ships. Pierced with bitter grief, she stayed her course, and then, shaking her head, pours from her heart words like these: 'Ah, that hated stock! those destinies of Phrygia that hold my destinies in check! Did the dead really fall on the plains of Sigeum? were the captives captured in truth? did the flames of Troy burn the men of Troy? Through the heart of the battle, through the heart of the fire they have found a way. Ay, belike, my power at last lies gasping and spent; my hatred is slaked and I am at peace. I, who followed them with a foe's zeal over the water even when tossed from their country's arms, and met the exiles front to front on every sea! Spent on these Teucrians is all that sky and surge can do. Have Syrtes, has Scylla, has Charybdis' yawning gulf stood me aught in stead? They have gained the channel of Tiber, the haven of their wishes, and may laugh at ocean and at me. Mars had strength to destroy the Lapithan nation, huge as they were ; the father of the gods gave up the honoured land of Calydon to Diana's vengeance ; and what had Lapithans or Calydon done to earn such penal ruin ? But I, Jove's great consort, who have stooped, miserably stooped, to leave nothing untried, who have assumed every form by turns, am vanquished by Æneas. Well, if my power be not august enough, I would not shrink from suing for other aid, be it found where it may ; if I cannot prevail above, I will stir up the fiends of the deep. It will not be mine to keep him from the crown of Latium—be it so fixed for him by fate unalterably is his bride Lavinia ; but delays and impediments may well be where the matter is so great ; but to cut off the subjects of our two monarchs—this may be done. So let father and son-in-law embrace, at the cost of their people's lives. The blood of Trojan and Rutulian shall be your dower, fair lady ; Bellona is waiting to lead you to your chamber. Nor is Hecuba the only mother that has teemed with a fire-brand and given birth to a nuptial blaze ; Venus sees the tale repeated in her own offspring—a second Paris—a funeral torch rekindled for reviving Troy.'

Having vented words like these, she flew down in black rage to the earth ; and now she summons Alecto the baleful from the dwelling of the dread goddesses and the darkness of the pit—Alecto, whom bitter wars, and strifes, and stratagems, and injurious crimes cheer like a cordial. Hateful even to Pluto her sire is the fiend, hateful to her Tartarean sisters, so many the forms she puts on, so terrible the mien of each, so countless the vipers that burgeon blackly from her head. Her, thus dreadful, Juno lashes to fiercer fury, speaking on this wise : 'Grant me, maiden daughter of Night, a boon all my own—thine undivided aid, that my praise and renown may not be dashed from their pedestal—that the children of Æneas may not be able to ensnare Latinus in a bridal alliance

or beset the Italian frontier. Thou canst make brothers of
one soul take arms and fight; canst make peaceful homes
dens of strife; thou canst gain entrance for the scourge and
the funeral torch: thou hast a thousand names, a thousand
means of ill. Stir up that prolific bosom, snap the formed
bands of peace, scatter the incentives of war, let the nation
in the same moment desire, demand, and seize the sword.'

So then Alecto, empoisoned with Gorgon venom, first repairs
to Latium and the lofty halls of the Laurentine monarch, and
sits down before the hushed chamber of queen Amata, who,
as she mused on the arrival of the Trojans and Turnus' bridal
hopes, was glowing and seething with all a woman's passion,
a woman's spleen. Snatching a snake from her dark venomed
locks, she hurls it at her, and lodges it in the bosom close to
the very heart, that, maddened by the pest, she may drive
the whole house wild. In glides the reptile unfelt, winding
between the robe and the marble breast, and beguiles her into
frenzy, breathing into her lungs its viperous breath; the linked
gold round her neck turns to the monstrous serpent; so does
the festoon of her long fillet; it twines her hair, it slides
smoothly from limb to limb. And while the first access of
contagion, stealing in with clammy poison, is pervading her
senses and threading her bones with flame, ere yet the soul
has caught fire through the whole compass of the bosom, she
speaks with gentle plaint, as mothers wont, shedding many
tears over her child and the Phrygian alliance: 'And are
fugitives from Troy to take Lavinia in marriage, good father?
have you no compassion for your daughter and yourself?
none for her mother, whom with the first fair gale the faithless pirate will leave and make for the deep, carrying off his
maiden prey? Ay, things were not so when the Phrygian
shepherd stole into Lacedæmon, and bore away Leda's Helen
to Troy town. Where is your pledged faith? where your old

tenderness for your own blood, and your hand plighted so oft to your kinsman Turnus? If Latian folk must have a son-in-law fetched from a foreign stock, and this is unalterably fixed, and your father Faunus' command sits heavy on your soul, I hold that every nation is foreign whose independence severs it from our rule, and that such is Heaven's intent. Turnus, too, if you go back to the first foundation of his house, has Inachus and Acrisius for his ancestors, and the heart of Mycenæ for his home.' But when, having tried in vain what these words can do, she sees Latinus obstinately bent, and meantime the serpent's fiendish mischief has sunk deep into her vitals, and is thrilling every vein, then at last the miserable queen, unsexed by the portentous enormity, raves in ungoverned frenzy through the city's length and breadth; as oft you may see a top spinning under the lash, which boys are flogging round and round in a great ring in an empty courtyard, with every thought on their game: driven by the whip it keeps making circle after circle: the beardless faces hang over it in puzzled wonder, marvelling how the box-wood can fly, as though the blows made it a living thing. With motion as furious she courses through crowded streets and unruly peoples. Nay, more than this, she feigns the inspiration of Bacchus, nerving herself to more atrocious deeds, and climbing new heights of madness—flies into the woods, and hides her daughter among the leafy hills, all to snatch from the Teucrians the bridal bed and delay the kindling of Hymen's torch. 'Evoe Bacchus!' is her cry; 'thou, and none but thou art fit mate for a maid like this. See! for thee she takes up the sacred wand, for thee she leads the dance, for thee she grows her dedicated hair.' Fame flies abroad; other mothers are instinct with frenzy, and all have the same mad passion driving them to seek a new home. They have left their houses, and are spreading hair and shoulders to the wind;

while some are filling the sky with quivering shrieks, clad in
fawn-skins, and carrying vine-branch spears. There in the
middle is the queen all aglow, lifting high a blazing pine, and
singing the bridal song of Turnus and her daughter, her eye
red and glaring ; and sudden she shouts like a savage : ' Ho !
mothers of Latium all, where'er ye be, if ye have human
hearts and kindness left there for poor Amata, if ye are stung
to think of a mother's rights, off with the fillets from your
hair, and join the orgie with me.' Such is the queen, driven
among the woods, among the wild beasts' lairs far and wide,
by Bacchus' goad in Alecto's hand.

And now, judging that she had barbed enough the young
fangs of frenzy, upheaving from their bases the royal purpose
and the royal house, the grim goddess next soars in air on her
murky wings on to the walls of the bold Rutulian, the city
which they say Danae built for her Argive settlers, landing
there under stress of wind. Ardea was the name which past
generations gave the place, and Ardea still keeps her august
title; but her star is set. Here, in his lofty palace, Turnus
at deep of night was in the midst of his sleep. Alecto puts
off her hideous features and her fiendish shape, transforms
herself to an old woman's countenance and furrows her loathly
brow with wrinkles, assumes hoary locks and woollen fillet,
lastly twines them with an olive spray, and so becomes Calybe,
the aged priestess of Juno's temple ; and presents herself to
the young warrior's eyes with such words as these : ' And can
Turnus calmly see all his toils poured out in vain, and the
crown that is his own transferred to settlers from Dardania ?
See, the king is refusing you your bride and your blood-bought
dowry, and search is being made for a foreign heir to fill the
throne. Go on now, confront ungracious perils, and earn
derision ; go, mow down the Tuscan ranks, and spread over
Latium the shield of peace. These very words Saturn's

almighty daughter with her own lips bade me say to you when you should be slumbering in the still of night. Rise, then, bid your soldiery arm and move from city to camp, set fire to the Phrygian chiefs who have anchored in our fair river and to their painted ships. The dread voice of heaven speaks by me. Nay, let king Latinus, unless he consent to give you your bride and respect his promise, feel at last and find what it is to have Turnus for a foe.'

Laughing scornfully at the old seer, the youth thus spoke in reply: ' The news that a fleet has arrived in the Tiber has not, as you imagine, escaped my ear. Conjure me no such mighty terrors, nor think that queen Juno has forgotten me. No, it is you, good mother, whom mouldering dotage, drained dry of truth, is vexing to no end, mocking your prophetic soul with false alarms in an atmosphere of royal armaments. You are in your place watching over statues and temples; but war and peace must be wielded by men, whose work war is.'

At these words Alecto kindled into wrath. Even in the act of speaking a shudder seized the youth's frame and his eyes grew stiff and stony, so fierce the hissing of the Fury's thousand snakes, so monstrous the features that rose on his view. Instant with a roll of her fiery orbs she thrust him back as he faltered and tried to speak further; on either brow she upreared a serpent lock, and cracked her whip, and with infuriate lips followed thus: ' Here is the mouldering mother, whom dotage, drained dry of truth, is mocking with false alarms in an atmosphere of royal armaments. Turn your eyes hither; I am come from the dwelling of the Dread Sisters : war and death are wielded by this hand.'

Saying thus, she hurled a torch full at the youth, and lodged in his breast the pine-wood with its lurid smoke and glare. The bonds of sleep are broken by the giant terror, and a burst of sweat all over bathes the whole man, bone and limb. 'My sword!' he screams in frenzy; for his sword he searches pillow and palace: the fever of the steel, the guilty madness of bloodshed rage within him, and angry pride tops all: even as when loud-crackling a fire of sticks is heaped round the sides of a waving caldron, and the heat makes the water start; there within is the flood, steaming and storming, and bubbling high in froth, till at last the wave cannot contain itself, and the black vapour flies up into the air. So then, trampling on treaties, he gives the word to the chiefs of his soldiery for a march upon king Latinus, and bids arms be got ready. Italy must be protected, the foe must be driven from the frontier; he and his men will be enough for both, Teucrians and Latians. So he says and appeals to Heaven: and the Rutulians with emulous zeal encourage each other to the fight. This one is fired by his leader's peerless beauty and youth; this by the kings in his pedigree; this by the glorious deeds of his hand.

While Turnus is filling the Rutulians with the spirit of daring, Alecto is putting her infernal wings in motion against the Teucrians. A new device working in her mind, she fixed her eye on the spot where on the winding coast Iulus was hunting game with the snare and the course. Hereon the maiden of Cocytus suddenly presents to the hounds a maddening lure, and touches their nostrils with the scent they know so well, making them chase a stag in full cry; which was the first origin of the trouble, and put the spark of war to the spirit of the countryside.. There was a stag of beauteous form and lofty horns, taken by the sons of Tyrrheus from its mother's breast, and brought up by them and their father Tyrrheus, who had the control of the royal herds and the charge of the whole range of lawn. Trained to obey, it was the chief care of their sister Silvia; she would deck and wreathe its horns with delicate festoons, and comb its rough coat, and wash it in the clear stream. Grown tame to the hand, and accustomed to its master's table, it would run free in the forest and take itself back home to the well-known door, however late the night. Now, in one of its wanderings the maddened hounds of Iulus started it in the hunt, as it happened to be floating down the stream or allaying its heat on the verdant bank. Ascanius himself, fired with a proud ambition, bent his bow and levelled a shaft: nor did his hand err for want of heavenly aid: the reed sped with a loud hurtling sound and pierced the belly and the flank. The wounded creature took refuge under the roof it knew, and moaning crept into its stall, and bleeding all over filled, like a human suppliant, the house with its piteous plaints. Sister Silvia first, smiting on her arms with her flat hands, calls for help and summons the rough country folk. They—for the fell fiend is lurking in the silence of the forest—are at her side ere she looks for them, armed one with a seared brand, one with a heavy knotted stock: what each first finds as he gropes about, anger makes do weapon's service. Tyrrheus musters the company, just as the news found him, splitting an oak in four with convergent wedges, catching up an axe and breathing savage rage. But the cruel goddess, seizing from her watch-tower the moment of mischief, makes for the stall's lofty roof, and from its summit shrills forth the shepherd's clarion, pitching high on the wreathen horn her Tartarean note; at the sound the whole line of forest was convulsed, and the woods echoed to their depths: it was heard far off by Trivia's lake, heard by river Nar with his whitening sulphurous waters, and by the springs of the Veline: and terror-stricken mothers clasped their children to their breasts.

At once running to the sound with which the dread clarion gave the signal, the untamed rustics snatch up their weapons and gather from all sides; while the forces of Troy, on their part, pour through the camp's open gates their succour for Ascanius. It is no longer a woodman's quarrel waged with heavy clubs or seared stakes; they try the issue with two-edged steel; a dark harvest of drawn swords bristles over the field; the brass shines responsive to the sun's challenge, and flings its radiance skyward; as when the wave has begun to whiten under the rising wind, the ocean gradually upheaves itself, and raises its billows higher and higher, till at last, from its lowest depths, it mounts up to heaven. See! as the arrow whizzes, a young warrior in the first rank, once Tyrrheus' eldest born, Almo, is laid low in death; for the wound has lodged in his throat, and has cut off, with the rush of blood, the passage of the liquid voice and the vital breath. Round him lie many gallant frames, and among them old Galæsus, while throwing himself between the armies and pleading for peace; none so just as he, none so wealthy before to-day in Ausonian land; five flocks of sheep had he, five herds of oxen went to and fro from his stalls, and his land was furrowed by a hundred ploughs.

While thus on the plains the impartial war-god deals out fortune, the goddess, having achieved her promise, soon as she had inaugurated the war with blood, and brought the battle to its first murderous shock, flies from Hesperia, and rounding the cope of heaven, addresses Juno in the haughty tones of triumph: ' See here the work of discord complete in the horrors of war! Now bid them come together in friendship and strike truce. Thou hast seen that I can sprinkle the Trojans with Ausonian blood; let me but be assured of thy wish, I will give thee a further boon: I will sow rumours and bring the neigh-bouring cities into the war, and inflame their souls with mad martial passion to crowd from all sides with succour; I will scatter arms broadcast.' Juno returns: ' There is panic and treachery enough; the seeds of war are sown deep; men are

fighting hand to hand; the weapons which chance first supplied
are being seasoned with new-spilt blood. Such be the alliance,
such the nuptial rites solemnised by Venus' virtuous son
and good king Latinus. For thee to walk the upper air
with larger freedom would displease the great Father, the
monarch of high Olympus. Give place; should any chance
emerge in the struggle, myself will deal with it.' So spoke
Saturn's daughter: the Fury lifts her wings that hurtle with
serpent plumage, and seeks her home in Cocytus, leaving
the altitudes above. There is a place in the bosom of
Italy, under the shadow of lofty hills, known to fame and
celebrated in far-off lands, the vale of Amsanctus; pent between
two woody slopes, dark with dense foliage, while at the bottom
a broken torrent makes a roaring among the rocks along its
winding bed. Here men show an awful cavern, the very
gorge of the fell infernal god, and a deep gulf through which
Acheron breaks open its baleful mouth: there dived the Fury,
and relieved of her loathed presence earth and heaven.

Meanwhile, for her part, Saturn's royal daughter gives
the last touch that brings down the war. From the battle-
field there pours into the city the whole company of shepherds, with their slain in their arms, young Almo and
Galæsus' disfigured countenance, calling on the gods and
adjuring Latinus. Turnus is on the spot, and, in the fury
and fire of the blood-cry, sounds again and again the note
of terror: 'The Teucrians are invited to reign in Latium;
a Phrygian shoot is to be grafted on the royal tree; the
palace-gate is closed on himself.' Moreover, the kinsmen of
the matrons, who in Bacchic madness are footing the pathless
woods—for Amata's name weighs not lightly—muster from
all sides, and strain the throat of Mars to hoarseness. All at
once, defying omens and oracles, under the spell of a cursed
deity, they clamour for an atrocious war. With emulous zeal

they swarm round Latinus' palace ; he, like a rock in the sea, stands unshaken ; like a rock in the sea before the rush and crash of waters, which, amid thousands of barking waves, is fixed by its own weight; the crags and the spray-foamed stones roar about it in vain, and the lashed seaweed falls idly from its side. But when he finds no power given him to counterwork the secret agency, and all is moving at relentless Juno's beck, then with many an appeal to the gods and the soulless skies, ' Alas ! ' exclaims the good sire, ' shattered are we by destiny and whirled before the storm ! On you will come the reckoning, and your impious blood will pay it, my wretched children ! You, Turnus, you will be met by your crime and its fearful vengeance, in a day when it will be too late to pray to Heaven. For me, my rest is assured ; my ship is just dropping into port; it is but of a happy departure that I am robbed.' No more he spoke, but shut himself in an inner chamber, and let the reins of empire go.

A custom there was in the Hesperian days of Latium, observed as sacred in succession by the Alban cities, and now honoured by the observance of Rome, the greatest power on earth, when men first stir up the war-god to battle, whether their purpose be to carry piteous war among the Getæ, the Hyrcanians, or the Arabs, or to march as far as India, track the Morning-star to its home, and wrest the standards from the grasp of Parthia. There are two folding-gates of War—such the title they bear—clothed with religious awe and with the terrors of Mars the cruel: they are closed by a hundred brazen bars and by the everlasting strength of iron, and Janus never quits his guard on the threshold. When the fathers finally conclude for battle, the consul him-self, in the pride of Quirinus' striped robe and the Gabine cincture, unbars the grating portals, and with his own voice invokes battle ; the rest of the warriors take up the cry, and brazen horns blare out in unison their hoarse assent. Thus it was that then, too, Latinus was urged to declare war against the family of Æneas and to unclose the grim gates. The good old king recoiled from the touch, turned with averted eyes from the service he loathed, and shrouded himself in impenetrable gloom. Then darted· down from the sky the queen of heaven, smote with her own royal hand the unwilling portals, and from their bursten fastenings, as Saturn's daughter might, flung back the valves on their hinges. All Ausonia, sluggish and moveless till then, blazes into fury ; some commence their footmarch over the plain, some from the height of their steeds storm through the dust ; one and all cry out for arms. Some are rubbing their shields smooth and their javelins bright with unctuous lard, and putting their axes under the grindstone ; there is joy in the carrying of the standard, joy in the hearing of the trumpet's sound. And now there are five great cities with anvils everywhere set up, giving a new edge to their weapons : Atina the mighty and Tiber the proud, Ardea, and they of Crustumium, and tower-crowned Antemnæ. Helmets are hollowed to guard the head ; willows are twisted into wicker frames for shields ; others are beating out brass into breastplates, or stretching ductile silver into polished greaves. All the pride of sickle and share, all the passion for the plough are swallowed up in this ; they bring out their fathers' swords, and smelt them anew in the furnace. Here, in wild haste, is one snatching his helm from the chamber-wall ; there is another bringing his snorting steeds to the yoke, clothing himself with shield and corslet of three-piled gold, and girding to his side his trusty sword.[1]

---

[1] The remaining lines of this Book are not translated.—[ED.]

BOOK VIII.

Soon as Turnus set high on Laurentum's tower the ensign of war, and the horns clanged forth their harsh music, soon as he shook the reins in the mouth of his fiery steeds, and clashed his armour, at once came a stirring of men's souls : all Latium conspires in tumultuous rising, and the warrior bands are inflamed to madness. The generals, Messapus and Ufens and Mezentius, scorner of the gods, assume the lead; mustering succour from all sides and unpeopling the fields of their tillers far and wide. Venulus too is sent to the town of mighty Diomede to entreat help, and set forth that the Teucrians are planting foot in Latium; that Æneas is arrived by sea and intruding his vanquished home-gods, and announcing himself as the Latians' destined king; that many tribes are flocking to the standard of the Dardan chief, and the contagion of his name is spreading over Latium's length and breadth. What is to be the end of such a beginning, what, should fortune favour him, he promises to himself as the issue of the battle, Diomede will know better than king Turnus or king Latinus.

So go things in Latium. The chief of Laomedon's line sees it all, and is tossed on a sea of cares ; now on this point, now on that, he throws in a moment the forces of his mind, hurrying it into all quarters and sweeping the whole range of thought : as in water a flickering beam on a brazen vat, darted back by the sun or the bright moon's image, flits far and wide over the whole place, now at last mounting to the sky and striking the

T

ceiling of the roof. Night came, and tired life the earth over, bird and beast alike, were lapped deep in slumber, when Æneas, good king, troubled at heart by the anxious war, stretched himself on the bank under heaven's chilly cope, and let repose at last steal over his frame. Before him appeared in person the god of the place, old Tiber of the pleasant stream, rising among the poplar foliage : a gray mantle of transparent linen floated about him, and his hair was shaded with bushy reeds : and thus he began to address the chief and relieve his care : ' O offspring of heaven's stock, who are bringing back to us safe from the foe the city of Troy, and preserving Pergamus in enduring life, yourself looked for long on the Laurentian soil and in the fields of Latium, here is your abiding place of rest, here, distrust it not, permanence for your home-gods : let not war's threatenings make you afraid, the swellings of the anger of heaven have all given way. Even now, that you may not think this the idle coinage of sleep, under the oaks on the bank you shall find an enormous swine lying with a litter of thirty head just born, white herself throughout her lazy length, her children round her breasts as white as she : a sign that when thirty years have made their circuit, Ascanius shall found that city known by the illustrious name of the White. Of no doubtful issue are these words of mine. Now for the way in which you may triumphantly unravel the present knot, grant me your attention, and I will show you in brief. On this my coast, Arcadians, a race sprung from Pallas, who have followed king Evander and his banner, have chosen themselves a site and built a city on the hills, called from the name of their ancestor Pallas, Pallanteum. These are for ever engaged in war with the Latian nation : let them join your camp as allies, and make league with them. I myself will lead you between the banks, straight along my stream, that as you journey up your oars may surmount the

adverse current. Up then, goddess-born, and ere the stars
have well set, offer prayer in due course to Juno, and overbear with suppliant vows her anger and her menace. Once
triumphant, you shall pay your worship to me. I am he
whom you see here with brimming flood grazing the banks
and threading rich cultured lands, sea-green Tiber, the river
whom gods love best. Here rises my royal palace, the crown
of lofty cities.' The river-god said, and plunged into his
deep pool, down to the bottom ; night and sleep at once fled
from Æneas. He rises, and with his eyes fixed on the sun's
rays just dawning on the sky, he lifts up in due form water
from the river in the hollow of his hands, and pours forth
to heaven words like these : 'Nymphs, Laurentian nymphs,
whence rivers derive their birth, and thou, father Tiber, with
thy hallowed flood, take Æneas to your bosom, and at last
relieve him from perils. Whatever the spring of the pool
where thou dwellest in thy pity for our troubles, whatever
the soil whence thy goodly stream arises, ever shalt thou be
honoured by me with sacrifice, ever with offerings, the river
with the crescent horn, the monarch of Hesperian waters.
Be but thou present, and confirm by thy deed thy heavenly
tokens.' So saying, he chooses two biremes from the fleet
and fits them with rowers, while he gives his comrades arms
to wear.

When lo, a sudden portent marvellous to view—stretched
in milk-white length along the sward, herself of one hue with
her white litter, conspicuous on the verdant bank is seen a
sow, whom pious Æneas to thee, even to thee, mightiest Juno,
immolates in sacrifice, and sets her with all her brood before the
altar. That whole night long Tiber smoothed his brimming
stream, and so stood with hushed waves, half recoiling, as to lay
down a watery floor as of some gentle lake or peaceful pool, that
the oar might have nought to struggle with. So they begin their

voyage and speed with auspicious cheers. Smooth along the surface floats the anointed pine : marvelling stand the waters, marvelling the unwonted wood, to see the warriors' shields gleaming far along the stream, and the painted vessels gliding between the banks. The rowers give no rest to night or day, as they surmount the long meanders, sweep under the fringe of diverse trees, and cut through the woods that look green in the still expanse. The sun had climbed in full blaze the central cope of heaven, when from afar they see walls, and a citadel, and the roofs of straggling habitations—the place which the power of Rome has now made to mate the skies : then it was but Evander's poor domain. At once they turn their prows to land and approach the town.

It happened that on that day the Arcadian monarch was performing a yearly sacrifice to Amphitryon's mighty child and the heavenly brotherhood in a grove before the city. With him his son Pallas, with him all the prime of his warriors and his unambitious senate were offering incense, and the new-shed blood was steaming warm on the altar. Soon as they saw tall ships gliding toward them through the shadowy trees, and plying the oar in silence, alarmed by the sudden apparition, each and all start up from the sacrificial board. Pallas, bolder than the rest, bids them not break the sacred observance, and snatching up a weapon flies himself to meet the strangers, and from a height at distance, 'Warriors,' he cries, 'what cause has led you to venture on a path you know not? whither are you bound? what is your nation, your family? is it peace you bring us or war?' Then father Æneas bespeaks him thus from the lofty stern, stretching forth in his hand a branch of peaceful olive : 'These are Trojans you see. These weapons mean hostility to the Latins, who have driven us from their land by a tyrannous war. Our errand is to Evander. Take back our message, and say that chosen chiefs

of Dardany are at his gate, praying for an armed alliance.'
That mighty name struck awe into Pallas. 'Disembark,' he
cries, 'whoever you be, and speak to my sire in person, and come
beneath our home-gods' hospitable shelter,' and gave his hand
in welcome, and clung to the hand he clasped. They advance
under the shade of the grove, and leave the river behind.

Then Æneas addresses the king with friendly courtesy :
'Best of the sons of Greece, to whom it has pleased Fortune
that I should make my prayer and stretch out boughs wreathed
with fillets, I felt no fear for that you were a Danaan leader,
an Arcadian, allied by lineage with the two sons of Atreus : I
felt that my own worth, and the gods' hallowed oracles, and
the old connection of our ancestry, and your world-wide fame,
had linked me to you, and brought me before you at once by
destiny and of my own will. Dardanus, first father and
founder of the town of Ilion, born, as Greeks tell, of Electra,
daughter of Atlas, came among Teucer's people : Electra's
father was mighty Atlas, he that bears up on his shoulders the
spheres of heaven. Your progenitor is Mercury, whom beauteous Maia conceived and brought forth on Cyllene's chill
summit; but Maia, if tradition be credited, is the child of Atlas,
the same Atlas who lifts up the stars of the firmament. Thus
our two races part off from one and the same stock. Trusting
to this, I sent no embassy, nor contrived the first approaches
to you by rule and method : in myself, in my own person, I
have made the experiment, and come to your gate as a suppliant. The same tribe which persecutes you, the Daunians,
is now persecuting us with cruel war : should they drive us
away, they foresee nought to hinder their subduing all Hesperia
utterly to their yoke, and mastering either sea, that washes it
above or below. Take our friendship and give us yours. On
our side are hearts valiant in war, and a gallant youth approved
by adventure.'

Æneas ended. Long ere this the other's eye was scanning the speaker's countenance and eyes, and surveying his whole frame. Then he returns in brief : 'With what joy, bravest of the Teucrians, do I welcome and acknowledge ye! how well I call to mind the words, the voice, the look of your sire, the great Anchises! For I remember how Priam, son of Laomedon, journeying to Salamis, to see the kingdom of his sister Hesione, went on to visit the chill frontier of Arcadia. In those days the first bloom of youth was clothing my cheeks. I admired the Teucrian leaders, I admired Laomedon's royal son ; but Anchises' port was nobler than all. My mind kindled with a youth's ardour to accost one so great, and exchange the grasp of the hand. I made my approach, and eagerly conducted him to the walls of Pheneus. On leaving he gave me a beauteous quiver with Lycian arrows, and a scarf embroidered with gold, and two bridles which my Pallas has now, all golden. So now I both plight you herewith the hand you ask, and soon as to-morrow's light shall restore to the earth its blessing, I will send you back rejoicing in an armed succour, and reinforced with stores. Meanwhile, since you are arrived here as my friends, join in gladly solemnising with us this our yearly celebration, which it were sin to postpone, and accustom yourselves thus early to the hospitalities of your new allies.'

This said, he bids set on again the viands and the cups, erewhile removed, and himself places the warriors on a seat of turf, welcoming Æneas in especial grace with the heaped cushion of a shaggy lion's hide, and bidding him occupy a throne of maple wood. Then chosen youths and the priest of the altar with emulous zeal bring in the roasted carcases of bulls, pile up in baskets the gifts of the corn-goddess prepared by art, and serve the wine-god round. Æneas and the warriors of Troy with him regale themselves on a bull's long chine and on sacrificial entrails.

When hunger had been quenched and appetite allayed, king Evander begins: 'Think not that these solemnities of ours, these ritual feastings, this altar so blest in divine presence, have been riveted on us by idle superstition, unknowing of the gods of old; no, guest of Troy, it is deliverance from cruel dangers that makes us sacrifice and pay again and again worship where worship is due. First of all cast your eyes on this rock-hung crag: observe how the masses of stone are flung here and there, how desolate and exposed stands the mountain's recess, and how the rocks have left the trail of a giant downfall. Here once was a cave, retiring in enormous depth, tenanted by a terrible shape, Cacus, half man, half brute: the sun's rays could never pierce it; the ground was always steaming with fresh carnage; fixed to its imperious portals were hanging human countenances ghastly with hideous gore. This monster's father was Vulcan: Vulcan's were the murky fires that he disgorged from his mouth as he towered along in enormous bulk. To us also at length in our yearning need time brought the arrival of a divine helper. For the mightiest of avengers, Alcides, triumphing in the slaughter and the spoils of the triple Geryon, was in our land, and was driving by this road as a conqueror those giant oxen, and the cattle were filling valley and river-side. But Cacus, infatuated by fiendish frenzy, not to leave aught of crime or craft undared or unessayed, carries off from the stalls four bulls of goodly form, and heifers no fewer of surpassing beauty. And these, that they might leave no traces by their forward motion, he dragged by the tail to his cave, haled them with reversed footprints to tell the story, and so concealed them in the dark rocky den. Thus the seeker found no traces to lead him to the cavern. Meantime, when Amphitryon's son was at last removing from their stalls his feasted herds and preparing to quit the country, the oxen gave a farewell low, filling the whole woodland with their plainings, and taking clamorous leave of the hills. One of the heifers returned the sound, lowing from the depth of the vast cavern, and thus baffled the hopes of her jealous guardian. Now, if ever, Alcides' wrath blazed up from the black choler of his heart : he snatches up his weapons and his club with all its weight of knots, and makes at full speed for the skiey mountain's height. Then first the men of our country saw Cacus' limbs tremble and his eyes quail : away he flies swifter than the wind, and seeks his den ; fear has winged his feet. Scarce had he shut himself in, and let down from its burst fastenings the huge stone, suspended there by his father's workmanship in iron, and with that barrier fortified his straining doorway, when lo ! the hero of Tiryns was there in the fury of his soul : scanning every inlet he turns his face hither and thither, gnashing with his teeth. Thrice in white heat of wrath he surveys the whole mass of Aventine ; thrice he attempts in vain the stony portal; thrice, staggering from the effort, he sits down in the hollow. Before him stood a pointed crag with abrupt rocky sides rising over the cave behind, high as the eye can reach, a fitting home for the nests of unclean and hateful birds. This, as sloping down it inclined towards the river on the left, pushing it full on the right he upheaved and tore it loose from its seat, then suddenly sent it down, with a shock at which high heaven thunders, the banks start apart, and the river runs back in terror. Then the cave and the vast halls of Cacus were seen unroofed, and the dark recesses lay open to their depths—even as if earth, by some mighty force laid open to her depths, should burst the doors of the mansions below, and expose the realms of ghastly gloom which the gods hate, and from above the vast abyss were to be seen, and the spectres dazzled by the influx of day. So as Cacus stares surprised by the sudden burst of light, pent by the walls of his cave, and roars in strange and hideous sort,

Alcides from above showers down his darts, and calls every weapon to his aid, and rains a tempest of boughs and huge millstones. But he, seeing that no hope of flight remains, vomits from his throat huge volumes of smoke, marvellous to tell, and wraps the whole place in pitchy darkness, blotting out all prospect from the eyes, and in the depth of the cave masses a smothering night of blended blackness and fire. The rage of Alcides brooked not this: headlong he dashed through the flame, where the smoke surges thickest and the vast cavern seethes with billows of black vapour. Here while Cacus in the heart of the gloom is vomiting his helpless fires he seizes him, twines his limbs with his own, and in fierce embrace compresses his strangled eyeballs and his throat now bloodless and dry. At once the doors are burst and the black den laid bare, and the plundered oxen, the spoil that his oath had disclaimed, are exposed to light, and the hideous carcase is dragged out by the heels. The gazers look unsatisfied on those dreadful eyes, those grim features, the shaggy breast of the half bestial monster, and the extinguished furnace of his throat. Since then grateful acknowledgments have been paid, and the men of younger time have joyfully observed the day: foremost among them Potitius, founder of the ceremony, and the Pinarian house, custodian of the worship of Hercules. He himself set up in the grove this altar, which shall ever be named by us the greatest, and shall ever be the greatest in truth. Come then, warriors, and in honour of worth so glorious wreathe your locks with leaves, and present in your hands brimming cups, and invoke our common deity, and pour libations with gladness of heart.' As he ended, the white-green poplar cast its Herculean shade over his locks and hung down with a festoon of leaves, and the sacred goblet charged his hand. At once all with glad hearts pour libations on the board and make prayers to heaven.

Meantime evening is approaching nearer the slope of heaven, and already the priests and their chief Potitius were in procession, clad in skins in ritual sort, and bearing fire in their hands. They renew the solemn feast, and bring delicious offerings for a fresh repast, and pile the altars with loaded chargers. Then come the Salii to sing round about the blazing altars, their temples wreathed with boughs of poplar, a company of youths and another of old men; and these extol in song the glories and deeds of Hercules: how in his cradle, by the pressure of his young hand he strangled his stepmother's monstrous messengers, the two serpents; how in war that same hand dashed to pieces mighty cities, Troy and Œchalia; how he endured those thousand heavy labours, a slave to king Eurystheus, by ungentle Juno's fateful will. 'Yes, thou, unconquered hero, thou slayest the two-formed children of the cloud, Hylæus and Pholus, thou slayest the portent of Crete, and the enormous lion that dwelt 'neath Nemea's rock. Thou never quailedst at aught in bodily shape, no, nor at Typhoeus himself, towering high, weapons in hand; thy reason failed thee not when Lerna's serpent stood round thee with all her throng of heads. Hail to thee, authentic offspring of Jove, fresh ornament of the sky! come to us, come to these thine own rites with favouring smile and auspicious gait.' Such things their songs commemorate; and they crown all with Cacus' cave and the fiend himself, the fire panting from his lungs. The entire grove echoes with their voices, and the hills rebound.

The sacrifice over, the whole concourse returns to the city. There walked the king, mossed over with years, keeping at his side Æneas and his son as he moved along, and lightening the way with various speech. Æneas admires, and turns his quick glance from sight to sight: each scene enthralls him; and with eager zest he enquires and learns one by one the records of men of old. Then spoke king Evander, the builder of Rome's tower-crowned hill: 'These woodlands were first inhabited by native Fauns and Nymphs, and by a race of men that sprung from trunks of trees and hard oaken core; no rule of life, no culture had they : they never learnt to yoke the ox, nor to hive their stores, nor to husband what they got; the boughs and the chase supplied their savage sustenance. The first change came from Saturn, who arrived from skiey Olympus, flying from the arms of Jove, a realm-less exile. He brought together the race, untamed as they were and scattered over mountain heights, and gave them laws, and chose for the country the name of Latium, because he had found it a safe hiding-place. The golden age of story was when he was king, so calm and peaceful his rule over his people; till gradually there crept in a race of worse grain and duller hue, and the frenzy of war, and the greed of having. Then came the host of Ausonia and the Sicanian tribes, and again and again Saturn's land changed its name; then came king after king, savage Thybris with his giant bulk, from whom in after days we Italians called the river Tiber: the authentic name of ancient Albula was lost. Myself, an exile from my country, while voyaging to the ends of the sea, all-powerful Fortune and inevitable Destiny planted here ; at my back were the awful hests of my mother, the nymph Carmentis, and the divine sanction of Apollo.' Scarce had he finished, when moving on he points out the altar and the Carmental gate, as the Romans call it, their ancient tribute to the nymph Carmentis, the soothsaying seer, who first told of the future greatness of Æneas' sons and of the glories of Pallanteum. Next he points out a mighty grove, which fiery Romulus made the Asylum of a later day, and embowered by the chill dank rock, the Lupercal, bearing after Arcadian wont the name of Lycæan Pan. He shows, moreover, the forest of hallowed

Argiletum, and appeals to the spot, and recounts the death of Argus, once his guest. Thence he leads the way to the Tarpeian temple, even the Capitol, now gay with gold, then rough with untrimmed brushwood. Even in that day the sacred terrors of the spot awed the trembling rustics; even then they shuddered at the forest and the rock. 'This wood,' he says, 'this hill with the shaggy brow, is the home of a god of whom we know not; my Arcadians believe that they have seen there great Jove himself, oft and oft, shaking with his right hand the shadowy Ægis and calling up the storm. Here, too, in these two towns, with their ramparts overthrown, you see the relics and the chronicles of bygone ages. This tower was built by father Janus, that by Saturn; the one's name Janiculum, the other's Saturnia.' So talking together they came nigh the palace where Evander dwells in poverty, and saw cattle all about lowing in the Roman forum and Carinæ's luxurious precinct. When they reached the gate, 'This door,' said the host, 'Alcides in his triumph stooped to enter; this mansion contained his presence. Nerve yourself, my guest, to look down on riches, and make your own soul, like his, such as a god would not disdain, and take in no churlish sort the welcome of poverty.' He said, and beneath the slope of his narrow roof ushered in the great Æneas, and laid him to rest on a couch of leaves and the skin of a Libyan bear.

Down comes the night, and flaps her sable wings over the earth. But Venus, distracted, and not idly, with a mother's cares, disturbed by the menaces of the Laurentines and the violence of the gathering storm, addresses Vulcan, and in the nuptial privacy of their golden chamber begins her speech, breathing in every tone the love that gods feel: 'In old days of war, while the Argive kings were desolating Pergamus, their destined prey, and ravaging the towers which were doomed to hostile fire, no help for the sufferers, no arms of thy resourceful workmanship did I ask; no, my dearest lord, I chose not to task thee and thy efforts to no end, large as was my debt to the sons of Priam, and many the tears that I shed for Æneas' cruel agony. Now, by Jove's commands, he has set his foot on Rutulian soil; so, with the past in my mind, I appear as a suppliant, to ask of his power whom I honour most, as a mother may, armour for my son. Thee the daughter of Nereus, thee the spouse of Tithonus, found accessible to tears. See but what nations are mustering, what cities are closing the gate and pointing the steel against me and the lives I love.' The speech was ended, and the goddess is fondling her undecided lord on all sides in the soft embrace of her snowy arms. Suddenly he caught the wonted fire, the well-known heat shot to his vitals and threaded his melting frame, even as on a day when the fiery rent burst by the thunderclap runs with gleaming flash along the veil of cloud. His spouse saw the triumph of her art and felt what beauty can do. Then spoke the stern old god, subdued by everlasting love : ' Why fetch your excuses from so far? whither, my queen, has fled your old affiance in me? had you then been as anxious, even in those old days it had been allowed to give arms to the Trojans ; nor was the almighty sire nor the destinies unwilling that Troy should stand and Priam remain in life for ten years more. And now, if war is your object and so your purpose holds, all the care that it lies within my art to promise, what can be wrought out of iron and molten electrum, as far as fire can burn and wind blow—cease to show by entreaty that you mistrust your power.' This said, he gave the embrace she longed for, and falling on the bosom of his spouse wooed the calm of slumber in every limb.

Then, soon as rest, first indulged, had driven sleep away, when flying night had run half her course; just when a woman, compelled to support life by spinning, even by Pallas'

slender craft, wakes to light the fire that slumbered in the
embers, adding night to her day's work, and keeps her hand-
maids labouring long by the blaze, all that she may preserve
her husband's bed unsullied, and bring up his infant sons;
even so the lord of fire, at an hour not less slothful, rises from
his couch of down to the toils of the artisan.   There rises an
island hard by the Sicanian coast and Æolian Lipari, towering with fiery mountains; beneath it thunders a cavern, the
den of Ætna, blasted out by Cyclop forges; the sound of
mighty blows echoes on anvils : the smeltings of the Chalybes
hiss through its depths, and the fire pants from the jaws of
the furnace; it is the abode of Vulcan, and the land bears
Vulcan's name.   Hither, then, the lord of fire descends from
heaven's height.   There, in the enormous den, the Cyclops
were forging the iron, Brontes, and Steropes, and Pyracmon,
the naked giant.   In their hands was the rough cast of the
thunder-bolt, one of those many which the great Father
showers down on earth from all quarters of heaven—part was
polished for use, part still incomplete.   Three spokes of frozen
rain, three of watery cloud had they put together, three of
ruddy flame and winged southern wind; and now they were
blending with what they had done the fearful flash, and the
noise, and the terror, and the fury of untiring fire.   In another
part they were hurrying on for Mars the car and the flying
wheels, with which he rouses warriors to madness, ay, and
whole cities; and with emulous zeal were making bright with
golden serpent scales the terrible Ægis, the armour of angry
Pallas, snakes wreathed together, and full on the breast of the
goddess the Gorgon herself, her neck severed and her eyes
rolling.   'Away with all this,' cries the god; 'take your
unfinished tasks elsewhere, you Cyclops of Ætna, and give
your attention here.   Arms are wanted for a fiery warrior.
Now is the call for power, now for swiftness of hand, now for

all that art can teach. Turn delay into despatch.' No more
he said; but they with speed put their shoulder to the work,
sharing it in equal parts. Copper flows in streams and golden
ore, and steel, that knows how to wound, is molten in the
huge furnace. They set up in outline a mighty shield, itself
singly matched against all the Latian weapons, and tangle together seven plates, circle and circle. Some with their gasping bellows are taking in and giving out the wind; others are
dipping the hissing copper in the lake. The cave groans
under the anvil's weight. They, one with another, with all a
giant's strength, are lifting their arms in measured cadence,
and turning with their griping tongs the ore on this side and
on that.

While the father of Lemnos makes this despatch on the
Æolian shores, Evander is roused from his lowly dwelling by
the genial light and the morning songs of birds under the
eaves. Up rises the old man, and draws a tunic over his
frame, and puts Tyrrhenian sandals round his feet; next he
fastens from below to side and shoulder a sword from Tegea,
flinging back over him a panther's hide that drooped from
the left. Moreover, two guardian dogs go before him from
his palace door, and attend their master's steps. So he made
his way to the lodging of his guest, and sought Æneas' privacy,
their discourse of yesterday and the gift then promised fresh
in his heroic soul. Æneas likewise was astir not less early.
This had his son Pallas, that had Achates walking by his
side. They meet, and join hand in hand, and sit them down
in the midst of the mansion, and at last enjoy the privilege of
mutual talk. The king begins as follows:—

'Mightiest leader of the Teucrians, whom while heaven
preserves I shall never own that Troy's powers are vanquished
or her realm overturned, we ourselves have but small means
of martial aid to back our great name; on this side we are

bounded by the Tuscan river: on that our Rutulian foe beleaguers us, and thunders in arms around our walls. But I have a mighty nation, a host with an imperial heritage, which I am ready to unite with you—a gleam of safety revealed by unexpected chance. It is at the summons of destiny that you bend your steps thither. Not far hence, built of ancient stone, is the inhabited city of Agylla, where of old the Lydian nation, renowned in war, took its seat on Etruscan mountains. This city, after long and prosperous years, was held by king Mezentius, by stress of tyrant rule and the terror of the sword. Why should I recount the despot's dreadful murders and all his savage crimes? may the gods preserve them in mind, and bring them on his own head and his family's! Nay, he would even link together the dead and the living, coupling hand with hand and face with face—so inventive is the lust of torture—and in the slime and poison of that sickening embrace would destroy them thus by a lingering dissolution. At last, wearied by oppression, his subjects in arms besiege the frantic monster himself and his palace, slay his retainers, shower firebrands on his roof. He, mid the carnage, escapes to Rutulian territory, and shelters himself under Turnus' friendly power. So all Etruria has risen in righteous wrath; at once, at the sword's point, they demand that the king be surrendered to their vengeance. Of these thousands, Æneas, I will make you general. For along the seaboard's length their ships are swarming and panting for the fray, and calling on the trumpet to sound, while an aged soothsayer is holding them back by his fateful utterance: "Chosen warriors of Mæonian land, the power and soul of an ancient nation, whom just resentment launches against the foe and Mezentius inflames with righteous fury, no Italian may take the reins of a race so proud: choose foreigners to lead you." At this the Etruscan army settled down on yonder plain, awed by the heavenly warning. Tarchon himself has sent me ambassadors with the royal crown and sceptre, and given to my hands the ensigns of power, bidding me join the camp, and assume the Tyrrhene throne. But age, with its enfeebling chill and the exhaustion of its long term of years, grudges me the honour of command ; my day of martial prowess is past. Fain would I encourage my son to the task, but that the blood of a Sabine mother blending with mine makes his race half Italian. You, in years and in race alike the object of Fate's indulgence—you, the chosen one of Heaven—assume the place that waits you, gallant general of Teucrians and Italians both. Nay, I will give you, too, Pallas here, the hope and solace of my age ; under your tutelage let him learn to endure military service and the war-god's strenuous labours ; let your actions be his pattern, and his young admiration be centred on you. To him I will give two hundred Arcadian horsemen, the flower of my chivalry, and Pallas in his own name shall give you as many more.'

Scarce had his words been uttered—and the twain were holding their eyes in downcast thought, Æneas Anchises' son and true Achates, brooding each with his own sad heart on many a peril, had not Cythera's goddess sent a sign from the clear sky. For unforeseen, flashed from the heaven, comes a glare and a peal, and all around seemed crashing down at once, and the clang of the Tyrrhene trumpet appeared to blare through ether. They look up : a second and a third time cracks the enormous sound. Armour enveloped in a cloud in a clear quarter of the firmament is seen to flash redly in the sunlight and to ring as clashed together. The rest were all amazement ; but the Trojan hero recognised the sound, and in it the promise of his goddess mother. Then he cries : ' Nay, my host, nay, ask not in sooth what chance these wonders portend ; it is I that have a call from on high. This

U

was the sign that the goddess who gave me birth foreshowed me that she would send, should the attack of war come, while she would bring through the air armour from Vulcan for my help. Alas! how vast the carnage ready to burst on Laurentum's wretched sons! what vengeance, Turnus, shall be mine from thee! how many a warrior's shield and helm and stalwart frame shalt thou toss beneath thy waters, father Tiber! Ay, clamour for battle, and break your plighted word!'

Thus having said, he rises from his lofty seat, and first of all quickens the altars where the Herculean fires were smouldering, and with glad heart approaches the hearth-god of yesterday, and the small household powers; duly they sacrifice chosen sheep, Evander for his part and the Trojan youth for theirs. Next he moves on to the ships and revisits his crew: from whose number he chooses men to follow him to the war, eminent in valour: the rest are wafted down the stream and float lazily along with the current at their back, to bring Ascanius news of his father and his fortunes. Horses are given to the Teucrians who are seeking the Tyrrhene territory, and one is led along, reserved for Æneas; a tawny lion's hide covers it wholly, gleaming forth with talons of gold.

At once flies rumour, blazed through the little city, that the horsemen are marching with speed to the gates of the Tyrrhene king. In alarm the matrons redouble their vows; fear treads on the heels of danger, and the features of the war-god loom larger on the view. Then Evander, clasping the hand of his departing son, hangs about him with tears that never have their fill, and speaks like this: 'Ah! would but Jupiter bring back my bygone years, and make me what I was when under Præneste's very walls I struck down the first rank and set a conqueror's torch to piles of shields, and with this my hand sent down to Tartarus king Erulus, whom at his birth his mother Feronia endowed with three lives—

fearful to tell—and a frame that could thrice bear arms : thrice had he to be struck down in death : yet from him on that day this hand took all those three lives, and thrice stripped that armour—never should I, as now, be torn, my son, from your loved embrace. Never would Mezentius have laid dishonour on a neighbour's crest, dealt with his sword that repeated havoc, and bereaved my city of so many of her sons. But you, great powers above, and thou, Jupiter, mightiest ruler of the gods, have pity, I implore you, on an Arcadian monarch, and give ear to a father's prayer ; if your august will, if destiny has in store for me the safe return of my Pallas, if life will make me see him and meet him once more, then I pray that I may live ; there is no trial I cannot bear to outlast. But if thou, dark Fortune, threatenest any unnamed calamity, now, oh, now, be it granted me to snap life's ruthless thread, while care wears a double face, while hope cannot spell the future, while you, darling boy, my love and late delight, are still in my arms : nor let my ears be pierced by tidings more terrible.' So was the father heard to speak at their last parting ; his servants were seen carrying within doors their fallen lord.

And now the cavalry had passed the city's open gates, Æneas among the first and true Achates, and after them the other Trojan nobles ; Pallas himself the centre of the column, conspicuous with gay scarf and figured armour ; even as the morning-star just bathed in the waves of the ocean, Venus' favourite above all the stellar fires, sets in a moment on the sky his heavenly countenance, and melts the darkness. There are the trembling matrons standing on the walls, following with their eyes the cloud of dust and the gleam of the brass-clad companies. They in their armour are moving through the underwood, their eye on the nearest path : hark ! a shout mounts up, a column is formed, and the four-foot beat of the hoof shakes the crumbling plain. Near the cool stream of Caere stands a vast grove, clothed by hereditary reverence with wide-spread sanctity; on all sides it is shut in by the hollows of hills, which encompass its dark pine-wood shades. Rumour says that the old Pelasgians dedicated it to Silvanus, god of the country and the cattle, a grove with a holiday—; the people who once in early times dwelt on the Latian frontier. Not far from this Tarchon and the Tyrrhenians were encamped in a sheltered place, and from the height of the hill their whole army spread already to the view, as they pitched at large over the plain. Hither come father Æneas and the chosen company of warriors, and refresh the weariness of themselves and their steeds.

But Venus had come in her divine beauty through the dark clouds of heaven with the gifts in her hand, and soon as she saw her son far retired in the vale in the privacy of the cool stream, she thus accosted him, appearing suddenly before him : 'See, here is the present completed by my lord's promised skill : now you will not need to hesitate to-morrow about daring to the combat the haughty Laurentians or fiery Turnus' self.' So said the lady of Cythera, and sought her son's embrace: the arms she set up to glitter under an oak that faced his view. He, exulting in the goddess' gifts, and charmed with their dazzling beauty, cannot feast his eyes enough as he rolls them from point to point, admiring and turning over in his hands and arms the helmet with its dread crest, vomiting flame, the fateful sword, the stiff brazen corselet, blood-red and huge, in hue as when a dark cloud kindles with sunlight and gleams afar; the polished cuishes, too, of electrum and gold smelted oft and oft, and the spear, and the shield's ineffable frame-work. On this was the story of Italy and the triumphs of the Romans wrought by the Lord of the fire; no stranger he to prophecy nor ignorant of the time to come: on it was the whole royal line of the future from Ascanius onward, and their foughten fields in long succession. There, too, he had portrayed the mother-wolf stretched in Mars' green cavern ; around her teats were the twin boys in play climbing and clinging, and licking their dam without dread ; while she, her lithe neck bent back, was caressing them by turns and with her tongue shaping their young limbs. Near this he had inserted Rome and the lawless rape of the Sabine maidens amid the crowded circus, while the great games were in course, and the sudden rise of a new war between the sons of Romulus and ancient Tatius with his austere Cures. Afterwards were seen the two kings, the conflict set at rest, standing in arms before the altar of Jove with goblets in their hands and cementing a treaty with swine's blood. Not far off Mettus had already been torn asunder by the chariots driven apart—ah ! false Alban, were you but a keeper of your word !—and Tullus was dragging the traitor's flesh through the woodland, while the bushes were sprinkled with the bloody rain. There, too, was Porsenna insisting that exiled Tarquin should be taken back and leaguering the city with a mighty siege : Æneas' sons were flinging themselves on the sword in freedom's cause. In his face might be seen the likeness of wrath, and the likeness of menace, that Cocles should have the courage to tear down the bridge, that Cloelia should break her prison and swim the river. There was Manlius standing sentinel on the summit of the Tarpeian fortress in the temple's front, holding the height of the Capitol, while the Romulean thatch looked fresh and sharp on the palace-roof. And there was the silver goose fluttering its wings in the gilded cloister, and shrieking that the Gauls were at the door. The Gauls were at hand marching among the brushwood, and had gained the summit sheltered by the darkness and the kindly grace of dusky night. Golden is their hair and golden their raiment; striped cloaks gleam on their shoulders; their milk-white necks are twined with gold; each brandishes two Alpine javelins, his body guarded by the long oval of his shield. There he had shown in relief the Salii in their dances and the naked Luperci, and the woolly peaks of their caps, and the sacred shields which fell from heaven : chaste matrons were making solemn progress through the city in their soft-cushioned cars. At distance from these he introduces too the mansions of Tartarus, Pluto's yawning portals, and the torments of crime, and thee, Catiline, poised on the beetling rock and quailing at grim Fury-faces : and the good in their privacy, with Cato as their lawgiver. Stretching in its breadth among these swept the semblance of the swelling sea, all of gold, but the blue was made to foam with whitening billows; and all about it dolphins of bright silver in joyous circles were lashing the surface with their tails and cutting the tide. In the midst might be seen fleets of brazen ships, the naval war of Actium; you might remark the whole of Leucate aglow with the war-god's array, and the waves one blaze of gold. On this side is Augustus Cæsar leading the Italians to conflict, with the senate and the people, the home-gods and their mighty brethren, standing aloft on the stern : his auspicious brows emit twin-born flames, and his ancestral star dawns over his head. Elsewhere is Agrippa with the winds and the gods at his back, towering high as he leads his column; his brows gleam with the beaked circle of a naval crown, the glorious ornament of war. On that side is Antonius with his barbaric powers and the arms of divers lands, triumphant from the nations of the dawn-goddess and the red ocean's coast, carrying with him Egypt and the strength of the East and the utmost parts of Bactria, and at his side—shame on the profanation !—his Egyptian spouse. All are seen at once in fierce onward motion : the whole sea-floor foams up, torn by the backward pull of the oars and by the three-fanged beaks. On to the deep! you would deem that uprooted Cyclades were swimming the sea, or that tall hills were meeting hills in battle ; such the giant effort with which the warriors urge on their tower-crowned ships. From the hand is scattered a shower of flaming tow and flying steel : the plains of Neptune redden with unwonted carnage. In the midst of them the queen is cheering on her forces with the timbrel of her native land ; casting as yet no glance on the twin-born snakes that threaten her rear. There are the portentous gods of all the nations, and Anubis the barking monster, brandishing their weapons in the face of Neptune and Venus and in the face of Pallas. Midmost in the fray storms Mavors, relieved in iron, and fell Fury-fiends swooping from the sky ; and Discord sweeps along in the glory of her rent mantle, and at her back Bellona with blood-dropping scourge. There was Actium's Apollo, with his eye on the fray, bending his bow from above ; at whose terror all Egypt and Ind, all Arabia, all the sons of Saba were turning the back in flight. The queen herself was shown spreading her sails to friendly. breezes, and just loosing the sheets. On her face the Lord of the Fire had written the paleness of foreshadowed death, as she drove on among corpses before the tide and the zephyr ; over against her was Nile, his vast body writhing in woe, throwing open his bosom, and with his whole flowing raiment inviting the vanquished to his green lap and his sheltering flood. But Cæsar, entering the walls of Rome in threefold triumph, was consecrating to the gods of Italy a votive tribute of deathless gratitude, three hundred mighty fanes the whole city through. The ways were ringing with gladness and with games and with plausive peal ; in every temple thronged a matron company, in every temple an altar

blazed; in front of the altars slaughtered bullocks strewed
the floor. The hero himself, throned on dazzling Phœbus'
snow-white threshold, is telling over the offerings of all the
nations and hanging them up on the proud temple gates;
there in long procession move the conquered peoples, diverse
in tongue, diverse no less in garb and in armour. Here had
Mulciber portrayed the Nomad race and the zoneless sons of
Afric: here, too, Leleges and Carians and quivered Gelonians:
Euphrates was flowing with waves subdued already; and the
Morini, furthest of mankind, and Rhine with his crescent
horn, and tameless Dahae, and Araxes chafing to be bridged.
Such sights Æneas scans with wonder on Vulcan's shield, his
mother's gift, and joys in the portraiture of things he knows
not, as he heaves on his shoulder the fame and the fate of
grandsons yet to be.

BOOK IX.

WHILE these things are in progress far away, Juno, Saturn's daughter, has sent down Iris from above on an errand to Turnus the bold. It chanced that then Turnus was sitting in the grove of his sire Pilumnus, deep in the hallowed dell. Him then the child of Thaumas bespoke thus from her rosy lips : 'Turnus, what no god would have dared to promise to your prayers, lo ! the mere lapse of time has brought to you unasked. Æneas, leaving behind town, comrades, and fleet, is gone to seek the realm of the Palatine, the settlement of Evander. Nor is that all : he has won his way to Corythus' farthest towns, and is arming the Lydian bands, the crowds of country folk. Why hesitate ? now, now is the moment to call for horse and car ; fling delay to the winds, and come down on the bewildered camp.' So saying, she raised herself aloft on the poise of her wings, and drew as she fled along the clouds her mighty bow. The warrior knew his visitant, lifted his two hands to heaven, and pursued her flight with words like these : ' Iris, fair glory of the sky, who has sent thee down from heaven to earth on an errand to me ? I see the firmament parting asunder, and the stars reeling about the poles. Yes ! I follow thy mighty presage, whoe'er thou art thus calling me to arms.' With these words he went to the river-side, and took up water from the brimming flood, calling oft on the gods and burdening heaven with a multitude of vows.

And now his whole army was in motion along the open

plain, richly dowered with horses, richly dowered with gold and broidered raiment. Messapus marshals the van, Tyrrheus' warrior-sons the rear: Turnus himself, the general, is in the centre—like Ganges with his seven calm streams proudly rising through the silence, or Nile when he withdraws from the plain his fertilising waters and has at last subsided into his bed. Suddenly the Teucrians look forth on a cloud massed with murky dust, and see darkness gathering over the plain. First cries Caicus from the rampart's front: 'What mass have we here, my countrymen, rolling towards us, black as night? Quick with the steel, bring weapons, man the walls, the enemy is upon us, ho!' With loud shouts the Teucrians pour themselves through all the gates and through the bulwarks. For such had been the charge of Æneas, that best of soldiers, when going on his way; should aught fall out meantime, let them not venture to draw out their lines or try the fortune of the field: enough for them to guard camp and wall safe behind their earthworks. So now, though shame and anger prompt to an engagement, they shield themselves nevertheless with closed gates in pursuance of his bidding, and armed, within the covert of their towers, await the foe. Turnus, just as he had galloped on in advance of his tardy column, appears unforeseen before the gate with a chosen following of twenty horse: with a Thracian steed to carry him, spotted with white, and a golden helm with scarlet crest to guard his head. 'Now, gallants, which of you will venture with me first against the foe? Look there!' he cries, and with a whirl sends his javelin into the air, the overture of battle, and proudly prances over the plain. His friends second him with a shout and follow with dreadful cries; they wonder at the Teucrians' sluggish hearts—men-at-arms, not to trust themselves to a fair field or fight face to face, but keep nursing their camp. Enraged, he rides round and round the walls,

and looks out for an opening where way is none. Even as a
wolf, lying in wait to surprise a crowded fold, whines about
the enclosure, exposed to wind and rain, at mid of night; the
lambs, nestling safe under their mothers, keep bleating loudly;
he maddened and reckless, gnashes his teeth at the prey beyond his reach, tormented by the long gathered rage of hunger
and his dry bloodless jaws: just so the Rutulian scans wall
and camp with kindling wrath; grief fires the marrow of his
iron bones—how to essay an entrance? what way to dash the
prisoned Trojans from the rampart and fling them forth on
level ground? Close to the camp's side was lying the fleet, shored
round by earthworks and by the river; this he assails, calling
for fire to his exulting mates, and filling his hand with a blazing
pine, himself all aglow. Driven on by Turnus' presence, they
double their efforts: each soldier of the band equips himself
with his murky torch. See, they have stripped the hearths:
the smoking brand sends up a pitchy glare, and the Fire-god
wafts clouds of soot and flame heaven-high.

What god, ye Muses, shielded the Teucrians from a fire
so terrible? who warded off from the ships so vast a conflag-
ration? Tell me, the faith in the tale is old, but its fame is
evergreen.

In early days, when Æneas in Phrygian Ida was first fashion-
ing his fleet and making ready for the high seas, the great
mother of the gods, they say, the Berecyntian queen, thus
addressed almighty Jove: 'Grant, my son, to thy mother's
prayer the boon she asks thee on thy conquest of Olympus.
A pine-forest is mine, endeared by the love of many years, a
sacred grove on the mountain's height, whither worshippers
brought their offerings, bedarkened with black pitch-trees and
trunks of maple: these I was fain to give to the youth of
Dardany when he needed a fleet; now my anxious heart is
wrung by disturbing fears. Release me from my dread, and

let a mother's prayer avail thus much: let them be overcome
by no strain of voyage, no violence of wind; give them good
of their birth on my sacred hill.' To her replied her son, who
wields the starry sphere: 'O mother, whither wouldst thou
wrest the course of fate? what askest thou for these thy
favourites? should vessels framed by mortal hand have charter
of immortality? should Æneas, himself assured, meet perils
all unsure? What god had ever privilege so great? Nay,
rather, when their service is over and they gain one day the
haven of Ausonia, from all such as escape the waves and con-
voy the Dardan chief safe to Laurentian soil, I will take away
their perishable shape, and summon them to the state of goddesses of the mighty ocean, in form like Nereus' children, Doto
and Galatea, when they breast the foaming deep.' He said;
and by the river of his Stygian brother, by the banks that
seethe with pitch and are washed by the murky torrent, he
nodded confirmation, and with his nod made all Olympus
tremble.

So now the promised day was come, and the Destinies had
fulfilled the time appointed, when Turnus' lawless violence
gave warning to the mighty mother to ward off the firebrand
from her consecrated ships. Now in a moment a strange light
flashed on the eyes of all, and a great cloud was seen from the
quarter of the dawn-goddess running athwart the sky, with
the choirs of Ida in its train; then came darting through the
air a voice of terror, thrilling the ranks of Trojan and Rutulian
from end to end: 'Busy not yourselves, ye Teucrians, to
defend my ships, nor take weapons into your hands: Turnus
shall have leave to burn up the ocean sooner than to consume
my sacred pines. Go free, my favourites: go and be goddesses
of the sea: it is the mother's voice that bids you.' And
at once each ship snaps her cable from the bank, and like a
dolphin dips her beak and makes for the bottom. Then all

emerge in maiden forms, a marvel to behold, and breast the main, as many as stood a moment ago with their brazen prows to the shore.

Amazement seized the Rutulians ; terror came on Messapus himself, confusion on his steeds ; even Tiber, the river, pauses, murmuring hoarsely, and retraces his seaward course. But bold Turnus' confidence felt no check ; no, his words are ready to encourage and upbraid : 'It is at the Trojans that these portents point : Jove himself has robbed them of their wonted resource ; they wait not for Rutulian fire and sword to do the work. Yes, the sea is impassable to the Teucrians; hope of flight have they none ; one half of nature is taken from them ; as for earth, it is in our hands, thanks to the thousands here standing in arms, the tribes of Italy. I care not for the fateful utterances of heaven that these Phrygians vaunt, be they what they may : fate and Venus have had license enough, in that the Trojans have set foot on the soil of our rich Ausonia. I, too, have a fate of my own, to mow down with the sword the guilty nation that has stolen my bride ; that wrong of theirs comes not home to the Atridæ alone, nor has Mycenæ alone the privilege of going to war. But one destruction is enough for them—ay, had one transgression been enough, so that they had henceforth loathed the sex well-nigh to a woman. Men who trust in their intervening rampart, whom the pause at the trench, those few feet of distance from death, inspires with courage. Why, did they not see their city of Troy sink into the fire, though built by the hand of Neptune ? But you, my chosen mates, who is there ready to hew down the rampart and rush with me on their bewildered camp ? I need not the arms of Vulcan nor a thousand sail for *my* Trojan war. Let all Etruria join them in a body. Night alarms, cowardly thefts of their guardian image, slaughterings of the sentry on the height, they need fear none of these ; we will not skulk in a horse's murky womb: in broad day, in the sight of all, I stand pledged to put a ring of fire round their walls. I will not let them fancy they are dealing with the Danaans and the Pelasgian chivalry, whom Hector kept ten years waiting for their due. Now, since the better part of the day is spent, for what remains, gallants, refresh yourselves after your good service, and be assured that battle is getting ready.'

Meantime the charge is given to Messapus to leaguer the gates with relays of watchmen, and throw a girdle of fire round the ramparts. Twice seven Rutulian chiefs are chosen to keep armed observation of the walls : a hundred warriors attend on each, red with scarlet crests and gleaming with gold. They move from place to place and relieve one another, and stretched on the grass give wine its fling and tilt the brazen bowl. Bright shine the fires : the warders speed the wakeful night with sport and game.

The Trojans look forth on the scene from their earth-works, as in arms they man the summit; with anxious fear they test the gates, and link bridge and bulwark, their weapons in their hands. First in the work are Mnestheus and keen Serestus, whom father Æneas, should adverse crisis call for action, left to command the warriors and govern affairs at home. The whole army along the wall, dividing the danger, keeps guard, each relieving each at the post assigned.

The warder of the gate was Nisus, a soldier of keenest mettle, Hyrtacus' son, whom Ida the huntress sent to attend Æneas, quick with the dart and the flying arrow : and at his side Euryalus, than who was none fairer among Æneas' children, none that ever donned the arms of Troy, a stripling whose unrazored cheeks just showed the first bloom of youth. Theirs was a common love : side by side they wont to rush into the battle : and even then they were keeping watch at the gate in joint duty. Nisus exclaims : 'Is it the gods, Euryalus, that make men's hearts glow thus ? or does each one's ungoverned yearning become his god? My heart has long been astir to rush on war or other mighty deed, nor will peaceful quiet content it. You see the Rutulians there, delivered up to confidence in the future : their line of lights gleams brokenly: unnerved with sleep and wine, yonder they lie : all around is still. Listen on, and learn on what I am brooding, and what thought is this moment uppermost. "Æneas should be recalled"—so cry people and leaders as one man ; "messengers should be sent to tell him the truth." If they pledge themselves to what I ask for you—for me the fame of the deed is sufficient—methinks under the mound yonder I could find a way to the city walls of Pallanteum.' A thrill of generous ambition struck wonder into Euryalus, as thus he addressed his glowing friend : 'And would you shrink from taking me with you, Nisus, on this high occasion ? Am I to send you out alone on such perilous errand? It was not thus that my father, the veteran Opheltes, reared and bred me among Argive terrors and Trojan agonies, nor have such been my doings at your side, since I followed our hero Æneas and his desperate fate. Here, here, within me is a soul that thinks scorn of happy sunshine, and deems that the glory at which you aim were cheaply bought with life.' 'Nay,' returns Nisus, 'trust me, I had no such fear of you—none such had been just: so may I return to you in triumph, by grace of mighty Jove, or whosoever now looks down on us with righteous eyes. But should aught—and a venture like this, you see, has a thousand such—should aught sway things amiss, be it chance or heaven's will, I would fain have you spared : yours is the meeter age for life. Let me have one to rescue me in fight, or redeem me by ransom paid, and so consign me to the burial all receive : or should Fortune grudge even that, to pay me the rites of the absent, and give

me the adornment of a tomb. Nor let me be the cause of
grief so terrible to that unhappy parent, who alone of many
matrons has had a heart to follow you, dear boy, nor cares
for the city of great Acestes.' He replied : 'Spinning empty
pretexts is idle work : there is no change or faltering in my
resolve. Up and despatch !' At once he rouses the guard,
who take his place and fulfil their time, while he, departing
from the post, walks side by side with Nisus, and they seek
the prince together.

All else that breathed on earth were asleep, their load of
care unbound, their hearts oblivious of toil; the chief leaders
of the Teucrians, the flower of the host, were holding council
on the crisis in their realm's fortune, what they should do,
or who should at length be sent with the news to Æneas.
There they stand propped on their long spears, their shields
still in their hands, in the midst of camp and plain. At this
moment Nisus and Euryalus eagerly crave instant admission
—the affair is great, say they, and well worth the pause it
claims. Iulus was the first to welcome and reassure them,
and bid Nisus speak. Then began the son of Hyrtacus :
'Listen, ye sons of Troy, with kindly heed, nor let these our
proffers be judged by our years. The Rutulians, unnerved by
sleep and wine, are hushed in silence : we have ourselves
observed a place for a stealthy move, open through the passage
of the gate which abuts on the sea. The line of fires is
broken, and only dusky smoke rises to the sky : give us but
leave to make use of fortune, and go in quest of Æneas and
the walls of Pallanteum, soon shall you see us here again after
a mighty carnage, laden with spoils. Nor can the way
mislead us as we go : we have seen in the dimness of the
vale the outskirts of the city while persevering in our hunting, and have made acquaintance with the whole river's
course.' Then spoke Aletes, weighty with years and ripe of

understanding : 'Gods of our fathers, whose constant presence watches over Troy, not yet in spite of all do ye purpose to make an utter end of us Teucrians, when such are the spirits and so steadfast the hearts ye breed in our youth.' As he said this, he kept embracing the necks and hands of both, and bathing his cheeks in floods of tears. 'What guerdons, gallant men, what can I fancy of worth enough to pay you for glories like these? First and richest of all will be the praise of heaven and your own hearts : next to these you will receive the rest without fail from good Æneas and young Ascanius, who will never forget a service so great.' 'Nay,' cries Ascanius, 'let me speak, me, whose safety is bound up with my sire's return : by our great household gods I adjure you, Nisus, by the deity of Assaracus' house and the shrine of reverend Vesta—all my fortune, all my trust, I place in your hands : bring back my father, let me see him again ; he once restored, all grief is over. I will give you a pair of goblets wrought with silver and rough from the chasing-tool, which my father took when he conquered Arisba, a couple of tripods, two great talents of gold, and an ancient bowl, Sidonian Dido its donor. But if it be our victorious fortune to conquer Italy and attain the crown, and appoint the lot for the booty—you saw the horse which Turnus rode, the arms in which he moved all golden—that horse, that shield, and the scarlet crest I will set apart from the lot, and count it, Nisus, yours already. Moreover, my sire shall give you twelve matron captives of choicest beauty, male prisoners too, each with his armour, and, to crown all, the portion of domain held by king Latinus himself. But you, whose years are followed at nearer distance by my own, revered youth, I take at once to my heart, and fold you there, my comrade for whatever betides. Never will I seek glory for my own estate apart from you : whether I have peace or war on hand,

x

yours shall be my utmost confidence in deed and in word.'
To him spoke Euryalus in reply: 'No length of time shall
find me false to the promise of my bold essay: let but fortune
speed and not thwart us. But one boon I would ask of you
beyond all others: I have a mother of Priam's ancient
house, whom not the land of Ilium, not the city of king
Acestes, could keep, poor soul, from going with me. Her I am
now leaving, ignorant of this peril, be it what it may, with
no word of greeting—Night and your right hand are my
witnesses—because I could not bear a parent's tears. But
you, I pray, comfort her need and support her lonely age.
With this trust in you to bear along with me, I shall meet all
that happens with a bolder spirit.' Touched to the heart, the
children of Dardanus broke into tears—chief of all the fair
Iulus, as the picture of his own filial love flashed upon his
soul. Thus he speaks: 'Assure yourself that all shall be
done that your mighty deeds deserve. Yes, she shall be my
own mother, nought wanting but the name to make her Creusa's
self; to have borne you lays up no mean store of gratitude.
Whatever the fortune that attends your endeavour, I swear by
this my head, by which my father has been wont to swear, all
that I promise to you in the event of your prosperous return,
shall remain in its fulness assured to your mother and your
house.' This he says weeping, and unbelts from his shoulder a
gilded sword wrought with rare art by Lycaon of Crete, and
fitted for use with a scabbard of ivory. To Nisus Mnestheus
gives a skin, a lion's shaggy spoils: Aletes, true of heart, makes
an exchange of helmets. Their arming done they march along;
and as they go, the whole band of nobles, young and old, escorts
them to the gate with prayers for their safety. There too was
fair Iulus, in heart and forethought manlier than his years, giving them many a charge to carry to his father. But the winds
scatter all alike, and deliver them cancelled to the clouds.

Passing through the gate, they cross the trenches, and through the midnight shade make for the hostile camp—destined, though, first to be the death of many. All about the grass they see bodies stretched at length by sleep and wine, cars tilted up on the shore, men lying among wheels and harness, with armour and pools of wine about them. First spoke the son of Hyrtacus : 'Euryalus, daring. hands are wanted ; the occasion now calls for action; here lies our way. Do you keep watch and wide look-out, lest any hand be lifted against us from behind ; I will lay these ranks waste, and give you a broad path to walk in.' So saying, he checks his voice, and at once with his tyrannous sword assails Rhamnes, who, pillowed on a vast pile of rugs, was breathing from all his breast the breath of sleep—a king himself, and king Turnus' favourite augur ; but his augury availed him not to ward off death. Close by he surprises three attendants, stretched carelessly among their weapons, and Remus' armour-bearer and charioteer, catching him as he lay at the horses' side : the steel shears through their drooping necks; then he lops the head of their lord, and leaves the trunk gurgling and spouting blood, while ground and couch are reeking with black streams of gore. Lamyrus too, and Lamus, and young Serranus, who had played long that night in the pride of his beauty, and was lying with the dream-god's hand heavy upon him ; happy, had he made his play as long as the night, and pushed it into morning. Like a hungry lion making havoc through a teeming fold—for the madness of famine constrains him—he goes mangling and dragging along the feeble cattle, dumb with terror, and gnashing his bloody teeth. Nor less the carnage of Euryalus : he, too, all on fire, storms along, and slays on his road a vast and nameless crowd, Fadus and Herbesus, and Rhœtus and Abaris —unconscious these : Rhœtus was awake and saw it all, but in his fear he crouched behind a massive bowl; whence, as he rose, the conqueror plunged into his fronting breast the length of his sword, and drew it back with a torrent of death. The dying man vomits forth his crimson life, and disgorges mingled wine and blood : the foe pursues his stealthy work. And now he was making for Messapus' followers, for there he saw the flicker of dying fires, and horses tied and browsing at their ease; when thus spoke Nisus in brief, seeing him hurried on by passion and excess of slaughter : 'Forbear we now ; the daylight, our enemy, is at hand; we have supped on vengeance to the full; a highway is open through the foe.' Many warriors' arms they leave, wrought of solid silver, many bowls and gorgeous coverlets. Euryalus lays hand on Rhamnes' trappings and his belt with golden studs, sent by wealthy Cædicus of old as a present to Remulus of Tibur, when he fain would make him his friend from a distance ; he, dying, leaves them to his grandson, after whose death the Rutulians won them in battle ; these he strips off, and fits them to his valiant breast, all for nought. Then he puts on Messapus' shapely helm, with its graceful crest. They leave the camp, and pass into safety.

Meanwhile a troop of horse, sent on from the town of Latium, while the rest of the force abides drawn up on the field, was on its way with a message to king Turnus, three hundred, shield-bearers all, with Volscens, their chief. They were just nearing the camp, and passing under the wall, when at distance they spy the two bending to the left, and the helmet, seen in the glimmering twilight, betrayed the heedless Euryalus, as the moonbeam flashed full upon it. The sight fell not on idle eyes. Volscens shout from his band : 'Halt, gallants ; tell your errand, who you are thus armed, and whither you are going.' They venture no reply, but hasten the faster to the woods, and make the night their friend.

The horsemen bar each well-known passage right and left and set a guard on every outlet. The wood was shagged with thickets and dark ilex boughs; impenetrable briars filled it on every side; through the concealed tracks just gleamed a narrow path. Euryalus is hampered by the darkness of the branches, and the encumbrance of his booty, and fear makes him miss the right line of road. Nisus shoots away: and now in his forgetfulness he had escaped the foe, and gained the region afterwards called Alban from Alba's name; in that day king Latinus had there his stately stalls; when he halted, and looked back in vain for the friend he could not see. 'My poor Euryalus! where have I left you? what way shall I trace you, unthreading all the tangled path of that treacherous wood?' As he speaks, he scans and retraces each step, and wanders through the stillness of the brakes. He hears the horses, hears the noise and the tokens of pursuit. Pass a few moments, and a shout strikes on his ear, and he sees Euryalus, who is in the hands of the whole crew, the victim of the ground and the night, bewildered by the sudden onslaught, hurried along, and making a thousand fruitless efforts. What should he do? with what force, what arms can he attempt a rescue? should he dash through the thick of their swords with death before his eyes, and hurry to a glorious end in a shower of wounds? Soon, with his arm drawn back, he poises his spear-shaft, looking up to the moon in the sky, and thus prays aloud: 'Thou, goddess, be thou present, and befriend my endeavour, Latona's daughter, glory of the heavens and guardian of the woods: if ever my father Hyrtacus brought gift for me to thine altar, if ever my own hunting swelled the tribute, if ever I hung an offering from thy dome or fastened it on thy hallowed summit, suffer me to confound this mass, and guide my weapons through the air.' This said, with an effort of his whole frame he hurled the steel. The flying spear strikes through the shades of night, reaches the turned back of Sulmo, there snaps short, and pierces the midriff with the broken wood. Down he tumbles, disgorging from his breast the warm life-torrent that leaves him cold, and long choking gasps smite on his sides. They look round this way and that: while the same fell arm, nerved by success, is levelling, see! another weapon from the ear-tip. While all is confusion, the spear has passed through Tagus' two temples with whizzing sound, and lies warmly lodged in his cloven brain. Volscens storms with fury, yet sees nowhere the author of the wound, nor on whom to vent his rage: 'You, however, shall pay both debts meanwhile with your heart's blood,' cries he; and speaking, rushes with drawn sword on Euryalus. Then, indeed, in frantic agony, Nisus shouts aloud; no more care had he to hide himself in darkness, no more strength to bear grief so terrible: 'Me, me! behold the doer! make me your mark, O Rutulians! mine is all the blame; he had no heart, no hand for such deeds; this heaven, these stars know that it is true; it was but that he loved his unhappy friend too well.' Thus he was pleading; but the sword, driven with the arm's full force, has pierced the ribs and is rending the snowy breast. Down falls Euryalus in death; over his beauteous limbs gushes the blood, and his powerless neck sinks on his shoulders; as when a purple flower, severed by the plough, pines in death, or poppies with faint necks droop the head, when rain has chanced to weigh them down. But Nisus rushes full on the foe, Volscens his one object among them all; he cares for none but Volscens: the enemy cluster round, and assail him on all sides; none the less he holds on his way, whirling his lightning blade, till at last he lodges it full in the Rutulian's face, as he shrieks for aid, and dying robs his foe of life. Then he flung himself on his breathless friend, pierced through and through, and there at length slept away in peaceful death.

Happy pair! if this my song has aught of potency, no lapse of days shall efface your names from the memory of time, so long as the house of Æneas shall dwell on the Capitol's moveless rock, and a Roman father shall be the world's lord.

The Rutulian conquerors, enriched with spoil and booty, were bearing Volscens' body to the camp with tears in their eyes. Nor less loud is the wailing in the camp, when they find Rhamnes drained of life, and those many chiefs slain by a single carnage—Serranus, Numa, and the rest. They flock in crowds to the bodies, the warriors yet breathing, the place fresh and reeking with slaughter, and the streams of gore full and foaming. They pass the spoils from hand to hand, and recognise Messapus' gleaming helm, and the trappings which it cost such sweat to recover.

Now at last the goddess of the dawn was sprinkling the world with new-born light, as she rose from Tithonus' saffron couch: the sun had streamed in and all was revealed by daybreak, when Turnus summons his men to arms, himself sheathed in armour; each general musters in battle array his brass-mailed bands, and, scattering divers speeches, stings them to fury. Nay, more, on uplifted spears, most piteous sight, they set up the heads, and follow them with deafening shouts—the heads of Euryalus and Nisus. Æneas' sturdy family, on the rampart's left side, set the fight in array—for the right is flanked by the river—guard the broad trenches and stand on the lofty towers, deep in sorrow—touched to see those lifted human countenances, which to their grief they knew so well, dripping with black corrupted gore.

Meantime, Fame spreads her wings and flies with the news through the wildered settlement, and reaches the ears of Euryalus' mother. At once the vital heat left her wretched frame : the shuttle was dashed from her hands, and the thread ran back. Forth flies the unhappy dame, and with a woman's piercing shriek, her tresses rent, makes madly for the walls and the van of battle, heeding not the eyes of men, heeding not the peril and the shower of javelins, while she fills the heaven with her plaints : 'Is it thus, Euryalus, that I see you again? have you, the late solace of my waning years, had the heart to leave me alone, unpitying? nor, when you ventured on such dangerous errand, might your wretched mother speak her farewell? Alas! on an unknown land you are lying, exposed to the ravin of Latium's dogs and birds; nor have I, your mother, followed your corpse to the tomb, or closed your eyes, or bathed your wounds, shrouding you with the robe which I worked so hard to finish day and night, and made the loom the medicine of an old wife's sorrow! Where shall I seek you? what land now contains those severed limbs, that mutilated corpse? is this the sole relic of yourself that you bring back to me, my son? is this what I followed over land and sea? Pierce me, if you have aught of human feeling—shower on me all your darts, ye Rutulians, let the sword make me its first meal; or do thou, great sire of the gods, have mercy, and with thy lightning-bolt strike down to Tartarus this hated life, since I cannot otherwise end the cruel pain of being.' Her wail shook every heart to its centre; a groan of sorrow passed through the ranks; their martial prowess flags and faints. At last, as her agony flames higher, Idæus and Actor, bidden by Ilioneus and the tearful Iulus, lay hold of her, and carry in their arms within.

But the trumpet from its brazen throat uttered afar a tremendous blare; a shout ensues, and heaven returns the roar. Quick speed the Volscians, carrying in level line their penthouse of shields, and strive to fill the moat and pluck down the palisade. Some look about for an access, and fain would scale the walls with ladders, where the line of defence is thin, and the ring of men, not too closely set, shows a gleaming interval. The Teucrians, on their part, shower missiles of every sort, and repulse the assailants with strong poles, taught by a long war's experience how to guard their walls. Stones, too, they kept rolling of fatal bulk, in hope to break through the foe's sheltered ranks, though beneath so firm a penthouse a soldier may well smile at all that can betide. Ay, and it ceases to avail them : for where a mighty mass threatens the rampart, the Teucrians push forward and roll down an enormous weight, which made wide havoc among the Rutulians, and burst the joints of their harness. And now the bold Rutulians care no longer to wage war in the dark, but aim at driving them from the ramparts with a storm of missiles. In another quarter, terrible to look upon, Mezentius waves an Etruscan pine and hurls fire and smoke, while Messapus, tamer of the steed, of the race of Neptune, plucks down the palisade, and calls for ladders to the battlement.

Vouchsafe, Calliope and thy heavenly sisterhood, to aid me while I sing, what slaughter, what deaths were dealt that day in that place by Turnus' sword, what foes each warrior sent down to the grave, and help me to unfold the length and breadth of the mighty war.

A tower there was, vast to look on from below, with lofty bridges, placed on a vantage-ground, which all the Italians, with utmost force and utmost strain of might, were essaying to storm, while the Trojans, on their side, were defending it with stones, and hurling showers of darts through its narrow eyelets. Turnus the first flung a blazing torch and fastened fire on its side ; fanned by the wind, the flame seized the planks and lodged in the consuming doors. The inmates are all in confusion, and in vain seek to escape the mischief.

While they huddle together and retire upon the part which the plague has spared, in an instant the tower falls heavily down, and the firmament thunders with the crash. Half dead they come to the ground, the huge fabric following on their backs, pierced by their own weapons, their breasts impaled by the cruel wood. Barely two escaped, Helenor and Lycus—Helenor in prime of youth, whom Licymnia the slave had borne secretly to the Mæonian king, and had sent to Troy in forbidden arms, with the light accoutrement of a naked sword, and a shield uncharged by an escutcheon. Soon as he saw himself with Turnus' thousands round him, the armies of Latium standing on this side and on that, like a beast that, hemmed in by the hunters' close-set ring, vents her rage on the darts and flings herself deliberately on death, and springs from high on the line of spears, even thus the doomed youth rushes on the midst of the foe, making for where he sees the darts are thickest. But Lycus, far swifter of foot, winds among ranks of foes and showers of steel and gains the wall, and strives to clutch the fabric's summit and reach the hands of his friends. Whom Turnus, following him at once with foot and javelin, taunts in victorious tone : 'Dreamed you, poor fool, that you could escape my hands ?' and with that he seizes him as he hangs in air, and pulls him down with a great fragment of the wall ; just as the bearer of Jove's thunder trusses in his hooked talons a hare or a snow-white swan and soars into the sky, or one of Mars' wolves snatches from the fold a lamb which its mother's bleatings reclaim in vain. On all sides rises the war-shout. They rush on the trenches and fill them with shattered earthworks, while others fling brazen firebrands to the roofs. Ilioneus with a rock, broken from a mighty mountain, brings down Lucetius as he assails the gates and waves his torch. Liger kills Emathion, Asilas Corynæus, one skilled with the javelin, one with the arrow that surprises from a distance. Cæneus slays Ortygius, Turnus the conqueror Cæneus, Turnus Itys and Clonius, Dioxippus and Promolus, and Sagaris, and Idas, who was standing on the turret's top. Capys kills Privernus : Themilla's flying spear had grazed him first ; he, poor fool, dropped his buckler and clapped his hand to the wound, so the arrow came on stealthy wing, and the hand was pinned to the left side, and the inmost seat of breath is rent asunder by the deadly wound. There stood the son of Arcens in conspicuous armour, his scarf embroidered with needlework, in the glory of Hiberian purple, fair of form, sent to war by his father Arcens, who had reared him in his mother's grove by the streams of Symæthus, where stands Palicus' rich and gracious altar : flinging his spears aside, Mezentius whirled the strained thong of the whizzing sling thrice round his head, and with the molten bullet burst in twain the forehead of the fronting foe, and stretched him at full length on the expanse of sand.

Then first, they say, Ascanius levelled in war his winged arrow, used till then to terrify the beasts of chase, and laid low by strength of hand the brave Numanus, Remulus by surname, who had lately won and wedded Turnus' younger sister. He was stalking in front of the host, vaunting aloud things meet and unmeet to tell, in the insolence of new-blown royalty, and venting his pride in clamorous tones : 'Are ye not ashamed to be imprisoned yet again in leaguer and rampart, twice-captured Phrygians, and to put your walls between you and death ? Lo, these are the men who demand our wives at the sword's edge ! What god, what madness, has driven you to Italy ? You will not find the Atridæ here, nor Ulysses the forger of speech. A hardy race even from the stock, we bring our sons soon as born to the river's side, and harden them with the water's cruel cold. Our boys spend long days in the chase, and weary out the forest; their sport is to rein the steed, and level shafts from the bow. Our youth, strong to labour and schooled by want, subdues the earth with the rake, or shakes the city's walls with battle. All our life we ply the steel; with the butt of our spears we belabour our cattle; old age, which dulls all else, impairs not the force of our hearts or changes our fresh vigour; the hoary head is clasped by the helmet; our constant joy is to bring home new booty and live by rapine. Yours are embroidered garments of saffron and gleaming purple; sauntering and sloth are your delight; your pleasure is to indulge the dance; your tunics have sleeves and your turbans strings. Phrygian dames in sooth—for Phrygian men ye are not—get you to the heights of Dindymus, where the pipe utters its two-doored note to your accustomed ears. The Idæan mother's cymbals, the Berecyntian flute are calling you to the revel; leave arms to men, and meddle no more with steel.'

Such boasting and such ill-omened talk Ascanius could bear no longer; setting his breast to the bow-string of horsehair he levelled his dart, and drawing his arms wide apart he stood, having first invoked Jove thus in suppliant prayer: 'Jove Almighty, smile on my bold essay; with my own hand I will bring to thy temple yearly offerings, and will set before thine altar a bullock with gilded brow, snowy white, rearing his head to the height of his mother's, fit to butt with the horn and spurn up sand with the hoof.' The father heard and from a cloudless quarter of the sky thundered on the left; at the same instant twanged the deadly bow. Forth flies the arrow from the string, whizzing fearfully, passes through the head of Remulus, and cleaves with its point his hollow temples. 'Go, make valour the sport of your boasting; the twice-captured Phrygians answer the Rutulians thus.' So far Ascanius:

the Teucrians second him with a cry, shout for joy, and mount
heavenward in their exultation. It chanced that then in the
realm of sky long-haired Apollo was surveying the armies of
Ausonia and the city, seated on a cloud; and thus addressed
Iulus in the moment of triumph : ' Rejoice, brave youth, in
your new-won laurels ; 'tis thus men climb the stars ; son of
gods that are, sire of gods that shall be! Well has Fate
ordered that beneath the house of Assaracus the wars of the
future shall find their end; nor can Troy contain your prowess.'
So saying he shoots down from heaven, parts before him the
breathing gales, and makes for Ascanius. He changes his
features to those of ancient Butes, who had once been armour-
bearer to Dardanian Anchises and trusty watcher at the gate ;
thence Ascanius' sire made him his son's guardian. Apollo
moved along, in all things like the aged veteran, the voice, the
colour, the white locks, the fiercely clanking armour ; and
thus he spoke to Iulus' glowing heart : 'Suffice it, child of
Æneas, that Numanus has met from your darts an unrequited
death : this your maiden glory great Apollo vouchsafes you
freely, nor looks with jealousy on weapons like his own ; for
the rest abstain from war, as stripling should.' So Apollo
began, and ere his speech was well done parted from mortal
eyes, and vanished from sight into unsubstantial air. The
Dardan chiefs knew the god and his divine artillery, and heard
his quiver hurtle as he fled. So now at Phœbus' present
instance they check Ascanius' ardour for battle ; themselves
take their place in the combat once more, and fling their lives
into the jaws of danger. All over the walls passes the shout
from rampart to rampart ; they bend their sharp-springing bows
and hurl their lashed javelins—the ground is all strewn with
darts ; shields and hollow helms ring with blow on blow ; a
savage combat is aroused ; fierce as the rain coming from the
west at the setting of the showery kid-stars scourges the earth,

plenteous as the hail which the stormclouds discharge into the sea, when Jove in the sullenness of southern blasts whirls the watery tempest and bursts the misty chambers of the sky.

Pandarus and Bitias, sons of Idæan Alcanor, brought up by Iæra the wood-nymph in the grove of Jupiter, youths tall as the pines and peaks of their birthplace, throw open the gate, which the general's order placed in their charge, relying on their good steel, and invite the foe to enter the town. Themselves within right and left stand before the bulwarks, sheathed in iron, the crest waving on their lofty heads : even as high in air beside the flowing streams, on Padus' banks it may be or by pleasant Athesis, uptower two oaks, raising to heaven their unshorn summits and nodding their lofty crowns. In rush the Rutulians when they see the entry clear. In a moment Quercens and Aquicolus in his brilliant armour and headlong Tmarus and Hæmon, scion of Mars, with all their followers are routed and turned to flight, or on the threshold of the gate have resigned their lives. At this the wrath of the combatants flames yet higher, and the Trojans rally and muster in one spot and venture to engage hand to hand and to advance farther into the plain.

Turnus, the chief, while venting his rage elsewhere and scattering ranks of warriors, hears tidings that the foe, fevered by the taste of blood, has thrown the gates open. He leaves the work he had begun, and stirred with giant fury hastens to the Dardan gate and the two haughty brethren. Hurling his dart, he first slays Antiphates, who happened first to meet him, bastard son of great Sarpedon by a Theban mother ; the shaft of Italian cornel flies through the yielding air, and lodging in the throat goes deep down into the chest ; the wound's dark pit spouts forth a foaming torrent, and the cold steel grows warm in the lungs it pierces. Then with strong hand he slays Merops and Erymas and then Aphidnus, then Bitias with his blazing eyes and his boiling valour—not with a dart, for to a dart he would not have surrendered his life—no ; it was a whirled phalaric lance that came hurtling fiercely, shot like a thunderbolt, which neither two bulls' hides nor a trusty corselet with double golden plait could withstand : the massive limbs sink and fall : earth groans, and the vast buckler thunders on the body. Even thus sometimes on Baiæ's Eubœan coast falls a pile of stone, which men compact with mighty blocks and then fling into the sea ; thus it comes down with protracted headlong ruin, and dashing on the shallows settles into its place ; the sea is all disturbed, and the murky sand rises to the surface ; the crash shakes Prochyta to her depths, and Inarime's rugged bed, laid by Jove's command upon Typhœus.

Now Mars, the lord of arms, inspires the Latians with strength and courage, and plants his stings deep in their bosoms, while among the Teucrians, he sends Flight and grisly Terror. They flock from this side and from that, now that scope for battle is given, and the warrior-god comes down on their souls. When Pandarus saw his brother's corpse laid low, and knew the posture of fortune and the chance that was swaying the day, with a mighty effort he turns the gate on its hinge, pushing with his broad shoulders, and leaves outside many of his comrades shut out from the camp all in the cruel battle, while others he shuts in with himself, admitting them as they stream onward—madman, to have failed to see the king of the Rutulians in the middle of the company storming in, and to have shut him wantonly within the walls, like a monstrous tiger among a herd of helpless cattle ! On the instant a strange light flashed from the eyes of the foe, and his arms gave a fearful clang ; on his helm quivers his crest, red as blood, and from his shield he darts gleaming lightnings. With sudden confusion the children of Æneas recognise that hated form and those giant limbs. Then forth springs mighty Pandarus, and with all the glow of wrath for his brother's death bespeaks him thus : 'This is not the bridal palace of Amata, nor is it Ardea that embraces Turnus in the walls of his fathers; the enemy's camp is before you; all escape is barred.' To him Turnus, smiling in quiet mood : 'Begin, if you have courage, and engage in combat. Priam shall learn from you that here too you have found an Achilles.' Thus he : Pandarus, with the full strain of his power, hurls his spear, rugged with knots and unpeeled bark. It was launched on the air; but Saturnian Juno turned aside the coming wound, and the spear lodged in the gate. 'But this my weapon you shall not escape, swayed as it is by my hand's full force; he from whom wound and weapon come is too strong for that.' So cries Turnus, and rises high upon his lifted sword, and cleaves with the steel the forehead in twain full between the temples, parting beardless cheek from cheek with a ghastly wound. A crash is heard : earth is shaken by the enormous weight : the unnerved limbs, the arms splashed with gore and brain are stretched in death on the ground ; and the head, shared in equal parts, hangs right and left from either shoulder. The routed Trojans fly here and there in wildering terror ; and had the thought at once seized the conqueror, to burst the gates by main force and give entrance to his friends, that day would have ended a war and a nation both. But rage and mad thirst for blood drove him in fury on the foe before him. First he surprises Phalaris and hamstrings Gyges ; plucks forth spears and hurls them on the backs of the fliers ; Juno gives supplies of strength and courage. He sends Halys to join them and Phegeus, pierced through the shield, and cuts down others as they stand unconscious on the walls and stir up the battle, Alcander and Halius, and Nœmon and Prytanis. As Lynceus moved to meet him and calls on

his comrades, with a sweep of his arm from the rampart on
his right he catches him with his whirling sword; swept off
by a single blow hand to hand, the head with the helmet on
it lay yards away. Next falls Amycus, the ravager of the
forest brood, than who was never man more skilled to anoint
the dart and arm the steel with venom, and Clytius, son of
Æolus, and Cretheus, darling of the Muses, Cretheus the
Muses' playmate, whose delight was ever in minstrelsy and
harp, and in stringing notes on the chord; songs of chargers
and warrior arms and battles were ever on his lips.

At last the Teucrian leaders, hearing of the slaughter of
their men, come together to the spot, Mnestheus and keen
Serestus, when they see their comrades flying in confusion,
and the foe lodged in the camp. Out cries Mnestheus:
'Whither now, whither are ye making in flight? what further
city have ye, what walls beyond? Shall it be said that a
single man, and he too, my countrymen, hemmed in on all
hands by your ramparts, has spread unavenged such havoc
through your streets, has sent down to death so many of your
bravest? As ye think of your unhappy country, your ancient
gods, your great Æneas, is there no pity, no shame in your
sluggish hearts?' Roused by these words they rally and halt
in close array. Turnus step by step withdraws from the
fight, making for the river and the part round which the
water runs. All the more keenly the Teucrians press on
him with loud shouts and close their ranks: as when a
company of hunters bears down on a savage lion javelin
in-hand: he, struck with fear, yet fierce and glaring angrily,
gives ground; wrath and courage suffer him not to turn
his back, nor yet may he charge, though he fain would
do so, through the huntsmen and the spears. Not unlike
to him Turnus in doubt retraces his lingering footsteps,
while his heart boils with rage. Even then twice had he

Y

dashed on the thick of the foe, twice he drives their ranks in huddled flight round the walls; but the whole army musters in a body from the camp, nor dares Saturnian Juno supply him with strength to oppose them; for Jove sent down from the sky celestial Iris, with no gentle message for his sister's ear, if Turnus retire not from the Teucrians' lofty ramparts. So now the warrior cannot hold his own with shield or sword; such a deluge of darts overwhelms him. Round his hollow temples the helmet echoes with ceaseless ringing; the solid plates of brass give way beneath the stones; the horsehair crest is struck from his head; his shield's boss cannot stand the blows; faster and faster they hail their spears, the Trojans and fiery Mnestheus. Over all his frame flows the sweat and trickles in a murky stream, while breathe he cannot; his sinking limbs are shaken with feeble panting. At last with headlong leap he plunged arms and all into the river. Tiber with his yellow gulf received the guest, upbore him on his buoyant waves, and washing off the stains of carnage, restored him in joy to his friends.

BOOK X.

MEANTIME the palace of strong Olympus is thrown open, and the sire of gods and monarch of men summons a council to the starry chamber, whence, throned on high, he looks down on the length and breadth of earth, the camp of the Dardans and the people of Latium. They take their seats in the double-gated mansion; he himself opens the court : ' Mighty denizens of heaven, wherefore is your judgment turned backward, and whence such discord in your unkindly souls? I had forbidden that Italy should meet the Teucrians in the shock of war. What strife is this in defiance of my law? What terror has prompted these or those to draw the sword and provoke the fight? There shall come a rightful time for combat—no need for you to hasten it—when fierce Carthage one day shall launch on the hills of Rome mighty ruin and the opening of Alpine barriers. Then will your rancours be free to contend, your hands to plunder and ravage; for the present let be, and cheerfully ratify the peace that I have willed.'

Thus Jupiter in brief; but not brief was the answer of golden Venus : ' O Father ! O eternal sovereignty of man and nature ! for what else can there be which is left us to implore? Seest thou how the Rutulians insult? how Turnus is whirled through the battle by his haughty coursers, borne on the flood-tide of war? No longer are the Teucrians safe even in the shelter of their walls; within the gates, amidst the very mounds of the ramparts combat is waged, and the trenches overflow with carnage. Æneas is away in his ignorance. Wilt thou never let us have respite from siege? Once more the enemy is stooping over the walls of our infant Troy, with a second army; once more Tydeus' son from his Ætolian Arpi is rising against the Teucrians. Ay, my wounds, I ween, are yet in the future, and I, thine own offspring, am delaying the destined course of a mortal spear. If it is without your leave and despite your will that the Trojans have won their way to Italy, let them expiate the crime and withdraw from them thine aid: but if they have but followed those many oracles given by powers above and powers underground, how can any now be able to reverse thine ordinance and write anew the page of fate? Why should I remind thee of our fleet consumed on Eryx' shore? why of the monarch of the storms and his raving winds stirred up from Æolia, or of Iris sent down from the clouds? Now she is even rousing the ghosts below —that portion of the world till then was untried—and on a sudden Alecto is launched on upper air, and rages through the Italian cities. It is not for empire that I am disquieted; for that we hoped in the past, while our star yet shone: let them conquer whom thou wouldst have conquer. If there is no country on earth which thy relentless spouse will allow the Teucrians, I adjure thee, father, by the smoking ruins of Troy overthrown, let me send away Ascanius safe from the war—let my grandson survive in life. Æneas, indeed, may be tossed on unknown waters, and follow such course as chance may give him: *him* let me have the power to screen and withdraw from the horrors of battle. Amathus is mine, and lofty Paphos, and high Cythera, and the mansion of Idalia: there let him pass his days unwarlike and inglorious. Let it be thy will that Carthage shall bow Ausonia beneath her tyrannous sway; the Tyrian cities need fear no resistance from him. What has it advantaged him to have

escaped the plague of war and fled through the hottest of the
Argive fires, to have drained to the dregs all those dangers by
sea and on broad earth, while the Teucrians are in quest of
Latium and a restored Pergamus? Give back, great sire, to
our wretched nation their Xanthus and their Simois, and let
the Teucrians enact once more the old tragedy of Ilium.' Then
outspoke queenly Juno, goaded by fierce passion: 'Why force
you me to break my deep silence, and give forth in words my
buried grief? Your Æneas—was it any man or god that
compelled him to draw the sword, and come down as a foe
on the Latian king? Grant that he went to Italy at the
instance of fate, at the impulse, in truth, of mad Cassandra;
was it our counsel that he should leave his camp and place
his life at the mercy of the winds? that he should trust
the control of battle and his city to a boy—should tamper
with Tyrrhenian loyalty and stir up a quiet nation? What
god, what cruel tyranny of ours drove him thither to his
hurt? is there a trace of Juno here, or of Iris sent down from
the clouds? Ay, it is foul shame that the Italians should throw
a belt of flame round the infant Troy—that Turnus should
plant a foot on the soil of his fathers, Turnus, whose grandsire was Pilumnus, whose mother the goddess Venilia. How
call you it for the Trojans to invade Latium with their
smoking torches, to put their yoke on a country that is none
of theirs, and harry away its plunder—to choose at will those
whose daughters they would wed, and drag the plighted bride
from the bosom—to bear suppliant tokens in the hand and
arm their vessels to the teeth? You have power to withdraw Æneas from the hands of the Greeks, and offer them
clouds and thin winds for the man they seek—power to
turn a fleet of ships into a bevy of Nymphs; and is it utterly
monstrous for us to give the Rutulians a measure of aid
in return? Æneas is away in ignorance, and in ignorance

flict of stubborn war; and now at midnight Æneas was ploughing the main. For soon as, leaving Evander, he entered the Etruscan camp, accosted the king, and told him of his name and his race, for what he sues and what he offers, explains what arms Mezentius musters on his side, and what the excess of Turnus' violence, warns him how little faith man can place in fortune, and seconds reasoning by entreaty, without a moment's pause, Tarchon combines his forces and strikes a truce; and at once, freed from the spell of destiny, the Lydian race embarks according to heaven's ordinance, under the charge of a foreign leader. First sails the vessel of Æneas, Phrygian lions harnessed on the prow; above them Ida spreads her shade, of happiest augury to exiled Troy. There sits great Æneas, brooding over the doubtful future of the war: and Pallas, close cleaving to his left side, keeps questioning him, now of the stars, the road-marks of the shadowy night, and now all that he has borne by land and by sea.

Now, ye goddesses, open wide your Helicon, and stir up the powers of song, to tell us what the army now following Æneas from the Tuscan shores, equipping its ships for adventure, and sailing over the sea.

First comes Massicus, cleaving the waters in his brass-sheathed Tiger: in his train a band of a thousand warriors, who have left the walls of Clusium and the city Cosæ; their weapons a sheaf of arrows, light quivers for the shoulder, and a bow of deadly aim. With him grim Abas: his whole band ablaze with gleaming armour, his vessel shining with a gilded Apollo. Populonia had sent him six hundred of her sons, all versed in war: Ilva three hundred, an island rich in the Chalybes' unexhausted mines. Third comes Asilas, the great interpreter 'tween gods and men, at whose bidding are the victims' entrails, the stars of the sky, the tongues of augurial birds, and the flame of the prophetic lightning. With him hurry a thousand in close array, bristling with spears—subjected to his command by the town of Pisa, which, sprung from Alphëus, took root on Etruscan soil. After these is Astur, fairest of form, Astur, proud of his steed and his glancing armour. Three hundred follow him, all with one loyal soul, from those who dwell in Cære and in the plains of Minio, in ancient Pyrgi, and Gravisca's tainted air.

I would not leave thee unsung, bravest chief of the Ligurians, Cinyras, or Cupavo with scanty retinue, whose helmet is surmounted by plumage of the swan : love was your joint crime ; for love you wear the cognisance of your father's form. For legend tells that Cycnus, all for grief over his darling Phaethon, while in the poplar shade and the leafage of the brotherless sisters he keeps singing and consoling his sad passion by the Muses' aid, drew over his form the soft plumage of downy eld, mounting up from earth and sending his voice before him to the stars. His son, with a band of martial peers sailing at his side, propels with his oars the enormous Centaur : the monster stands lowering over the water, and threatens the billows with a huge rock from his towering eminence, as he ploughs the deep sea with the length of his keel.

Great Ocnus too is leading an army from the coasts of his fathers, Ocnus, son of Manto the prophetess and the Etruscan river, who bestowed on thee, Mantua, thy city walls and the name of his mother, Mantua rich in ancestral glories : but not all her sons of the same blood ; three races are there, and under each race range four nations : herself the queen of the nations, her strength from Etruscan blood. Hence, too, Mezentius draws against his life five hundred unfriendly swords—Mincius, child of Benacus, with his gray covering of reeds, ushers into the deep their hostile bark.

On moves strong Aulestes, lashing the water as he rises with the stroke of a hundred oars : the sea spouts foam from

its upturned surface. His bearer is a huge Triton, whose
shell strikes terror into the green billows : his shaggy front,
breasting the water, down to the side bespeaks the man ; the
belly ends in a sea monster : under the half bestial bosom the
wave froths and roars.

So many chosen chiefs were journeying in thirty vessels
to the succour of Troy, and ploughing with brazen beak the
expanse of brine.

And now the day had withdrawn from the sky, and gracious
Dian was trampling over the cope of heaven with her night-
flying steeds : Æneas the while, for care refuses slumber to
his frame, is seated at his post, himself guiding the rudder
and trimming the sail—when lo ! in the middle of his voyage
he is met by a fair bevy of comrades of his own : the Nymphs
whom gracious Cybele had invested with the deity of the sea,
and changed from ships to goddesses, were swimming abreast
and cleaving the billow, a Nymph for each of the brazen
prows that erst had lined the shore. Far off they recognise
their king, and come dancing round him in state : Cymodoce,
their skilfullest in speech, swimming up behind, lays her right
hand on the stern, herself lifted breast high above the water,
while with her left she paddles in the noiseless wave. Then
thus she breaks on his wondering ear : 'Wake you, Æneas,
seed of the gods? be wakeful still, and let the sail-ropes go.
We it is you see, pines of Ida from the sacred summit, Sea-
nymphs now, your sometime fleet. When the false Rutulian
was hot at our backs with fire and sword, reluctantly we burst
your bonds, and are now in full quest of you over the sea. This
new shape the great mother gave us in her pity, and granted
us the state of goddesses and lives to lead beneath the water.
Meantime young Ascanius is hemmed in by rampart and
trench, with serried weapons all around him, and Latians
bristling with battle. Already the Arcadian horse mixed with

the brave Etruscan has gained the appointed spot: to bar their way with an intervening host and cut them off from the camp is Turnus' fixed intent. Rise, and with the earliest approach of dawn bid your allies be summoned to arms, and take in hand that shield which the Fire-god himself made to be invincible and bordered with a marge of gold. The morrow's sun, if you will but give credence to my words, shall survey mighty heaps of Rutulian carnage.' Her speech was done: and as she parted she gave with her hand an impulse to the lofty stern, well knowing the due measure of force: on it speeds over the wave, fleeter than dart and wind-swift arrow both. The rest in order mend their speed. Wondering he pauses, the great Trojan of Anchises' line, yet cheers his soul with the omen. Then, looking to the vault above, he prays in brief: 'Gracious mother of the gods, lady of Ida, whose joy is in Dindymus, and in turreted cities and harnessed lions at thy bridle-rein, be thou now to me the controller of the fight, do thou bring the presage nigh, and walk beside the Phrygians, mighty goddess, with favouring step.' Thus much he said: and meanwhile day was returning at speed, with its light grown to full strength, and night had vanished before it.

First he gives orders to his comrades to obey the heavenly token, and nerve their souls for combat, and make ready for the fight. And now at last from his station on the tall stern he has the Teucrians and his camp in view, when on the instant his blazing shield is raised high on his left arm. Up goes a shout to heaven from the Dardans on their ramparts; the gleam of hope quickens wrath to fury; they hurl a shower of javelins: even as amid dark clouds cranes from Strymon give token, sweeping sonorously over the sky, and flying from the southern gale with sequacious clamour. But the Rutulian king and the

Ausonian generals wonder at the sight, till, looking back, they behold the stems bearing to the shore, and the whole water floating on with vessels. There is a blaze on that helmet's summit, and from the crest on high streams the flame, and the shield's golden boss disgorges mighty fires, even as when on a clear night blood-hued comets glare with gloomy red, or as the Sirian blaze, that harbinger of drought and sickness to weak mortality, breaks into birth and saddens heaven with its ill-boding rays.

Yet pause was none in bold Turnus' confidence to forestall the landing-place, and beat off the comers from the shore. His words are ready at the moment to encourage and upbraid : ' See here the occasion you longed for, to break through them at the sword's point. A brave man's hand is the War-god's chosen seat. Now let each remember wife and home, recall the mighty deeds that made your fathers great. Let us meet them at once at the water's edge, while they are in the hurry of landing, and the foot falters in its first tread on shore. Valour has Fortune for its friend.' So saying, he ponders with himself whom to lead to the attack, and to whom he may trust the leaguer of the walls.

Meanwhile Æneas is landing his comrades from the tall ship-sides by help of bridges. Many of them watch for the ebb of the failing sea, and venture a leap among the shallows ; others resort to the oars. Tarchon, spying out a place on the beach where the waters seethe not nor the broken billows roar, but ocean without let glides gently up the shore as the tide advances, suddenly turns his prows thither, and exhorts his crew : ' Now, ye chosen band, ply your stout oars, lift the vessels and carry them home : cleave with your beaks this land that hates you ; let the keel plough its own furrow. Even from shipwreck in a roadstead like this I would not shrink, could I once get hold of the soil.' Tarchon having thus said, his crew rise on their oars and bear down on the Latian plains with vessels all foam, till the beaks have gained the dry land, and every keel has come scatheless to its rest. Not so thy ship, Tarchon : for while dashed on a sandbank it totters on the unequal ridge, poised in suspense awhile, and buffeting the waves, its sides give way, and its men are set down in the midst of the water : broken oars and floating benches entangle them, and their feet are carried back by the ebb of the wave.

No sluggish delay holds Turnus from his work : with fiery speed he sweeps his whole army against the Teucrians, and plants them in the foe's face on the shore. The clarions sound : first dashed Æneas on the rustic ranks, a presage of the fight's fortune, and disarrayed the Latians, slaying Theron, who in his giant strength is assailing Æneas : piercing through quilted brass and tunic stiff with gold the sword devours his unguarded side. Next he strikes Lycus, who was cut from the womb of his dead mother and consecrated to thee, Apollo, because his baby life had been suffered to scape the peril of the steel. Hard by, as iron Cisseus and gigantic Gyas were laying low his host with their clubs, he casts them down in death : nought availed them ; the weapons of Hercules or strong hands to wield them, or Melampus their sire, Alcides' constant follower, long as earth found for him those grievous tasks. See there, as Pharus is hurling forth words without deeds, he flings at him his javelin and plants it in the bawler's mouth. Thou, too, Cydon, while following with ill-starred quest the blooming Clytius, thy latest joy, hadst lain stretched on the ground by the Dardan hand, a piteous spectacle, at rest from the passions that were ever in thy heart ; but thy brethren met the foe in close band, the progeny of Phorcus : seven their number, seven the darts they throw ; some rebound idly from shield and helm, some as they grazed the frame were turned aside by Venus' gentle power. Quick spoke

Æneas to true Achates : ' Give me store of weapons ; not one shall my hand hurl in vain against the Rutulians, of all that have quivered in Grecian flesh on the plains of Troy.' With that he seizes his mighty spear and launches it : flying on it crashes through the brass of Mæon's shield and rends breast-plate and breast at once. Swift comes his brother Alcanor and props with his hand the falling man : piercing the arm the spear flies onward and holds its bloody course, and the dying hand dangles by the sinews from the shoulder-blade. Then Numitor, snatching the javelin from his brother's body, assails Æneas ; yet it might not lodge in the enemy's front, but just grazed the thigh of mighty Achates.

Now comes Clausus of Cures in the pride of his youthful frame, and strikes Dryops from a distance under the chin with the strong impact of his stark spear, and piercing his throat, robs him even as he speaks of life and breath alike : the wounded man strikes the earth with his forehead and vomits from his lips clotted blood. Three, too, from Thrace, of Boreas' noblest lineage, and three sent to battle by Idas their sire and Ismarus their country, he lays low by this chance or that. To his side runs Halesus and the Auruncan bands ; comes to his aid, too, the seed of Neptune, steed-famed Messapus. Now these, now those, strain to win the ground : the struggle is on Ausonia's very threshold. As in the spacious heaven jarring winds meet in battle, alike in spirit and in strength, winds, storm-clouds, and ocean, neither yields to the other : long doubtful hangs the fight ; all stand in death-grips, front to front : even such the meeting of the army of Troy and the army of Latium : foot is set close to foot, and man massed with man.

But in another part of the field, where a torrent had scattered wide whirling stones and trees uprooted from its banks, soon as Pallas saw his Arcadians, unused to wage war on foot, flying before the chase of Latium, in that the cragginess of the soil had driven them to discard their steeds, he tries the one remedy in sore distress, and now with prayers, now with bitter speeches, inflames their valour : ‘ Whither fly ye, mates ? By your gallant deeds I conjure you—by your chief Evander's name and victories won at his bidding—by my own promise, now shooting up in rivalry with my father's glory—trust not to your feet. It is the sword that must hew us a way through the foe. Where yonder host of men presses in thickest mass is the path by which our noble country is calling you and your general Pallas back to her arms. No deities sit heavy on us : by a mortal foe we are pressed, mortals ourselves : we have as many lives, as many hands as they. Lo there ! the sea hems us in with mighty ocean-barrier ; earth is closed to our flight : shall the sea or Troy be our goal ? ’ This said, he dashes at the midst of the hostile throng. The first that meets him is Lagus, brought to the spot by fates unkind ; him, while tugging a stone of enormous weight, he pierces with his whirled javelin, just where the spine running down the back was parting the ribs, and recovers the weapon from its lodgment among the bones. Nor can Hisbo surprise him in the fact, spite of his hopes ; for Pallas catches· him rushing on in blind fury for the pain of his comrade's death, and buries the sword in his distended lungs. Next his blow lights on Sthenelus, and Anchemolus of Rhœtus’ ancient line, who dared pollute his stepdame's couch. You, too, twin brethren, fell on those Rutulian plains, Larides and Thymber, Daucus’ resemblant offspring, undistinguished even by your kin, a sweet perplexity to those who bore you : but now Pallas has marked you with a cruel difference ; for you, poor Thymber, have your head shorn off by the Evandrian sword ; your hand, Larides, severed from the arm, is looking in vain for you its master; the fingers, half alive, are quivering yet and closing again on the steel.

Arcadia's sons, stung by their chief's rebuke and gazing on his glorious deeds, rush on the foe, strong in the armour of mingled rage and shame. Then Pallas strikes through Rhœtus as he flies past him on his car. So much space and respite from his end did Ilus gain; for 'twas at Ilus he had launched from the distance his stalwart spear: Rhœtus comes between and catches it, flying from thee, noble Teuthras, and Tyres thy brother; and tumbled from his car he beats with his dying heel the Rutulian plains. Even as when the winds have risen at his wish on a summer's day, a shepherd lets loose his scattered flames among the woods, in a moment catching all that comes between, the Fire-god's army in one bristling line stretches over the broad plains: he from his seat beholds the triumphant blaze with a conqueror's pride: even so the valour of thy friends musters from all sides on one point to aid thee, Pallas. But Halesus, that fiery warrior, moves against their opposing ranks, gathering himself up into his arms. Ladon he massacres, and Pheres, and Demodocus: Strymonius' right hand, raised against his throat, he lops away with his gleaming sword; with a stone he strikes the front of Thoas, and has crushed the bones mixed with gory brain. Halesus had been hidden in the woods by his prophetic sire; when the old man closed his whitening eyes in death, the Fates claimed their victim, and devoted him to Evander's darts. And now Pallas aims at him, after these words of prayer: 'Grant, Father Tiber, to the flying steel poised in my hand a prosperous passage through Halesus' hardy breast; thine oak shall have his arms and his warrior spoils.' The god gave ear: while Halesus shielded Imaon, he gives his own breast in evil hour unarmed to the Arcadian lance.

But Lausus, himself a mighty portion of the war, suffers

not his troops to be dismayed by the hero's dreadful carnage : first he slays Abas, who had met him front to front, the breakwater and barrier of fight. Down go the sons of Arcadia, down go the Etruscans, and ye, too, Teucrians, whose frames Greece could not destroy. The armies clash, their leaders and their powers the same. The rear ranks close up the battle ; nor weapon nor hand can be moved for the crowd. Here is Pallas pushing and pressing, there Lausus over against him : their years scarcely differ ; each has a comely form ; but Fortune had already written that neither should return to his home. Yet were they not suffered to meet man to man by great Olympus' lord : each has his fate assigned him ere long at the hand of a mightier enemy.

Turnus meanwhile is warned by his gracious sister to come to Lausus' aid ; and with his flying car he cleaves the intervening ranks. Soon as he met his comrades' eye : ' You may rest from battle now ; I alone am coming against Pallas. Pallas is my due, and mine alone ; would that his sire were here to see us fight.' He said ; and his friends retired from the interdicted space. But as the Rutulians withdraw, the young warrior, marvelling at the haughty command, gazes astonished on Turnus, rolls his eyes over that giant frame, and sweeps the whole man from afar with fiery glance, and with words like these meets the words of the monarch : ' I shall soon be famous either for kingly trophies won or for an illustrious death ; my sire is equal to either event ; a truce to menace.' This said, he marches into the middle space ; while the Arcadians' blood chills and curdles about their hearts. Down from his car leaps Turnus, and addresses himself to fight on foot. And as when a lion has seen from a high watch-tower a bull standing at distance in the field and meditating fight, he flies to the spot, even thus looks Turnus as he bounds along.

z

Soon as he judged his foe would be within reach of his spear-throw, Pallas begins the combat, in hope that Fortune may help the venture of unequal powers, and utters these words to the mighty heaven: 'By my sire's hospitality and the board where thou satest as a stranger, I pray thee, Alcides, stand by me in my great endeavour. Let Turnus see me strip the bloody arms from his dying frame, and may his glazing eyes endure the sight of a conqueror.' Alcides heard the youth, and stifled a heavy groan deep down in his breast, and shed forth unavailing tears. Then the Almighty Father bespeaks his son with kindly words: 'Each has his fixed day: short and irretrievable is the span of all men; but to propagate glory by great deeds, this is what worth can do. Think of those many sons of gods who fell beneath Troy's lofty walls: among whom died even Sarpedon, my own offspring. For Turnus, too, the call of his destiny has gone forth, and he has reached the term of his allotted days.' So he speaks, and turns away his eyes from the Rutulian plain.

But Pallas with a mighty effort sends forth his spear, and plucks from the hollow scabbard his flashing sword. On flies the weapon, strikes where the margin of the harness rises toward the shoulder, and forcing its way through the buckler's edge, at last even grazed the mighty frame of Turnus. Then Turnus, long poising his beam with its point of sharp steel, hurls it at Pallas, with these words: 'See whether our weapon be not the keener.' So he: while cleaving those many plates of iron and brass, spite of the bull-hides wound oft and oft about, the point strikes through the shield's midst with quivering impact, and pierces the corselet's barrier and the mighty breast beyond. In vain the youth tears the reeking dart from the wound: as it parts, blood and life follow on its track. He falls forward on his wound: his arms resound upon him, and with his bloody jaws in death he bites the hostile earth. Standing over him, Turnus began : ' Men of Arcady, take heed and carry my words to Evander : I send back Pallas handled as his sire deserves. If there be any honour in a tomb, any solace in burial, let him take it freely ; his welcome of Æneas will be costly notwithstanding.' Then with his left foot as he spoke, he trod on the dead, tearing away the belt's huge weight and the crime thereon engraved : that band of youths slain foully all on one wedding night, and the chambers dabbled with blood : Clonus Eurytides had chased it on the broad field of gold : and now Turnus triumphs in the prize, and exults in his winning. Blind are the eyes of man's soul to destiny and doom to be, nor knows it to respect the limit, when upborne by prosperous fortune ! Turnus shall see the day when he will fain have paid a high price for Pallas unharmed, when he will hate the spoils and the hour he won them ! But Pallas' followers, with many a groan and tear, are bearing off their chief on his shield in long procession. Oh, vision of sorrow and great glory, soon to meet thy father's eye ! this day first gave thee to battle, this day withdraws the gift, yet vast are the heaps thou leavest of Rutulian carnage !

And now not the mere rumour of a blow so dreadful, but surer intelligence flies to Æneas, that his army is but a hand-breadth's remove from death—that it is high time to succour the routed Teucrians. With his sword he mows down all that crosses him, and all on fire hews a broad pathway through the ranks with the steel, seeking thee, Turnus, fresh flushed with slaughter. Pallas, Evander, the whole scene stands before his eyes—the board where he had first sate as a stranger, the outstretched hands of fellowship. At once he takes alive four youths born of Sulmo, and other four reared by Ufens, that he may offer them as victims to the dead, and sprinkle

the funeral flame with their captive gore. Next he had
levelled his spear from afar at Magus. Magus deftly runs
beneath, while the quivering spear flies over his head, and
clasping the enemy's knees, utters these words of suppliance :
' By your dead father's soul, and the dawning promise of
Iulus, I pray you spare my poor life for my son and my sire.
I have a lofty palace : deep in its vaults lie talents of chased
silver ; masses of gold are mine, wrought and unwrought
both. The victory of Troy hangs not on my fortunes, nor
can a single life make difference so great.' He spoke, and
Æneas thus makes reply : ' Those many talents you name of
silver and gold, keep them for your sons. Turnus was the
first to put an end to such trading usages of war at the moment
when he slew Pallas. My sire Anchises' ghost, and my son
Iulus, speak their thoughts through me.' This said, with
his left hand he grasps the helmet and drives his sword
hilt-deep through the suppliant's back-drawn neck. Hard by
was Hæmonides, priest of Phœbus and Trivia, his temples
wreathed with the fillet's sacred band, glittering all over with
gay raiment and goodly armour. Him he meets, drives over
the plain, stands over him fallen, sacrifices the victim, and
whelms him in a mighty shade ; the arms are stripped and
carried off on Serestus' shoulders, a trophy to thee, royal
Gradivus. The ranks are rallied by Cæculus, scion of Vulcan's
stock, and Umbro, who comes from the Volscian hills. The
Dardan chief puts forth his rage against them. Already had he
mowed down with his sword Anxur's left hand and the whole orb
of the shield he bore—that foe, I ween, had uttered a haughty
boast, and deemed that his hand would second his tongue,
and was swelling in spirit to the stars, with an assured hope
of gray hairs and length of days—when Tarquitus, in the
pride of gleaming armour, borne by the nymph Dryope to
woodland Faunus, crossed his fiery path. Drawing back

his spear, he hampers the corselet and the buckler's weighty mass ; then he sweeps to the ground the head, as the lips were vainly praying and essaying to say a thousand things, and dashing before him the reeking trunk, utters thus the fierceness of his heart : ' Lie there, doughty warrior ! never shall your tender mother give you burial, or pile your father's tomb above your limbs ; no, you will be left to savage birds, or the river will carry you whelmed by its eddies, and hungry fish will lick your wounds.' Next he hunts down Antæus and Lucas, of Turnus' first rank, and gallant Numa, and yellow Camers, son of noble Volscens, who was wealthiest in land of Ausonia's children, and reigned over voiceless Amyclæ. Even as Ægæon, who, fable tells, had a hundred arms and a hundred hands, and flashed fire through fifty mouths from the depths of fifty bosoms, what time against Jove's lightning he thundered on fifty strong shields, and drew forth fifty sharp swords, so Æneas slakes his victorious fury the whole field over, when once his blade had grown warm with blood. See ! he is advancing against Niphæus' four harnessed steeds, and setting his breast against theirs. At once they, soon as they saw his lofty stride and his fierce gestures, turn round affrighted, and, rushing backward, unseat their master and hurry the car to the beach. Meanwhile Lucagus forces his way into the midst, drawn by two white horses, with Liger his brother ; but the brother guides the steeds with the rein, while Lucagus sweeps fiercely round his naked sword. Æneas brooked not the fury of their fiery onset, but rushed against them, and stood fronting them in his giant bulk with threatening spear. To him cried Liger : ' These are not Diomede's steeds you see, nor this Achilles' chariot, nor are these the Phrygian plains ; your warfare and your life shall end here on Italian ground.' So fly abroad the random words of frantic Liger. The chief of

Troy seeks not to meet him with words, but hurls his javelin at the foe. Even as Lucagus, bending forward over the stroke, pricked on his horses with the steel, and advancing his left foot prepares himself for fight, the spear pierces the last margin of the radiant shield and enters the groin at the left: down he falls from the car and wallows in death on the plain; while good Æneas bespeaks him with words of gall: 'So, Lucagus, it is no craven flight of your steeds that has played your car false; no empty shadow cast by the foe has turned them; no, it is you that spring down from the wheels, and leave the horses to their fate.' With these words he laid hold of the bridles, while the wretched brother, gliding down from the car, was stretching his recreant hands: 'Oh, by yourself, by the parents that gave such greatness birth, spare this poor life, brave hero of Troy, and let prayer find compassion.' Æneas cut short his entreaties: 'Not such were your words a moment ago; die, and forsake not your brother, as brother should:' and cleaving the bosom with his sword, he laid bare the seat of breath. Such were the deaths that the Dardan leader dealt about the plains, storming along like torrent wave or murky tempest. At length the prisoners burst forth and leave their camp, the young Ascanius and the soldiery beleaguered in vain.

Jupiter meanwhile first addresses Juno: 'Sister mine and sweetest wife in one, Venus it is, even as thou didst suppose —for thy judgment is never at fault—that upholds the powers of the Trojans, not the warriors' own keen right hand and the courageous soul that braves every peril.' Juno returned, meekly: 'Why, my fairest lord, dost thou vex a sick spirit that quails before thy cruel speeches? Had my love the force it once had, and which should still be its own, this at least thou wouldst not deny me, almighty as thou art, the power to withdraw Turnus from the fight and preserve him in safety for Daunus his father. As it is, let him perish, and glut the Teucrian vengeance with his righteous blood. Yet he draws his name from our lineage, and Pilumnus is his grandsire's grandsire; and often has thy temple been loaded with store of offerings from his bounteous hand.' To whom, in brief reply, the lord of skiey Olympus: 'If thy prayer for the doomed youth is respite and breathing-space from present death, and so thou readest my will, bear thou Turnus away in flight, and snatch him from the destiny that presses on his heels. Thus far is room for compliance. But if any deeper favour be hidden under these prayers of thine, and thou deemest that the war's whole course can be moved or changed, thou art nursing an empty hope.' Juno answered with tears: 'What if thy heart were to grant what thy tongue grudges, and Turnus' life were pledged to continue? As it is, a heavy doom hangs over his guiltless head, or I am void of truth and wandering in delusion. But oh, that I might rather be the sport of lying terrors, and thou, who canst, lead back thy counsels by a better road!'

This said, from the lofty sky she shot forthwith, driving storm before her through the air and girt with the rain-cloud, and sought the army of Ilium and the camp of Laurentum. Then, as goddesses may, she fashions a thin, strengthless shadow of hollow cloud in the likeness of Æneas, a marvel to the eyes, accoutres it with Dardan weapons, and counterfeits the shield and the crest of the god-like head, gives it empty words and tones without soul, and renders to the life the step and the gait: even as the shapes that are said to flit when death is past, or the dreams that mock the sense of slumber. So the phantom strides triumphant in the van, goading the enemy with brandished weapons and defiant speech. Turnus comes on, and hurls from far his hurtling spear; it turns its back and retires. Then, when Turnus thought Æneas flying in retreat, and snatched in the vehemence of his soul at the empty hope : ' Whither so fast, Æneas ? ' cries he : ' nay, leave not your promised bridal ; this hand shall give you the soil you have sought for the ocean over.' So with loud shouts he follows, waving his drawn sword, nor sees that the winds are bearing off his triumph. It chanced that a ship was standing moored to the edge of a lofty rock, its ladder let down, its bridge ready to cross—the ship which had carried king Osinius from the borders of Clusium. Hither, as in haste, the semblance of the flying Æneas plunged for shelter. Turnus follows as fast, bounds over all obstacles, and springs across the high-raised bridge. Scarce had he touched the prow when Saturn's daughter breaks the mooring and sweeps the sundered ship along the receding flood. Æneas meanwhile is claiming the combat with his absent foe, and sending down to death many a warrior frame that crosses his way. Then the airy phantom seeks shelter no longer, but soaring aloft blends with the murky atmosphere, while Turnus is borne by the wind down the middle of the tide. Ignorant of the event, and unthankful for escape, he looks back, his hands and his voice addressed to the sky : ' Almighty sire ! hast thou judged me worthy of an infliction like this, and sentenced me to this depth of suffering ? Whither am I bound ? whence have I come ? what is this flight that is bearing me home, and what does it make of me ? Shall I look again on Laurentum's camp and city ? what of that warrior troop who followed me and my standard ? Are they not those whom I left—horror to tell—all of them in the jaws of a cruel death—whom I now see scattered in rout, and hear their groans as they fall ? What can I do ? what lowest depth of earth will yawn for me ? Nay, do you, ye winds, have compassion—on reef, on rock— see, it is I, Turnus, who am fain to plead—dash me this vessel, and lodge it on the sandbank's ruthless shoal, where none that know my shame, Rutuli or rumour, may find me out !' So speaking, he sways in spirit to this side and to that : should he for disgrace so foul impale his frenzied breast on the sword's point, and drive the stark blade through his ribs, or fling himself into the midst of the waves, and make by swimming for the winding shore, and place himself again among the Teucrian swords? Thrice he essayed either way : thrice mighty Juno kept him back, and of her great pity withheld the youth from action. On he flies, ploughing the deep with wave and tide to speed him, and is borne safely to the ancient town of Daunus his sire.

Prompted meanwhile by Jove, Mezentius, all on fire, takes up the war, and charges the triumphant Teucrians. The Tyrrhene host flocks to the spot, bending all their fury, all their showering darts on one, one only man. Even as a rock which juts into the mighty deep, exposed to the rage of the wind and braving the sea, bears all the violence and menace of heaven and ocean, itself unshaken, he stands unmoved ; now he lays low Hebrus, Dolichaon's child, and with him Latagus and craven Palmus : Latagus he strikes on the face and front with a stone, a hill's enormous fragment, Palmus he suffers to roll ham-strung in his cowardice ; their harness he gives to Lausus to wear on his shoulders, their crests to adorn his head. Euanthes, too, the Phrygian, and Mimas, Paris' playmate, borne by Theano to Amycus his sire, the self-same night when Cisseus' royal daughter, teeming with a fire-brand, gave birth to Paris ; he sleeps beneath his father's walls, while Mimas has his rest on Laurentum's unknown shore. Like as the mighty boar driven by fangs of hounds from mountain heights, the boar whom pine-crowned Vesulus or Laurentum's pool shelters these many years, pastured on the reedy jungle, soon as he finds himself among the nets, stands at bay, snorting with fury and bristling his back ; none has the courage to flame forth and come near him ; at safe distance they press him with their darts and their cries; even so of them who hate Mezentius with a righteous hate, none has the heart to face him with drawn steel; with missiles and deafening shouts they assail him from afar; while he, undaunted, is pausing now here, now there, gnashing his teeth, and shakes off the javelins from his buckler's hide. There was one Acron from Corythus' ancient borders, a Grecian wight, who had fled forth leaving his nuptials yet to celebrate; him, when Mezentius saw at distance scattering the intervening ranks, in pride of crimson plumage and the purple of his plighted bride, even as oft a famished lion ranging through high-built stalls—for frantic hunger is his prompter—if he chance to mark a flying goat or towering-antlered deer, grins with huge delight, sets up his mane, and hangs over the rent flesh, while loathly blood laves his insatiate jaws—so joyfully springs Mezentius on the foe's clustering mass. Down goes ill-starred Acron, spurns the blackened ground in the pangs of death, and dyes with blood the broken spear. Nor did the chief deign to strike down Orodes as he fled, or deal from a spear-throw a wound unseen: full in front he meets him, and engages him as man should man, prevailing not by guile but by sheer force of steel. Then with foot and lance planted on the back-flung body: 'See, gallants, a bulwark of the war has fallen in tall Orodes,' and his comrades shout in unison, taking up the triumphal pæan. The dying man returns: 'Whoever thou art, thy victorious boasting shall not be long or unavenged; for thee, too, a like fate is watching, and thou shalt soon lie on these self-same fields.' Mezentius answers, with hate mantling in his smile: 'Die now. The sire of gods and king of men shall make his account with me.' So saying, he drew forth the spear from the body: the heavy rest of iron slumber settles down on its eyes, and their beams are curtained in everlasting night.

Cædicus slaughters Alcathous, Sacrator Hydaspes, Rapo

.kills Parthenius and Orses of iron frame, Messapus slays Clonius and Ericetes, Lycaon's son, that grovelling on the ground by a fall from his unbridled steed, this encountered foot to foot. Prancing forward came Agis of Lycia; but Valerus, no unworthy heir of his grandsire's prowess, hurls him down : Thronius falls by Salius, and Salius by Nealces, hero of the javelin and the shaft that surprises from far.

And now the War-god's heavy hand was dealing out to each equal measures of agony and carnage; alike they were slaying, alike falling dead, victors and vanquished by turns, flight unthought of both by these and by those. The gods in Jove's palace look pityingly on the idle rage of the warring hosts—alas, that death-doomed men should suffer so terribly ! Here Venus sits spectator, there over against her Saturnian Juno. Tisiphone, ashy pale, is raving among thousands down below. But see ! Mezentius, shaking his giant spear, is striding into the field, an angry presence. Think of the stature of Orion, as he overtops the billows with his shoulders, when he stalks on foot through the very heart of Nereus' mighty depths that part before him, or as carrying an aged ash in triumph from the hill-top he plants his tread on the ground, and hides his head among the clouds above : thus it is that Mezentius in enormous bulk shoulders his way. Æneas spies him along the length of the battle, and makes haste to march against him. He abides undismayed, waiting for his gallant foe, and stands like column on its base ; then, measuring with his eye the distance that may suffice for his spear, 'Now let my right hand, the god of my worship, and the missile dart I am poising, vouchsafe their aid ! I vow that you, my Lausus, clad in spoils torn from yonder robber's carcase, shall stand in your own person the trophy of Æneas.' He said, and threw from far his hurtling lance : flying onward, it glances aside from the shield, and strikes in the distance noble Antores twixt side and flank, Antores, comrade of Hercules, who, sent from Argos had cloven to Evander's fortunes and sat him down in an Italian home. Now he falls, ill-fated, by a wound meant for other, and gazes on the sky, and dreams in death of his darling Argos. Then good Æneas hurls his spear; through the hollow disk with its triple plating of brass, through the folds of linen and the texture wherein three bulls joined, it won its way and lodged low down in the groin, but its force held not on. In a moment Æneas, gladdened by the sight of the Tuscan's blood, plucks his sword from his thigh and presses hotly on his unnerved foe.

Soon as Lausus saw, he gave a heavy groan of tenderness for the sire he loved, and tears trickled down his face. And here, gallant youth, neither the cruel chance of thy death, nor thy glorious deeds, if antiquity may gain credence for so great a sacrifice, nor thine own most worthy memory shall be unsung through fault of mine. The father, dragging back his foot, disabled and entangled, was quitting the field, his enemy's spearshaft trailing from his buckler. Forth dashed the youth and mingled in the duel, and even as Æneas was rising with hand and body and bringing down a blow from above, met the shock of the sword, and gave the swordsman pause; his comrades second him with a mighty shout, covering the father's retreat as sheltered by his son's shield he withdraws from the fray, hurl a rain of darts, and strive with distant missiles to dislodge the foe. Æneas glows with anger, and keeps within the covert of his arms. Even as on a time when storm-clouds sweep down in a burst of hail, every ploughman, every husbandman has fled scattering from the field, and the traveller lies hid in a stronghold of safety, either some river bank or vault of lofty rock, while the rain is pelting on the lands, in the hope that with the returning sun they may task the day once more, even so, stormed on by javelins from all sides, Æneas endures the thunder-cloud of war till all its artillery be spent, and keeps chiding Lausus and threatening Lausus: 'Whither are you rushing on your death, with aims beyond your strength ? Your duteous heart blinds your reckless valour.' Yet he bates not a jot in his frantic onslaught ; and now the Dardan leader's wrath surges into fury, and the fatal sisters are gathering up Lausus' last thread, for Æneas drives his forceful blade sheer through the youth's body, and buries it wholly within him. Pierced is the shield by the edge, the light armour he carried so threateningly, and the tunic embroidered by his mother with delicate golden thread, and his bosom is deluged with blood ; and anon the life flits through the air regretfully to the shades and the body is left tenantless. But when the son of Anchises saw the look and countenance of the dying—the countenance with its strange and varying hues of pallor—heavily he groaned for pity and stretched forth his hand, and the portraiture of filial love stood before his soul. 'What now, hapless boy, what shall the good Æneas give you worthy of your merit and of a heart like yours? Let the arms wherein you took pride be your own still; yourself I restore to the company of your ancestors, their shades and their ashes, if that be aught to you now. This at least, ill-starred as you are, shall solace the sadness of your death : it is great Æneas' hand that brings you low.' Then without more ado he chides the slackness of his comrades, and lifts their young chief from the earth, as he lay dabbling his trim locks with gore.

Meanwhile the father at the wave of Tiber's flood was stanching his wounds with water, and giving ease to his frame, leaning on a tree's trunk. His brazen helmet is hanging from a distant bough, and his heavy arms are resting on the mead. Round him stand his bravest warriors : he, sick and panting, is relieving his neck, while his flowing beard scatters over his bosom : many a question asks he about Lausus, many a messenger he sends to call him off and convey to him the charge of his grieving sire. But Lausus the while was being carried breathless on his shield by a train of weeping comrades, a mighty spirit quelled by a mighty wound. The distant groan told its tale to that ill-boding heart. He defiles his gray hairs with a shower of dust, stretches his two palms to heaven, and clings to the body. 'My son! and was I enthralled by so strong a love of life as to suffer you, mine own offspring, to meet the foeman's hand in my stead? Are these your wounds preserving your sire? is he living through your death? Alas! now at length I know the misery of banishment! now the iron is driven home! Ay, it was I, my son, that stained your name with guilt, driven by the hate I gendered from the throne and realm of my father! Retribution was due to my country and to my subjects' wrath : would that I had let out my forfeit life through all the death-wounds they aimed! And now I live on, nor as yet leave daylight and humankind—but leave them I will.' So saying, he raises himself on his halting thigh, and though the deep wound makes his strength flag, calls for his war-horse with no downcast mien. This was ever his glory and his solace : this still carried him victorious from every battle-field. He addresses the grieving creature and bespeaks it thus: 'Long, Rhæbus, have we twain lived, if aught be long to those who must die. To-day you shall either bear in victory the bloody spoils and head of Æneas yonder, and join with me to avenge my Lausus' sufferings, or if our force suffice not to clear the way, we will lie down together in death : for never, I ween, my gallant one, will you stoop to a stranger's bidding and endure a Teucrian lord.' He said, and mounting on its back settled his limbs as he was wont, and charged his two hands with pointed javelins, his head shining with brass and shaggy with horse-hair crest. So he bounded into the midst—his heart glowing at once with mighty shame, madness and agony commingled. Then with a loud voice he thrice called on Æneas : ay, and Æneas knew it, and prays in ecstasy : 'May the great father of the gods,

may royal Apollo grant that you come to the encounter ! ' So
much said, he marches to meet him with brandished spear.
The other replies : ' Why terrify me, fellest of foes, now you
have robbed me of my son ? this was the only way by which
you could work my ruin. I fear not death, nor give quarter to
any deity. Enough : I am coming to die, and send you this
my present first.' He said, and flung a javelin at his enemy :
then he sends another and another to its mark, wheeling round
in a vast ring : but the golden shield bides the blow. Three
times, wheeling from right to left, he rode round the foe that
faced him, flinging darts from his hand : three times the hero
of Troy moves round, carrying with him a vast grove planted
on his brazen plate. Then, when he begins to tire of the
long delay and the incessant plucking out of darts, and feels
the unequal combat press him hard, meditating many things, at
last he springs from his covert, and hurls his spear full between
the hollow temples of the warrior-steed. The gallant beast
rears itself upright, lashes the air with its heels, and, flinging
the rider, falls on and encumbers him, and itself bowed to earth
presses with its shoulder the prostrate chief. Up flies Æneas,
plucks forth his sword from its scabbard, and bespeaks the
fallen : ' Where now is fierce Mezentius and that his savage
vehemence of spirit ? ' To whom the Tuscan, soon as opening
his eyes on the light he drank in the heaven and regained his
sense : ' Insulting foe, why reproach me and menace me with
death ? You may kill me without crime : I came not to battle
to be spared, nor was that the league which my Lausus ratified
with you for his father. One boon I ask, in the name of that
grace, if any there be, which is due to a vanquished enemy :
suffer my corpse to be interred. The hot hatred of my subjects,
well I know, is blazing all round me : screen me, I pray, from
their fury, and vouchsafe me a share in the tomb of my son.'
So saying, with full resolve he welcomes the sword to his throat,
and spreads his life over his armour in broad streams of blood.

BOOK XL.

MEANWHILE, the Goddess of Dawn has risen and left the ocean. Æneas, though duty presses to find leisure for interring his friends, and his mind is still wildered by the scene of blood, was paying his vows to heaven as conqueror should at the day-star's rise. A giant oak, lopped all round of its branches, he sets up on a mound, and arrays it in gleaming arms, the royal spoils of Mezentius, a trophy to thee, great Lord of War: thereto he attaches the crest yet raining blood, the warrior's weapons notched and broken, and the hauberk stricken and pierced by twelve several wounds: to the left hand he binds the brazen shield, and hangs to the neck the ivory-hilted sword. Then he begins thus to give charge to his triumphant friends, for the whole company of chiefs had gathered to his side: 'A mighty deed, gallants, is achieved already: dismiss all fear for the future: see here the spoils, the tyrant's first-fruits: see here Mezentius as my hands have made him. Now our match is to the king and the walls of Latium. Set the battle in array in your hearts and let hope forestall the fray, that no delay may check your ignorance at the moment when heaven gives leave to pluck up the standards and lead forth our chivalry from the camp, no coward resolve palsy your steps with fear. Meanwhile, consign we to earth the unburied carcases of our friends, that solitary honour which is held in account in the pit of Acheron. 'Go,' he says, 'grace with the last tribute those glorious souls, who have bought for us this our fatherland with the price of their blood : and first to Evander's sorrowing town send we Pallas, who, lacking nought of manly worth, has been reft by the evil day, and whelmed in darkness before his time.'

So he says weeping, and returns to his tent-door, where the body of breathless Pallas, duly laid out, was being watched by Accetes the aged, who had in old days been armour-bearer to Evander his Arcadian lord, but then in an hour less happy was serving as the appointed guardian of the pupil he loved. Around the corpse were thronging the retinue of menials and the Trojan train, and dames of Ilion with their hair unbound in mourning fashion. But soon as Æneas entered the lofty portal, a mighty wail they raise to the stars, smiting on their breasts, and the royal dwelling groans to its centre with their agony of woe. He, when he saw the pillowed head and countenance of Pallas in his beauty, and the deep cleft of the Ausonian spear in his marble bosom, thus speaks, breaking into tears : 'Can it be, unhappy boy, that Fortune at the moment of her triumphant flood-tide has grudged you to me, forbidding you to look on my kingdom, and ride back victorious to your father's home? Not such was the parting pledge I gave on your behalf to your sire Evander, when, clasping me to his heart, he sent me on my way to mighty empire, and anxiously warned me that the foe was fierce and the race we should war with stubborn. And now he belike at this very moment in the deep delusion of empty hope is making vows to Heaven and piling the altars with gifts, while we are following his darling, void of life, and owing no dues henceforward to any power on high, with the vain service of our sorrow. Ill-starred father! your eyes shall see what cruel death has made of your son. And is this the proud return, the triumph we looked for? has my solemn pledge shrunk to this? Yet no beaten coward shall you see,

2 A

Evander, chastised with unseemly wounds, nor shall the father pray for death to come in its terror while the son survives. Ay me ! how strong a defender is lost to our Ausonian realm, and lost to you, my own Iulus !'

So having wailed his fill, he gives order to lift and bear the poor corpse, and sends a thousand men chosen from his whole array to attend the last service of woe, and lend their countenance to the father's tears, a scant solace for that mighty sorrow, yet not the less the wretched parent's due. Others, nothing slack, plait the framework of a pliant bier with shoots of arbute and oaken twigs, and shroud the heaped-up bed with a covering of leaves. Here place they the youth raised high on his rustic litter, even as a flower cropped by maiden's finger, be it of delicate violet or drooping hyacinth, unforsaken as yet of its sparkling hue and its graceful outline, though its parent earth no longer feeds it or supplies it with strength. Then brought forth Æneas two garments stiff with gold and purple, which Dido had wrought for him in other days with her own hands, delighting in the toil, and had streaked their webs with threads of gold. Of these the mourner spreads one over his youthful friend as a last honour, and muffles the locks on which the flame must feed : moreover he piles in a heap many a spoil from Laurentum's fray, and bids the plunder be carried in long procession. The steeds too and weapons he adds of which he had stripped the foe. Already had he bound the victims' hands behind their backs, doomed as a sacrifice to the dead man's spirit, soon to spill their blood over the fire : and now he bids the leaders in person carry tree-trunks clad with hostile arms, and has the name of an enemy attached to each. There is Accetes led along, a lorn old man, marring now his breast with blows, now his face with laceration, and anon he throws himself at his full length on the ground. They lead too the car, all spattered with Rutulian blood. After it the warrior steed, Æthon, his trappings laid aside, moves weeping, and bathes his visage with big round drops. Others carry the spear and the helm : for the rest of the harness is Turnus' prize. Then follows a mourning army, the Teucrians, and all the Tuscans, and the sons of Arcady with weapons turned downward. And now after all the retinue had passed on in long array, Æneas stayed, and groaning deeply uttered one word more : 'We are summoned hence by the same fearful destiny of war to shed other tears : I bid you hail for ever, mightiest Pallas, and for ever farewell.' Saying this and this only, he turned to the lofty walls again, and bent his footsteps campward.

And now appeared the ambassadors from the town of Latium, with the coverings of their olive boughs, entreating an act of grace : the bodies which were lying over the plains as the steel had mowed them down they pray him to restore, and suffer them to pass under the mounded earth : no man wars with the vanquished and with those who have left the sun : let him show mercy to men once known as his hosts and the fathers of his bride. The good Æneas hearkens to a prayer that merits no rebuke, grants them the boon, and withal bespeaks them thus : 'What undeserved ill chance, men of Latium, has entangled you in a war so terrible and made you fly from us your friends ? Ask you peace for the dead, for those on whom the War-god's die has fallen ? Nay, I would fain grant it to the living too. I were not here had not fate assigned me a portion and a home : nor wage I war against your nation : it was the king that abandoned our alliance, and sought shelter rather under Turnus' banner. Fairer it had been that Turnus should have met the death-stroke ye mourn. If he seeks to end the war by strength of arm and expel the Trojan enemy, duty bade him confront me with weapons like mine, and that one should have lived who had earned life from heaven or his own right hand. Now go and kindle the flame beneath your ill-starred townsmen.' Æneas' speech was over: they stood in silent wonder, their eyes and countenances steadfastly fixed on each other. Then Drances, elder in birth, ever embroiled with the youthful Turnus by hatred and taunting word, thus speaks in reply: 'O mighty in fame's voice, mightier in your own brave deeds, hero of Troy, what praise shall I utter to match you with the stars? Shall I first admire your sacred love of right, or the toils of your hand in war? Ours it shall be gratefully to report your answer to our native town, and should any favouring chance allow, make you the friend of king Latinus. Let Turnus look for alliance where he may. Nay, it will be our pride to uprear those massive walls of destiny, and heave on our shoulders the stones of your new Troy.' He spoke, and the rest all murmured assent. For twelve days they make truce, and with amity to mediate, Trojans and Latians mingled roam through the forest on the mountain slopes unharming and unharmed. The lofty ash rings with the two-edged steel : they bring low pines erst uplifted to the sky, nor is there pause in cleaving with wedges the oak and fragrant cedar, or in carrying ashen trunks in the groaning wains.

And now flying Fame, the harbinger of that cruel agony, is filling with her tidings the ears of Evander, his palace and his city. Fame that but few hours back was proclaiming Pallas the conqueror of Latium. Forth stream the Arcadians to the gates, with funeral torches in ancient fashion, snatched up hurriedly ; the road gleams with the long line of fire, which parts the breath of fields on either hand. To meet them comes the train of Phrygians, and joins the wailing company. Soon as the matrons saw them pass under the shadow of the houses, they set the mourning city ablaze with their shrieks. But Evander—no force can hold him back ; he rushes into the midst : there as they lay down the bier he has flung himself upon Pallas, and is clinging to him with tears and groans, till choking grief at last lets speech find her way : ' No, my Pallas ! this was not your promise to your sire, to trust yourself with caution in the War-god's savage hands. I knew what a spell there lay in the young dawn of a soldier's glory, the enrapturing pride of the first day of battle. Alas for the ill-starred first-fruits of youth, the cruel foretaste of the coming war ! alas for those my vows and prayers, that found no audience with any of the gods ! alas too for thee, my blessed spouse, happy as thou art in the death that spared thee not for this heavy sorrow ! while I, living on, have triumphed over my destiny, that I might survive in solitary fatherhood. Had I but followed the friendly standards of Troy, and fallen whelmed by Rutulian javelins ! had I rendered my own life up, so that this funeral train should have borne *me* home, and not my Pallas ! Nor yet would I blame you, men of Troy, nor the treaty we made, nor the hands we plighted in friendship ; it is but the portion ordained long ago as fitting for my gray hairs. If it was written that my son should die ere his time, it shall be well that he fell after slaying his Volscian thousands, while leading a Teucrian army to the gates of Latium. Nay, my Pallas, I would wish for you no worthier funeral than that accorded to you by Æneas the good and his noble Phrygians, by the Tyrrhene leaders, and the whole Tyrrhene host. Each bears you a mighty trophy whom your right hand sends down to death. And you, too, proud Turnus, would be standing at this moment, a giant trunk hung round with armour, had your age been but as his, the vigour of your years the same. But why should misery like mine hold back the Teucrians from the battle ? Go, and remember · to bear my message to your king. If I still drag the wheels of my hated life now my Pallas is slain, it is because of your right hand, which owes the debt of Turnus' life to son and sire, yourself being witness. This is the one remaining niche for your valour and your fortune to fill. I ask not for triumph to gild my life: that thought were crime: I ask but for tidings that I may bear to my son down in the spectral world.'

Meantime the Goddess of Dawn had lifted on high her kindly light for suffering mortality, recalling them to task and toil. Already father Æneas, already Tarchon, have set up their funeral piles along the winding shore. Hither each man brings the body of friend or kinsman as the rites of his sires command; and as the murky flames are applied below, darkness veils the heights of heaven in gloom. Thrice they ran their courses round the lighted pyres, sheathed in shining armour; thrice they circled on their steeds the mournful funeral flame, and uttered the voice of wailing. Sprinkled is the earth with their tears, sprinkled is the harness. Upsoars to heaven at once the shout of warriors and the blare of trumpets. Others fling upon the fire plunder torn from the Latian slain, helms and shapely swords and bridle-reins and glowing wheels; some bring in offering the things the dead men wore, their own shields and the weapons that sped so ill. Many carcases of oxen are sacrificed round the piles: bristly swine and cattle harried from the country round are made to bleed into the flame. Then along the whole line of coast they gaze on their burning friends, and keep sentry over the half-quenched fire-bed, nor let themselves be torn away till dewy night rolls round the sky with its garniture of blazing stars.

With like zeal the ill-starred Latians in a different quarter set up countless piles; of the multitude of corpses some they bury in the earth, some they lift up and carry off to neighbour districts, and send them home to the city; the rest, a

mighty mass of promiscuous carnage, they burn uncounted
and unhonoured; and thereon the plains through their length
and breadth gleam with the thickening rivalry of funeral
fires. The third morrow had withdrawn the chill shadows
from the sky: the mourners were levelling the piles of ashes
and sweeping the mingled bones from the hearths, and heap-
ing over them mounds of earth where the heat yet lingers.
But within the walls, in the city of Latium's wealthy king,
the wailing is pre-eminent, and largest the portion of that
long agony. Here are mothers and their sons' wretched
brides, here are sisters' bosoms racked with sorrow and love,
and children orphaned of their parents, calling down curses
on the terrible war and on Turnus' bridal rites; he, he himself, they cry, should try the issue with arms and the cold
steel, who claims for himself the Italian crown and the
honours of sovereignty. Fell Drances casts his weight into
the scale, and bears witness that Turnus alone is challenged
by the foe, Turnus alone defied to combat. Against them
many a judgment is ranged in various phrase on Turnus' side,
and the queen s august name lends him its shadow; many an
applauding voice upholds the warrior by help of the trophies
he has won.

Amid all this ferment, when the blaze of popular turmoil is
at its height, see, as a crowning blow, comes back the sorrowing embassy with tidings from Diomede's mighty town: the
cost of all their labours has gained them nought: gifts and
gold and earnest prayers are alike in vain: the Latians must
look for arms elsewhere, or sue for peace from the Trojan
chief. King Latinus himself is crushed to earth by the
weight of agony. The wrath of the gods, the fresh-made
graves before his eyes, tell him plainly that Æneas is the man
of destiny, borne on by heaven's manifest will. So he summons by royal mandate a mighty council, the chiefs of his

nation, and gathers them within his lofty doors. They have mustered from all sides, and are streaming to the palace through the crowded streets. In the midst Latinus takes his seat, at once eldest in years and first in kingly state, with a brow that knows not joy. Hereupon he bids the envoys returned from the Ætolian town to report the answers they bear, and bids them repeat each point in order. Silence is proclaimed, and Venulus, obeying the mandate, begins to speak :

'Townsmen, we have looked on Diomede and his Argive encampment: the journey is overpast, and every chance surmounted, and we have touched the hand by which the realm of Ilion fell. We found him raising his city of Argyripa, the namesake of his ancestral people, in the land of Iapygian Garganus which his sword had won. Soon as the presence was gained and liberty of speech accorded, we proffer our gifts, inform him of our name and country, who is our invader, and what cause has led us to Arpi. He listened, and returned as follows with untroubled mien : " O children of fortune, subjects of Saturn's reign, men of old Ausonia, what caprice of chance disturbs you in your repose, and bids you provoke a war ye know not ? Know that all of us, whose steel profaned the sanctity of Ilion's soil—I pass the hardships of war, drained to the dregs under those lofty ramparts, the brave hearts which that fatal Simois covers—yea, all of us the wide world over have paid the dues of our trespass in agonies unutterable, a company that might have wrung pity even from Priam : witness Minerva's baleful star, and the crags of Eubœa, and Caphereus the avenger. Discharged from that warfare, wandering outcasts on diverse shores, Menelaus, Atreus' son, is journeying in banishment even to the pillars of Proteus ; Ulysses has looked upon Ætna and her Cyclop brood. Need I tell of Neoptolemus' portioned realms, of Idomeneus' dismantled home, of Locrian settlers on a Libyan coast? Even the monarch of Mycenæ, the leader of the great Grecian name, met death on his very threshold at the hand of his atrocious spouse; Asia fell before him, but the adulterer rose in her room. Cruel gods, that would not have me restored to the hearth-fires of my home, to see once more the wife of my longing and my own fair Calydon! Nay, even my flight is dogged by portents of dreadful view; my comrades torn from me are winging the air and haunting the stream as birds—alas that the followers of my fortunes should suffer so!—and making the rocks ring with the shrieks of their sorrow. Such was the fate I had to look for even from that day when with my frantic steel I assailed the flesh of immortals, and impiously wounded Venus' sacred hand. Nay, nay, urge me no longer to a war like this. Since Pergamus fell, my fightings with Troy are ended; I have no thought, no joy, for the evils of the past. As for the gifts which you bring me from your home, carry them rather to Æneas. I tell you, I have stood against the fury of his weapon, and joined hand to hand with him in battle; trust one who knows how strong is his onset as he rises on the shield, how fierce the whirlwind of his hurtling lance. Had Ida's soil borne but two other so valiant, Dardanus would have marched in his turn to the gates of Inachus, and the tears of Greece would be flowing for a destiny reversed. All those years of lingering at the walls of stubborn Troy, it was Hector's and Æneas' hand that clogged the wheels of Grecian victory, and delayed her coming till the tenth campaign had begun. High in courage were both, high in the glory of martial prowess; but piety gave *him* the pre-eminence. Join hand to hand in treaty, if so you may; but see that your arms bide not the shock of his." Thus, gracious sire, have you heard at once the king's reply, and the judgment he passed on this our mighty war.'

The envoys had scarcely finished when a diverse murmur
runs along the quivering lips of the sons of Ausonia, as when
rapid streams are checked by rocks in their course, confused
sounds rise from the imprisoned torrent, and neighbouring
banks re-echo with the babbling of the waves. Soon as their
passions were allayed, and their chafed countenances settled
in calm, the monarch, first invoking heaven, begins from his
lofty throne :

'To have taken your judgment, Latians, ere this on the
state of the common-weal, would have been my pleasure, and
our truer interest, rather than summon a council at a crisis
like this, when the foe has sat down before our walls. A
grievous war, my countrymen, we are waging, with the seed of
heaven, a nation unsubdued, whom no battles overtire, nor
even in defeat can they be made to drop the sword. For any
hope ye have cherished in the alliance of Ætolian arms, resign
it for ever. Each is his own hope; and how slender is this
ye may see for yourselves. As to all beside, with what utter
ruin it is stricken is palpable to the sight of your eyes, to the
touch of your hands. I throw the blame on none : manly
worth has done the utmost it could : all the sinews of the
realm have been strained in the contest. Now then I will set
forth what is the judgment of my wavering mind, and show
you it in few words, if ye will lend me your attention. There
is an ancient territory of mine bordering on the Tuscan river,
extending lengthwise to the west, even beyond the Sicanian
frontier ; Auruncans and Rutulians are its tillers, subduing
with the ploughshare its stubborn hills, and pasturing their
flocks on the rugged slopes. Let this whole district, with the
lofty mountain and its belt of pines, be our friendly gift to the
Teucrians ; let us name equal terms of alliance, and invite
them to share our kingdom ; let them settle here, if their
passion is so strong, and build them a city. But if they have

a mind to compass other lands and another nation, and are free to quit our soil, let us build twenty ships of Italian timber, or more if they have men to fill them : there is the wood ready felled by the river side ; let themselves prescribe the size and the number ; let us provide brass, and hands, and naval trim. Moreover, to convey our proffers and ratify the league, I would have an embassy of a hundred Latians of the first rank sent with peaceful branches in their hands, carrying also presents, gold and ivory, each a talent's weight, and the chair and striped robe that are badges of our royalty. Give free counsel and help to support a fainting commonwealth.'

Then Drances, hostile as ever, whom the martial fame of Turnus was ever goading with the bitter stings of sidelong envy, rich, and prodigal of his riches, a doughty warrior with the tongue, but a feeble hand in the heat of battle, esteemed no mean adviser in debate, and powerful in the arts of faction: his mother's noble blood made proud a lineage which on his father's side was counted obscure :—he rises, and with words like these piles and heaps anger high :

' A matter obscure to none, and needing no voice of ours to make it plain is this that you propound, gracious king. All own that they know what is the bearing of the state's fortune ; but their tongues can only mutter. Let him accord freedom of speech, and bate his angry blasts, to whose ill-omened leadership and inauspicious temper—ay, I *will* speak, let him threaten me with duel and death as he may —we owe it that so many of our army's stars have set before our eyes, and the whole city is sunk in mourning, while he is making his essay of the Trojan camp, with flight always in reserve, and scaring heaven with the din of his arms. One gift there is over and above that long catalogue which you would have us send and promise to the Dardans : add but this to them, most excellent sovereign, nor let any man's violence prevent you from bestowing your daughter in the fulness of a father's right on a noble son-in-law and a worthy alliance, and basing the peace we seek on a covenant which shall last for ever. Nay, if the reign of terror is so absolute over our minds and hearts, let us go straight to him with our adjurations and ask for grace at his own hands—ask him to yield, and allow king and country to exercise their rights. Why fling your wretched countrymen again and again into danger's throat, you, the head and wellspring of the ills which Latium has to bear? There is no hope from war; peace we ask of you, one and all—yes, Turnus, peace, and the one surety that can make peace sacred. See, first of all I, whom you give out to be your enemy—and I care not though I be—come and throw myself at your feet. Pity those of your own kin, bring down your pride, and retire as beaten man should. Routed we are; we have looked on corpses enough, and have left leagues enough of land unpeopled. Or if glory stirs you, if you can call up into your breast the courage needed, if the dowry of a palace lies so near your heart, be bold for once, and advance with bosom manned to meet the foe. What! that Turnus may have the blessing of a queenly bride, are we, poor paltry lives, a herd unburied and unwept, to lie weltering on the plain? It is your turn: if you have any strength, any touch of the War-god of your sires, look him in the face who sends you his challenge.'

At these words Turnus' violence blazed out: heaving a groan, he vents from the bottom of his heart such utterance as this: 'Copious, Drances, ever is your stream of speech in the hour when war is calling for hands; when the senate is summoned, you are first in the field. Yet we want not men to fill our court with talk, that big talk which you hurl from a safe vantage-ground, while the rampart keeps off the foe and the moat is not foaming with carnage. Go on pealing your eloquence, as your wont is: let Drances brand Turnus with cowardice, for it is Drances' hand that has piled those very heaps of Teucrian slaughter, and is planting the fields all over with its trophies. What is the power of glowing valour, experience may show you: enemies in sooth are not far to seek : they are standing all about the walls. Well, are we marching to the encounter? why so slow? will you never lodge the War-god better than in that windy tongue, those flying feet? What? beaten? I? who, foulest of slanderers, will justly brand me as beaten, that shall look on Tiber still swelling with Ilion's best blood, on Evander's whole house prostrate root and branch, and his Arcadians stripped naked of their armour? It was no beaten arm that Bitias and giant Pandarus found in me, or the thousand that I sent to death in a single day with my conquering hand, shut up within their walls, pent in by the rampart of the foe. No hope from war? Croak your bodings, madman, in the ears of the Dardan and of your own fortunes. Ay, go on without cease, throwing all into measureless panic, heightening the prowess of a nation twice conquered already, and dwarfing no less the arms of your king. See, now the lords of the Myrmidons are quaking at the martial deeds of Phrygia, Tydeus' son, Thessalian Achilles, and the rest, and river Aufidus is in full retreat from the Hadrian sea. Or listen when the trickster in his villany feigns himself too weak to face a quarrel with me, and points his charges with the sting of terror. Never, I promise you, shall you lose such life as yours by hand of mine—be troubled no longer—let it dwell with you and retain its home in that congenial breast. Now, gracious sire, I return to you and the august matter that asks our counsel. If you have no hope beyond in aught our arms can do, if we are so wholly forlorn, destroyed root and branch by one reverse, and our star can never rise again, then pray we for peace and stretch craven hands in suppliance. Yet, oh, had we but one spark of the worth that once was ours, that man I would esteem blest beyond others in his service and princely of soul, who, sooner than look on aught like this, has lain down in death and once for all bitten the dust. But if we have still store of power, and a harvest of youth yet unreaped, if there are cities and nations of Italy yet to come to our aid, if the Trojans as well as we have won their glory at much bloodshed's cost—for they too have their deaths —the hurricane has swept over all alike—why do we merely falter on the threshold? why are we seized with shivering ere the trumpet blows? Many a man's weal has been restored by time and the changeful struggles of shifting days: many a man has Fortune, fair and foul by turns, made her sport and then once more placed on a rock. Grant that we shall have no help from the Ætolian and his Arpi: but we shall from Messapus, and the blest Tolumnius, and all the leaders that those many nations have sent us; nor small shall be the glory which will wait on the flower of Latium and the Laurentine land. Ay, and we have Camilla, of the noble Volscian race, with a band of horsemen at her back and troops gleaming with brass. If it is I alone that the Teucrians challenge to the fight, and such is your will, and my life is indeed the standing obstacle to the good of all, Victory has not heretofore fled with such loathing from my hands that I should refuse to make my venture for a hope so glorious. No, I will confront him boldly, though he should prove great as Achilles, and don harness like his, the work of Vulcan's art. To you and to my royal father-in-law have I here devoted this my life, I, Turnus, second in valour to none that went before me. "For me alone Æneas calls." Vouchsafe that he may so call! nor let Drances in my stead, if the issue be Heaven's vengeance, forfeit his life, or, if it be prowess and glory, bear that prize away!'

So were these contending over matters of doubtful debate : Æneas was moving his army from camp to field. See, there runs a messenger from end to end of the palace amid wild confusion, and fills the town with a mighty terror, how that in marching array the Trojans and the Tuscan force are sweeping down from Tiber's stream over all the plain. In an instant the minds of the people are confounded, their bosoms shaken to the core, their passions goaded by no gentle stings. They clutch at arms, clamour for arms : arms are the young men's cry : the weeping fathers moan and mutter. And now a mighty din, blended of discordant voices, soars up to the skies, even as when haply flocks of birds have settled down in a lofty grove, or on the fishy stream of Padusa hoarse swans make a noise along the babbling waters. 'Ay, good citizens,' cries Turnus, seizing on his moment, 'assemble your council and sit praising peace ; they are rushing on the realm sword in hand.' Without further speech he dashed away and issued swiftly from the lofty gate. 'You, Volusus,' he cries, 'bid the Volscian squadrons arm, and lead out the Rutulians. You, Messapus, and you, Coras and your brother, spread the horse in battle array over the breadth of the plain. Let some guard the inlets of the city and man the towers ; the rest attack with me in the quarter for which I give the word.' At once there is a rush to the ramparts from every part of the city : king Latinus leaves the council and the high debate unfinished, and wildered with the unhappy time, adjourns to another day, ofttimes blaming himself that he welcomed not with open arms Æneas the Dardan, and bestowed on the city a husband for the daughter of Latium. Others dig trenches before the gates or shoulder stones and stakes. The hoarse trumpet gives its deathful warning for battle. The walls are hemmed by a motley ring of matrons and boys : the call of the last struggle rings in each one's ear. Moreover the queen among a vast train of Latian mothers is drawn to the temple, even to Pallas' tower on the height, with presents in her hand, and at her side the maid Lavinia, cause of this cruel woe, her beauteous eyes cast down. The matrons enter the temple and make it steam with incense, and pour from the august threshold their plaints of sorrow : ' Lady of arms, mistress of the war, Tritonian maiden, stretch forth thy hand and break the spear of the Phrygian freebooter, lay him prostrate on the ground, and leave him to grovel under our lofty portals.' Turnus with emulous fury arms himself for the battle. And now he has donned his ruddy corselet, and is bristling with brazen scales ; his calves have been sheathed in gold, his temples yet bare, and his sword had been girded to his side, and he shines as he runs all golden from the steep of the citadel, bounding high with courage, and in hope already forestalls the foe : even as when a horse, bursting his tether, escapes from the stall, free at last and master of the open champaign, either wends where the herds of mares pasture, or wont to bathe in the well-known river darts forth and neighs with head tossed on high in wanton frolic, while his mane plays loosely about neck and shoulders. His path Camilla crosses, a Volscian army at her back, and dismounts from her horse at the gate with queenly gesture ; the whole band follow her lead, quit their horses, and swim down to earth, while she bespeaks him thus : 'Turnus, if the brave may feel faith in themselves, I promise boldly to confront the cavalry of Troy and singly ride to meet the Tyrrhene horse. Let me essay the first hazard of the combat ; do you on foot remain by the walls and be the city's guard.' Turnus replies, gazing steadfastly on the dreadful maid : ' O maiden, glory of Italy, what thanks shall I strive to speak or render ? but seeing that soul of yours soars above all, partake the toil with me. Æneas,

as rumour and missioned spies tell me for truth, has cunningly
sent on his light-armed cavalry to scour the plain, while he,
surmounting the lonely steeps of the hill, is marching town-
ward. I meditate a stratagem of war in that woodland gorge,
to beset the narrow thoroughfare with an armed band. Do
you in battle array receive the Tuscan horse. With you will
be keen Messapus, and the Latian cavalry, and Tiburtus' troop :
take your share of a general's charge.' This said, he exhorts
Messapus and the federate leaders with like words to the
fight, and advances to meet the enemy. A glen there is,
narrow and winding, suited for ambush and stratagems of
arms, pent in on both sides by a mountain-wall black with
dense foliage; a scant pathway leads to it, with straitened
gorge and jealous inlet. Above it on the mountain's watch-
tower height lies a concealed table-land, a post of sheltered
privacy, whether one be minded to face the battle right and
left, or, standing on the slope, to roll down enormous stones.
Hither repairs the warrior along the well-known road : he has
occupied the spot and sat him down in the treacherous forest.
　Meantime, in the mansions above Latona's daughter was
addressing Opis the swift, a maiden comrade of her sacred
train, and was uttering these words in tones of sorrow : ' Ah,
maiden, Camilla is on her way to the ruthless war ; in vain
she girds herself with the arms of our sisterhood, dear to me
that she is beyond all beside : for no new tenderness this that
has come on Diana, nor sudden the spell wherewith it stirs her
heart. When Metabus, exiled for the hate which tyranny gen-
ders, was parting from Privernum, his ancient city, as he fled
from the heart of the combat, he bore away his infant child to
share his banishment, and varying Casmilla, her mother's name,
called her Camilla. The father, carrying her in his bosom, was
making for the long mountain slopes of the solitary woods,
while bitter javelins were showering all around him, and the
Volscians with circling soldiery hovering about : when lo !

intercepting his flight was Amasenus, brimming and foaming over its banks, so vast a deluge of rain had burst from the clouds. Preparing to plunge in, he is checked by tenderness for his child, and fears for the precious load. At last, as he pondered over every course, he hit suddenly on this resolve. There was a huge weapon, which he chanced to be carrying in his stalwart hand as warriors use, sturdy with knots and seasoned timber : to it he fastens his daughter, enclosed in the cork-tree's forest bark, and binds her neatly round the middle of the shaft ; then, poising it in a giant's grasp, he thus exclaims to heaven : "Gracious lady, dweller in the woods, Latona's maiden daughter, I vow to thy service this my child : thine are the first weapons that she wields as she flies from the foe through air to thy protection. Receive, I conjure thee, as thine own her whom I now entrust to the uncertain gale." He said, and, drawing back his arm, hurled the javelin : loud roared the waves, while over the furious stream fled poor Camilla on the hurtling dart. But Metabus, pressed closer and closer by the numerous band, leaps into the river, and in triumph plucks from the grassy bank his offering to Trivia, the javelin and the maid. No cities opened to him house or stronghold, for his wild nature had never brooked submission : among the shepherds' lonely mountains he passed his days. There in the woods, among beasts' savage lairs, he reared his daughter on milk from the breast of an untamed mare, squeezing the udder into her tender lips. And soon as the child first stood on her feet, he armed her hands with a pointed javelin, and hung from her baby shoulder a quiver and a bow. For the golden brooch in her hair, for the long sweeping mantle, there hang from her head adown her back a tiger's spoils. Even then she launched with tiny hand her childish missiles, swung round her head the sling's well-turned thong, and brought down a crane from Strymon or a snow-white swan. Many a mother in Tyrrhene

town has wooed her for her son in vain : with no thought but
for Dian, she cherishes in unsullied purity her love for the
hunter's and the maiden's life. Would she had never been
pressed for warfare like this, essaying to strike a blow at the
Teucrians : so had she still been my darling and a sister of my
train. But come, since cruel destiny is darkening round her,
glide down, fair nymph, from the sky, and repair to the Latian
frontier, where now in an evil hour the tearful battle is joining. Take these arms, and draw from the quiver an avenging
shaft : therewith let the foe, whoever he be, Trojan or Italian,
that shall profane with the stroke of death that sacred person,
make to me in like manner the atonement of his blood. Afterwards in the hollow of a cloud I will bear off the body of my
lost favourite undespoiled of its arms, and lay her down in her
own land.' Thus she : and Opis hurtled downward through
the buoyant air, a black whirlwind enswathing her form.

But the Trojan band meanwhile is nearing the walls with
the Etruscan chiefs and the whole array of cavalry, marshalled
into companies. Steeds are prancing and neighing the whole
champaign over, and chafing against the drawn bridle as they
face hither and thither : the field, all iron, bristles far and
wide with spears, and the plains are ablaze with arms reared
on high. Likewise Messapus on the other side and the swift-
paced Latians, and Coras and his brother, and maid Camilla's
force appear in the plain against them, couching the lance in
their backdrawn hands and brandishing the javelin : and the
onset of warriors and the neighing of steeds begin to wax hot.
And now each army had halted within a spear-throw of the
other : with a sudden shout they dash forward, and put spurs
to their fiery steeds : missiles are showered from all sides in
a moment, thick as snow-flakes, and heaven is curtained with
the shade. Instantly Tyrrhenus and fierce Aconteus charge
each other spear in hand, and foremost of all crash together
with sound as of thunder, so that the chest of either steed is

burst against his fellow's ; Aconteus, flung off like the levin-bolt or a stone hurled from an engine, tumbles headlong in the distance, and scatters his life in air. At once the line of battle is broken, and the Latians, turned to flight, sling their shields behind them and set their horses' heads cityward. The Trojans give them chase : Asilas in the van leads their bands. And now they were nearing the gates, when the Latians in turn set up a shout, and turn their chargers' limber necks ; the others fly, and retreat far away at full speed. As when the sea, advancing with its tide that ebbs and flows, one while sweeps towards the land, deluges the rocks with a shower of spray, and sprinkles the sandy margin with the contents of its bosom, one while flees in hasty retreat, dragging back into the gulf the recaptured stones, and with ebbing waters leaves the shore. Twice the Tuscans drove the Rutulians in rout to their walls ; twice, repulsed, they look behind as they sling their shields backward. But when in the shock of a third encounter the entire armies grapple each other, and man has singled out man, then in truth upsoar the groans of the dying, and arms and bodies and death-stricken horses blended with human carnage welter in pools of gore : and a savage combat is aroused. Orsilochus hurls a spear at Remulus' horse—for the rider he feared to encounter—and leaves the steel lodged under the ear. Maddened by the blow, the beast rears erect, and, uplifting its breast, flings its legs on high in the uncontrolled agony of the wound : Remulus unseated rolls on earth. Catillus dismounts Iollas, and likewise Herminius, giant in courage, and giant too in stature and girth : his bare head streams with yellow locks, and his shoulders also are bare: wounds have no terrors for him, so vast the surface he offers to the weapon. Through his broad shoulders comes the quivering spear, and bows the impaled hero double with anguish. Black streams of gore gush on all sides : the combatants spread slaughter with the steel, and rush on glorious death through a storm of wounds.

But Camilla, with a quiver at her back, and one breast put
forth for the combat, leaps for joy like an Amazon in the
midst of carnage : now she scatters thick volleys of quivering
javelins, now her arm whirls unwearied the massy two-edged
axe : while from her shoulder sounds the golden bow, the
artillery of Dian. Nay, if ever she be beaten back and
retreating rearward, she turns her bow and aims shafts in
her flight. Around her are her chosen comrades, maid Larina,
and Tulla, and Tarpeia, wielding the brazen-helved hatchet,
daughters of Italy, whom glorious Camilla herself chose to
be her joy and pride, able to deal alike with peace and war :
even as the Amazons of Thrace when they thunder over the
streams of Thermōdon and battle with their blazoned arms,
encompassing Hippolyte, or when Penthesilea, the War-god's
darling, is careering to and fro in her chariot, and the woman
army, amid a hubbub of shrill cries, are leaping in ecstasy
and shaking their moony shields. Who first, who last,
fierce maiden, is unhorsed by your dart ? How many stalwart bodies lay you low in death ? The first was Eunēus,
Clytius' son, whose unguarded breast as he stood fronting
her she pierces with her long pine-wood spear. Down he
goes, disgorging streams of blood, closes his teeth on the
gory soil, and dying writhes upon his wound. Then Liris,
and Pagasus on his body : while that, flung from his stabbed
charger, is gathering up the reins, and this is coming to the
rescue and stretching his unarmed hand to his falling comrade, they are overthrown in one headlong ruin. To these
she adds Amastrus, son of Hippotas : then, pressing on the
rout, pursues with her spear-throw Tereus, and Harpalycus,
and Demophoon, and Chromis : for every dart she launched
from her maiden hand there fell a Phrygian warrior. In the
distance rides Ornytus accoutred strangely in hunter fashion
on an Iapygian steed : a hide stripped from a bullock swathes
his broad shoulders in the combat, his head is sheltered by a

wolf's huge grinning mouth and jaws with the white teeth
projecting, and a rustic pike arms his hand: he goes whirling through the ranks, his whole head overtopping them.
Him she catches, an easy task when the hosts are entangled
in rout, pierces him through, and thus bespeaks the fallen in
the fierceness of her spirit: 'Tuscan, you thought yourself
still chasing beasts in the forest; but the day is come which
shall refute the vaunts of your nation by a woman's weapons.
Yet no slight glory shall you carry down to your fathers'
shades, that you have fallen by the dart of Camilla.' Next
follow Orsilochus and Butes, two of the hugest frames of
Troy: Butes she speared behind 'twixt corselet and helm,
where the sitter's neck is seen gleaming, and the shield is
hanging from the left arm: Orsilochus, as she pretends to
fly and wheels round in a mighty ring, she baffles by ever
circling inwards, and chases him that chases her: at last,
rising to the stroke, she brings down on the wretch again
and again, spite of all his prayers, her massy battle-axe that
rives armour and bone: the brain spouts over the face
through the ghastly wound. Now there stumbles upon her,
and pauses in terror at the sudden apparition, the warrior
son of Aunus, dweller on the Apennine, not the meanest
of Liguria's children while Fate prospered his trickery. He,
when he sees no speed of flight can escape the combat, or
avoid the onset of the dreadful queen, essaying to gain his
base end by policy and stratagem, thus begins: 'What,
great glory is it after all, if you, a woman, trust your
mettled steed? Put away the chance of flight, and dare to
meet me hand to hand on equal ground, and gird you for
battle on foot: soon shall you see which of us gains honour
from this windy boasting.' He said: but she, all on fire,
stung with bitter grief, gives her horse to her comrade, and
stands ready to meet him in arms, fearless though on foot,
with naked sword and maiden shield. But the youth, deem-

ing that his wiles had sped, darts away without more ado, and turning his bridle, rides off in flight, and wearies his beast with the strokes of his iron heel. 'False Ligurian, vainly puffed up with overweening fancies, to no end have you tried your sire's slippery craft, nor shall your lying bring you safe to Aunus the liar.' So cries the maiden, and with lightning-like pace crosses at full speed the horse's path, and seizing the reins, fronts and encounters him, and gluts her vengeance with his hated blood: easily as a hawk, the bird of augury, darting from a lofty rock, comes up with a dove high in the clouds, holds her in his gripe, and with crooked talons tears out her heart, while gore and plucked feathers come tumbling from the sky.

But no blind spectator of the scene is sitting throned on high Olympus, even the father of men and gods. The sire urges Tarchon the Tuscan to the ruthless fray, and goads him to wrath by no gentle stings. So among heaps of carnage and yielding bands Tarchon goes riding, and rouses the cavalry with words of diverse purport, calling each by his name, and gives the beaten new strength for battle. 'What terror, O ye Tuscan hearts that will not feel, that will still be sluggish, what strange cowardice has come on you? To what end is this steel, these idle weapons our right hands bear? But slow ye are not to hear the call of love, or when the wry-necked fife gives the word for the Bacchic dance: ay, there is your passion, there your delight, till the favouring seer announce the sacrificial feast, and the fat victim invite you to the tall trees of the grove.' So saying, he spurs his steed into the midst, ready for the death he brings to others, and charges in fury on Venulus, snatches the foe from his horse, folds his arms round him, and carries him on his saddle before him with wild and violent speed. Upsoars a shout to heaven, and every Latian eye is turned to the scene. Over the plain like lightning flies Tarchon, bearing the warrior and his arms. Then from the top of the chief's own spear he breaks off the point, and feels for an unguarded part where to plant the deadly blow: the foe, struggling, keeps off Tarchon's hand from his throat, and repels force with force. As when the golden eagle soaring on high carries a serpent he has caught, trussing it in his claws, and adhering with his taloned gripe; the wounded reptile writhes its spiral coils, stiffens with erected scales, and hisses from its mouth, surging and swelling; the eagle, undismayed, plies it despite its struggles with his hooked beak, while his pinions beat the air: even thus Tarchon carries his prize in triumph from the bands of Tibur's folk. Following their chief's auspicious lead, the sons of Mæonia charge the foe. Then Arruns, the man of fate, compasses swift Camilla about, dart in hand, with many a forestalling wile, and tries what chance may be readiest. Wherever the fiery maid dashes into the midst of the battle, Arruns threads his way after her, and scans her steps in silence: wherever she returns in triumph, escaping safely from the foe, that way the youth turns his swift and stealthy rein; now makes proof of this approach, now of that, and traverses the whole circle, and shakes with relentless malice his inevitable lance. It chanced that one Chloreus, sacred to Cybele and once her priest, was shining conspicuous from afar in Phrygian armour, urging on a foaming charger, whose covering was a skin adorned with golden clasp and brazen scales set plume-wise. He, in the blaze of foreign purple, was launching Gortynian shafts from a Lycian bow; golden was the bow that rang from his shoulder, golden the helm on his sacred head; his saffron scarf with its rustling gauzy folds was gathered up by a golden brooch, and his tunic and his hose decked with barbaric broidery. He it was that the maiden, eager, it may be, to fasten on the temple-gate the arms of Troy, or to flaunt herself in the golden spoil, singled out from all the battle, and was following with a hunter's blind devotion, raging recklessly through the ranks, enkindled with a woman's love for prey and plunder ; when at length, seizing his opportunity, Arruns awakes his dart from its ambush, and thus prays aloud to heaven : 'Greatest of gods, Apollo, guardian of divine Soracte, whom we are the first to worship, for whom the pine-tree glow is fed by heaps of wood, while ourselves, thy votaries, strong in our piety, walk through the flame over living embers, grant, all-powerful sire, that my arms may wipe this scandal away. I seek no plunder or spoil, no trophy for the conquest of a maid ; the rest of my deeds shall secure my fame ; let but this terrible fiend fall vanquished by wound of mine, I will return to the cities of my fathers an unhonoured man.' Phœbus heard, and vouchsafed in his heart that half the vow should speed, while half he scattered among the flying breezes : to strike and slay Camilla with sudden death-wound, so much he grants the suppliant : to return and meet the eyes of his noble fatherland, this he allows not ; the gusts of air turned the accents into wind. So when the spear, launched from the hand, was heard along the sky, each keen Volscian mind flew to one centre, every Volscian eye was bent on the queen. She alone had no thought for wind or sound or weapon sweeping down from heaven, till the spear had made its passage and lodged beneath her protruded breast, and deeply driven, drank her maiden blood. Her comrades run together in alarm, and support their falling mistress. Arruns, more terrified than all, flies away, half joy, half fear, nor puts further confidence in his lance, nor dares to meet the darts of the maiden. Even as the caitiff wolf, ere the weapons of vengeance can follow him, has fled at once to the pathless privacy of the mountain steep, on slaying a shepherd or mighty bullock, conscious of his daring deed, and drawing back his quivering tail with lithe action has clapped it to his belly and made for the woods, in like

manner Arruns all wildered has stolen away from sight, and
contented to escape has plunged into the thick of the battle.
With dying hand the maiden pulls at the spear; but the steely
point stands lodged among the bones at the ribs in the deep
wound it made.   Drained of blood, she sinks to earth; sink,
too, her death-chilled eyes; her once bright bloom has left
her face.   Then at her last gasp she accosts Acca, one of her
maiden train, who beyond the rest was Camilla's friend
and shared her thoughts, and speaks on this wise: 'Thus
far, sister Acca, has strength been given me: now the cruel
wound overcomes me; and all around me grows dim and dark.
Haste and carry Turnus my dying charge, to take my place in
the battle and keep off the Trojans from the town.   And now
farewell.'   As she spoke she dropped the bridle, swimming
down to earth with no willing act.   Then as the death-chill
grows she gradually discumbers herself of the entire weight of
the body, droops her unstrung neck and her head on which
fate has seized, quitting too her armour, and her soul, resenting
its lot, flies groaningly to the shades.   Then indeed, rising
unmeasured, the uproar strikes the golden stars : Camilla overthrown, the fight waxes fiercer : on they rush thickening, at
once the whole force of the Teucrians, and the Tyrrhene
leaders, and Evander's Arcad cavalry.

But Trivia's sentinel Opis has long been seated high on
the mountain top, an undismayed spectator of the combat.   And when far off, deep among the din of raging
warriors, she spied Camilla shent by ruthless death, she
groaned, and fetched these words from the bottom of her
breast : 'Poor maiden! too, too cruel the penalty you have
paid for provoking the Teucrians to battle.   Nought has it
bestead you at your need to have served Dian in the forest,
and carried on your shoulder the shafts of our sisterhood.
Yet not unhonoured has your queen left you even here in
death's extremity; nor shall this your end be without its

glory in the world, nor yourself bear the ignominy of the
unrevenged; for he, whoever he be, whose wound has profaned your person, shall atone it by the death he has earned.'
Under the lofty mountain's shade there stood a vast mound
of earth, the tomb of Dercennus, an old Laurentine king,
shrouded with dark ilex: here the beauteous goddess first
alights with a rapid bound, and spies out Arruns from the
barrow's height. Soon as she saw him gleaming in his
armour, and swelling with vanity, 'Why stray from the
path?' cries she; 'turn your feet hitherward! come hither
to your death, and receive Camilla's guerdon! Alack! and
are you too to be slain by the shafts of Dian?' She said,
and with the skill of Thracian maiden drew a swift arrow
from her gilded quiver, bent the bow with deadly aim, and
drew it far apart, till the arching ends met together, and with
her two hands she touched, the barb of steel with her left,
her breast with her right and the bowstring. Forthwith the
hurtling of the shaft and the rush of the breeze reached
Arruns' ear at the moment the steel lodged in his body.
Him gasping and groaning his last his comrades leave
unthinking in the unmarked dust of the plain: Opis spreads
her wings, and is borne to skiey Olympus.

First flies, its mistress lost, Camilla's light-armed company;
fly the Rutules in rout, flies keen Atinas; leaders in disarray
and troops in devastation make for shelter, turn round, and
gallop to the walls. None can sustain in combat the Teucrians' deadly onset or resist the stream; they throw their
unstrung bows on their unnerved shoulders, and the hoof of
four-foot steeds shakes the crumbling plain. On rolls to the
ramparts a cloud of dust, thick and murky; and the matrons
from their sentry-posts, smiting on their breasts, raise a shriek
as women wont to the stars of heaven. Who first pour at
speed through the open gates are whelmed by a multitude of
foemen that blends its crowd with theirs; they scape not the

agony of death, but on the very threshold, with their native walls around them, in the sanctuary of home, they breathe away their lives. Some close the gates: they dare not give ingress to their friends nor take them within the walls, implore as they may : and a piteous carnage ensues, these guarding the approach sword in hand, those rushing on the sword's point. Some, borne on by the deluge, stream headlong into the moat ; some in blind agony, spurring their horses, charge as with battering-rams the portals and their stubborn barriers. Nay, the very matrons on the walls in the intensity of the struggle, prompted by true patriot spirit at sight of Camilla, fling darts from their quivering hands, and make hard oak-stakes and seared truncheons do the work of steel, hot and headlong, and fain would be the first to die for their city.

Meantime the cruel news floods Turnus' ears in his forest-ambush, as Acca tells the warrior her tale of mighty terror : the Volscian ranks destroyed, Camilla slain, the enemy coming on like a torrent, sweeping all before their victorious onslaught, the alarm already wafted to the walls. He, all on fire (for even such is Jove's stern requirement), quits his post on the hills, leaves the impregnable forest. Scarce had he passed from their sight and occupied the plain, when father Æneas, entering the unguarded pass, scales the hill-top, and issues through the shadowy wood. So the two rivals march cityward at full speed, each with all his army, nor long is the intervening distance ; at the same moment Æneas looked far over the plains all smoking with dust, and saw the host of Laurentum, and Turnus was aware of fell Æneas in battle array, and heard the onward tramp of feet and the neighing of steeds. Instantly they were for closing in fight and throwing for the stake of combat ; but the time was come for reddening Phœbus to bathe his wearied team in the Hiberian flood, and bring back night on the steps of retreating day. So they encamp before the city, and make their ramparts strong.

BOOK XII.

WHEN Turnus sees that the War-god's enmity has broken the spirit of Latium, that men are beginning to claim his promise, and make him the mark of their eyes, he bursts at once into fury unappeasable, and swells his pride to the height. As in Punic land, when the hunters have wounded him deep in the breast, the lion at last rouses himself to fight, tosses with fierce joy his mane from his neck, snaps fearlessly the brigand's spear in the wound, and roars from his gory mouth: even so, Turnus once kindled, his vehemence grows each moment. Then he addresses the king, and dashes hotly into speech: 'Turnus stops not the way: Æneas and his cowards have no plea for retracting their challenge or disowning their plighted word; I meet the combat; bring the sacred things, good father, and solemnise the truce. Either will I with my own right hand send the Dardan down to Tartarus, the runaway from Asia—let the Latians sit by and see—and with my single weapon refute the slander of a nation; or let the vanquished own their master and Lavinia be the conqueror's bride.'

With calm dignity of soul the king makes answer: 'Gallant youth, the greater your impetuous valour, the more watchful must needs be my foresight, the more anxious my scrutiny of all that may happen. You have your father Daunus' kingdom, you have many a town won by your own sword: I that speak have gold and a heart to give it; in Latium and Laurentum's land are other unwedded maidens, of no unworthy lineage. Suffer me without disguise to give voice to these unwelcome sayings, and take home what I speak further: I was forbidden by Fate to give my daughter to any of her early suitors: so sang gods and men alike. Conquered by my love for you, conquered by the ties of kindred and the sorrow of my weeping queen, I set all pledges at naught, I snatched the bride from her plighted husband. I drew the unhallowed sword. From that fatal day you see what troubles, what wars are let loose upon me; you know the weight of the sufferings which *you* are the first to feel. Twice vanquished in a mighty conflict, we scarce protect by our bulwarks the hopes of Italy: Tiber's waters are yet steaming with our blood, and the spacious plains are whitened by our bones. Whither am I drifting again and again? what madness turns my brain? If on the death of Turnus I am ready to welcome these new allies, why should I not end the strife while he lives and is safe? What will our Rutulian kinsmen say, what the rest of Italy, if—may Fortune forefend the omen!—I give you up to death, you, a suitor for my alliance, for my daughter's hand? Think of the uncertainties of war; have pity on your aged sire, now biding forlornly far away in his Ardean home!'

These words abate not Turnus' vehemence a whit: it starts up fiercer, more virulent for the healing hand. Soon as he can find utterance, he thus begins: 'The care you take for my sake, best of fathers, lay down for my sake, I beg, and suffer me to pledge my life for my honour. My hand, too, can scatter darts and fling steel with no feeble force; my blows, too, fetch blood. He will not have his goddess-mother within call, to hide her craven son in an unmanly cloud, and conceal herself by help of treacherous shadows.'

But the queen, appalled by the new hazard of the combat, was all in tears, clinging to her fiery son-in-law with the convulsive grasp of death: 'Turnus, by these my tears, by any regard you cherish for Amata—you are now our only hope, our only solace in our forlorn old age—the honour and power of the king are in your hands; on you, its one pillar, the whole house leans. I ask but this—forbear to cross swords with the Teucrians. Whatever chance waits on you in this unhappy combat, waits on me, too, my Turnus; along with you I shall leave the hated light, nor see in Æneas my son-in-law and my conqueror.'

As Lavinia heard her mother's voice, her glowing cheeks were bathed in tears; a deep blush kindled a fire, and shot over her flushing face. As when a man has stained Indian ivory with blood-red purple, or like a bed of lilies and roses mixed: such hues were seen on the maiden's countenance. He, bewildered with passion, fixes his eyes upon her: the sight makes him burn the more for battle, and thus he addresses Amata in brief: 'Let me not have tears nor aught so ominous, dear mother, as my escort to the iron battle; Turnus is not free to postpone the call of death. Go, Idmon, and bear the Phrygian despot a message that will like him not: Soon as the goddess of to-morrow's dawn shall fire the sky with the glow of her chariot, let him not spur the Teucrians against the Rutulians; let Teucrian and Rutulian sheath their swords, while we twain with our own life-blood decide the war. Let Lavinia's hand be sought and won in yonder field.'

So he spoke, and rushed back within doors: he calls for his steeds, and joys to look on them snorting and neighing—the steeds which Orithyia gave as a present to Pilumnus, to surpass the snows in whiteness, the winds in speed. Round them stand the bustling charioteers, patting their chests with hollow palms and combing their maned necks. Next he throws round his shoulders his hauberk, stiff with scales of gold and dazzling orichalc, and adjusts to his wear the sword, the shield, and the cones of the crimson crest—that sword the Fire-god's own hand had made for his father Daunus, and tempered it glowing in the Stygian wave. Lastly, the spear which was standing in the palace-hall, propped by a mighty column, the spoil of Auruncan

Actor, he seizes forcefully, sturdy as it is, and shakes till it quivers, crying aloud: 'Now, my good spear, that hast never failed my call, now is the time; once wast thou swayed by giant Actor, now by Turnus: grant that I may lay low the emasculate Phrygian, strip and rend his hauberk by strength of hand, and soil in the dust those ringlets curled with hot iron and moist with myrrh.' So he rages, fury-driven: sparks flash from the furnace of his countenance, lightnings dart from his fiery eyes; as when a bull in view of a fight raises fearful bellowing, and calls up rage into his horns by butting against a tree's trunk, challenges the wind with his blows, and spurns the flying sand in prelude for the fray.

With equal fierceness Æneas, clad in his mother's armour, sharpens valour's edge, and lashes his heart with wrath, joying that proffered truce should end the war. Then he calms his comrades' fear and the grief of Iulus, talking of destiny, and sends envoys with an answer to the Latian king, to name the conditions of peace.

Scarce had the next morrow begun to sprinkle the mountain-tops with light, at the time when the sun's steeds first come up from the deep and breathe flakes of radiance from their upturned nostrils, when Rutulians and Teucrians were at work, measuring out lists for combat under the ramparts of the mighty town, with hearths in the midst, and altars of turf for their common gods. Others were carrying fire and spring water, begirt with aprons, vervain wreaths on their brows. Forth moves the Ausonian army, bands with lifted javelins issuing from the crowded gates. From yonder quarters pours the Trojan and Tuscan force, with the arms of their several countries, harnessed as if summoned by the War-god's bloody fray. In the midst of either squadrons the generals flash along, glorious in gold and purple, Mnestheus, Assaracus' seed, and Asilas the brave, and Messapus, tamer of horses, the progeny of Neptune. At a given signal each army retreats within its confines; spears are fixed in the ground, and bucklers rested at ease. Matrons in yearning eagerness, and unarmed masses, and tottering old men, fill turret and roof, or stand by the lofty portals.

But Juno, from the top of the mount now styled Alban— in those days it had no name, nor glory, nor honour—was looking in prospect on the plain, the two armies, Trojan and Laurentine, and the Latian town. At once she addressed Turnus' sister, a goddess herself, who presides over the pool and the brawling stream—such dignity Jove, the king of heaven, solemnly made hers in return for violated maidenhood: 'Sweet Nymph, glory of the rivers, favourite of my heart, you know how I have preferred you to all Latium's daughters who have climbed the odious bed of our great Master and have gladly given you a seat in the sky; and now, Juturna, learn from me your sorrow, for which I am not to blame. So long as Fortune seemed favourable and Fate allowed Latium to prosper, I spread my shield over Turnus and these your walls : now I see the youth engaged with a destiny mightier than his own, and the day of doom and the power of the enemy are at hand. I cannot look on the combat, nor on the league that ushers it in. If you have the nerve to dare aught for your brother, go on; it is a sister's part : perhaps the down-trodden have a better lot in store.' Ere she had well ended, Juturna's tears sprang forth, and thrice and again her hand smote on her lovely breast. 'No time for tears,' cries Saturn's daughter : 'quick, and if any way there be, snatch your brother from death : or at least revive the war, and mar the treaty while yet on their lips. Remember, I warrant the attempt.' With such advice she left her wavering in purpose and staggering under the cruel blow.

Meantime the monarchs appear, the stately form of the Latian king riding in a four-horse car, his brows gleaming with a circle of twelve gilded rays, the cognisance of the Sun

2 o

his grandsire : Turnus is drawn by a snow-white pair, two spears with broad iron points quivering in his hands. Then comes father Æneas, the parent stock of the Roman tree, blazing with his starry shield and celestial armour, and at his side Ascanius, the second hope of mighty Rome, both issuing from their camp : while a priest in stainless robe has brought the young of a bristly boar and an unclipped sheep of two years old, and placed the victims by the blazing altar. They, turning their eyes to the rising sun, offer the salted barley, score with the steel the brows of the cattle, and make libations from their chargers. Then thus prays good Æneas, his sword drawn in his hand : 'Let the Sun above and the Earth beneath witness my invocation, this very Earth for which I have had the heart to endure so much, and the almighty Sire, and thou, his goddess-bride, Saturn's daughter, now—may I hope it?—now at last made gracious : thou, too, glorious Mars, whose princely nod controls every battle : Springs also and Rivers I invoke, all the majesty of the sky, all the deities of the purple deep : if chance award the victory to Turnus the Ausonian, reason claims that the vanquished shall retire to Evander's town : Iulus shall quit the land, nor shall Æneas' children in after-days draw the sword again, or threaten this realm with war. But should conquest vouch-safe to us the smiles of the battle-field, as I rather deem, and pray that Heaven will rather grant, I will not bid the Italians be-subject to Troy, or ask I the crown for myself : no, let the two great nations, one unconquered as the other, join on equal terms in an everlasting federation. The gods and their ritual shall be my gift : let my good father-in-law still wield the sword and the lawful rights of empire : the Teucrians shall raise me a city, and Lavinia shall give it her name.' Thus first Æneas : the Latian king follows, with eyes lifted to heaven, and right hand stretched to the stars : 'I swear as you swore, Æneas, by Land and Ocean and Lights above,

Latona's twofold offspring, and two-faced Janus, the potency of the gods below and the shrine of relentless Pluto: and let the Father too give ear, who ratifies covenants with thunder. My hand is on the altars; I adjure the fires and powers that part us: so far as rests with Italy, no length of time shall break this bond of friendship, let things issue as they may: no violence shall make me swerve in will, not though deluge and chaos come again, ruining the earth into the water and crushing down heaven into Tartarus: even as this sceptre'— for a sceptre chanced to be in his hand—'shall never more burgeon with light foliage into branch or shade, now that once cut down in the woods it is orphaned of that which gave it life, and has resigned to the axe its leaves and its sprays— once a tree, now the workman's hand has cased it with seemly brass, and given it to be wielded by Latium's elders.' With words like these were they ratifying the treaty, all the nobles looking on. Then, as the rite ordains, they cut the throats of the hallowed victims into the fire, flay the yet breathing flesh, and pile the altars with laden chargers.

But the Rutulians have long been thinking the combat unequal: their bosoms are swayed by rival emotions, all the more, the nearer they observe the ill-matched champions. Turnus aids the feeling by the quietness of his step and the downcast reverential look which he turns on the altar, his wan cheeks, and the pallor of his youthful frame. Soon as his sister Juturna heard such whispers spreading, and saw the hearts of the multitude wavering to and fro, she plunges among the ranks, taking the form of Camers, great in ancestral dignity, great in the name of his father's worth, and himself a valiant warrior—plunges among the ranks, knowing well what she would have, and scatters her sayings abroad in words like these: 'Blush ye not, Rutulians, with souls such as yours, to make one a sacrifice for all? are we not equal to our foes in strength or in numbers? See, here is their whole army, Trojan and Arcadian, ay, and that fated band of Etruria, which seeks Turnus' life. Though but half of us should engage, each would scarce have an enemy to fight with. He, no doubt, will rise on the wings of fame to the gods for whose altars he gives himself to die, and will live in the mouths of men : we, stripped of our country, shall be the slaves of haughty masters, we, I say, now seated passively on the ground.' By such words the flame is fanned more and more in those young warrior hearts, and murmurs run from rank to rank: not Rutulian alone, but Laurentian and Latian are changed men. They who a short while since were hoping for their own repose and their state's prosperity, now burn for arms, would have the treaty undone, and pity Turnus' cruel fate. And now Juturna gives them one thing more, even a sign from heaven, no spell so potent to work on Italian minds and make them dupes of the marvel. Flying through the ruddy sky, Jove's golden bird was chasing the river fowl, a winged noisy multitude, when suddenly swooping on the water he carries off in his tyrant claws a stately swan. The Italians are all attention, when lo ! the whole mass of birds face about with a scream, marvellous to see, their wings darkening the air, and in dense cloud press on their enemy, till overborne by sheer weight he gives way, drops the booty from his talons into the river, flying aloft, and vanishes in the distant sky. Oh, then the Rutulians welcome the omen with a shout and spread their hands on high ; and first of all cries the augur Tolumnius. ' Here, here is the thing I have prayed for so often. I embrace it, I own the hand of Heaven. Follow me—yes, me—and seize your weapons, my poor countrymen, whom the felon stranger is scaring with battle, as if ye were feeble birds, and ravaging your coasts. He too will turn to flight and sail far away on the deep. Close your ranks with one accord, and rally round the prince of whom the battle robs you.' He spoke, and running forward hurls his dart full at the enemy : the

hurtling cornel sounds, and cuts the air on no doubtful errand.
A deafening shout follows on the act, the ranks are confused,
and men's hearts stirred with mad bewilderment. On flew
the spear, just where nine goodly brethren chanced to stand
facing it, all born of one true Tuscan mother to Gylippus the
Arcadian. One of these just at the waist where the quilted
belt chafes against the belly and the buckle presses the sides
—a youth of goodly form and clad in refulgent armour—it
strikes through the ribs and lays him grovelling on the yellow
sand. But his brothers, a gallant company and stung by
grief, draw their swords or seize their javelins, and charge in
headlong fury. To meet them rush the Laurentian columns :
while from their side surge forth in a flood Trojans and
Agyllans and Arcadians with inlaid harness. All are possessed by one passion, to try the issue with the steel. The altars
are stripped bare : through the whole sky drives a flickering
storm of weapons and an iron sleet comes thick : bowls and
hearths are carried away. King Latinus flies, bearing away his
gods in discomfiture, the truce unratified. Others rein the
chariot or vault on horseback, with swords ready drawn.

Messapus, all on fire to annul the treaty, spurs his horse full
on the Tuscan Aulestes, a king and wearing kingly cognisance :
he draws quickly back, and gets entangled in piteous sort with
the altars that meet him behind, falling on them head and
shoulders. Up flashes Messapus spear in hand, and towering
on horseback brings down on him the massy beam in the
midst of his prayers, and delivers himself thus : 'He is sped :
here is a better victim for the mighty gods.' The Italians
cluster round, and strip the yet warm body. As Ebusus comes
up and aims a blow, Corynæus meets him with a brand half-
burnt from the altar and dashes the fire in his face : his long
beard burst into a blaze and made a smell of burning hair :
the enemy presses on, grasps in his left hand the locks of the
wildered man and with the impact of his knee pins him to

earth; then buries the stark falchion in his side. Podalirius gives chase to Alsus the shepherd as he rushed in the first rank through a shower of darts, and hangs over him with naked sword: he swinging back his axe, splits full in front the foe's forehead and chin, and splashes his arms right and left with the blood. The heavy rest of iron slumber settles down on the dying eyes, and their beams are curtained in everlasting night.

But good Æneas, his head bare, was stretching forth his unarmed hand and shouting to his men: 'Whither are you driving? what is this sudden outburst of strife? Oh, curb your passions! the truce is stricken, and all the terms arranged: none but I has a right to engage: give way to me and have done with alarm: my sword shall ratify the treaty: this sacrifice has put Turnus in my power.' While he is crying thus and uttering words like these, lo! full at the chief flies a hurtling arrow, none knew by what hand launched, by what wind wafted, who graced the Rutulians so highly, chance or deity: the glory of the proud achievement was lost, nor was any known to boast of having wounded Æneas.

Soon as Turnus sees Æneas retiring from the battle, and the Trojan leaders in confusion, he glows with swift access of hope, calls for horses and armour, bounds like a conqueror into the chariot, and takes the reins in hand. Many a heroic frame he slaughters as he whirls along, many he tumbles and leaves to live or die, crushes whole ranks by the onset of his car, or plucks forth spears and hurls them at the fliers. Just as storming along by Hebrus' icy flood gore-stained Mars smites on his shield, and stirring battle lets loose his fiery steeds: they fly over the plains faster than winds southern or western: Thrace groans to her extremity under the beat of their hoofs: around him circle the frowns of black-visaged Terror, and the powers of Wrath and Treachery, liege followers of the god: with like eagerness through the thickest of the battle Turnus whirls his straining horses, trampling in piteous sort on the slaughtered foe : the flying hoof spirts gory dew, and blood and sand are kneaded in a mass. Sthenelus he has slain already, and Thamyris and Pholus, these hand to hand, that from a distance : a distant death, too, has found the Imbrasidæ, Glaucus and Lades, trained in Lycia by Imbrasus their sire, and by him harnessed alike, warriors who could stand and fight or outride the winds. In another part of the field Eumedes is riding through the fray, the gallant son of ancient Dolon, with the name of his grand-sire, the heart and hand of his sire, who of old, offering to spy out the Danaan camp, dared to ask Achilles' chariot as his guerdon ; far other guerdon was it with which Diomed requited his daring, and his hopes are set on Achilles' steeds no longer. Marking him at distance along the plain, Turnus first sends after him a flying spear through the inter-vening space, then stops the car and dismounts, comes on the wretch gasping and laid low, and setting his foot on his neck, wrests the sword from his hand, bathes it flashing deep in his throat, and thus accompanies the blow : 'Lie there, Trojan, and measure the Hesperian soil you came to invade : such are their guerdons who draw their swords on me ; so build they up their city.' Then with a spear throw he sends Asbutes to join the dead. Chloreus and Sybaris and Dares and Ther-silochus, Thymœtes too, thrown off by a restiff horse. As when the blast of Thracian Boreas roars on the deep Ægean and drives the billows to the shore, wherever the winds push on, the clouds scurry over the sky, so when Turnus cleaves his path, the ranks give way, the armies turn in rout ; the motion bears him along, and the gale which blows on the car tosses his flickering crest. Phegeus, indignant at his over-weening onset, meets the car and grasping the bridle wrenches aside the foaming jaws of the impetuous steeds. While he is dragged along clinging to the yoke, the broad spear-head reaches his unguarded breast, cleaves the two-plated corselet, and tastes the surface of the flesh. Yet he, his shield before him, kept fronting and threatening the foe, and protecting himself with his drawn sword, when the wheel careering onward strikes and flings him on the ground, and Turnus with a sweep of his blade between the bottom of the helmet and the breastplate's topmost rim has lopped the head and left the trunk to welter.

While Turnus thus is dealing havoc over the field, Mnestheus, true Achates, and Ascanius have helped Æneas to the camp, all bleeding, and staying his halting steps by the help of a spear. There he frets and struggles to pull out the broken shaft, and calls for help the readiest way, bidding them enlarge the wound with a broad sword, cut the weapon's lodgment to the bottom, and send him to combat again. And now at his side was Iapis, son of Iasus, dearest of mankind to Phœbus, he to whom the god in his passionate fondness would fain have given his own function, his own hand's cunning, the augur's insight, the lyre, the weapons of archery; but he, wishing to lengthen out the span of his bed-rid sire, chose rather to know the virtue of simples and the laws of the healing art, and to practise in silence an unambitious craft. There stood Æneas, fretting impatiently, propped on his massy spear, with a warrior concourse about him, and Iulus all in tears, yet himself unmoved by their sorrow. The aged leech, his garments swathed round him in Pæon's fashion, is plying busily the healing hand and Phœbus' sovereign remedies all to no end, all to no end pulling at the dart and griping the steel with the pincer. No Fortune guides the course of skill, no patron Phœbus lends his aid; and meanwhile the fierce alarms of the field grow louder and louder, and the mischief is nearer at hand. They see dust-clouds propping the sky, the horsemen gallop in, darts fall thick in the midst of the camp, and heavenward mounts the cruel din of warriors battling or falling in the stern affray:—when, lo! Venus, struck to the heart by her son's undeserved suffering; with a mother's care plucks dittany from Cretan Ida, a plant with downy leaves and a purple flower: wild goats know that simple well, if the flying arrow should lodge in their flesh. Veiled by a dim cloud, the goddess brings it down; with it she impregnates the spring water gleaming in the caldron, imparting unseen powers, and sprinkles ambrosia's healthful juice and fragrant panacea. The old man rinsed the wound with the water so transformed, all unwitting, and in a moment all pain was fled from the frame, and the blood was stanched in the wound. The arrow obeys the hand, and falls unforced, and strength is restored as before. 'Quick! give the warrior his arms! why so tardy?' cries Iapis, himself the first to stir up the martial spirit. 'No human aid has done this, no power of leech-craft; it is not my hand, Æneas, that restores you; a mightier power than man's is at work, sending you back to mightier deeds.' The chief, greedy for the fight, has cased his legs in gold, chafing at delay and brandishing his spear. Soon as the shield is fitted to his side, the cuirass to his back, he clasps Ascanius to his mailed breast, and kissing his lips through the helmet addresses him thus: 'Learn valour from me, my son, and genuine hardihood, success from others. To-day it is my hand that shall shield you in war and lead you through the walks of honour; be it your care, when your age has ripened into manhood, to bear the past in mind, seek patterns among those of your own blood, and be stirred to action by Æneas your sire and Hector your uncle.'

So having said, he passed towering through the gate, a huge spear quivering in his hand: Antheus and Mnestheus close their ranks and rush forth, and the whole multitude streams from the empty camp. The field is clouded by blinding dust, and earth throbs and shudders with the tramp of feet. Turnus saw them coming towards him from their battlements, the Ausonians saw, and a cold shudder ran through their vitals:

first before all the Latians Juturna heard and knew the sound and shrank back in terror. As a storm-cloud bursting through the sky sweeps down to earth along the main : hapless husbandmen know it ere it comes, and shudder at heart; yes, it will bring havoc to their trees, devastation to their crops, will lay all low far and wide ; the winds fly before it and waft the sound to the shore : with as strong a rush the Rhœteian chief sweeps his army full on the foe; they close in firm masses and form severally at his side. Thymbræus' sword cuts down mighty Osiris, Mnestheus slays Archetius, Achates Epulo, and Gyas Ufens ; falls too the augur Tolumnius, the first to fling his javelin at the enemy. The din mounts to the sky, and the Rutulians routed in turn fly through the plains in a whirlwind of dust. The hero himself neither stoops to slaughter the flying nor encounter such as would fain meet him foot to foot, weapon in hand : Turnus alone he tracks winding through the thick darkness, him alone he challenges to combat. The terror struck Juturna's manly mind : she plucks from his seat Metiscus, Turnus' charioteer, as he drives the horses, and leaves him fallen at distance behind the car : herself takes his place and handles the flowing rein, assuming all that Metiscus had, voice and person and armour. Like a black swallow that flies through the house of some wealthy man and traverses the lofty hall, in quest of scraps of food for her twittering nestlings ; now she is heard in the empty cloisters, now about the water-tanks ; so drives Juturna through the thick of the foe, and flies on rapid wheel from spot to spot, now here, now there she gives a glimpse of her victorious brother, yet never lets him stop and fight, but whirls far away in the distance. Æneas for his part winds through sinuous paths in hope to meet him, tracks his steps, and shouts to him aloud across the weltering ranks. Oft as he spies out the foe and tries by running to match the horses' winged speed, each time

Juturna wheels the car aside. What can he do? he tosses in aimless ebb and flow, thoughts distracting his mind this way and that:—when lo! Messapus, with sudden movement, happening to carry two limber spear-shafts tipped with steel, levels one at him and flings it true to its mark. Æneas stopped and gathered his arms about him, sinking on his knee; yet the fierce spear took the top of the helmet and struck the crest from the cone. Then at last his wrath mounts high; and under the duresse of treachery, as he sees the steeds and chariot whirling away from him, after many an appeal to Jove and the altars of the violated league, he falls on the ranks before him, and fanned to dreadful vengeance by the War-god's breath, lets loose a carnage cruel and unsparing, and flings the reins on the neck of his passion.

And now what god will tell me all those horrors and relate for me in verse the several scenes of slaughter, the deaths of the leaders whom Turnus here, the Trojan hero there, is chasing over the plain? Was it thy will, great Jove, that nations destined in time to come to everlasting amity, should first clash in such dread turmoil? Æneas confronted by Rutulian Sucro (that combat first brought the Trojan onset to a stand) after brief delay catches him on the side and drives his stubborn sword death's nearest way through the ribs that fence the bosom. Turnus in foot-encounter slays Amycus, whose horse had thrown him, and his brother Diores, striking one with the spear ere he came up, the other with the sword-blade, lops the heads of both, hangs them from his car, and carries them dripping with blood. That sends down Talos to death and Tanais and brave Cethegus, those at one onslaught, and hapless Onytes, of the house of Echion, brought forth by Peridia: that kills the brethren who came from Apollo's land of Lycia, and young Menœtes the Arcadian, who shrunk from war in vain; he plied his craft and lived in poverty by the fishy waters of Lerna, a stranger to the halls of the great;

and his father tilled land for hire. Like two fires launched
from different quarters on a dry forest with bushes of crackling bay, or as when two foaming rivers pouring from lofty
heights crash along and run towards the ocean, each ploughing his own wild channel : with no less fury rush through the
fight Æneas and Turnus both : now, now the wrath is boiling
within them; their unconquered bosoms swell to bursting :
they throw their whole force on the wounds they deal. This
with the whirl and the blow of a mighty rock dashes Murranus headlong from his car to the ground, Murranus who had
ever on his tongue the ancient names of sires and grandsires and a lineage stretching through the series of Latium's
kings : the wheels throw forward the fallen man under the
reins and yoke, and he is crushed by the quick hoof-beat of
the steeds that mind not their lord. That meets Hyllus as
he rushed on in vehement fury, and hurls a javelin at his
gold-bound brows : the spear pierced the helmet and stood
fixed in the brain. Nor did your prowess, Cretheus, bravest
of Greeks, deliver you from Turnus, nor did the gods Cupencus
worshipped shield him from the onset of Æneas : his bosom
met the steel, and the check of the brazen buckler stood the
wretch in small stead. You, too, great Æolus, the Laurentian
plains looked on in death, spreading your frame abroad over
their surface : fallen are you, whom the Argive bands could
never overthrow, nor Achilles the destroyer of Priam's realm :
here was your fatal goal : a princely home under Ida's shade :
at Lyrnesus a princely hope, in Laurentian soil a sepulchre.
The two armies are in hot conflict : all the Latians, all the
sons of Dardanus, Mnestheus, and keen Serestus, and Messapus
tamer of the steed, and brave Asilas, the Tuscan band, and
Evander's Arcad cavalry, each man for himself straining every
nerve : no stint, no stay ; they strive with giant tension.

    And now Æneas had a thought inspired by his beauteous
mother, to march to the walls, throw his force rapidly on the

town, and stun the Latians with a sudden blow. Tracking Turnus through the ranks he swept his eyes round and round, and beholds the city enjoying respite from all that furious war, and lying in unchallenged repose. At once his mind is fired with the vison of a grander battle : Mnestheus he summons and Sergestus and brave Serestus, the first in command, and mounts an eminence round which the rest of the Teucrian army gathers in close ranks, not laying shield or dart aside. Standing on the tall mound, he thus bespeaks them : ' Let nothing stay my orders ; the hand of Jove is here ; nor let any move slower because the enterprise is sudden. The town, the cause of the war, the royal home of the Latian king, unless they submit the yoke and confess themselves vanquished, I will overthrow this day, and lay its smoking turrets level with the ground. What ? am I to wait till Turnus choose to bide the combat, and once conquered, meet me a second time ? This, my men, is the well-spring, this the head and front of the monstrous war. Bring torches with speed, and reclaim the treaty fire in hand.' He said, and all with emulous spirit of union close their ranks and stream to the walls in compact mass. Scaling ladders and brands are produced suddenly and in a moment. Some run to the several gates and slay those stationed there : some hurl the steel and overshadow the sky with javelins. Æneas himself among the foremost lifts up his hand under the city wall, loudly upbraids the king, and calls the gods to witness that he is once more forced into battle, the Italians twice his foes, the second treaty broken like the first. Strife arises among the wildered citizens : some are for throwing open the town and unbarring the gates to the Dardans : nay, they even drag the monarch to the ramparts : others draw the sword and prepare to guard the walls : as when a countryman has tracked out bees concealed in a cavernous rock and filled their hiding-place with pungent smoke, they in alarm for the common wealth flit about their waxen realm and stir themselves to wrath by vehement buzzing: the murky smell winds from chamber to chamber: a dull blind noise fills the cavern: vapours ascend into the void of air.

Yet another stroke fell on Latium's wearied sons, shaking with its agony the city to her foundations. When the queen from her palace saw the enemy draw near, the walls assailed, flames flying roofward, the Rutulian army, the soldiers of Turnus nowhere in sight, she deemed, poor wretch, her warrior slain in the combat, and maddened with the access of grief, cries aloud that she alone is the guilty cause, the fountainhead of all this evil; and flinging out wild words in the fury of her frenzied anguish, rends with desperate hand her purple raiment, and fastens from a lofty beam the noose of hideous death. Soon as Latium's wretched dames knew the blow that had fallen, her daughter Lavinia is first to rend yellow hair and roseate cheek, and the rest about her ran as wildly: the palace re-echoes their wail. The miserable story spreads through the town: every heart sinks: there goes the old king with garments rent, all confounded by his consort's death and his city's ruin: he soils his hoary locks with showers of unseemly dust, and oft and oft upbraids himself that he embraced not sooner Æneas the Dardan nor took him for son-in-law of his own free will.

Turnus, meantime, is plying the war far away on the plain, following here and there a straggler with abated zeal, himself and his steeds alike less buoyant. The air wafted to him the confused din, inspiring unknown terror, and on his quickened ears smote the sound of the city's turmoil and the noise not of joy. 'Alas! what is this mighty agony that shakes the walls? what these loud shouts pouring from this quarter and that?' So he cries, and drawing his bridle halts bewildered. His sister, just as she stood in guise of Metiscus the driver, guiding car, horse, and reins, thus meets his question: 'Proceed we still, Turnus, to chase the Trojans, where victory's dawn shows us the way: others there are whose hands can guard the city: Æneas bears down on the Italians and stirs up the battle: let us send havoc as cruel among his Teucrians: so shall your slain be as many and your martial fame as high.' Turnus answered: 'Sister, I both knew you long since, when at first you artfully disturbed the truce and flung yourself into our quarrel, and now you vainly hide the goddess from my eyes. But tell me by whose will you are sent from Olympus to cope with toils like this? Is it that you may look on the cruel end of your hapless brother? For what can I do? what chance is there left to give me hope of safety? With my own eyes I saw Murranus die, his giant frame laid low by a giant wound: he called me by name, he, than whom I had no dearer friend. Dead, too, is ill-starred Ufens, all because he would not see me disgraced: his body and his arms are the Teucrians' prize. Am I to let the nation's homes be razed to the ground, the one drop that was wanting to the cup, and not rather with my own right hand give Drances' words the lie? Shall I turn my back? shall this land see Turnus flying? is death after all so bitter? Be gracious to me, gentle powers of the grave, since the gods above are against me! Yes, I will come down to you a stainless spirit, guiltless of that base charge, worthy in all my acts of my great forefathers.'

Scarce had he spoken, when lo! there flies through the midst of the foe, on a foaming steed, Saces, with an arrow full in his face: up he spurs, imploring Turnus by name: 'Turnus, our last hope is in you: have compassion on your army. Æneas thunders with sword and spear, and threatens that he will level in dust and give to destruction the Italians' topmost battlements: even now brands are flying to the roofs. Every Latian face, every eye turns to you: the king himself mutters in doubt whom to call his son-in-law, to whose alliance to incline. Nay, more, your fastest friend the queen is dead by her own hand, scared and driven out of life. Only Messapus and keen Atinas are at the gates to uphold our forces. About them are closed ranks, and an iron harvest of naked blades : you are rolling your car over a field from which war has ebbed.' Turnus stood still with silent dull regard, wildered by the thoughts that crowd on his mind: deep shame, grief and madness, frenzy-goaded passion and conscious wrath all surging at once. Soon as the shadows parted and light came back to his intelligence, he darted his blazing eyes cityward with restless vehemence, and looked back from his car to the wide-stretching town. Lo ! there was a cone of fire spreading from story to story and flaring to heaven : the flame was devouring the turret which he had built himself of planks welded together, put wheels beneath it, and furnished it with lofty bridges. 'Fate is too strong for me, sister, too strong ; hold me back no longer : we needs must follow where Heaven and cruel Fortune are calling us. Yes, I *will* meet Æneas : I will endure the full bitterness of death : no more, my love, shall you see me disgraced: suffer me first to have my hour of madness.' He said, and in a moment leapt to the ground, rushes on through foes, through javelins, leaves his sister to her sorrow, and dashes at full speed through the intervening ranks. Even as from a mountain's top down comes a rock headlong, torn off by the wind, or washed down by vehement rain, or loosened by the lapse of creeping years : down the steep it crashes with giant impulse, that reckless stone, bounding over the ground and rolling along with it trees, herds, and men: so, dashing the ranks apart, rushes Turnus to the city walls, where the earth is wet with plashy blood, and the gale hurtles with spears: he beckons with his hand, and cries with a mighty voice: 'Have done, ye Rutulians ! ye Latians, hold back your darts ! whatever Fortune brings she brings to me : 'tis juster far that I in your stead should singly expiate the treaty's breach and try the issue of the steel.' All at the word part from the midst, and leave him a clear space.

But father Æneas, hearing Turnus' name, quits his hold on the walls and the battlements that crown them, flings delay to the winds and breaks off the work of war, steps high in triumph, and makes his arms peal dread thunder: vast as Athos, vast as Eryx, vast as father Apennine himself, when he roars with his quivering holms and lifts his snowy crest exultingly to the sky. All turn their eyes with eager contention. Rutulians, Trojans, and Italians, those alike who were manning the towers and those whose battering-rams were assailing the foundations. All unbrace their armour. Latinus himself stands amazed to see two men so mighty, born in climes so distant each from each, thus met together to try the steel's issue. At once, when a space is cleared on the plain, first hurling their spears, they advance with swift onset, and dash into the combat with shield and ringing harness. Earth groans beneath them : their swords hail blow on blow : chance and valour mingle pell-mell. As when on mighty Sila or Taburnus' summit two bulls, lowering their brows for combat, engage fiercely : the herdsmen retreat in dread : the cattle all stand dumb with terror, the heifers wait in suspense who is to be the monarch of the woodland, whom the herds are to follow henceforth : they each in turn give furious blows, push and lodge their horns, and bathe neck and shoulders with streams of blood : the sound makes the forest bellow again : with no less fury Æneas the Trojan, and the Daunian chief clash shield on shield : the enormous din fills the firmament. Jupiter himself holds aloft his scales poised and level, and lays therein the destinies of the two, to see whom the struggle dooms, and whose the weight that death bears down. Forth darts Turnus, deeming it safe, rises with his whole frame on the uplifted sword, and strikes. Trojans and eager Latians shout aloud : both armies gaze expectant. But the faithless sword snaps in twain and fails its fiery lord midway in the stroke, unless flight should come to his aid. Off

2 D

he flies swifter than the wind, seeing an unknown hilt in his defenceless hand. Men say that in his headlong haste, when first he was mounting the car harnessed for battle, he left behind his father's falchion and snatched up the steel of Metiscus, his charioteer: so long as the Teucrians fled straggling before him, the weapon did good service; soon as it came to the divine 'Vulcanian armour, the mortal blade, like brittle ice, flew asunder at the stroke: the fragments sparkle on the yellow sand. So now in his distraction Turnus flies here and there over the plain, weaving vague circles in this place and in that: for the Trojans have closed in circle about him, and here is a spreading marsh, there lofty ramparts to bar the way.

Nor is Æneas wanting, though at times the arrow wound slackens his knees and robs them of their power to run: no, he follows on, and presses upon the flier foot for foot: as when a hound has got a stag pent in by a river, or hedged about by the terror of crimson plumage, and chases him running and barking: the stag, frighted by the snare and the steep bank, doubles a thousand times: the keen Umbrian clings open-mouthed to his skirts, all but seizes him, and as though in act to seize, snaps his teeth, and is baffled to find nothing in their gripe. Then, if ever, uprises a shout, echoing along bank and marsh, and heaven rings again with the noise. Turnus, even as he flies, calls fiercely on the Rutulians, addressing by name, and clamours for his well-known sword. Æneas, for his part, threatens death and instant destruction, should any come near, and terrifies his trembling foes, swearing that he will raze their city to the ground, and presses on in spite of his wound. Five times they circle round, five times they retrace the circle: for no trivial prize is at stake, no guerdon of a game: the contest is for Turnus' life, for his very heart's blood. It chanced that there had stood there a wild olive with its bitter leaves, sacred to Faunus, a tree in old days reverenced by seamen, where when saved from ocean they used to fasten their offerings to the Laurentian god and hang up their votive garments : but the unrespecting Trojans had lately lopped the hallowed trunk, that the lists might be clear for combat. There was lodged Æneas' spear : thither its force had carried it, and was now holding it fast in the unyielding root. The Dardan chief bent over it, fain to wrench forth the steel that his weapon may catch whom his foot cannot overtake. Then cried Turnus in the moment of frenzied agony : 'Have mercy, I conjure thee, good Faunus, and thou, most gracious earth, hold fast the steel if I have ever reverenced your sanctities, which Æneas' crew for their part have caused battle to desecrate.' He said, nor were his vows unanswered by heavenly aid. Hard as he struggled, long as he lingered over the stubborn stock, by no force could Æneas make the wood unclose its fangs. While he strains with keen insistence, the Daunian goddess, resuming the guise of charioteer Metiscus, runs forward and restores to her brother his sword. Then Venus, resenting the freedom taken by the presumptuous Nymph, came nigh, and plucks the weapon from the depth of the root. And now towering high, with restored weapons and recruited force, this in strong reliance on his sword, that fiercely waving his spear tall as he, the two stand front to front in the breath-draining conflict of war.

Meanwhile the king of almighty Olympus accosts Junó, as from a golden cloud she gazes on the battle : ' Where is this to end, fair spouse ? what last stroke have you in store ? you know yourself, by your own confession, that Æneas has his place assured in heaven among Italia's native gods, that destiny is making him a ladder to the stars. What plan you now ? what hope keeps you seated on those chilly clouds ? was it right that mortal wound should harm a god, or that Turnus— for what power could Juturna have apart from you ?—should receive back his lost sword and the vanquished should feel new forces? At length have done, and let my prayers bow your will. Let this mighty sorrow cease to devour you in silence: let me hear sounds of sullen disquiet less often from your lovely lips. The barrier has been reached. To toss the Trojans over land and sea, to kindle an unhallowed war, to plunge a home in mourning, to blend a dirge with the bridal song, this it has been yours to do: all further action I forbid.' So spake Jupiter: and so in return Saturn's daughter with downcast look: 'Even because I knew, great Jove, that such was your pleasure, have I withdrawn against my will from Turnus and from earth: else you would not see me now in the solitude of my airy throne, exposed to all that comes, meet or unmeet: armed with firebrands, I should stand in the very line of battle, and force the Teucrians into the hands of their foes. As for Juturna, I counselled her, I own, to succour her wretched brother, and warranted an unusual venture where life was at stake: but nought was said of aiming the shaft or bending the bow: I swear by the inexpiable fountain-head of Styx, the one sanction that binds us powers above. And now I yield indeed, and quit this odious struggle. Yet there is a boon I would ask, a boon which destiny forefends not. I ask it for the sake of Latium, for the dignity of your own people: when at last peace shall be ratified with a happy bridal, for happy let it be: when bonds of treaty shall be knit at last, let it not be thy will that the native Latians should change their ancient name, become Trojans or take the Teucrian style: let not them alter their language or their garb. Let there be Latium still: let there be centuries of Alban kings: let there be a Roman stock, strong with the strength of Italian manhood: but let Troy be fallen as she is, name and nation alike.' The Father of men and nature answered with a smile: 'Ay, you are Jove's own sister, the other branch of Saturn's line; such billows of passion surge in your bosom !

but come, let this ineffectual frenzy give way : I grant your wish, and submit myself in willing obedience. The Ausonians shall keep their native tongue, their native customs : the name shall remain as it is : the Teucrians shall merge in the nation they join—that and no more : their rites and worship shall be my gift : all shall be Latians and speak the Latian tongue. The race that shall arise from this admixture of Ausonian blood shall transcend in piety earth and heaven itself, nor shall any nation pay you such honours as they.' Juno nodded assent, and turned her sullenness to pleasure ; meanwhile she departs from the sky, and quits the cloud where she sat.

This done, the sire meditates a further resolve, and prepares to part Juturna from her brother's side. There are two fiends known as the Furies, whom with Tartarean Megæra dismal Night brought forth at one and the same birth, wreathing them alike with coiling serpents, and equipping them with wings that fan the air. They are seen beside Jove's throne, at the threshold of his angry sovereignty, goading frail mortality with stings of terror, oft as the monarch of the gods girds himself to send forth disease and frightful death, or appals guilty towns with war. One of these Jove sped with haste from heaven's summit, and bade her confront Juturna in token of his will. Forth she flies, borne earthward on the blast of a whirlwind. Swift as the arrow from the string cleaves the cloud, sent forth by Parthian—Parthian or Cydonian—tipped with fell poison's gall, the dealer of a wound incurable, and skims the flying vapours hurtling and unforeseen, so went the Daughter of Night and made her way to earth. Soon as she sees the forces of Troy and the army of Turnus, she huddles herself suddenly into the shape of a puny bird, which oft on tombstone or lonely roof sitting by night screams restlessly through the gloom ; in this disguise the fiend again and again flies flapping in Turnus' face, and beats with

her wings on his shield.. A strange chilly terror unknits his
frame, his hair stands shudderingly erect, and his utterance
cleaves to his jaws. But when Juturna knew from far the
rustling of those Fury pinions, she rends, hapless maid, her dishevelled tresses, marring, in all a sister's agony, her face with
her nails, her breast with her clenched hands: 'What now,
my Turnus, can your sister avail? what more remains for an
obdurate wretch like me? by what expedient can I lengthen
your span? can I face a portent like this? At last, at last I
quit the field. Cease to appal my fluttering soul, ye birds of
ill omen : I know the flapping of your wings and its deathful
noise; nor fail I to read great Jove's tyrannic will. Is this
his recompense for lost virginity? why gave he me life to last
for ever? why was the law of death annulled? else might I
end this moment the tale of my sorrows, and travel to the
shades hand in hand with my poor brother. Can immortality, can aught that I have to boast give me joy without him?
Oh, that earth would but yawn deep enough, and send me
down, goddess though I be, to the powers of the grave !' So
saying, she shrouded her head in her azure robe, with many a
groan, and vanished beneath the river of her deity.

Æneas presses on, front to front, shaking his massy, tree-
like spear, and thus speaks in the fierceness of his spirit :
' What is to be the next delay? why does Turnus still hang
back? ours is no contest of speed, but of stern soldiership,
hand to hand. Take all disguises you can : muster all your
powers of courage or of skill: mount on wing, if you list, to
the stars aloft, or hide in the cavernous depth of earth.'
Shaking his head, he replied : 'I quail not at your fiery words,
insulting foe: it is Heaven that makes me quail, and Jove
my enemy.' No more he spoke : but, sweeping his eyes
round, espies a huge stone, a stone ancient and huge, which
chanced to be lying on the plain, set as some field's boundary,
to forefend disputes of ownership : scarce could twelve picked

men lift it on their shoulders, such puny frames as earth produces now-a-days : he caught it up with hurried grasp and
flung it at his foe, rising as he threw, and running rapidly, as
hero might. And yet all the while he knows not that he is
running or moving, lifting up or stirring the enormous stone :
his knees totter under him, and his blood chills and freezes :
and so the mass from the warrior's hand, whirled through the
empty void, passed not through all the space between nor
carried home the blow. Even as in dreams, at night, when
heavy slumber has weighed down the eyes, we seem vainly
wishing to make eager progress forward and midway in the
effort fail helplessly : our tongue has no power, our wonted
strength stands not our frames in stead, nor do words or
utterance come at our call : so it is with Turnus : whatever
means his valour tries, the fell fiend bars them of their issue.
And now confused images whirl through his brain : he looks
to his Rutulians and to the city, and falters with dread, and
quails at the threatening spear : how to escape he knows not,
nor how to front the foe, nor sees he anywhere his car or the
sister who drives it.

Full in that shrinking face Æneas shakes his fatal weapon,
taking aim with his eye, and with an effort of his whole
frame hurls it forth. Never stone flung from engine of siege
roars so loud, never peal so rending follows the thunderbolt. On flies the spear like dark whirlwind with fell destruction on its wing, pierces the edge of the corselet, and the
outermost circle of the seven-fold shield, and with a rush
cleaves through the thigh. Down with his knee doubled
under him comes Turnus to earth, all his length prostrated
by the blow. Up start the Rutulians, groaning as one man :
the whole mountain round rebellows, and the depths of the
forest send back the sound far and wide. He in lowly suppliance lifts up eye and entreating hand : 'It is my due,' he cries,
'and I ask not to be spared it : take what fortune gives you.

Yet, if you *can* feel for a parent's misery—your father, Anchises, was once in like plight—have mercy on Daunus' hoary hairs, and let me, or if you choose my breathless body, be restored to my kin. You are conqueror : the Ausonians have seen my conquered hands outstretched : the royal bride is yours : let hatred be pressed no further.' Æneas stood still, a fiery warrior, his eyes rolling, and checked his hand : and those suppliant words were working more and more on his faltering purpose, when, alas ! the ill-starred belt was seen high on the shoulder, and light · flashed from the well-known studs—the belt of young Pallas, whom Turnus conquered and struck down to earth, and bore on his breast the badge of triumphant enmity. Soon as his eyes caught the spoil and drank in the recollection of that cruel grief, kindled into madness and terrible in his wrath : ' What, with my friend's trophies upon you, would you escape my hand ? It is Pallas, Pallas, who with this blow makes you his victim, and gluts his vengeance with your accursed blood.' With these words, fierce as flame, he plunged the steel into the breast that lay before him. That other's frame grows chill and motionless, and the soul, resenting its lot, flies groaningly to the shades.

THE END.

www.ingramcontent.com/pod-product-compliance
Lightning Source LLC
Chambersburg PA
CBHW031030030726
47497CB00004B/1073